THE PATINA OF PLACE

THE PATINA OF PLACE

*The Cultural Weathering of a
New England Industrial Landscape*

KINGSTON WM. HEATH

THE UNIVERSITY OF TENNESSEE PRESS

Knoxville

Chapter 4 was published, in part, as "The Howland Mill Village:
A Missing Chapter in Model Workers' Housing," *Old-Time New England*
75 (263) (1997): 64–111. It was awarded the 1999 Catherine Bauer Wurster
prize for best scholarly article by the Society for American City and Regional
Planning History.

Unless otherwise noted, the photographs were taken by the author or are
part of his private collection, and the illustrations were prepared by him.

This book is printed on acid-free paper. The binding materials have been
chosen for strength and durability.

LIBRARY OF CONGRESS CATALOGING-IN-PUBLICATION DATA

Heath, Kingston Wm.
    The patina of place: the cultural weathering of a New England
industrial landscape / Kingston Wm. Heath.
    p. cm.
Includes bibliographical references and index.
ISBN 1-57233-138-0 (cl.: alk. paper)
1. Working class—Dwellings—Massachusetts—New Bedford.
2. Working class—Housing—Massachusetts—New Bedford.
3. Apartment houses—Massachusetts—New Bedford.
4. Urban renewal—Massachusetts—New Bedford.
5. Architecture, Domestic—Massachusetts—New Bedford.
I. Title.

HD7304.N35 H4 2001
728'.314'0974485—dc21   2001001841

Contents

ACKNOWLEDGMENTS .... *xiii*

INTRODUCTION
Architecture as Cultural Production .... *xvii*

PART I

NEW BEDFORD
One Generation and Many

1. GROWING UP IN A NEW BEDFORD THREE-DECKER:
   An Environmental Autobiography *3*
2. FROM WHALING PORT TO LEADING TEXTILE CENTER
   An Overview of the City's Shift in Economies *24*

PART II

CORPORATE HOUSING AS AN INDEX TO SOCIAL CHANGE

3. HOUSING THE NEW INDUSTRIAL WORKFORCE *61*
4. HOWLAND MILL VILLAGE
   The Dashed Dream for an Industrial Utopia *86*

PART III

FROM CORPORATE PATERNALISM TO A
SPECULATIVE BUILDING MARKET
The Three-Decker in New Bedford

5. THE ANATOMY OF A NEW BEDFORD THREE-DECKER
   AND THE FORCES THAT SHAPED IT AT THE HEIGHT
   OF THE TEXTILE ERA *119*

6. THE CULTURAL TRANSFORMATION OF THE
   THREE-DECKER AT THE CLOSE OF THE TEXTILE
   ERA IN NEW BEDFORD *162*

CONCLUSION
*Cultural Weathering as a Vehicle for
Exploring the Process of Place Making* *182*

NOTES *187*

SELECTED BIBLIOGRAPHY *227*

INDEX *239*

ILLUSTRATIONS

FIGURES

1. Ship *Niger* of New Bedford,
   Built at Mattapoisett in 1844 ....*4*

2. Detail of Wamsutta Mills Looking
   North from Fairhaven Bridge *4*

3. Bringing Home Firewood in Wamsutta's
   Tenements during the Depression *5*

4. Three-Deckers on North Street,
   New Bedford's North End *7*

5. Amanda and Harold Pitts Sr.,
   90 Nelson Street, c. 1947 ....*8*

6. Drawing of 90 Nelson Street
   during the Late 1940s *9*

7. Harold and Amanda Pitts, Emilie
   Medeiros on the Piazza, c. 1941 ....*10*

8. Harold and Amanda Pitts on Their
   First-Floor Piazza during the mid-1950s *10*

9. Extending the Object into Its
   Social Setting *12*

10. Drawing of the Backyard Neighborhood,
    90 Nelson Street, during the Late 1940s *13*

11. Amanda Pitts on the Laundry Deck
    at 90 Nelson in 1941 ....*14*

12. The Author in the Backyard of
    90 Nelson in 1947 ....*14*

13. John and Elaine Dias on Their
    Wedding Day, June 28, 1947 ....*15*

14. Social Context of a Three-Decker:
    New Bedford, Massachusetts *17*

15. Harold and Amanda Pitts with
    Their Niece, c. 1950 ....*18*

16. The Spatial Dynamics of a 1912
    Three-Decker Flat as Built *19*

17a. First-floor Use Pattern of the Pitts
     Family, 1939–50 ....*20*

17b. First-floor Use Pattern of the Pitts
     Family, 1950–66 ....*20*

18. Second-Floor Use Pattern of the
    Pitts Family, 1966–79 ....*21*

19. The Winter Climate Context of the
    Three-Decker in New Bedford *22*

20. The Summer Climate Context of the
    Three-Decker in New Bedford *23*

21. Stereograph of Whaleships and Casks
    of Whale Oil, New Bedford, c. 1870 ....*26*

22. The John Avery Parker Estate
    of 1833, c. 1870 ....*27*

23. Joseph Grinnell Mansion,
    County Street, 1832 ....*28*

24. William R. Rodman Mansion
    Built in 1833 ....*29*

25. Detail of William J. Rotch Cottage/Villa *32*

26. First Mill of Wamsutta Mills, Incorporated
    on April 8, 1846 ....*35*

27. "Wamsutta Mills," Oil on Canvas, by
    William Allen Wall *36*

28. 1895 Photograph of Wamsutta Mills by
    Joseph G. Tirrell *37*

29. 1924 Photograph of Wamsutta's Mill
    No. 2, Built in 1854 ....*41*

30. 1890 Photograph of Wamsutta's Mill
    No. 4, Built in 1868 ....*42*

31. Postcard of the Manomet Mill, c. 1910 . . . . *43*

32. Corliss Steam Engines in Machinery Hall, 1876 . . . . *44*

33. Mule Spinning Room at the Potomska Mills, c. 1880 . . . . *45*

34. Young French-Canadian Women in the Warping Room at the Whitman Mill, 1910 . . . . *46*

35. View from the Downtown Business District Looking to the South End Mill Development, c. 1910 . . . . *47*

36. Drawings for Edward Mandell Estate *49*

37. Residence of Edward D. Mandell, Published in William L. Sayer, *New Bedford 1889.* *50*

38. 1893 Formal Flower Garden Design Proposal and Driveway Study by Olmsted, Olmsted, and Eliot *52*

39. Portuguese Immigrant Family, 1912, Lewis W. Hine *53*

40. 1912 Lewis W. Hine Photograph of a Kitchen/Living Room of the Alfred Benoit Family *54*

41. Bronze Statue of *The Whaleman* by Bela L. Pratt *56*

42. Buttonwood Park Commemorative Statue to New Bedford's Rise to Manufacturing Greatness *57*

43. Louise Pitts behind the Laundry Deck, 90 Nelson Street, 1942 . . . . *57*

44. Greek Revival Roominghouse of the Whaling Era along South Water Street *62*

45. Eight Brick "Four-Tenements" Constructed for Wamsutta's Skilled Operatives, c. 1848 . . . . *63*

46. Four-Tenements at Wamsutta Mills *67*

47. A Group of Fifty Wamsutta Four-Tenements in 1913 . . . . *69*

48. Potomska Workers' Housing, Corner of Rivet and Second Streets, 1871 . . . . *71*

49. Evolution of New Bedford Mill-Housing Typology *72*

50. "New England—Sketches among the Weavers," 1898 . . . . *79*

51. Gable-End Workers' Housing near Wamsutta Mills, c. 1892 . . . . *80*

52. Evolution of New Bedford Mill-Housing Typology *81*

53. Grinnell Mill Housing in 1915 . . . . *82*

54. The Howland Mill Village in 1996 . . . . . *87*

55. Howland Mill No. 1 Under Construction, 1888 . . . . *93*

56. Superintendent's House, 1889 . . . . . . *93*

57. Howland Mills at Its Furthest Development, c.1901 . . . . *94*

58. Howland Mills Boardinghouse, c. 1905 . . . . *97*

59. Howland Mills Single-Family Housing for Skilled Workers by Architects Wheelwright and Haven *98*

60. The Bungalow, Wheelwright Family Cottage, Vinalhaven *99*

61. The Oaks, 1880, Willimantic Linen Company, Willimantic, Connecticut *105*

62. Duplex Housing at Hopedale under Construction, c. 1898 . . . . *114*

63. The 1840 Haile Luther House, Corner of Elm and Second Streets, New Bedford *122*

64. Examples of Town Row Houses, Which May Have Inspired the Three-Decker *123*

65. Early Example of a Three-Tenement in Fall River, Massachusetts *123*

66a. Plan of an Early Boston Three-Decker *124*

66b. Detail of Boston Three-Decker *124*

67. Cross-sectional Stereoview of a Gable-end Three-Decker, Worcester, Massachusetts, 1868 . . . . *126*

68. Drawing of a Three-Family Dwelling Designed in 1894 by Jacob Luippold *128*

69. Gable-end Three-Family Dwelling by architect Samuel Rantin, 1897 . . . . . . *128*

70. Drawing by T. J. Moriarty for Store and Tenements, New Bedford, 1904 . . . . . . *130*

71. 1896 Side-hall, Gable-end Workers' Houses across from the Dartmouth Mill .. *131*

72. 1892 Flat-top Three-Deckers on Upper Nelson Street *131*

73. Earliest Set of Blueprints on File in the New Bedford City Hall for a Three-Decker, 1904 .... *132*

74. Elevation and Plans for Six-Block Tenement Built over a Store *134*

75. Elevation and Plans for Neocolonial Six-Block designed in 1924 by Oscar Crapo *135*

76. Three-Tenement at Northeast Corner of Newton and Union Streets, New Bedford *137*

77. Two-story Three-Tenement with "Portuguese Dormers" *138*

78. Formal and Typological Evolution of the New Bedford Three-Tenement *139*

79. Three-story Tenement Block *140*

80. Sectional Views of a 1912 Three-Tenement *141*

81. Two First-Floor Plans by Jacob Luippold for Three-Family Dwellings *144*

82. Front Elevations by Jacob Luippold for Two Three-Family Dwellings in 1909 Showing "Clothes Yard: Placed on the Roofs" *145*

83. Street View of 90 Nelson *147*

84. Piazzas in New Bedford, being used for Surveillance during the 1928 Labor Strike *148*

85. A Two-Family Twin House by Architect C. E. Schermerhorn *150*

86a. Three-Decker at 5 Orchard Street, Built in 1915 by Joseph Motta *152*

86b. Three-Decker near the Former Rotch Mill, Built during the 1910s *152*

87. Side Yard Illustrating Required Minimum of Eight Feet between Tenements *153*

88. Canyons of Three-Decker Housing, across from Former Rotch Mill *153*

89. New Bedford Female Worker on the Winding Floor *154*

90. Angled Porch in Response to Corner Site condition, New Bedford, South End *155*

91. Raised Fieldstone Retaining Wall for a North End Three-Decker *155*

92. The Washington Social and Music Club,1905 .... *157*

93. Mt. Carmel Roman Catholic Church, 1903 .... *158*

94. Broadening Realms of Contextual Awareness: Home, Yard, Street *159*

95. Broadening Realms of Contextual Awareness: Neighborhood, District *160*

96. Broadening Realms of Contextual Awareness: City, State, Region *161*

97. South Water Street Shopping District after the Demolition *169*

98. Demolition of the Rotch Mill Site Exposing Former Mill Housing *170*

99. Portuguese Feast of the Blessed Sacrament *171*

100. Sunbeam Bread Shop Front Advertisement in Portuguese *171*

101. Laundry Pole Serving as a Mount for a Satellite Dish, 90 Nelson Street *172*

102. Removal of Piazzas and Conversion of Former Porch Doorways to More Energy-Efficient Window Openings, New Bedford's North End *173*

103. Cladding of a Three-Decker in Vinyl Siding, New Bedford's North End *173*

104. 1924 Cement-block "Gang Garages" Built by Architect Oscar Crapo for Six-block Tenements at 99 Nelson Street *174*

105. Side Yard Living Space Used as Off-Street Parking *174*

106. Joseph Soares in Front of His Two-Decker, Corner of Norwell Street and Bolton *175*

107. Gloria Medeiros in Provocao, Sao Miguel, Azores............ *176*

108. Rebuilt Piazzas on Norwell Street Mimicking Portuguese Wrought-Iron Verandas............ *177*

109. "New Vernacular" Response to the Traditional Three-Decker in New Bedford............ *177*

110. An Adapted Grape Arbor Serving as a Carport and Picnic Area............ *178*

111. Clarks Cove at Dawn, Showing the Kilburn Mill's Chimney Stack............ *179*

112. Traditional and Adaptively Used Three-Family Tenement Side by Side, Former Rotch Mill Neighborhood............ *181*

MAPS

1. New Bedford, 1815............ *27*

2. James Arnold Home on the Corner of County and Union Streets............ *30*

3. 1871 Walker Map, *The City of New Bedford,* Part of First Ward............ *64*

4. 1895 Beers *Atlas of Bristol County, Massachusetts*............ *65*

5. 1887 Walker Map, *The City of New Bedford* Showing Wamsutta Mills and Its Workers' Housing............ *66*

6. 1906 Sanborn Map Indicating Potomska's Four-Family Tenement Blocks............ *74*

7. Computer-enhanced Detail of the 1875 City Engineers' Map showing parcels later purchased for the Howland Mills Corporation and Mill Roads Nos. 2, 3, and 4............ *91*

8. The Curvilinear Plan of the Howland Mill Village............ *96*

9. Plan of Pullman,1885............ *103*

10. Detail of the Forty Cottages at "The Oaks"............ *104*

11. Lost Proposal of Olmsted, Olmsted, and Eliots' Plan for a "System of Parks" in New Bedford............ *109*

12. Map and Listing of All the City's Corporate-owned and -rented Workers' Housing............ *115*

13. Arthur Krim's Three-Decker Distribution Map for New England............ *127*

TABLES

1. Housing Distribution of Potomska Mill Workers............ *75*

2. New Bedford Three-Tenements. 1893–1930............ *130*

ACKNOWLEDGMENTS

The author would like to thank the following individuals for their assistance in the preparation of this book. John Roza III, deputy building commissioner for the City of New Bedford, allowed me to have access to the city building permits and offered his generous assistance on many research issues; the late Clement E. Daley, the former director of the Marketing Department of the City of New Bedford, shared his grandfather's three-decker building ledger with me; Tony Souza, director of W.H.A.L.E., put me in contact with several individuals in New Bedford who assisted me on the project; both Michael Steinitz of the Massachusetts Historical Commission and Arthur Krim, a consultant for Survey Systems in Cambridge, Massachusetts, were generous with their own research on the subject of the three-decker and offered several insights at various stages of the project. Deedee Jacobsohn, a doctoral candidate in the American Studies Program at Boston University working under Richard Candee, was most generous with her research data on three-deckers in south Boston. Thomas Beardsley of the Windham Textile and History Museum provided significant insights into the 1880 model mill village at Willimantic, Connecticut. His personal interpretation of the industrial site, which he offered to my American Architecture and Technology seminar, both enriched the class experience and informed this study. George Sanchez, an associate professor of American studies and history at the University of Michigan, offered valuable commentary as session chair at the American Studies Association Conference held in Boston, where my paper on the Portuguese-American transformation of the three-decker flat was presented in 1993.

Also, Tina Furtado and Joan Barney of the New Bedford Free Public Library offered effective and generous assistance whenever asked and provided many avenues for local research that otherwise would have gone unnoticed. Llewellyn Howland III offered many significant insights into his family history, shared his family correspondence, and reviewed earlier versions of the chapter on the Howland Mill Village. Kathryn Grover, contributing editor for *Old-Time New England*, helped me to become a more effective writer in my essay on the Howland Mill Village, arranged for a public lecture on the three-decker at the New Bedford Whaling Museum, and believed in the project when I needed it most. Patrick Malone, associate professor of American Civilization and Urban Studies at Brown University, arranged a public lecture (co-sponsored by the Portuguese and Brazilian Studies Department) on the social dimensions of the three-decker in New Bedford. This talk also provided the opportunity for me to discuss the conceptual framework of the larger study with Professors Malone, Jordy, and Almeida. Terrance Goode, editor for the Journal of Architectural Education *(J.A.E.)* and professor of architecture at Syracuse University, provided important critical commentary on my article "Cultural Weathering: Vernacular Architecture as Cultural Production." His insights into the notion of the transformative consumption of "type" both improved the article and led to an enriched discussion in the text.

Pamela Simpson, Arthur Krim, Michael Steinitz, John Garner, Richard Longstreth, and Kathryn Grover read the entire manuscript and contributed significantly to the present state of the book.

I would like to thank the following members of the University of North Carolina at Charlotte College of Architecture faculty: Gregor Weiss and Greg Snyder generously offered their talents for many issues on visual representation; Randy Swanson and Michael Swisher reviewed the written work at various stages and provided commentary on several occasions; Dale Brentrup offered professional insights on issues of environmental design; James B. Asbel provided insights into the relevance of my theoretical position to the design profession; and Robert Sandkam helped to resolve countless technical difficulties with computer modeling and photo manipulation. I cannot thank enough the dean of the College of Architecture, Charles Hight, for his patience and continued support of this project. Also, the University of North Carolina at Charlotte provided a paid leave of absence in the form of a University Reassignment of Duties grant (Fall 1991), which led to the preparation of the original manuscript; a University Research Grant (1996–97) provided the funding to undertake additional field research during the manuscript revisions; and two UNC Charlotte Faculty Grants Committee and Graduate School publication grants (1999–2000) helped to offset the final photographic preparation costs.

Special thanks to my mentors at Brown University—the late William Jordy, the late James Deetz, and Patrick Malone—for their guidance and inspiration in the fields of architectural history, material culture, and history of technology. A warm thank you is due to Donia Larth Schauble,

Todd Williams, Ed Portis, John Truitt, Matthew Draughn, Sean Gallagher, and Matt Jenkins for their research, typing, and illustrative assistance throughout the many stages of the manuscript. Their enthusiasm, skill, and patience have meant so much. The dedication of Matthew Draughn, in particular, not only ensured the timely publication of this work but contributed to what merit it may hold. He is a true friend. I am very grateful as well to my relatives in New Bedford, Massachusetts, for the use of their family photographs and personal histories. These resources enabled me to reconstruct life in my grandparent's three-decker flat after World War II with a level of richness and honesty that the subject deserved. Finally, my immediate family (Keay, Corey, and Wilder) and special friends Robert Meeker, Vince Kohl, and Amy Gottfried have suffered through this process with me, and they have provided the encouragement, direction, and emotional support so necessary for the completion of a work of this scale.

Front Elevation for C...
Proposed to be built a...
Drawn by Jacob Shippe...

INTRODUCTION
Architecture as Cultural Production

From the end of the Civil War to the collapse of the textile market in New England after 1923,[1] the explosion of urban growth tied to the industrial manufacture of textile goods in New England created a remarkably diverse regional stock of single-family and multifamily dwellings. This marked shift to industrial urbanism was fueled by two major forces—the introduction of Corliss steam power to supply the energy for cotton manufacturing and the large-scale immigration of Europeans into the American workplace. The wood-frame urban housing types that accompanied the large-city phase of industrialization often were designed specifically to accommodate the flood of immigrants that poured into New England to work in the mills. The magnitude of this residential building response resulted in not only unique housing solutions but often in new regional identities for many towns and villages now transformed into truly industrialized cities.

Unfortunately, the history of the conception and design of company-built industrial workers' housing in New England is still an underexplored topic, with the exception of the houses of Slater's village in Rhode Island and the early stages of Lowell's boardinghouses. Articles and monographs on late-nineteenth-century developments by scholars such as Garner, Gross, Beardsley, and Candee provide exceptions, as does Margaret Crawford's recent comprehensive study on the design of company towns in America up through the 1920s; but most—as in the case of John Garner's significant study on Hopedale, Massachusetts—have concentrated on corporate housing for model villages *outside* the major cities.[2]

Consequently, the circumstances surrounding the development of standard workers' housing in New England cities, as opposed to the model mill villages of the countryside, have received little attention. Largely missing from our understanding of the late stages of textile growth in the region, for example, are the specifics of the evolution of single-family and multifamily workers' housing, and the transition from company-built housing to a speculative building market in different locales, which introduced entirely different housing alternatives to the textile work force. In particular, the emergence of the wood-frame "three-decker" as the region's urban multifamily housing solution of choice has never received book-length treatment, even though it is widely acknowledged as a unique and characteristically New England form.

Finally, the nineteenth-century industrialization of New England might be thought of as one big boom-and-bust building cycle that resulted in a vast urban landscape abandoned by corporate capital. Perhaps because the lasting effects of industrial decline in New England are still present in many communities, the subject is both a complex and a painful one to address. As a result, little has been written that can add to our understanding of how those who were left behind or who inherited the landscape have used and reshaped it; further, little has been written about how this process characterizes the urban neighborhoods of New England as distinct regional places in their own right. (A welcome exception is Laurence Gross's recent study, *The Course of Industrial Decline: The Boott Cotton Mills of Lowell, Massachusetts, 1835–1955.*)

This study documents the cotton textile industry of New Bedford, Massachusetts—at one point the nation's leading producer of fine woven goods—with primary data otherwise previously unavailable. In doing so, it offers a multidisciplinary investigation of workers' housing as an index to social change and cultural identity within New Bedford from 1848 to 1925. The work addresses the specifics of the entire range of corporate-built and -owned housing in the city, and then focuses on the speculative building market that established the three-decker rental flat (a three-story, multifamily dwelling with individual living units on each floor) as the city's predominant residential building form. After 1925 (when the general economic slowdown in textiles within the region began to affect New Bedford), a broader story unfolds about the cultural imprints left on the built environment by the more recent city dwellers who inherited this industrial setting as the mills began to shut down. I contend that the story of this leading whaling port and textile city should not be seen as ending with the eclipse of its two "golden ages." Instead, through the record of ongoing change in the face of industrial decline and demographic shifts, New Bedford's evolving regional character within New England is further revealed. This study, then, brings together four inter-related and sequential spheres of investigation: the changing regional dynamics that bring textiles and industrial housing to a former whaling port; the history of workers' housing in New Bedford as part of the change in economies; the specific role that the three-decker plays within this class of housing as local mill owners begin to rely on a speculative building market to house their workers; and the record of change witnessed in the three-decker (after the collapse of the textile economy) that speaks to New Bedford's changing regional expression. This record of incremental change left on the built environment by its inhabitants I refer to as "cultural weathering."

In brief, the main purposes and arguments put forth in this book are as follows:

Part I of this study (chapters 1 and 2) provides the economic and cultural context for the emergence of the three-decker as the predominant multifamily workers' housing type in New Bedford. Chapter 1 prepares the reader for the discussion of the three-decker as a building type that appears and evolves in direct response to the changing demands of the New England textile economy through the literary device of an environmental autobiography. Here, the text not only examines the three-decker as a lived-in residential space, but addresses the issue of immigration in industrialized New England from the perspective of people's daily lives. It views immigrant life in New England, as immigration historian Donna Gabaccia refers to it, through "ethnic-particularism."[3] That is, this chapter interprets immigrant life in the host country by recalling neighborhoods and specific daily activities, thereby offering a vantage point of the world peopled only by those of the same ethnic background.

In order to assist the reader in understanding the socio-spatial dynamics of the three-decker living environment from an "insider's" perspective, I draw upon my own Portuguese heritage in the city and use personal, family, and community history for insights into the folkways, resources, and technologies of the area. In choosing to include this vantage point, I recognize that I have undertaken the difficult challenge of what anthropologist James Clifford refers to as the "participant observer"; namely, someone who is *in* the culture while at the same moment attempting to look *at* the culture. However, my motivation is to break, momentarily, from the historical narrative of the remaining sections of work where, as a virtual "outsider," I rely on standard primary and secondary sources of evidence to reconstruct the nature of place. By contrast, in this opening chapter I gaze with knowing eyes upon *who* lived in these buildings, *when* and *why* they did, in order to provide a vivid impression of how these individuals shaped their surroundings in ways expressive of their human condition and personal values. By focusing on life in and around my grandparents' three-decker rental flat in New Bedford after World War II, I attempt to illustrate how those who occupy buildings years after they were initially designed and built (and thereby invest them with new uses and meanings) play a central role in creating, or recreating, our built environment in a manner that contributes to its regional character. This vivid picture of the New Bedford of my youth offers a child's landscape awash in sensory images and distorted physical scales borne of childhood sensibilities. It is a mental reconstruction defined by physical artifacts from the locale and memories of human interaction in and around the three-deckers that were omnipresent in the immigrant industrial quarters of the city. Interpretive drawings (by the author, Greg Snyder, and Gregor Weiss of the College of Architecture at the University of North Carolina, Charlotte) are used to illustrate underlying patterns of spatial usage and climatic response within and surrounding the domestic sphere of the three-decker. Measured and sectional drawings of the 1912 three-decker rented by my grandparents for forty years, coupled with spatial readings of the changing use of the generic plan over their extended occupation of the flat, reveal how standardized building plans are imprinted with—and controlled by—local intentions.

From this narrow and personal vantage point, which once formed my *only* reality of what New Bedford was, I look backward and then forward to fold others' lives, events, aspirations, and needs into a broadly conceived account of the changing forces that shaped the residential development of this important New England industrial city. Following the experiential reading of the three-decker in chapter 1, the narrative voice shifts from an insider's to an outsider's perspective. I begin by posing the question "whence came they?" referring to the appearance of this particular aspect of workers' housing in New Bedford. Chapter 2 probes the circumstances governing community planning and housing design by local and national figures alike who originally shaped the regional character of New Bedford from the seventeenth century up to the turn of the twentieth century. This section of the book illustrates how New Bedford's elite society self-consciously constructed the geographical, cultural, and public identities of place through the large-scale production of corporate structures, palatial estates, public art, and park planning schemes. The focus is on chronicling the change in economies in late-nineteenth-century New Bedford from the whaling trade to textile production. Documentary evidence, including period maps, photographs, city directories, U.S. Census figures, local newspaper accounts, correspondence by mill owners, mill and housing blueprints, New Bedford city documents for the Board of Public Works and early historical accounts, is used to depict New Bedford's transformation from a river port village given to enterprise and trade to a city on the brink of a phase of large-scale industrialization. The change in regional economies also reveals New Bedford's transformed identity from a residential landscape defined largely during the whaling era by aloof patrician mansions sitting on large lots situated west of the city's commercial district, to one of densely packed workers' housing built in the service of an adjacent textile mill in the immigrant industrial neighborhoods of the north and south ends.

Part II addresses corporate housing in New Bedford. Bridging the gulf of extremes between New Bedford's mansions and its workers' housing was the vision of one mill owner, William D.

Howland. He attempted to extend to his workers similar benefits of a healthful and pleasant natural and built surroundings that the mill owners provided for themselves in the "suburban" villas and gardens of the western sector of the city. The case study of the Howland Mill Village (chapter 4) illustrates the shift from company-built and -managed workers' housing in the city (discussed in chapter 3) to a speculative building market (chapter 5), and represents more broadly the cusp of change in New Bedford from a workers' landscape shaped by the paternalistic visions of a powerful few to one transformed by the entrepreneurial efforts of the many at the beginning of this century.

In Part III (chapter 5) the social significance of the three-decker is analyzed as a transplanted building type that arrived in New Bedford during the 1870s at the very moment that the city was being transformed into a leading center for textile production. The social dimensions of this architectural form are traced by exploring the competing motivations of promoters, architects, builders, developers, and housing reformers within New Bedford and in surrounding shoe and textile cities in the same decades. This investigation was accomplished in New Bedford by examining building permits and blueprints in the New Bedford City Hall from their inception in 1893 to 1925, when the three-decker ceased to be built in the city. These sources reveal that an archetypal three-decker form emerged in the city by 1904, and they determined the years of greatest three-decker building activity and clarified three-decker typological preferences. Also, the complete collection of insurance, planning, and bird's-eye view maps for the city (located in the planning office of City Hall and the New Bedford Free Public Library) were consulted and augmented by three-decker distribution studies undertaken by Arthur Krim. The building ledger of Michael E. Daley, who began documenting his three-decker projects in 1909, proved to be an invaluable resource. It revealed the financing practices between builder and client, as well as the sequence and cost of various stages of construction. This document was in the possession of his grandson, the late Clement Daley. Morphology charts, prepared by the author, of representative three-tenement buildings in New Bedford, coupled with building chronology charts (indicating the number of three-deckers built each year with the notation of their respective roof types) also were useful in establishing the localization of the building type.

Blueprints by three-decker builders outside of the city, such as those in Lynn, Massachusetts, by architect Dana A. Sanborn (in the possession of the Lynn Historical Society), Jacob Luippold of Jamaica Plain, and Samuel Rantin and Son of Boston (the latter are in the possession of the Society for the Preservation of New England Antiquities), provided comparative analyses for work undertaken during the same era in New Bedford. These works, though highly selective because they were among some of the most sophisticated treatments of the three-decker design formulas, nevertheless reflected broad-ranging design intentions, economic determinants, aesthetic considerations, and client concerns that served to illustrate how this popular residential form addressed the needs and sensibilities of a broad user group in its day. This evidence also clarified the regional differences among the building forms.

The prescriptive goals behind the builders' guides, where the three-decker was often represented as a bridge between the suburban ideal of a single-family dwelling on a lot and a two- or three-family "home" in a more compressed urban circumstance, were explored by consulting such works as William T. Comstock's *Two Family and Twin Houses* (1908). Also, the attack on the "evils of the three-decker" by social reformers, particularly during the early teens, was researched largely through the proceedings from the annual conference entitled "Housing Problems in America." This last source, coupled with local newspaper editorials, was used to gauge the conflicting interpretations between social reform claims and concerns and the actual design and ordinance responses implemented at the local level.

This section of the study shifts the attention away from the rather extraordinary manipulations of industrial and residential space on the part of the mill magnates, politicians, urban planners, and banking officials discussed in Parts I and II to the construction of an urban, industrial, residential landscape shaped by land speculators and local builders. Collectively, these two spheres of design—the corporate designer/planner and speculative builder—defined the parameters of a common living experience shared by the majority of New Bedford mill workers from 1848 to 1925.

Chapter 6 explores the social accommodation of the three-decker building type by successive users. Chapter 5 relies principally on documentary evidence to reveal an archetypal example of the New Bedford three-decker. The same sources serve to identify individual builders, buildings, and generic living spaces common to the locale within the time frame of 1893 to 1925. In contrast, the three-decker is addressed in Chapter 6 as a culturally transformed living environment. Here, I draw upon a material culture analysis—the examination of everyday objects, neighborhood photographs, oral histories, field research of buildings and their adjacencies as built and transformed—to reveal patterns of human behavior and belief within three-decker neighborhoods in the era of decline following the collapse of the textile economy in the region (c. 1925–59). The story of the three-decker in New Bedford is only initially a story of the textile industry in that city and the design efforts by architects and builders to house the largely poor and unskilled labor force of the working population. Indeed, we cannot fully understand the nature of the three-decker as an agent of the rapidly industrializing Northeast without considering the domestic settings of the immigrant industrial workforce beyond what the speculative builder had envisioned. Further, to ignore the issue of how the three-decker was appropriated by users of this industrial landscape to meet their particularized needs, to assign meaning to things, and to negotiate power leaves much of the meaning of the type (as a shared experiential living environment within the locale) untouched.

This final chapter addresses two phases of the transformation of the building type; it shows how the type was altered during the decline of the textile economy in the region (1925–59), and how the type changed after the passage of the 1965 U.S. Immigration Act that brought a large in-migration of a foreign population into New Bedford. This latter aspect of cultural-landscape analysis considers the impact of new ethnic social patterns on building modifications of the three-decker up to the present. The subject is addressed principally by an examination of the field evidence and by personal interviews with recent arrivals from the Portuguese Azore Islands—the source of the largest immigrant population in New Bedford. Emphasis is placed on how objects, consumer goods, and social rituals serve to define and subvert status within the local community.

While the first two sections of the text offer a broad contextual framework for understanding the forces that brought industrial housing to New Bedford, the final section presents a detailed investigation of the various scales and modes of influence that drive the production and consumption of New Bedford's most popular multifamily housing form—the three-decker flat. Historical, economic, and urban forces are discussed at regional and local scales (in terms of the city and neighborhoods within it), then the discussion focuses on the local cultural and familial scales that reveal the transformative consumption of the three-decker up to the present. I argue that out of these complex and varied range of forces, the three-decker in New Bedford was, in effect, "reproduced" several times within its locale. Area builders adopted the regional type to address local conditions; local economic and legal factors overlapped and fostered the formal and spatial optimization of the type as built; and demographic shifts tied to the national economy and national immigration policies led to changes in aesthetic preference and use that contribute to the social construction of a different regional identity for New Bedford. Accordingly, architecture is interpreted in this section of the text as an act of cultural production, rather than as an act of individual inspiration, in order to account for the full range of forces acting upon it at various points in time.

Hence, while much of the focus on workers' housing culminates with an in-depth analysis of the three-decker, the object of the work is *not* to produce a monograph on this regional building type. To be sure, the three-decker tenement is central to the discussion, and the documentary evidence, detailed analysis, and historical interpretation offered in the three chapters that address this building type provide, arguably, the most comprehensive examination to date of this important multifamily housing form. But it is the issue of place making that is paramount: Is the three-decker a generic type—an architectural blank—capable of being grafted onto the middle-class suburbs of Roxbury or Dorchester with the same functional and symbolic import as when it is introduced into working-class neighborhoods such as Lynn, Fall River, or New Bedford? Or do the ethnic, economic, and geographic conditions of a locale (to cite only a few factors) serve as regional filters that reshape the meaning, utility, and character of a building form? By witnessing the entire range of forces that account for the conception, design, use, and transformation of this regionally significant building type, we can learn not only about basic design characteristics of a certain building type that are shared broadly within a region, but also about a particular human and physical setting to which it is bound inextricably. It is my contention that only through such an integrated, contextual approach can the subregional forces acting upon a building form be defined effectively and, in turn, place-specific and culturally reflexive qualities be clarified. It is the goal of this study, therefore, to chronicle the formation and transformation of this important New England industrial city through an examination of the building stock designed to accommodate its labor force. The notion of "cultural weathering" (discussed as a theoretical position at the end of the field study) is used as an interpretive tool to demonstrate how the layers of cultural evidence left on the built environment by its inhabitants reveal the collective choices made in response to the subregional determinants of the locale. In the end, the manner in which different forces merge, overlap, collide, reveal, and conceal one another determines the distinctive patina of place.

PART I

NEW BEDFORD
One Generation and Many

GROWING UP IN A NEW BEDFORD THREE-DECKER
An Environmental Autobiography

New Bedford is situated on the western shore of the Acushnet River near its outlet to Buzzard's Bay. Its location on the southeastern coast of Massachusetts anchors its economic, social, and historical identities to the sea. Historically, life in this part of New England has turned on two points of reference: whaling and textiles (figs. 1–2). For more than a century (from approximately 1818 to 1928), the expressive character and regional identity of New Bedford have been linked inextricably to these two sequential and overlapping economic forces that account for relatively unbridled growth and development. Today, the city's cultural memory still draws upon the creative energy and pride of that era. The memories are, perhaps, the only tonic for much of the human despair that has taken hold since the collapse of New Bedford's textile economy. With 82 percent of New Bedford's inhabitants employed

Fig. 1. Ship *Niger* of New Bedford, built at Mattapoisett in 1844. Courtesy of Old Dartmouth Historical Society–New Bedford Whaling Museum.

Fig. 2. Detail of Wamsutta Mills (built 1848) looking north from Fairhaven Bridge. Used with the permission of the Board of Trustees of the New Bedford Free Public Library.

solely in textiles at its peak, this downturn in textile production was devastating.[1]

The 1919 to 1929 regional textile depression hit New Bedford by 1925. In the five years between 1928 and 1933, 21 mills went under. In 1933 alone, the city lost 7 of its remaining 42 textile mills, putting 5,000 operatives out of work. Derelict mills were torn down as part of a 1934 economic recovery act; in turn, the neighborhoods became weather-beaten by economic hardship (fig. 3). Unlike industrial centers elsewhere that also suffered through the ill effects of the Depression, New Bedford's one-industry economy had been irrevocably transformed by economic pressures that eventually moved textiles permanently from New England to the South.[2] There was to be no recovery in this industry which, by the 1880s, had so completely governed the life and character of the city.

By the end of the Depression, the aging mill tenements stood, as before, in harsh contrast to the mansions of the mill magnates. Yet, something had changed. The mansions now seemed to represent, almost mockingly, the greatness that *had* been New Bedford's. Similarly, the symbiotic link between mill and mill housing was broken with the closing of the mills. As a result,

Fig. 3. New Bedford youth and adult woman bringing home firewood in front of Wamsutta's four-family workers' tenements during the Depression. Courtesy of Jack Delano, Spinner Publications.

the north and south ends of the city, which once had been stable immigrant industrial neighborhoods, lost the economic support vital to their social operation.

As inhabitants of a newly depressed factory town, New Bedford's citizens developed a different self-image. Where once its civic leaders spoke of New Bedford in superlatives—"the largest whaling port in the world" or "the leading textile center in the country"—quiet desperation replaced bravado, and memories softened harsh realities. The generations of New Bedford youths that followed the Depression years never experienced the gritty vibrancy of seventy textile mills signaling their productive potency in clouds of smoke from coal-fed engine houses. Instead, they inherited the despair of decline and the physical remnants of an industrial landscape undergoing wrenching change. These generations were part of New Bedford's history, but not part of its triumph.

The city began to turn more emphatically than before the Depression to a cod-fishing economy and, later, to an economy based on scallop fishing. Gradually its residents acquired a different consen-

sus image of place, as fishing boats replaced smokestacks as artifacts of regional expression.[3] Yet the visible presence of an abandoned factory landscape bespoke a heritage that was still locked in the memories, emotions, and experience of its citizenry.

Though the physical setting of giant textile mills surrounded by workers' housing stayed largely unchanged in the two decades following New Bedford's economic descent, there was a hidden dimension that indicated a new way of life within the former textile city. What follows is an environmental autobiography of the working-class architectural environments in which I was raised as experienced principally through the lens of a child. This section of the study offers what Heinz Kohut refers to as an "experience-near" reading of place and probes the social use and meaning of domestic space during a time of transition within the city following a regional depression, a world depression, and World War II. It invokes the power of memory in order to capture the texture of ethnic life and aims at interpreting the cultural milieu within which one three-decker flat existed. In doing so, it demonstrates how the generic living spaces as defined by the original three-decker builders of the textile era are rein-scribed by subsequent human experience. The intent is to see the three-decker *relationally* and to explore subregional realities rooted in the life of the locale. The following family photographs and recollections not only evoke my own child-hood, but attempt to bring a particular human set-ting into clearer focus.[4]

References to the vantage point of a child's landscape seek to tap the full sensory engagement with place that comes with the pre-intellectualiza-tion of space. This, in actuality, is the basis upon which most people relate to their living environ-ments. Children, for example, do not simply experience *their* houses, or the *outsides* of build-ings—they make the entire neighborhood their playground. They make clubhouses in damp cel-lars; they rummage through hot attics, investigate the tops of garage roofs, and explore abandoned textile mills. They play baseball in cluttered alley-ways and hang by their ankles (held by their friends) to retrieve balls from storm drains. In their own way, children "survey" every house and space on the block. These direct experiences later become part of the memory framework that constitutes one's awareness of—and attachment to—place.

EXTENDING THE THREE-DECKER INTO ITS EXPERIENTIAL LANDSCAPE: THE INFLUENCE OF THE USER IN THE SOCIAL CONSTRUCTION OF SPACE

No land ever again has such power over him as that in which a man was once a child.
— Whittaker Chambers, *Witness,* 1952

Growing up in New Bedford always seemed at once a world apart and world within. The world within was composed of my Portuguese American identity that played out along the wharves lined with fishing boats, where immigrants from the Azores, Madeira, and Cape Verde Islands drew upon their experience with the sea and carried on their traditional ways in their adopted home. Sharing an experience not wholly my own, my maternal grandfather on rare occasions would show me a world more like his than mine—the Portuguese feasts such as the Azorean Stackhouse festival in the south end. Antonio Jose Medeiros came to America from Povacao, St. Michael, in 1900 and moved to New Bedford by 1901, just as the second textile boom was underway. The feasts reconnected him to the world he had left behind at age fourteen. Viola music, sweet bread, fava beans, linguica, kale soup, and the language I never learned evoked a cultural experience I was tied to more by birth than by daily ritual. It was not entirely a world "within." There is, after all, a difference between a Portuguese and a Portuguese American world view.

Away from the fishing economy of the wharves and the displays of social and religious ritual offered by both the feasts and an abundance of Catholic churches throughout the city, other confusing and overlapping boundaries that served to define the edges of "within" and "without" asserted themselves. Among the mills and mill neighborhoods, "place" was the hypnotic rhythm of three-decker after three-decker that formed sweeping canyons of wood that halted suddenly at the looming figure of a red-brick mill (fig. 4). Such recurring images defined the immigrant industrial neighborhoods of the North and South Ends of New Bedford to which I belonged.

This world of massive factories was relieved by the blocks and half blocks where family and friends lived. In my child's landscape, I spent a good deal of time at the home of my paternal grandparents, a three-decker flat on 90 Nelson Street in the South End industrial district. Here, Amanda (Souza) Paes and her husband, Harold Pitts Sr., rented various floors of the same three-decker for forty years (from 1939 to 1979) in

Fig. 4. These three-deckers line North Street, which ends at the former Nashawena Mill B on Belleville Avenue in New Bedford's North End.

response to their changing family structure.[5] This three-tenement (as a three-decker was referred to in the *New Bedford Record of Building Permits*) was built by Joseph Blier in 1912 for his client Francis Cardinand at a cost of forty-five hundred dollars. Like all the others at this end of the block, it was the product of speculative development linked to the construction of the Page Mill, built itself from 1906 to 1909.[6] The Pitts family, like many of the occupants of these three-decker neighborhoods who worked in the mills, would never own their own home.

Both of my paternal grandparents had worked briefly in the South End mills after World War II. Harold was a night watchman in the Holmes Mills and Amanda was a carder and winder in the Kilburn Mill. One of their daughters, Louise, worked as a stitcher for Page Mill at the foot of Nelson Street; my great uncle, Charlie Paes (anglicized to Page), had been a foreman in a

silk mill in Warren, Rhode Island, until it closed. After that he sold cars. When my father had worked for Charlie he learned additional skills at the New Bedford Textile School (which first opened in 1899 to help operatives advance their positions in the mills) until it was clear that textiles essentially had left the city. My father left with them. My aunt Elaine (Pitts) Dias worked as a foreman in a former textile mill converted to making refrigerator valves. Early on, her husband, John Dias, went from being a bobbin changer at the Acushnet Mills to going into the laundry business. All these people at one time or another lived at 90 Nelson Street.

This was the web of family, work, and place that shaped my childhood memories of New

Fig. 5. Amanda and Harold Pitts Sr. in front of 90 Nelson Street, c. 1947. Note the ice truck in the background, off-loading blocks of ice for the iceboxes, which were accessed through the rear of the three-deckers.

Bedford. In the background of a family photo taken on the sidewalk of their tenement in 1946 is an ice truck (fig. 5). Before 1947 when refrigerators were finally available after the wartime shortages, ice truck drivers delivered large blocks of ice to the rear of the flats for the ice boxes. As a child, I would gather around the truck with my cousin and friends to grab broken pieces of ice to eat, though often the chips of ice were covered in sawdust or straw used to keep the ice from melting.

The ice truck was just one of several delivery trucks, peddler's carts, and work wagons that brought coal, fish, produce, milk, even ice cream down the street for sale in what amounted to a mobile economic infrastructure vital to a community not yet wholly dependent upon the automobile. The scarcity of automobiles in the South End during the 1940s was partly the result of situational constraints brought on by the lingering effects of the worldwide depression, followed by World War II gas and tire rationing, and partly the result of sustained patterns of inconsistent employment in the city after the war ended. Yet, the frequency of horse-drawn wagons in this community reflected as well the rural roots of the new ethnic population, which, following the regional textile decline of 1919 to 1929, had settled in the

South End from the Azore Islands. Willing to work for lower wages, operate more equipment, and forfeit the representation of a trade union, the Portuguese changed the largely French-Canadian ethnic makeup of both the mills and adjoining neighborhoods.[7]

While purchasing from street vendors had long been frowned upon by prescriptive texts such as *Plain Facts for Future Citizens* (1914) because of contamination by flies, it was nevertheless part of Old World custom and, therefore, maintained by the newly arrived Portuguese (fig. 6).[8] The street became an extension of the social sphere of the old mill tenements, and a setting for the reenactment of the farming village life many of these transplants from the Portuguese islands had lived prior to their immigration. Such a transference of culture lent continuity to their lives amidst dramatic social and economic change and, in turn, temporarily transformed urban industrial neighborhoods into approximations of Portuguese village life just a few miles from the city's metropolitan center. The street, then, was both an urban activity space and a residential transition zone in such changing mill neighborhoods. As part of the street life, common American practices merged with Old World living patterns; Portuguese

Fig. 6. Interpretive drawing of 90 Nelson Street in its streetscape social context during the late 1940s.

American children in the neighborhood played basketball late into the night under street lamps using bottomless peach baskets nailed to a telephone pole. During the day, when street market activities were taking place, widows (traditionally Portuguese widows wear black all of their remaining lives) would work their way back from their daily visit to corner grocery stores to prepare traditional family meals. The family meals, in turn, immersed both young and old in the rituals of the homeland by maintaining foodways customs. In such a manner, the interior and exterior worlds of three-decker neighborhoods were addressed through the street in vitally important ways.

Most often during the 1950s, the day was marshaled by the flow of human activity that occurred at (and between) mill shift changes from the nearby Goodyear Tire Company—once the Rotch Spinning Mill—or the Page Mill garment factory (more familiarly referred to as a sweatshop). The time during second shift (from 2:00 P.M. to 10:00 P.M.) on Saturday, for example, would blend a multitude of street events that were forced to accommodate one another. Coal trucks emptied fuel down long chutes into wooden bins through the cellar windows of the three-deckers, displacing children who, moments earlier, had been playing street baseball by throwing a rubber ball against a cellar window sill.

Once on the sidewalk, another contested spatial realm existed that represented both public

Fig. 7. (Right) Harold and Amanda Pitts, Emilie Medeiros on the piazza, c. 1941. Note the use of clapboard siding prior to its conversion to shingles in 1947, and the use of screen inserts in the window bay for cross-ventilation.

Fig. 8. (Below) Harold and Amanda Pitts sitting on their first-floor piazza during the mid-1950s. Note the Page Mill (built 1906) at the end of the block.

and private spheres of activity. Since each tenement owner was given the choice of either paving the sidewalk in front of his or her building or leaving it as gravel, there was often the sound of a staccato beat of changing textures along the length of the streetscapes. As a child, when I wanted to roller skate on the sidewalk in front of my grandparents' tenement, I was inevitably frustrated by the lack of uniformity in the paving surfaces as I proceeded to move down the block. Often, I would be yelled at (in any number of foreign tongues still spoken in the neighborhood) if I was playing on someone else's front walk, since the foreground space of a three-decker generally was conceived of as an "owned space." (In actuality, all three-deckers were built only two feet from the

front lot line or the inside edge of the sidewalk.) Some children took advantage of ordinary gravel paving and used it as a setting to play marbles or just to dig in. Also in evidence on the sidewalk were ash cans that held the refuse of coal stoves or furnaces on garbage day. They unceremoniously marked the transition from street to sidewalk, where they were left on axis with the ash can sheds provided to each tenant at the rear of the three-decker.

Once one reached the front piazza, another spatial zone was broached (figs. 7–8). While used generally after summer work hours to catch breezes off the cove nearby, the front porch held multiple meanings. It, too, was a transition zone, a boundary from semipublic space such as the front walkway to a semiprivate zone. Raised above the ground plane, the piazza offered both surveillance of the public realm of the street and entertainment. During the 1920s, courting rituals also took place here under the watchful eye of a Portuguese grandmother, who had a clear vantage point through the bay window of the front parlor.

While the front hallway leading from the piazza was conceived of as a central feature of public performance and daily use in the original three-decker design scheme (particularly since the boarder's entrance to the bedroom was directly off of the front stair hall), it was effectively a ceremonial entrance for the Pitts family, as for most New Bedford residents, used in conjunction with the front parlor for First Communions, weddings, funerals, Christmas, Easter, and other holidays. When not in use, the entrance hallway served as a weather baffle or for cold storage. Instead, the *rear* entry that led directly into the dining room (formerly the kitchen in 1912) was the primary everyday entrance. Apart from holiday visitors, any person who came to the front door could be presumed to be from *outside* the community. Such spatial practices illustrate how the users often subvert the formal spatial hierarchies prescribed by the designer. They also emphasize the dichotomy between the perceived awareness of physical space and the hidden reality of socially constructed space (fig. 9).[9]

The distinction between ceremonial and utilitarian entrances was, from the start, implied in the aesthetic handling of the three-decker itself (compare figs. 6 and 10). As a living unit, the organization of the apartment space ran from streetfront to deep into the backyard lot (the flat measured 26 feet by 40 feet), and followed a pattern of decreasing aesthetic embellishment and social formality. Front and rear, semi-enclosed porches (called piazzas) were distinctly less formal from streetside to backyard in terms of architectural detail and, in turn, in their usage. But in spite of such symbolic distinctions, these were in actuality consistently negotiated and interconnected spheres of social interaction (as were other aspects of outdoor living space), making such "exterior-but-included" spaces settings for important social relationships. Hence, the social relevance of the three-decker can be defined as much by its lot utilization and physical adjacencies as by the building's form and plan, and *all* aspects of the household are best understood as part of an integrated domestic unit.[10]

Because the actual entry was through the rear, the side yard and rear passageways leading to the flat became meaningful extensions of the household (fig. 10). The side and rear yard spaces between frame tenements—intended as firebreaks originally and as a means of containing contagious diseases among the working population—now became the product of claimed communal-use patterns. For my grandparents, who lived in the same three-decker flat for forty years and whose children often rented a different floor in the same building, the backyard was essentially *their* private space. Wooden outdoor chairs, flower beds, birdhouses, children's swings, and a side-yard shrine to the Virgin Mother established their spatial "claim" amidst such overwhelming uniformity of housing stock.

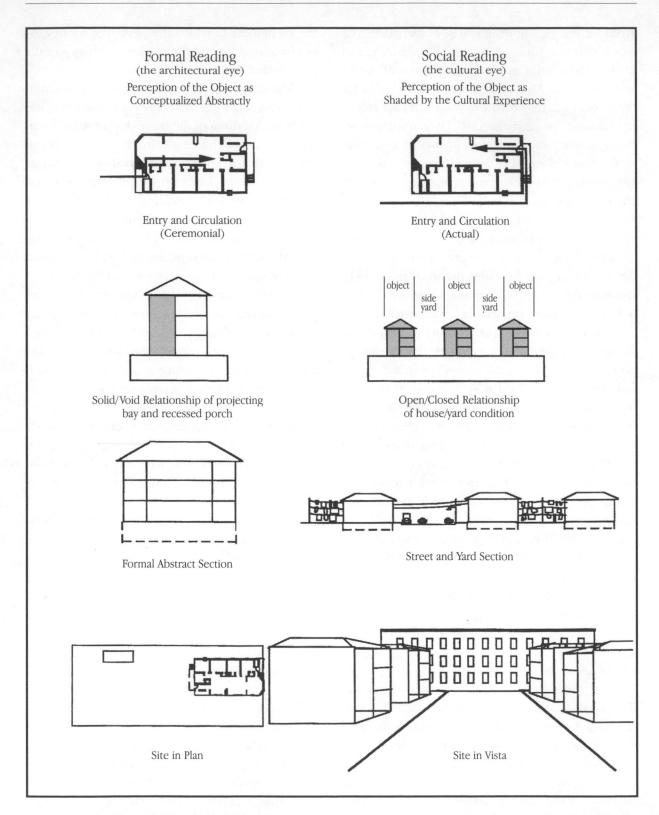

Formal Reading
(the architectural eye)
Perception of the Object as
Conceptualized Abstractly

Social Reading
(the cultural eye)
Perception of the Object as
Shaded by the Cultural Experience

Entry and Circulation
(Ceremonial)

Entry and Circulation
(Actual)

Solid/Void Relationship of projecting
bay and recessed porch

Open/Closed Relationship
of house/yard condition

Formal Abstract Section

Street and Yard Section

Site in Plan

Site in Vista

Fig. 9. Extending the object into its social setting.

Fig. 10. Extending the object into its cultural landscape: Interpretive drawing of the backyard neighborhood at 90 Nelson Street during the late 1940s.

Fig. 11. Amanda Pitts on the laundry deck at 90 Nelson in 1941.

rear "decks" to a pole on the corner of the lot. This busy flurry of lines was carefully calculated within the framework of local tenement etiquette so that laundry from the other flats would not drip on those below or get tangled with someone else's wash. Each day, the bedding hung on lines linking women, through similar work patterns, together across backyard neighborhoods.

Unlike some other New Bedford urban dwellers, who purchased multifamily dwellings and rented them to friends and relatives as a means of controlling the character of their living environment, my grandparents were unable to provide such a living arrangement for their family because of economic limitations. They could, however, reconstruct through proximity the *notion* of

In contrast to the often generous side-yard condition of the privately owned two-deckers, where Portuguese homeowners purchased adjoining house lots to be used for gardens and vineyards in concert with cellar kitchens, the social life of the household in the larger three-decker rental units traditionally concentrated on activities located at the rear of the tenement in connection with housekeeping and childrearing responsibilities (figs. 11–12). As a child, my cousins and I played here under the scrutiny of our grandmother, who did laundry in her cold-water flat in the family tub with boiling water from the stove. Laundry was hung on lines connected from the

Fig. 12. The author in the backyard of 90 Nelson in 1947.

an extended family living in a single-family dwelling. In the Pitts household, family members lived on the first two floors of the three-decker on 90 Nelson; on the second floor of the three-decker flat to the immediate left; and on the first-floor apartment across the street. Therefore, the cultural continuity of the households often extended from floor to floor, and from flat to flat, reinforcing the social, economic, and ethnic cohesiveness of the neighborhood. Such a close proximity to family and friends offered not only neighborhood ties, but also visual access from the vantage point of parallel stacks of porches forming streetside and backyard corridors of community (fig. 13). Often, relatives communicated with one another by yelling across porches or between households through parallel window openings. Of course, there was also little privacy in such surroundings; the neighborhood stood witness to family joy and calamity alike.

From the minute I entered the rear landing of my grandparents' rental flat, coats, sweaters, and household items hanging from wall hooks began to establish the individual character of their apartment (see item "f" on the floor plan in fig. 14). Covered with inexpensive linoleum, the rear entry was steeped in the aroma of exotic smells from vinegar-based marinades and red-pepper dishes, whose odors were absorbed into the wall surfaces from generations of Portuguese cooking. Upon entering directly from the hallway into the dining room (item "e" in fig. 14), I was invited to have something to eat as part of the ritual of family acceptance. In many ways the dining room was the heart of the household; here, the entire family gathered on Sundays and talked at meal times— exchanging sentences at rapid speed and at intervals as closely packed as the weave from the power looms in neighboring mills.

With regard to the house plan as reconstituted by the Pitts family over the years, there was still an evident procession of spaces leading from the front to rear entries; however, the sequence was

Fig. 13. John and Elaine Dias on their wedding day June 28, 1947, with Mr. Piva, the landlord, looking on from his second-floor laundry deck. Note the shingle siding that has replaced the clapboard cladding on 90 Nelson in the background and the simplified treatment of the rear laundry deck compared with the classical columns on the front piazzas.

generally experienced in reverse order. Instead of the original zonal organization of social spaces leading from the formal parlor to the dining room and finally to the kitchen (as prescribed in the Victorian-era plans), one entered through the dining room (the former kitchen) and, hence, through the more utilitarian end of the house. (The concern about tracking in dirt from the mill onto the parlor floor coverings may have had something to do with this shift in the circulation path.) Further, the old dining room by the 1940s had become utilized instead as a "double parlor" (item "d" in fig. 14), and the formal parlor now terminated the spatial sequence. The "double parlor" by the 1940s served as a sitting or living room for daily usage, while the front parlor (item "c" in fig. 14) was generally closed off by sliding pocket doors to conserve heat or to protect furniture for special occasions of public and private ritual.

Among Portuguese, there is almost a shrine-like reverence for the front parlor. Therefore, in attempting to understand the sociology of the parlor today in terms of its relationship, for example, to the formal entry, the double parlor, and the front bedroom,[11] we observe that its selection as the "best room" is consistent with the design intent of the original builder. But it is in the degree of nonarchitectural decorative embellishment and in the degree of respect accorded to it by the user that we see additional clues as to its symbolic importance within the home. It is in the double parlor, for instance, where the majority of family portraits are on display and where often the television is placed. It is a space for informal social gatherings. In the formal or front parlor, on the other hand, all the best furniture is gathered (sometimes hermetically sealed in plastic), to be used as a setting for First Communion celebrations or other Catholic observances. It is more a place to *look at* than to use—an icon of social and religious propriety. The bedrooms, bathroom, and kitchen, on the other hand, are part of the private sphere off to the side (items "k"–"o" in fig. 14). But even here private versus public space is not straightforward. The master bedroom (item "m" in fig. 14), where in 1939 my great-grandparents

lived, eventually became my grandparents' bedroom. Its social relationship to the household ranged from simple sleeping, to a place for private family discussions, to where my grandmother said her rosary and maintained a "bureau shrine," complete with votive candles, a crucifix, and palms. The kitchen (item "n" in fig. 14), small as it was, became the staging area for a sequence of ethnic dishes throughout the day—made more complicated by the fact that my grandfather was of Irish descent and my uncle Charlie, the family boarder, preferred Portuguese cooking. The cooking stove in the original design had been moved from the present dining room into what had previously been designated as the pantry or sink room to form the present kitchen space. A hot-water heater was finally added to the kitchen facilities during the 1970s as prescribed by a newly instituted Massachusetts state law.

In large households, such as the Pitts family, with occupants sharing rent in a collective-family living arrangement, these spaces were often more complex than they might first appear. In the 1940s, as noted, Amanda (Paes) Pitts had her father-in-law and mother-in-law living in the master bedroom. Later, her brother and his daughter moved into the three-decker upon the death of the mother-in-law, making a household of seven individuals for three bedroom spaces. After hours, domestic arrangements other than those shown in the house plan took place. For example, the living-room couch became a daybed for the niece, while the children slept, sometimes three to a bed, in the side rooms

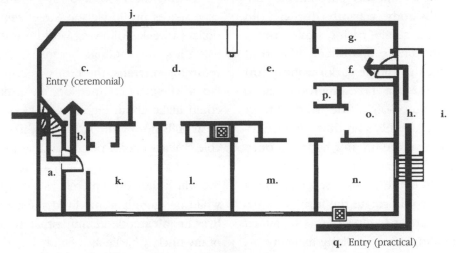

j.

g.

c.
Entry (ceremonial)

d.

e.

f.

p.

o.

h.

i.

b.

a.

k.

l.

m.

n.

q. Entry (practical)

N ←→ S

Plan

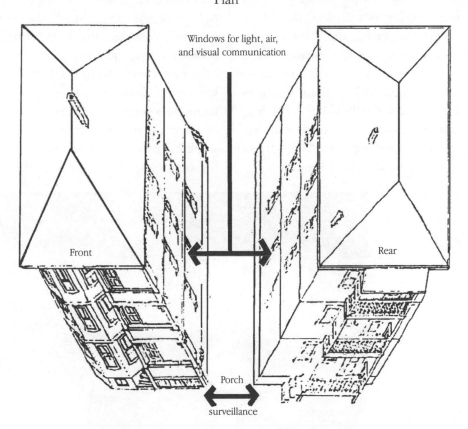

Windows for light, air,
and visual communication

Front

Rear

Porch

surveillance

Floor rental hierarchy (Social Concerns)

1st floor—easy access, expensive heat, ideal for children & elderly
2d floor—warm, cheap heat, noisy
3d floor—private, quiet, "free heat," difficult access

(fig. 15). The smallest child was placed in the middle for increased body warmth during cold evenings, when the single parlor stove proved unable to heat the entire apartment. The front bedroom (opposite the double parlor/living room) was designed in 1912 as a "boarding room," since it had its own entrance off of the front hallway. Here, Charlie Page, Amanda's brother, lived (rotating seasonally to the more interior bedroom once the children left the apartment) for over thirty years until his death in the 1970s. According to my grandmother, she would rotate the furniture during the seasonal changes to alter the wear pattern on the linoleum and, hence, prolong its utility.

While these living spaces may seem large in plan in comparison with other forms of urban housing for the working population, then, they were as densely packed *within* the living units as they were along the congested streetscapes.[12] But, since the congestion was the product of family members sharing space, rather than strangers being packed into tenement housing (as it may appear to an outsider), these three-deckers always seemed to me to be teeming with "life." These flats held people I knew and cared for deeply.

During the 1930s and early 1940s, these domestic spaces on 90 Nelson Street rented for three dollars a week. Following World War II, when there was a housing shortage because of the number of returning veterans, the rent was raised to six dollars a week. By comparison, an unskilled laborer could make about eighteen dollars a week in the local mills during the late 1930s, if work was available.[13] Years later, I pondered the fact that I never recalled a time in my grandparents' marriage during which they lived merely as a couple. However, while my grandparents lived their entire married lives in an extended family situation, the presence of my uncle Charlie as a family boarder, for example, provided my grandmother with some of the only economic certainty for supporting her household that she knew from the Depression era onward. Most important, the boarding income allowed her to quit her job as a winder in the Kilburn Mill after World War II to stay at home with her family. Certainly, issues of privacy presented themselves simply by having family boarders living in close proximity. This was particularly evident when bedroom doors had to be left open during the winter months in order to have access to the

Fig. 15. Harold and Amanda Pitts, c. 1950, with their niece, who also lived in the three-bedroom flat. During evening hours the daybed on which they are sitting became her bed.

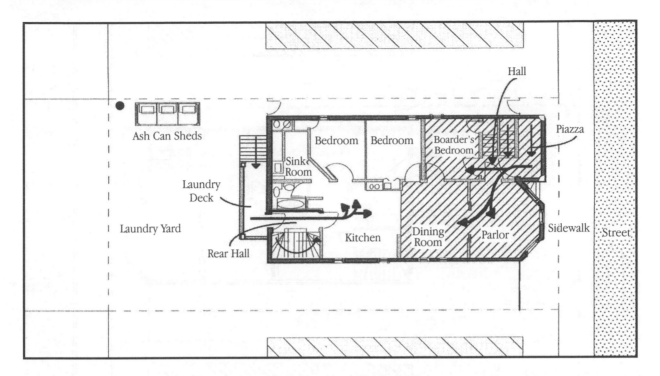

Fig. 16. The spatial dynamics of a 1912 three-decker flat as built. The author has overlaid the "mental structuring" of the spaces as anticipated by the client/landlord. Two interlocked domestic spaces signaled a shift in the house organization from the predominately formal/social activities toward the street side (marked in crosshatching) to the predominately utilitarian spaces toward the laundry yard. This spatial hierarchy was well suited to the sublet rental structure that existed within the separate flats. In effect, two interlocking L's separated the spatial domains of the principal renter (laundry deck, rear-hall entry, kitchen, sink room, and bedrooms), and the social sphere of the boarder (piazza, front-hall entry, parlor, dining room, and bedrooms). This spatial zoning helped to affirm the social relationship of agreed-upon domestic realms within the household. Drawing by Kingston Heath, Ed Portis, and Matt Jenkins.

space heater as the only heat source in the apartment. But these issues were accommodated within the living patterns of the household through a system of social negotiations. Such living situations, coupled with the stress and despair of industrial routine during the workday, demanded cooperation and tolerance from all parties. The route to family harmony can take many paths: some obvious, some subtle. The household is a spatial container for this hidden order.[14]

The useful roles of social memory and family and oral history have been explored here in an effort to not only understand "place" on a personal level, but to interpret a building form from the user's point of view. By choosing a point in my mental geography where I felt most at "home" in my youth, I gave priority as well to a single point in time during which the three-decker held its most palpable meaning for me. I am aware, however, that from its inception in 1912, *each* change in the domestic landscape of this three-decker spoke to the shifting familial circumstances of *all* its occupants and, more broadly, to the changing patterns of living within New Bedford itself. Therefore, in order to address how such buildings have been changed and adapted by owners and residents over time, it might be rewarding to approach the individual transformations of such standard pattern-book building types from additional vantage points that account for the flexibility of such schemes to meet the changing needs of its inhabitants (figs. 16–18). One can address the "social context" as historians of private life have done for the full range of

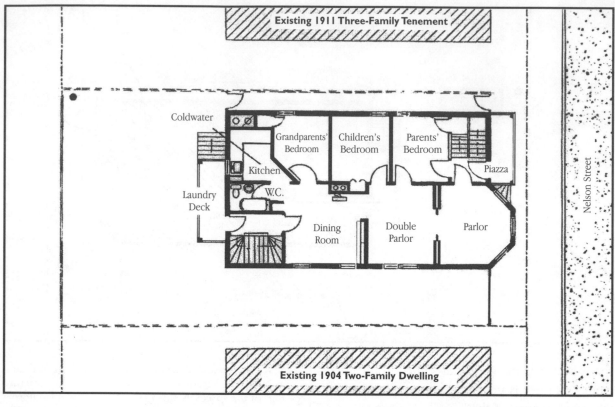

Existing 1911 Three-Family Tenement

Coldwater

Grandparents' Bedroom

Children's Bedroom

Parents' Bedroom

Kitchen

Piazza

Laundry Deck

W.C.

Dining Room

Double Parlor

Parlor

Nelson Street

Existing 1904 Two-Family Dwelling

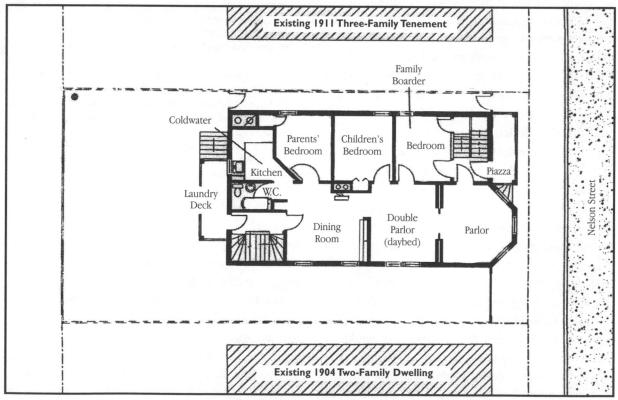

Existing 1911 Three-Family Tenement

Family Boarder

Coldwater

Parents' Bedroom

Children's Bedroom

Bedroom

Kitchen

Piazza

Laundry Deck

W.C.

Dining Room

Double Parlor (daybed)

Parlor

Nelson Street

Existing 1904 Two-Family Dwelling

socially constructed uses and meanings that exist (refer to fig. 14).[15] A "gender mapping" of these same spaces will reveal how the rooms were divided by behavior patterns related to gender, privacy, work, recreation, and public display for a better understanding of user demands as well as gender stratification related to status in the home.[16] Finally, a "climate context" of the building type will reveal how the domestic spaces were adapted by such factors as spatial manipulation (e.g., closing pocket doors to create a weather baffle) or the introduction of systems of appropriate (and sometimes inappropriate) technology to respond to changes in regional climate,[17] like energy-consuming window air-conditioning units, and so on (figs. 19–20). Though these various conditions may be separated as individual entities, they are, in fact, simultaneous forces that engage in dynamic interaction over the lifetime of a building. Such information offers a more nuanced perspective of the way inhabitants imprint themselves on their

Fig. 17a. (Opposite page top) Changing use patterns of the three-decker flat at 90 Nelson: First-floor use pattern of the Pitts family (1939–50). The married couple had Harold Pitts Sr.'s parents living with them as family boarders during the late stages of the Depression.

Fig. 17b. (Opposite page bottom) First-floor use pattern of the Pitts family (1950–66). Amanda Pitts had her brother and his daughter living in their first-floor unit as family boarders following the death of Harold's parents.

Fig. 18. (Below) Changing use patterns of a three-decker flat at 90 Nelson: Second-floor use pattern of the Pitts family (1966–79). With the children no longer living at home and not requiring first-floor access as readily, the Pitts family moved into the middle unit to conserve heat.

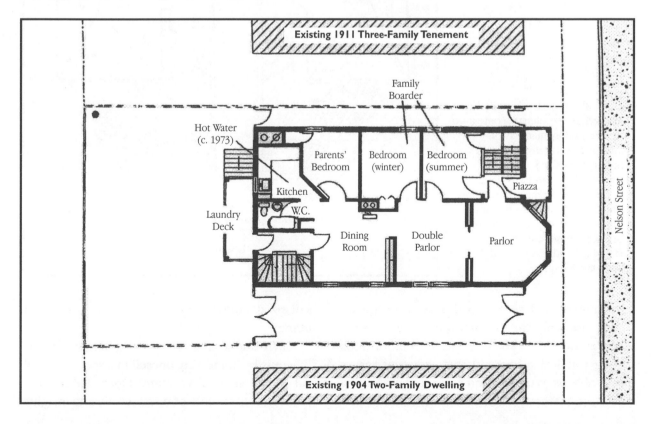

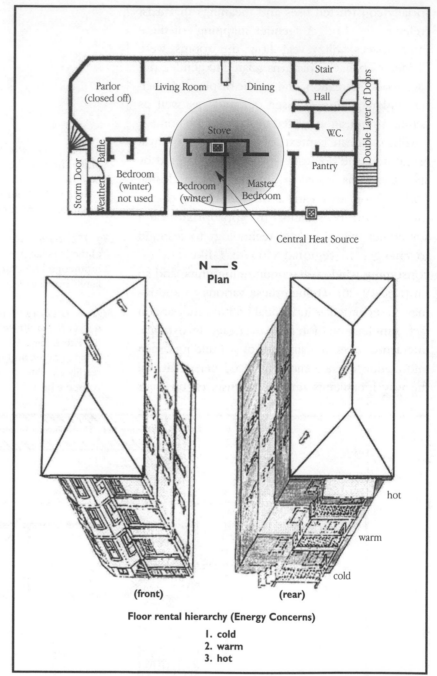

Parlor
(closed off)   Living Room   Dining   Stair

Hall

Stove

W.C.

Double Layer of Doors

Storm Door

Weather

Baffle

Bedroom
(winter)
not used

Bedroom
(winter)

Master
Bedroom

Pantry

Central Heat Source

N — S
Plan

hot

warm

cold

(front)   (rear)

Floor rental hierarchy (Energy Concerns)
1. cold
2. warm
3. hot

Fig. 19. Three-decker New Bedford, Massachusetts: Climate context— winter. Energy hierarchy: floors are zoned vertically within the building, creating temperature stratification. This factor indirectly becomes part of the rent structure. The middle tenement becomes the most cost-efficient in terms of energy requirements. Drawing by Kingston Heath and Dale Brentrup.

environment and serves to define, with greater clarity, not only the social experience of architecture but the socio-cultural relationships among physical forms and their adjacent spaces that enable us to understand a residential building type as an integrated domestic unit within its par-

ticularized cultural, physical and environmental setting.

Such evidence is often intangible, and accessible only by immersing oneself in a specific social and environmental situation. Once deciphered, however, it is capable of offering valuable insights

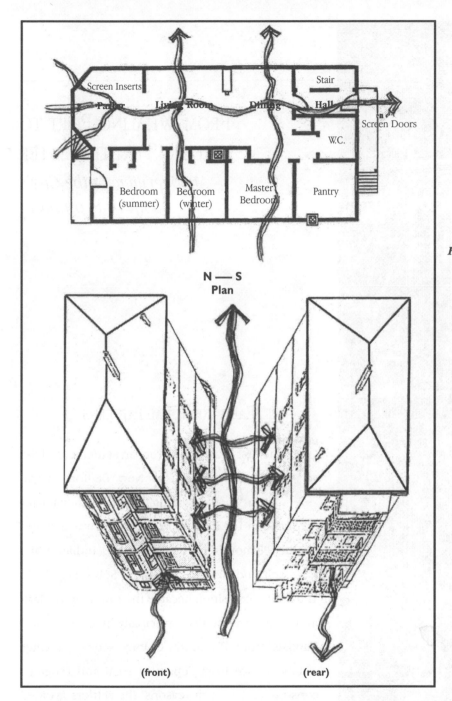

Screen Inserts

Parlor · Living Room · Dining · Hall

Stair

Screen Doors

W.C.

Bedroom (summer) · Bedroom (winter) · Master Bedroom · Pantry

N — S
Plan

(front)　(rear)

Fig. 20. Three-decker New Bedford, Massachusetts: Climate context—summer. Rooms are compact and clustered to reduce skin area. Allows for internal winter chambers, and other zoned activities to take place in warmer areas during cold periods (stove) and cooler areas in hot periods (porch); while the building was not necessarily designed to be used thermally for today's thermal and lighting criteria, the nature of its narrow section allows for lateral pulling of air and cross ventilation. It, then, was easy for people to adapt the heating and cooling requirements in a passive way. During the 1890s, perimeter daylighting and natural ventilation was all the user had to work within this plan and set of elements. For example, without transoms over windows and doors, and without stairwell skylight globe ventilators, stack ventilation cannot take place. Drawing by Kingston Heath and Dale Brentrup.

into the nature of everyday life. In this instance, it has offered a view of residential life in New Bedford filled with acts of human struggle, adjustment, perseverance and dignity that in some aspects are as heroic as those that shaped the physical contours of New Bedford initially.

In order to offer a more complete picture of the range of circumstances and collective human acts that brought textiles (and by extension—industrial housing) to New Bedford, it is necessary to go back in time. To invoke Melville, "Whence came they?"

FROM WHALING PORT TO LEADING TEXTILE CENTER
An Overview of the City's Shift in Economies

EARLY REGIONAL PATTERNS

The first recorded European settlement of the area now known as New Bedford began about 1630. It was first called Cushena, later Acushnet. In 1652, the Acushnet region was acquired by the Plymouth Colony from the Indian Chief Massasoit and his son Wamsutta. Subsequently, in 1664, this acquisition became the township of Dartmouth and was settled principally by Quakers and Baptists from Plymouth Colony seeking greater independence from Separatist legal and religious constraints. For such reasons, the settlers avoided developing a town center in order to prevent the Plymouth General Court from appointing a minister, who would encourage Separatist beliefs. Instead, scattered homesteads on large tracts prevailed in the settlement pattern of this early community. Ironically, Massasoit's youngest son, Metacomet—later called King Philip—would destroy most of the early settlement that his father helped bring about. The devastation of the isolated homesteads in the Dartmouth township during the King Philip's War of 1675 led the Plymouth General Court to pass a ruling requiring homes to be built in closer proximity for mutual protection.

By 1711, Joseph Russell bought a parcel of land for a farming homestead. During the 1750s this same parcel was laid out in village streets and house lots by John Russell III. He also began the first whale oil factory in the city, having been engaged in the business as early as 1755. Shipbuilding began in the village with the efforts of John Loudon in 1760. By 1765, Joseph Rotch brought his knowledge of the whaling industry and strong financial assets with him from Nantucket and started to build larger whaling ships that could make longer voyages in pursuit of sperm whales. Other encompassing whaling businesses soon followed and established the economic base of that industry in the village by the 1770s. In 1787, the Township of New Bedford was incorporated as a separate polity from Dartmouth, changing its name from Bedford village. New Bedford would enter its golden age of whaling by 1818 and surpassed Nantucket as the whaling capital of the world in 1829. The high point of the whaling industry in the city, in terms of capital and tonnage involved, was reached in 1857 with a fleet of 329 ships, 10,000 men employed, and an industry valued at nearly 12 million dollars. The city's registered tonnage by the 1850s also made New Bedford the fourth-largest port in the nation, behind only New York, Boston, and New Orleans; its tonnage was twice that of Philadelphia. New Bedford's population at this juncture was about 20,000.[1]

To New Bedford citizens of the mid-nineteenth century, then, theirs was a heritage of grand whaling vessels. These ships were built predominantly in their city, and returned from two- to three-year voyages with barrels of wealth wrought from the sea (fig. 21). The docks were choked with casks of whale oil covered with seaweed for insulation. The leakage was absorbed into the soil and left a distinctive odor, characteristic of the New Bedford industry. Docks cramped with whaling cargo were familiar sights, as were the vertical forests of mastheads that stood out against the skyline. As the largest whaling port in the world in the 1850s, New Bedford's city seal boasted, "We Light the World," referring to the industry that provided whale-oil fuel.

As a result of the shipping trade, during the 1850s New Bedford became one of the richest cities in the country in proportion to its population.[2] This prosperity was concentrated largely in the hands of shrewd Quaker (and after about 1830, Unitarian or Congregational) businessmen, who invested not only in whaling ships but also in associated industries, such as ropewalks, oil works (e.g., for grease refineries), boat building, waxworks (for both paraffin and spermaceti candles), and interlocking industries, such as banking and insurance offices to cover marine risks. These men, such as whaling vessel owner John Avery Parker, the city's first millionaire, built large urban estates in the burgeoning city as expressions of their status. Parker, for example, was involved in whaling, but he later branched out into investing in iron foundries, manufacturing, banking, local railroad construction, and eventually cotton textiles. In 1833, Russell Warren, the noted Greek Revival architect from Providence, Rhode Island, constructed Parker's estate on County Street (fig. 22).

County Street during the eighteenth century essentially established the western boundary of the main village. Here, following the War of 1812 and bolstered by nearly four decades of relatively uninterrupted prosperity in the whaling industry, city patricians built their large homes and established the precedent of setting aside a section of the city for houses of the sifted few. Along the length of County Street, the patriarchs of whaling and old-moneyed merchant families lived in a

Fig. 21. Whaleships and casks of whale oil at Central Wharf New Bedford. Stereograph, c. 1870, by Stephen F. Adams. Courtesy of Nicholas Whitman, Spinner Publications.

clearly distinguishable neighborhood that was at the end of a "wealthy wedge." This economic perimeter, by mid-century, began with the banking establishments along Water Street and included a handful of large, older homes built by the earliest whaling masters a few streets from the wharves; more modest homes were located just beyond this residential district to the west, and then the area of housing fanned out to include the newer residential district at the western part of the city (map 1).

To be sure, the migration to the "hill," as the land parcels along the County Road were referred to, reflected a shift in the settlement pattern among the elite. Wealthy Quaker whaling masters, such as Abraham Howland, had lived in unpretentious homes only three blocks from the water. Similarly, Joseph Grinnell, who was born in 1788

and was one of six sons of a Quaker whaling captain, lived in a small brick house near the waterfront of the old town settlement. The prosperity borne of whaling, however, soon crowded out these earlier homes as the wharf area filled in with ship chandlers, sail lofts, block makers' shops, bakeries for hardtack, sailmakers, blacksmiths for harpoons and chains, ropewalks, cooperages, counting houses, waxworks, and sailors' bars. Eventually, the most prosperous whaling masters abandoned the dock setting for the hill. By 1832, Joseph Grinnell moved into his prominent, but austere, Greek Revival mansion on County Street (fig. 23). Constructed of Quincy granite and designed by Russell Warren, its simplicity and solidity must have appealed to Grinnell's Quaker sensibilities.[3] It took Abraham Howland, however, until 1856 to move to the hill, when he purchased

Fig. 22. The John Avery Parker Estate of 1833 was designed by Russell Warren, the noted Greek Revival architect from Providence, Rhode Island. Photograph by Thomas E. M. White, c. 1870. Courtesy of Nicholas Whitman, Spinner Publications.

Map 1. New Bedford, 1815. Arrow indicates County Street to the west of the early waterfront commercial district. From Leonard B. Ellis, *History of New Bedford and Its Vicinity*, 1892. Used with the permission of the Board of Trustees of the New Bedford Free Public Library.

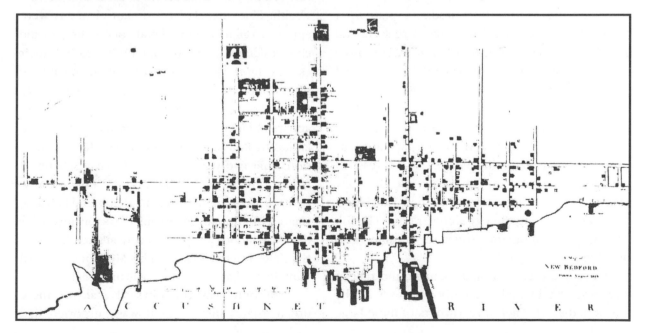

Fig. 23. Joseph Grinnell Mansion, County Street (1832).
Courtesy of the *Standard Times*/Spinner Publications.

at auction the William Rotch Rodman estate for a mere $2,500 (fig. 24). The stately Greek Revival mansion had been built in 1833 at exactly three times the amount paid by Howland, but tastes had begun to turn away from neoclassicism, and such mansions could no longer demand the highest sums. In the end it was likely the reasonable cost of the estate that appealed to the parsimonious Quaker, rather than the prestigious address on the hill. Reluctantly purchased or not, this new residence on County Street solidified Howland's new station among the city's power elite. The following year, Abraham Howland became New Bedford's first mayor.[4]

County Street occupied high ground that at one time overlooked the harbor as well as the business district. Therefore, owners of these large estates (often with the aid of distinctive New Bedford cupolas, or "widow's walks," as they were referred to) had visual access to the source of their wealth. Since neoclassical design elements were applied to all manner and scale of buildings, some elite residents of the hill attempted to link their estates more symbolically to their means of income by having the architects of their homes mimic the façades of their businesses, as Parker apparently instructed Russell Warren to do in the façade treatment of his 1833 Greek Revival mansion, built two years after his Merchants National Bank. Others, as in the case of one of New Bedford's leading whaling merchants and bankers, Charles W. Morgan, maintained surveillance over their livelihood. Morgan visually aligned his 1825 Greek Revival mansion with his Mechanic National Bank located at the foot of William Street.

Not only was the physical scale of these urban estates imposing—it was purported that

the John Avery Parker mansion was the largest Greek Revival residence ever built in the United States—the grounds were equally commanding.[5] As the colonial economy of New Bedford underwent a fundamental alteration after 1812 with the large infusion of capital from whaling interests, the concentrated wealth that resulted accentuated the transformation of the landscape. Prior to 1812, for example, there had been only two brick houses and no stone houses in New Bedford.[6] How these prosperous New Bedford citizens—many of whom were bound to Quaker principles of moderation, thrift, tolerance, and equality—conceived of owning property is reflected in the reorganization of their habitats into statements of power and belief. Most affirmed the virtues of private ownership of property and set their estates physically apart, using the barrier of landscaped grounds; yet simultaneously these same urban dwellers emphasized economic, philosophical—

Fig. 24. The William R. Rodman Mansion built in 1833 on County Street was located diagonally across from the Grinnell Estate. In 1856, it became the home of Abraham Howland, New Bedford's first mayor.

even moral—unity by the design treatment of their homes and grounds.

James Arnold, the son of a prominent Providence Quaker, worked his way up in the counting house of William Rotch Jr. He became a partner in the firm and married Sarah Rotch, the boss's daughter. In 1821, Arnold built a stately brick Federal Period mansion on County Street that covered, in its eleven acres, three urban blocks bounded by Union, Orchard, Arnold, and County Streets. The grounds were illustrated in an 1881 engraving in the *Walker Atlas of New Bedford,* and the site was referenced on the street plat of the 1887 *Atlas of New Bedford* (Plate 7) (map 2). The estate was surrounded by a heavy

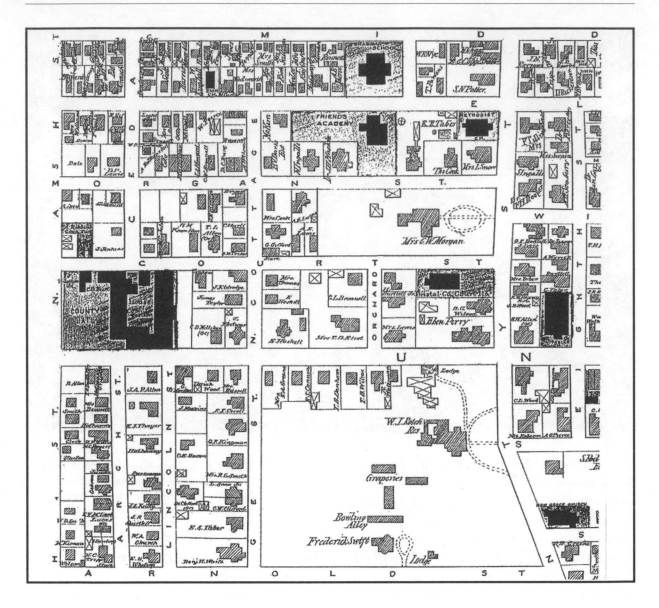

Map 2. In 1868, James Arnold died, leaving his home on the corner of County and Union Streets to William J. Rotch (bottom center of map). By the date of this Geo. H. Walker and Co. 1887 *Atlas of New Bedford* (Plate 7, Wards 4 & 5), the estate grounds included "graperies," five greenhouses, and an arbor. Used with the permission of the Board of Trustees of the New Bedford Free Public Library.

cover of trees randomly placed on the lot, reinforcing the aesthetic characteristics of a rural rather than an urban circumstance. There were by 1887 "graperies," five greenhouses, and an arbor. Local sources also indicate that there were boxwood gardens and formal flower beds with exotic plants collected from Arnold's travels abroad.[7] In essence, Arnold produced, with plantings drawn from elsewhere, a totally reconstructed landscape than previously existed in the colonial era for the edification of the public. A. J. Downing, having visited the James Arnold estate, wrote in his 1852 *A Treatise on the Theory and Practice of Landscape Gardening:* "There is scarcely a small place in New England where the *pleasure grounds* are so full of variety." Downing commented on its "winding walks, open bits of lawn, shrubs and plants grouped on turf, shady bowers, and rustic seats," all characteristics of romantic naturalism. An engraving of the grounds was provided opposite the description on page 57 of Downing's text.

Arnold was recognized in his day as a leading philanthropist and very active in the antislavery movement. It was said of him that "there was hardly an institution of charity in New Bedford without an 'Arnold fund.'" Upon his death in 1868, he bequeathed one hundred thousand dollars "for the benefit of the poor and needy in New Bedford who may be deserving." Such a lavish display for personal delight as exhibited in his estate gardens may have seemed unQuakerly to Arnold, for he opened them for public use as an expression of God's bounty, perhaps, rather than his own.[8]

Landscape gardening was a genteel activity in New Bedford as elsewhere in New England during the nineteenth century. The avocation not only brought many influential individuals together in the service of both home and village improvement, but inadvertently served as a means of disseminating forward-thinking social ideals as well. The New Bedford Horticultural Society was incorporated on March 12, 1847. On the list of signers of Articles of Intention are 107 members—the majority of whom were the city's most prominent individuals.[9]

The close proximity of these landscaped estates in the area west of the downtown commercial district allowed for a recognizable presence among New Bedford's elite as families and corporate leaders united in goals of social harmony and economic growth. Matthew Howland, for example, was one of the 107 signers of the Horticultural Society. His home on 81 Hawthorn Street was built in 1840, and by 1881 he had four greenhouses constructed on a separate parcel adjacent to the estate. As evidenced by the 1881 *Walker Atlas of New Bedford*, the home of this bank president and whaling merchant was flanked by homes and open land parcels belonging to his son, William D. Howland, and five other landowners, Thomas M. Stetson, Captain Joseph C. Delano, W. W. Crapo, William J. Rotch, and James Arnold—all related by birth, marriage, and/or business. Through shared religious beliefs, marriage partnerships, and interlocking business interests among bankers, whaling merchants, railroad promoters, and textile mill directors, the very economic destinies of the residents were as bound together as their domestic settings.

This elite society was not monolithic, however. Though joined by familial ties and business ventures, they were often at political odds. Moreover, the displays of privilege and prominence expressed in the size of the lots and the number and proportion of the rooms within some of these estates were beyond any practical justification that would be in keeping with Quaker principles of moderation. Partly because of such strict expectations of conduct, many influential Quakers during the 1830s split from the Society of Friends and joined the more liberal Unitarian movement. A. J. Davis was commissioned in 1838 to design the granite block Gothic Revival Unitarian Church on Union and Eighth Streets to accommodate this shift in religious preference.[10]

Davis was also commissioned to construct a "cottage-villa in the Rural Gothic Style"—a compromise, according to A. J. Downing, between the cottage for the workingman and the villa for the wealthy elite.[11] The home, listed in Downing's 1850 *The Architecture of Country Houses*, was constructed in 1846 for William J. Rotch shortly after his marriage to Emily Morgan, daughter of shipbuilder Charles W. Morgan (fig. 25). A handful of Gothic cottages, such as the 1840 Congdon estate or the estate of Mrs. William Gifford, had preceded the Rotch House in New Bedford. But

Fig. 25. Detail of William J. Rotch Cottage/Villa, 1846, designed by A. J. Davis. This photograph, c. 1870, by Thomas E. M. White depicts croquet in the front lawn. Courtesy of Spinner Publications.

these were placed in more undeveloped settings, such as the southern end of County Street in the case of the Gifford estate, or, further still, Clark's Point at the tip of the city facing Clark's Cove where the Congdon estate was located. With this introduction of the Gothic cottage tradition into the architectural heritage of the city proper, the English picturesque doctrine of romantic naturalism offered a counterpoint to the more commanding presence of the Greek Revival mansions that stood aloof along the crest of County Street.

The design principles of Downing and Davis called for a house to function as part of its natural landscape: floor plans were designed to take advantage of site conditions and favorable views,

while building materials were to be rendered in earth tones to further enhance the natural vitality of the cottage. It should also be noted that the Gothic cottage had clear associations of social reform and Christian benevolence attached to it (note, for instance, the cruciform arrangement of the intersecting gable roofs in fig. 25). The Gothic cottage, for example, was touted in 1869 as the very embodiment of the "Christian Home" in *American Woman's Home*, written by Catherine E. Beecher and her sister, Harriet Beecher Stowe.[12]

While the house was in harmony with its natural surroundings—almost cloistered from the forces of industrial urbanism which William J. Rotch would soon help to create—the "rural" cottage was considered "disgusting" by his Quaker father and out of place among other neighboring residences.[13] Built at a cost of six thousand dollars, A. J. Davis articulated the cottage's projected image: "Altogether, then, we should say, that the character expressed by the exterior of this design is that of a man or a family of domestic tastes, but with strong aspirations after something higher than social pleasures."[14]

Rotch's "aspirations" led ultimately to business and political interests. Prior to 1842, however, he had been a devout Quaker and was president of Friends Academy for many years. His strong leadership abilities and influence accounted for such early achievements as the founding of the highly successful New Bedford Cordage Company with his brother Benjamin in 1842. William J. Rotch then served two terms in the Massachusetts Legislature beginning in 1848, and at the age of thirty-three he served as New Bedford's second mayor. Rotch was one of the founders of the Republican Party in southeastern Massachusetts. This party would control city politics in New Bedford until the 1890s.

Still later, Rotch served on multiple corporation boards of directors, was vice president of the New Bedford Institution of Savings and president of the New Bedford and Howland Mills

Corporations. In 1872, he moved his family into the Federal Period mansion that had belonged to his late uncle, James Arnold, on County Street and symbolically expressed his preeminence in the community.[15] A mansard roof was added to the former Arnold residence by Rotch prior to 1876, no doubt to modernize its appearance, but also to expand the facilities to accommodate his nine children. His Gothic cottage eventually was home to his son Morgan Rotch.[16]

Because of the visible presence of such accumulated wealth and such evident signs of urban and residential development, leading architects were drawn to the city to share in the profits of New Bedford's golden age of whaling. These noted architects were joined, as well, by promising painters and writers anxious to launch their careers.[17] Herman Melville, who shipped out of Fairhaven on the whaler *Acushnet* in 1841, described New Bedford ten years later in his novel *Moby Dick:*

> New Bedford itself is perhaps the dearest place to live in, in all New England. It is a land of oil, true enough . . . nowhere in all America will you find more patrician-like houses: parks and gardens more opulent, than in New Bedford. Whence came they? . . . Go and gaze upon the iron emblematic harpoons round yonder lofty mansion, and your question will be answered. Yes, all these brave houses and flowery gardens from the Atlantic, Pacific, and Indian Oceans, one and all, they were harpooned and dragged up hither from the bottom of the sea.[18]

THE RISE OF THE TEXTILE ERA IN NEW BEDFORD: CHANGING REGIONAL PATTERNS

Given the concentrated wealth and fame that associated New Bedford with whaling the appearance of the Wamsutta Mill in 1849 on Front Street along the northern shoreline of the city marked a minor footnote at this particular time. After all, the textile industry had gotten underway in Pawtucket, Rhode Island, as early as 1793. Additionally, the city of Lowell, Massachusetts, in operation by 1823, had caught world attention not only in its ability to go from raw cotton to finished woven product within the confines of a single planned industrial complex but it had established, as well, an ideal, paternalistic scheme that housed, supplied, and educated its workers.

The importance of New Bedford in industrial history, in part, is as an exemplar of the impact that the introduction of steam power had on the industrialization of a former colonial port city. Where the earlier textile mill developments cited above were tied to water power technology, the introduction of Corliss steam power around 1850 allowed textile mills to be built anywhere. Harnessing cheap fuel and abundant labor available in a port city, New Bedford often led the way toward the development of the large steam cotton mill.[19]

In 1846, the same year that New Bedford was incorporated as a city, Abraham Howland chartered a Wamsutta Mills Manufacturing Company as a joint stock company producing either wool, cotton, or iron. But shortly afterwards Howland turned over the company's charter to his cousin, Joseph Grinnell, having secured only sixty thousand dollars of stock subscriptions from local investors. At this same moment, Thomas Bennett wanted to establish a cotton mill in Georgia, where cotton manufacturing had proven to be extremely profitable.[20] Bennett had recently worked for a colleague from Fairhaven, Massachusetts, Dwight Perry, in his small cotton mill in Wymansville, Georgia. Like his employer, Bennett hoped to raise funds to establish a factory in Georgia with himself as head of the enterprise.[21] When Bennett approached Joseph Grinnell, the president of the First National Bank, for financial support for his new mill, Grinnell stated that he preferred to keep the financial investment closer to home, where it would be under closer scrutiny. No doubt Grinnell realized the opportunity Bennett presented to provide the supervisory skills necessary to launch his own enterprise in the form of Wamsutta Mills. Ultimately, Thomas Bennett was appointed as superintendent of the new Wamsutta cotton mill in 1847 with Joseph Grinnell as president.

The initial difficulty Abraham Howland experienced in acquiring venture capital to sponsor cotton manufacturing in New Bedford stemmed largely from the certainty of profits and the low risk associated with investing in the city's whaling fleet. Potential investors also were against manufacturing by incorporated companies, preferring instead businesses conducted by individual capital and enterprise, such as those connected with the whaling and shipping interests. The longer hours and potential management conflicts related to organized and disciplined labor were additional factors that made the enterprise less desirable.[22]

Another consideration the mill investors faced prior to incorporation was what *type* of manufacturing enterprise was suited to New Bedford if any. Employing market and manufacturing analyses, they determined that cotton textile production would best reward them. "They figured that they could make fine sheetings at a cost of twelve cents a yard and sell it for fourteen cents. 'All other calculations that we have made,' their committee reported, 'show only from half to three-quarters a cent profit.'"[23] Such caution stemmed not only from an acquired business sense on the part of the potential investors, but the awareness that Samuel Rodman's New Bedford Steam Mill Company, established in 1846 to manufacture cotton cloth, was losing money.[24] The decision was to specialize in a superior line of shirting and sheeting. (Also, a contributing factor as to why New Bedford ultimately specialized in fine cottons, as Everett Allen has noted, was because the humidity was high enough that cotton threads could be spun finely without breaking.)

As these New Bedford merchants cautiously embarked on the transformation of the economic base of the city from whaling to textiles, they drew upon earlier patterns of business that had proven successful in whaling: they totally controlled the industrial development of the city by avoiding incorporations with outside investors (it would take until 1895 for a textile mill to be incorporated principally by outside capital); they worked together to reduce risk and to reduce competition with southern factories (as well as adjoining New England communities and among themselves) by forming business and family alliances; and, as Joseph Grinnell put it, they adopted "intelligent specialization."

With only $160,000 of the $300,000 raised to construct a facility, a site was chosen for the Wamsutta Mills on Front Street along the Acushnet River. This land was purchased for $7,500 from Benjamin Rodman and included approximately five acres, a wharf site, and water privileges in the mill pond. The freshwater pond provided pure water for the steam power plant.[25] The site also had access to the railroad and wharves for bringing in raw cotton and coal. Interestingly, Joseph Grinnell in 1840 had pushed through plans to construct the New Bedford and Taunton Railroad over the opposition of the stagecoach operators. Now the railroad became an integral component of his manufacturing process. Since there were only two outward and inward trains a day, sailing vessels were utilized as well. Coal arrived by large barges or schooners and was off-loaded into bins for the mill boilers. This transportation network also allowed for the shipping out of finished cotton goods, such as shirting, other fine and fancy cottons, and eventually percale sheeting—a fabric introduced by Wamsutta in the 1870s.[26] The harbor location also provided a cheap source of water for condensing purposes.

With advice from the recognized textile engineer, David Whitman from Warwick, Rhode Island, the mill was under construction by 1847 and was completed in the summer of 1848. Its architect was Seth H. Ingalls of New Bedford.[27] This first mill, based on the factory design of the Hope Mill in the Pawtuxet Valley of Rhode Island, was of granite rubble construction, measuring 212 feet by 70 feet and containing five stories under a Gothic Revival, stepped gable (fig. 26). The stone for the exterior walls was quarried locally on Marsh Island in the Acushnet River, but the remainder of the building materials had to be brought from neighboring cities by vessels. One of the first necessities for the smooth maintenance of the millworks was the establishment of a machine shop in the basement of the mill.[28]

Wamsutta produced its first cotton cloth in February 1849. The new mill's appearance, set amidst a backdrop of New Bedford's maritime industry and sections of undeveloped land, was depicted in an oil painting entitled "Wamsutta Mills" (fig. 27). Painted by William Allen Wall just after the mill's completion, the new factory is presented as anything but intrusive. In fact, it offers an emotionally validating image to the viewer of the "machine in the garden." Less grand than most of the mill landscape genre paintings of its day, where notions of industrial magnitude, productive potency, and social harmony were often stressed, a mood of rural tranquillity—rather than urban growth—is emphasized. Using the mill building compositionally to establish a diagonal, the viewer's eye is drawn from the pastoral scene in the foreground, to the mill, to the maritime

Fig. 26. Wamsutta Mills was incorporated on April 8, 1846. The first mill (shown here) was built of granite on Front Street by Seth H. Ingalls. It was completed in 1848 and started producing cotton cloth by February 1849. Courtesy of *The Standard Times*/Spinner Publications.

Fig. 27. Wamsutta Mills, oil on canvas (44 ½ by 54 ½ inches) by William Allen Wall (1801–1885) just after the mill's completion. This view was from the northwest corner of Mill No. 1, looking south toward Fairhaven. Note the parklike setting in the foreground of the mill. Courtesy of the Old Dartmouth Historical Society— New Bedford Whaling Museum.

activity along the Acushnet River, and finally to the neighboring settlements of Fairhaven (to the center) and New Bedford in the foreground (to the right) offering in effect an industrial "Peaceable Kingdom" guided by Quaker vision.

In place of a tree-covered grazing area that offered strollers the spectacle of benign corporate development, as depicted in Wall's painting, a very congested industrial landscape eventually emerged around the factory complex that was given over to efficient production and corporate growth. A circa 1895 photograph of Wamsutta Mills taken by Joseph G. Tirrell (1840–1907) demonstrates the difference in attitude toward industrial development by this date (fig. 28). Using the same pictorial convention of the diagonal line as had Wall, the railroad tracks lead the viewer's eye past off-loaded bales of raw cotton to feed the next cycle of production (bottom right under the shed roofs), beyond rows of corporate housing (to the left), past new construction for an elevated railroad crossing used to extend the transportation network critical for the distribution

Mill No. 1

of goods, and finally to a seemingly endless wall of mills that either belonged to Wamsutta or that have followed its lead on the western bank of the Acushnet River. Significantly, the attention of the scene has moved away from the growth of the older urban and residential core of the city to distant open areas for future mill expansion in the city's so-called "North End."

Between the dates of these two representations of Wamsutta Mills (c. 1850 to 1895), New Bedford underwent the first phase of industrial expansion related to textiles. Concurrently, the evolution of urban life and culture in New Bedford increasingly followed the transformation of the landscape as it changed from open tracts of cultivated or undeveloped land immediately to the north and south of the congested wharves to clearly defined mill districts hugging the river's edge all along the Acushnet River.

Fig. 28. C. 1895 photograph of Wamsutta Mills looking north. The stair tower for Mill No. 1 is visible at the top of the photograph (see arrow). The parklike setting formerly to the west of Mill No. 1 was by this date taken over as building sites for Mill Nos. 4 and 5. Note Wamsutta's four-tenements located west of the tracks. Photograph was taken by Joseph G. Tirrell. Courtesy of Spinner Publications.

By 1893, the Wamsutta corporation had built seven mills and became one of the largest cotton mill complexes in the country; it employed 2,100 operatives, running 230,000 spindles, 4,450 looms, and producing some two hundred varieties of fine cotton products from shirts to sheetings. The Wamsutta Mill proved to be a successful business venture for its local investors—realizing a 300-percent profit from the original capital investment by 1874.[29] However, the reluctance of New Bedford's citizenry to abandon whaling interests in favor of textiles is reflected in the fact that it would take twenty-five years from the date of incorporation of the Wamsutta Mills for another textile mill corporation to be established in the city.

Part of this reluctance can be ascribed to the shortage of textile labor, particularly from 1863 to 1865 due to the Civil War. At this point, active recruitment of French Canadian labor, mainly from Quebec and Acadia, began in the city.[30] Also worth noting with regard to the city's labor force is that by 1867 Wamsutta would experience its first strike by English skilled workers, who demanded a ten-hour workday. The specter of organized labor and the emergence of English socialist organizations in New Bedford may have accounted, as well, for the reluctance on the part of local investors to back further expansion of the new industry in the city, in spite of Wamsutta's marked success.

Throughout the 1830s and 1840s, the demand for a ten-hour workday built upon the protests of Lowell workers, who complained about the long working hours (5:00 A.M. to 7:00 P.M. with half-hour breaks for breakfast and dinner), wage cuts, and machine speedups. Hearings by the Massachusetts State House of Representatives were held in 1845 just prior to Wamsutta's incorporation. They listened to descriptions of the worsening industrial conditions, which included air filled with lint from the looms to smoke that filled the work space from the oil lamps.[31] Potential mill investors were understandably cautious about engaging in such controversial issues and dealing with such social conditions when establishing their businesses.

The working conditions aboard the whaling ships sailing out of New Bedford, of course, were equally abhorrent, but they were far less visible to the shipowners and were part of an entrenched economic system within New Bedford.[32] Further, the labor class represented by seamen on board whaling vessels consisted essentially of nonresidents. Almost all of the work of the whaling trade was done aboard ship during the long voyages, requiring little labor investment on shore other than to grade and package the products to transport them out of the city. In addition to the offshore whaling activities, though, a wide variety of whaling tradesmen functioned in the city and along the shore to augment this industry, including riggers, coopers, caulkers, sailmakers, ship chandlers, blacksmiths, and longshoremen.

Textile workers, on the other hand, represented a new resident labor class in the city. The factories brought together a highly visible and concentrated workforce capable, in the eyes of the mill owners, of posing organized opposition to the business goals of mill management. These concerns continually influenced the decision-making process of investors, as is reflected in the 1889 publication produced, significantly, by the New Bedford Board of Trade: "Labor troubles have been infrequent and usually unimportant and the toilers in New Bedford's cotton mills are ranked as the best of workers in the textile industries."[33] There were two major strikes at Wamsutta in the early stages of the corporation, however. Attempting to build on the success of the Fall River, Massachusetts mill workers, who won the ten-hour workday without a cut in pay on January 1, 1867, English strikers at Wamsutta also called for a ten-hour workday in 1867. Later, the 1877 strike protested against three wage cutbacks in three years as well as machine speedups. Here, the English and Irish workers were divided in the strike effort by the French Canadian workers, who did not support the strike.[34]

In spite of these early labor rumblings, the Potomska Mill was incorporated in 1871 in the South End and became only the second textile corporation in the city. It took another decade, however, for the Acushnet and Grinnell Mills (both 1882) to appear. The appearance of the Potomska Mill in 1871 came at a critical juncture in New Bedford's development with regard to its changing economic base and population density. The year 1870 had marked only a mild economic recovery of a five-year period of continued losses in the whaling industry. As a result, much of the fleet moved to San Francisco during the 1870s to engage in Arctic whaling. In addition, the city's population gain of only 467 residents in 1870 did not offset the population losses of previous years. In fact, the total population figures did not equal those for the census taken ten years earlier.

While the failing whaling industry continued to deplete the population related to that economic base, the growth of the immigrant population tied to textiles began to offset these numbers. Between 1870 and 1875, the population increased by 4,575 (for a total of 25,895). Hence, growth between the years of 1871 to 1875, which parallels the appearance of the first Potomska Mill structure in 1871 and Wamsutta Mill No. 5 in 1875, reflected an increase in the rate of population of over 200 percent since 1865–70. This growth trend continued at a steady pace, and by 1890 the number of inhabitants in New Bedford totaled 40,733—nearly doubling the low point of 1865.[35] It was becoming evident that whaling alone could no longer support New Bedford's economy and that it was time to diversify the city's economic base.

NEW REGIONAL IDENTITY

The whaling business seems running out and doomed to destruction, so that we may have no business and no way of earning a dollar.

— Matthew Howland to his middle son, Matthew Morris Howland, 2 Mar. 1881

In spite of the limited involvement on the part of New Bedford investors early on to embrace a new industrial base, the potential for large profits was too great to resist given the dramatic slowdown of the whaling economy following the Civil War. At the height of the whale-fishery in New Bedford (1857), the industry could boast of a fleet of 417 whalers producing 56,691 barrels of sperm oil and 153,413 barrels of whale oil. But this large fleet and yield had, in fact, caused a glut in the market. As the national economy slowed during the Panic of 1857, New Bedford investors reeled as the price of whale oil dropped from eighty cents to sixty-four cents a gallon, resulting in hundreds of barrels of oil sitting on the wharves awaiting a market recovery. Though the flame produced by spermaceti candles burned longer and cleaner than the conventional tallow candles and the whale oil used in lamps was second only to the best seed oils, refined mineral oils soon ended the demand. In 1859, petroleum was discovered in Titusville, Pennsylvania, and prices for many whale products began to fall yet again as consumers shifted to kerosene for lighting instead of whale oil or spermaceti candles and shifted to petroleum for lubricants. Even Abraham H. Howland, New Bedford's first mayor and prosperous whaling merchant, was involved in the early distillation of kerosene and coal oil and sought to establish manufacturing in the city to diversify the economy.[36] In addition to the loss of a large proportion of the whaling fleet during the Civil War (seventy New Bedford whalers were sunk intentionally at the harbor entrances of Savannah and Charleston as part of a blockade), in 1871 ice floes crushed the entire Arctic whaling fleet, including thirty-two ships from New Bedford. This tragedy was repeated in 1876, when the ice took 12 ships from New Bedford—most of them uninsured because of what was considered by many maritime companies as excessive insurance rates. It was now clear that the days when Jonathan Bourne's ship the *Lagoda* grossed more than six dollars an hour for the entire four-year voyage were over.[37] Whaling was no longer yielding high profits with little risk; the 6–8 percent dividends available in textiles became appealing.

An indication of the change in fortunes by a once prosperous whaling merchant and bank president, who had recently suffered large uninsured losses in the Arctic from his whaling fleet, is contained in the correspondence from the Howland family. In September 1871, the Howland

Company lost one-third of its vessels in the Arctic ice, amounting to a total loss of $300,000. In August 1876, additional losses of $442,000 in ships and $375,000 in cargo left the family economically compromised until 1884. This change of affairs is reflected in Rachel Howland's comment following the sale of the whaling vessel *The George and Susan* to the Swift family: "Well! She is gone from us after being in the family seventy years. It seems as though we are to part with everything of a material nature that is near and dear to us."[38]

In many ways, the Matthew Howland family would now look to their sons—particularly William D. Howland—for the economic and social regeneration of the family (see chapter 4). The sons of the family—Richard S. Howland (the oldest) and William D. Howland (the youngest)—during the 1880s began to seek new sources of income beyond whaling. William D. speculated in "prints," printed cloth from the local mills, and purchased Potomska Mill stock on margin. He also worked at this juncture as a clerk for Wamsutta. Richard, on the other hand, looked forward to the day when his father would give up outfitting whalers, liquidate his assets, and lend him money for his own business ventures, since Richard's firm in California (Hutchings and Co.) was on the brink of failure: "As you say, I hope another year will put us all in better shape. Father [Matthew Howland] writes me that you have made $500 by the rise in Wamsutta and Potomska Stock, which is not a bad operation for a beginning."[39] Soon thereafter, Richard Howland pointed out to William D. Howland: "As to your own position, I think you are making a mistake in going along at the Wamsutta Mills [as a clerk working long hours at little pay], when you might make much more joining forces with Morrie [Matthew Morris Howland, the middle son, who at this point was investing in lead mining]. . . . I have given up Jonathan Bourne's business [Arctic whaling out of San Francisco] since, it did not pay. If I can't earn a living, it will be because I am not fit to live; the sooner I begin to starve the sooner it will be over."[40]

Interesting here is the desperation on the part of the younger generation of New Bedford's Quaker elite to make their own mark. Well educated locally at Friends Academy and university trained at Harvard, Brown, and graduate schools abroad, these three sons had a difficult time meeting the expectations of success for which their privileged upbringing had prepared them (each son was given twenty thousand dollars upon reaching his twenty-first birthday, for example). In the middle of a national depression (from 1873 to 1879) and the shifting of local economies from whaling to textiles, New Bedford's younger generation could no longer count on the inevitable profits of whaling that had brought their parents wealth, power, and prestige.

As young men in their twenties, material evidence of their parents' success was visible at every turn. For example, William D. joined Art Grinnell at a farewell supper for their friend Morgan Rotch, who was to marry a member of the Grinnell family the next day, December 5, 1879. The opulence they were accustomed to is evident from the December 4, 1879, journal entry of William Morris Howland in which he discusses the rooms of the Greek Revival estate on County Street belonging to the Grinnells, which now appear to him somewhat small: "We had a very pleasant evening with good supper, songs, and plenty of Champagne. We all came away about 12 o'clock. Today, at half-past eleven, we put in an appearance at the Grinnells to make ourselves useful at the wedding. The ceremony went off smoothly, the rooms, though small, were not crowded and we all had a very sociable and enjoyable time." Meanwhile, the patriarch of the family, Matthew Howland, writes to his middle son, Matthew Morris, relating the economic success of local textiles: "I believe we wrote thee that Will bought 50 shares of Potomska stock two weeks ago at par. Today the stock sold at 106 1/4 [up from $103.12

on January 26] at auction; he expects to get 110 soon. But if he had sold today he could have made $300 in two weeks. Quite an operation for Will, and he did it without asking me for a dollar."[41]

Evident here is the growing fascination with the seemingly instantaneous profits from textile investment. These figures were in strong contrast to the devastating losses that the whale fisheries were showing, and they reflect the evolution of thought among New Bedford's business elite. Even the most frugal Quaker merchants seemed ready to shift their loyalties by 1880.

Between 1880 and 1910, New Bedford was transformed—seemingly overnight—from a whaling economy to a cotton textile city producing fine cotton yarn, cloth, and specialty goods. While in other urban settings such a shift in economic focus may have been resisted overtly by parties with vested interests in the older industry, the changeover was from *within* the community. As a result, the same families who had controlled the whaling interests now controlled textiles.

By 1897, there were twenty-five mill corporations in the city. Each corporation generally built

more than one mill; therefore, these twenty-five corporations represented several mill buildings that dotted the landscape in ever-increasing numbers. Brick mills became the norm following Wamsutta Mill No. 4 in 1868 (designed by Bennett himself), replacing the previous granite mills (figs. 29–30). As indicated by a statement in the 1892 *History of New Bedford*, "Everything [for the 1846 Wamsutta Mill] except the building stone had to be brought here, and all the stone used for the engine foundations, shafting supports and some other uses was brought from Fall River [Mass.]."[42]

The sole dependence on local granite as a primary building material was changed when Charles S. Paisler established a large business of lime, brick, cement, and other building materials in 1852. His business, located on North Water Street, established a new material and construction infrastructure for New Bedford builders. Between

Fig. 29. Wamsutta's Mill No. 2 was built in 1854 of granite. Photograph taken March 1924. Used with the permission of the Board of Trustees of the New Bedford Free Public Library.

Fig. 30. Wamsutta's Mill No. 4, built in 1868, was the first of the corporation's mills to be constructed of load-bearing brick. Photograph taken at lunchtime, c. 1890. Courtesy of Spinner Publications.

1876 and 1896 Paisler himself was credited with building fifteen of the largest cotton mills.[43] So quickly were these mills being erected that the 1888 Howland Mill Corporation in the South End had its brick work completed for the main building in just seven weeks.[44]

With the professionalization of mill construction technology, the shoreline of New Bedford rapidly took on the palette of red brick that marked the line of mills along the northern and southern reaches of the Acushnet River (fig. 31). Factory chimney stacks now replaced the mastheads of whaling ships that once were silhouetted against the sky. The visual presence of the chimney stacks separated these later mills, too, from the earlier

mills of New England that were driven predominately by water-power technology. Although there were steam-powered mills in Pawtucket, Rhode Island, as early as 1810, and in New Hampshire by the 1820s, the Corliss steam engine began to be adopted in greater numbers after 1850 throughout New England. These newer mills in New Bedford, such as the Potomska Mill Complex No. 1 (1871) and No. 2 (1877) in the South End, for example, were driven by Corliss double (twenty-eight-inch cylinder, five-foot stroke) steam engines of eight hundred horsepower each to run the line shafting of the textile machinery.[45]

Individuals such as Frederick Grinnell were particularly well informed about steam power technology. Born in New Bedford in 1836, he graduated from Rensselaer Polytechnic Institute in 1855. By 1860, he was a draftsman for the Corliss Steam Engine Company in Providence, Rhode Island. Due to his exceptional ability, he was chosen treasurer and then acted for a time as

Fig. 31. Postcard view of the Manomet Mill in the city's North End, c. 1910, looking south from Acushnet River.

superintendent of the works. Frederick Grinnell was also a director in the Mechanics National Bank of New Bedford and of Wamsutta Mills.[46]

The visible expression of industrial might that the city was rapidly attaining was characterized by the profusion of the brick stacks set against the skyline and by the enormous Corliss steam engines housed below in the boiler houses. The physical pairing of these two elements served as a source of pride for the city and as a consensus image that represented the burgeoning power of New Bedford as a new leader in American industry. Sayer, a chronicler of business affairs in the city, compared the larger scale and prior usage of the engines at New Bedford's textile mills with the one showcased at the Centennial Exposition at Philadelphia in 1876 (fig. 32).

> The magnitude of the motive power required to move the innumerable machines in the six great mills [of Wamsutta] is almost beyond imagination,

even aided by figures and descriptions. There is one single upright beam Corliss engine of three-hundred horse power, one pair of engines of eight hundred horse power, one pair of eleven hundred and one monster pair of two thousand horse power. Visitors to the Centennial Exposition at Philadelphia in 1876 will remember the great engine which was among the marvels of that collection of wonders, but though they could scarcely comprehend it, at that very time a larger engine was running in New Bedford. This enormous piece of machinery has a stroke of ten feet; the weight of the fly wheel is about fifty tons, and other parts are in like proportion.[47]

The appearance of steam-powered mills in New Bedford gains significance with regard to the textile growth of this city when it is coupled with the knowledge that coal was at least a dollar a ton cheaper when delivered to the waterfront than

Fig. 32. An illustration of the Corliss steam engines in Machinery Hall showcased at the Centennial Exposition in Philadelphia, 1876. Three years later, one of these engines powered George Pullman's Palace Car Factory in Illinois. From James D. McCabe, *The Illustrated History of the Centennial Exhibition* (Philadelphia: Jones Brothers & Co., 1876), 439. Private collection of Dr. Randy Swanson.

when delivered to the inland textile centers such as Lowell and Lawrence. This factor made mill locations along the Acushnet River invaluable with regard to reducing shipping and refueling costs. As a result, by 1900 there were twenty-one cotton mills along the waterfront alone.[48]

With the economic success of the Wamsutta Mills, New Bedford's transformation into the early phases of industrial urbanization was underway. Like many post–Civil War cities, particularly in New England when manufacturing became a general component of its urban economy, two forces fostered its urban growth: steam power (as has been demonstrated) and large-scale European immigration.[49] In terms of the latter, Wamsutta's decision to produce fine shirting and sheeting determined not only the source of power that would be used and the mill's location, but also the very nature of

the work force.[50] James Vance Jr. has argued that throttle-spinning, as in the water-frame under the Waltham system, could be carried out by women. The production of fine sheetings required mule-spun yarn, and mule spinning (as in most Rhode Island mills) required male labor (fig. 33).[51] Mule spinning also required *skilled* labor not available locally. Skilled workers were recruited from neighboring New England textile communities, such as Fall River, as well as from abroad—many were from Lancashire, England. Beyond spinners, other skilled mechanics, such as weavers and loom fixers, were required. Finally, there was a large demand for common labor to perform the more routine jobs of the industry. These lower-paid positions were filled by a largely immigrant European population that entered New Bedford's seaport desperate for work and shelter.

New Cultural Setting: Immigration and New Bedford's Changing Patterns of Settlement

As immigrants arrived in New Bedford by sea, the towering profile of brick smokestacks marked the mill sites along the shoreline. The smokestacks, in effect, served as divining rods for future urban growth, since they represented jobs to the ever increasing immigrant population.[52] Between 1880 and 1910, New Bedford underwent a 300-percent increase in population (from 26,845 in 1880 to 96,652 in 1910).[53] The maximum rate of acceleration of population growth was reached in 1897, and the maximum rate of growth was reached in 1905.[54] The great increase in population in the three decades between 1880 to 1910 was due almost solely to the building up of the city's

Fig. 33. Mule spinning room at the Potomska Mills, c. 1880. Skilled professions in the cotton mills were performed mostly by men from Lancashire, England. From Thomas L. Young, *The American Cotton Industry* (1902). Courtesy of Spinner Publications.

industries. During the same time period, New Bedford ranked third in the country in the number of spindles in operation among cotton-manufacturing cities, being exceeded only by Fall River and Lowell in 1893, and it ranked fourth in the number of looms after third-place Manchester, New Hampshire. Ranking among the top twenty-five manufacturing cities in the nation, the neighboring cities of New Bedford and Fall River now formed a major urbanized belt in the southern part of the state.[55]

The promise of good wages, steady employment, and housing (provided by the earliest mills) brought a broad spectrum of workers into the city. By 1900, 70 percent of the people living in New Bedford were first- or second-generation immigrants—an increase of 14 percent in ten years. Whereas earlier English and Irish mill workers dominated the work force, one-third of all the foreign-born people in New Bedford in 1900 were French Canadians and they accounted for 40 percent of all the mill operatives—about half of whom were female workers (fig. 34).[56] By 1905, with the city running 42 mills employing 14,545 people, fewer than one-fifth of the people in New Bedford had Yankee backgrounds.[57] French Canadian immigration would reach its highest point in 1910 with 12,241 entering the city, paralleling the high point of new mill incorporations.

The seventeen new textile corporations established between 1900 and 1910 elevated New Bedford to a new ranking in manufacturing within the United States. By 1911, New Bedford had a population of 104,000; its sixty-seven textile mills led the nation in the manufacturing of fine cotton goods and was second in the country in the number of spindles operated.[58] New Bedford sustained its growth through the teens, and by World War I it was the largest center of cotton textile production in America.

During this period of exponential growth, consciously celebratory accounts of the day reveled not only in the productivity of the mills but

Fig. 34. Young French Canadian women in the warping room at the Whitman Mill, 1910. Gift of Roland Jodoin, Spinner Publications.

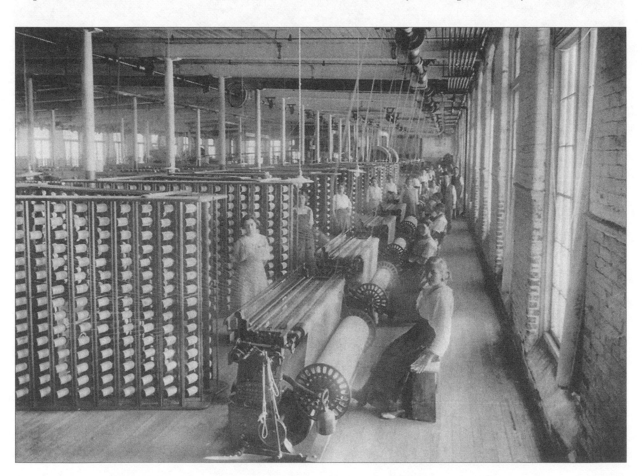

also in their enormous consumption. This 1889 description of Wamsutta's six factories captures the early optimism of the times: "The mills consume weekly when in full operation, four hundred fifty bales of cotton, making an annual consumption of over twenty thousand bales, out of which is manufactured twenty-four million yards of cloth—thousands upon thousands of miles."[59]

A DIVIDED CITY: CONFLICTING INTERESTS AND DIVERGENT SOCIOECONOMIC REALITIES SHAPE THE LANDSCAPE

This period of rapid growth and concentrated economic and industrial power demonstrated itself in harsh contrasts. As viewed from the comfort of the burgeoning downtown commercial district, the New Bedford skyline of 1910 exhibited veils of black smoke from the first and sixth wards of the North and South Ends where the factories were located and where the majority of the immigrants lived (fig. 35).

The use of the terms "North and South Ends" of New Bedford are descriptive labels for the topographic points at each end of the long, narrow city boundaries. But they were also, in essence, labels for the working-class industrial neighborhoods located at the distant reaches of the city. Ultimately, New Bedford merchants in the central business district and the wealthy residents living west of the downtown had reaffirmed the spatial zoning of the whaling era by allocating manufacturing to the outskirts of the city. To be sure, given the economic advantages of locating the mills along the river's edge for better access to coal supplies and for the shipments of raw materials and furnished goods, there was really nowhere else that the mills could be situated if not in the developable space along the Acushnet River and Clark's Cove in the North and South Ends. As a result, as early as 1871, when the Potomska Mill was incorporated in the undeveloped South End, New Bedford was on its way to becoming a use-segregated city as much through economic determinism as by political decree. Social isolation and economic cleavage for the over ten thousand mill workers was demonstrated in this geographic separation of the city. Not only did 56 percent of the urban population live in wards 1 and 6 in 1890; this division constituted 75 percent of the foreign population as well. The Yankee population, on the other hand, occupied the center wards.[60]

The extremes of empowerment, privilege, and wealth expressed themselves in contrasts within the area's building stock as well. Some later mill owners, anxious to transfer the mantle of success from whaling to textiles, bought the large estates of the former whaling merchants located in the center of the city or built large estates of their own on the remaining open lots in the western sector of New Bedford.

The 1833 Greek Revival mansion of William Rotch Rodman on County Street, for example, was the home of the Quaker whaling merchant family that, following the initial efforts of the Joseph Russell family, helped to shift the center of whaling trade to New Bedford from Nantucket. The change in ownership is interesting because it charts the conversion from whaling to textiles. Abraham Howland, as noted earlier, purchased the mansion at auction in 1856. Though he, too, was a prosperous whaling merchant and former sea captain, he obtained the original charter for the Wamsutta Mills and was on several local company boards of directors. Following Howland (who retained the property at least until 1889) the property was owned by Joseph Knowles and Thomas S. Hathaway, both from New Bedford whaling families that had turned to textiles in the North and South Ends. From 1919 until 1945 the mansion was owned by Walter Langshaw, an English immigrant who had worked his way up from clerk in the mills in Lawrence, Massachusetts, to president of the South End Dartmouth Manufacturing Company, and Bristol Manufacturing Company in New Bedford. Similarly, the John Avery Parker house, discussed earlier, was purchased in 1864 by Thomas Bennett, who was the first superintendent of Wamsutta Mills.[61]

The horticultural interests also continued among New Bedford mill magnates as they laid claim to the estates of the former whaling era or began their own impressive residences. It was simply a new generation of wealth demonstrating its economic power and reaffirming the cultural hegemony of the city's leadership. As part of the demonstration of privilege and power, the landscape architect Frederick Law Olmsted was hired to design the estate grounds of Edward D. Mandell in 1883. The home itself, though still under construction, had already caught the attention of New Bedford's established families. Rachel S. Howland, in a letter to her son Morris, stated: "We have told thee, I suppose, about the magnificent house E. Mandell is building on Hawthorn Street? By far the finest in town."[62]

Edward Mandell had taken over the responsibility of serving as Wamsutta Mills director from his father, Thomas Mandell. After much written correspondence between Mandell and Olmsted, an arched stone fence and a driveway following a contour plan was agreed upon (figs. 36–37). The lingering rural habits of the household that were capable of being carried out on these large lots are revealed in the letter to Olmsted dated September 4, 1883: "Dear Sir—The plans received last night thought very beautiful. We fear are not quite practicable. The lane is not just the place for carriages as it is used for driving cows and market wagons, therefore it seems desirable that the carriage drive should meet on Hawthorn Street."[63] Two days later, there was a stated desire to negotiate the spaces between the formal and service drives more effectively. Olmsted apparently wanted to widen the entrance lane: "Your letter and one from Mr. Emerson received this morning. Mr. Emerson agrees with you on the lane entrance . . . since it involves turning the carriages of visitors, and passing them in the drive. Of course a drive to stable and kitchen is necessary—but cannot one be differently arranged? We should be very glad to see either you or your son here at

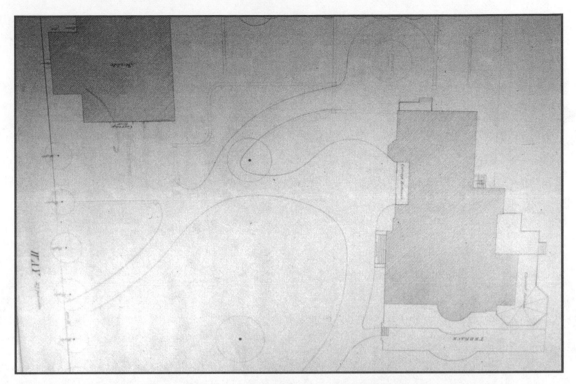

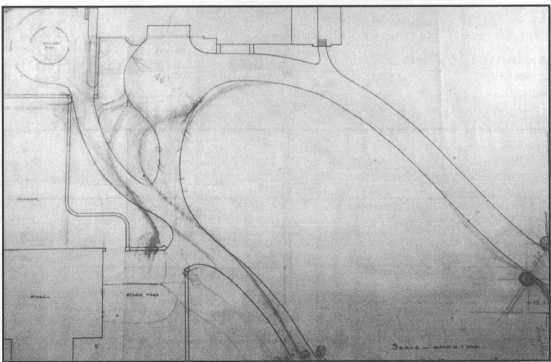

Fig. 36a (top). Drawings for Edward Mandell Estate: proposed approach to the estate, September 4, 1883. Courtesy of F. L. Olmsted National Historic Site.

Fig. 36b (bottom). Drawings for Edward Mandell Estate: Adjusted drive to stable and kitchen, September 6, 1883. Courtesy of F. L. Olmsted National Historic Site.

your earliest convenience as we hope surely to commence work on the middle of the month."[64]

A letter written by Mandell's contractor and builder, Lawrence Watson and Son, dated October 27, 1883, indicated that the plan for a "rockery and arch" was changed to a "simple wall similar to the rest of the walls." Mr. Olmsted was also informed that "Mr. Emerson drew a sketch of it" for him to follow and included it with the letter.[65] The reference to "Mr. Emerson" was likely to

William Ralph Emerson, an architect noted at this time for his designs of private homes in the so-called modern colonial style. His office by 1885 was located in Pemberton Square in Boston, requiring him to coordinate the design of the home and grounds by mail with Olmsted, the client, and the contractor. The high level of negotiation and even design censorship involved among the client (particularly Alice Mandell) and these famous practitioners underscores to what degree design is a collaborative process, and how the combined visions in this case of the landscape architect, designer, client, and contractor have been imprinted on New Bedford's landscape. These baseline statements of design later yield to additive and reductive design decisions by subsequent users that reflect, collectively, the changing nature of place. This is cultural weathering.

Such negotiations initially extended construction on the Mandell estate over approximately six years. In 1889, the Mandells moved from their former residence on 49 Fourth Street to their estate on 163 Hawthorn Street (beyond Page Street). The move paralleled the family's economic rise as well. Between 1879 to 1887 Edward Mandell's occupation is listed in the *New Bedford City Directory* as merchant and partner in the John F. Tucker Company and president of the recently established Pairpoint Manufacturing Company (1880). By 1889, Mandell had gone from being a partner to owning the E. D. Mandell and Company, and was also listed as vice president of the New Bedford Institute of Savings. He continued as president of Pairpoint, a well-established glass-manufacturing company by the time Mandell moved into his new home.[66]

At the same moment that Edward Mandell was constructing his impressive estate and grounds on Hawthorn Street, other large estates that had been built during the whaling era were being subdivided. Grounds that had formerly been given over to lavish pleasure gardens and greenhouses were now being filled with large homes owned by descendants of the original owners and prosperous mill investors anxious to leave their imprint on the prestigious "hill" yet again.

One such example is the 1840 estate of Matthew Howland (see map 2), the subdividing of which he describes in an 1884 letter: "Plummer and Captain Delano have deeded to me $1/3$ of the lot we owned together. I take the south end, and I have sold it to Willie [William D. Howland, Matthew's son], who is going to build on it this summer."[67] He later detailed the complexion of those plans: "Those four buildings near us are all up now and show what they are to look like. Clifford's is a very large house. Ingraham's overtops Willie's very considerably.

Many of Willie's windows are in and the glass is small, diamond shaped."[68] Similarly, the estates of William Hathaway Jr. and Jonathon Bourne (between Orchard Street and Cottage, from Maple Street to Arnold Street) were subdivided between 1897 and 1910.

Other New Bedford elites began to modernize the mansions of their forebears. Ten years after their work for Mandell, Olmsted, Olmsted, and Eliot returned to New Bedford and produced proposals, beginning in May 1893, to build "certain drives, walks, masonry and doing certain grading and cultivating on the estate of Frederick Grinnell, Esq. at New Bedford, Mass."[69] Grinnell, like Mandell, was now on the board of Wamsutta Mills (1893–1905). Up to this point, Grinnell had chosen to reside in Providence, Rhode Island. With the passing of Joseph Grinnell, the first president of the Wamsutta Mills, the 1832 Greek Revival mansion on County Street was left to Frederick Grinnell. The estate, now fifty years old and marred by a fire which destroyed the entrance portico, was in need of modernizing. Ultimately, the Olmsted firm was engaged to provide a complete planting list, design new drives, and supervise the installation of formal gardens (fig. 38). Concurrently, Frederick removed the Greek Revival parapet that had partially disguised the low hip roof and cupola and replaced it with a square, wooden monitor roof on the third floor. This roof form, a regional preference on early Providence estates, allowed Frederick unobstructed surveillance of his newly landscaped estate grounds, neighboring homes, and the harbor (refer to fig. 23).

While the cultural weathering of New Bedford's gentry houses from the whaling era was occurring under the direction of a new generation of industrialists enjoying the dividends of a new manufacturing empire, a very different cultural landscape was being defined in the manufacturing precincts of the city's North and South Ends where these same industrialists held controlling interests.

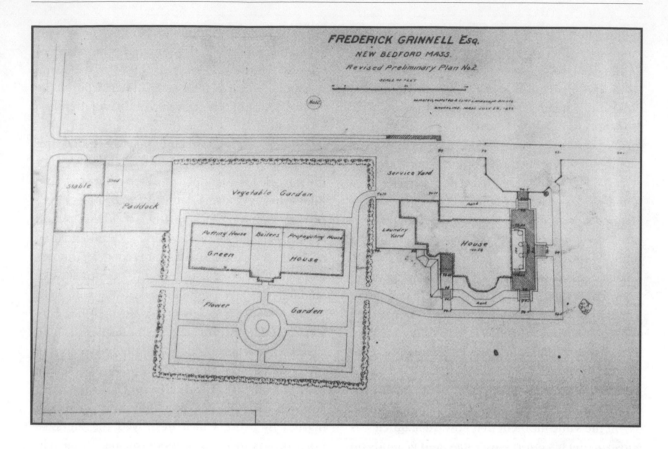

Fig. 38. The 1893 formal flower garden design proposal and driveway study by Olmsted, Olmsted and Eliot for the Frederick Grinnell estate. F. L. Olmsted National Historic Site.

Here, the immigrant mill workers lived in close proximity to their place of work in cramped corporate housing or in newer multifamily rental flats that steadily began (at least by 1871) to replace the tenement blocks and boardinghouses owned and operated by the earliest mills. The scale of these rental flats—built initially by the corporations for the skilled labor force and by the 1890s by speculative builders for the burgeoning unskilled labor force—increased dramatically after the turn of the century in an attempt to house the mill population in larger, detached, multifamily living units. Even by 1890 the "persons per dwelling averages" in Wards 1 and 6 approached eight people per dwelling (7.99 and 7.82 respectively), while the average

family size for the same areas was half that number (from 3.62 to 5.25).[70] Hence, boarders were likely to be a frequent occurrence in the overcrowded living environments that characterized the city's mill districts.

The 1895 persons per-room statistic demonstrates the overcrowding of the foreign population. In Ward 1, there was almost one room to each person. In Ward 3, which was most heavily Yankee and where the mansions discussed above were located, there was essentially one person to every two rooms.[71] Not only was the scale of the tenements increasing dramatically by the turn of the century, but the density of the human population living within those units increased as well. The wage differences account for such disparity. Mill managers earned nearly 100 dollars per week in 1890. Male skilled workers (such as spinners) earned 16 dollars a week; male operatives earned 8 dollars a week; and women operatives earned 4 dollars a week, while all averaged 10-hour days, 5 ½ to 6 days a week.[72]

Increasingly, textile mills in New Bedford became synonymous with immigrant labor. The 1900 U.S. Census reveals that 97 percent of New Bedford textile workers were first- or second-generation immigrants. These contrasts were emphasized by the spatial segregation of the city, where by 1900 90 percent of the foreign elements of the city's population (nearly 45,000 people) lived in Wards 1 and 6, and the persons per dwelling average in Ward 1 rose to 10 per living unit.[73]

A 1912 photograph taken in New Bedford by Lewis H. Hine illustrates the overcrowding of these tenements and the frequency of family boarders. Significantly, the photo was taken not to document overcrowding, but child-labor issues. Lewis Hine visited New Bedford in 1911, 1912,

and 1916 while being employed by the National Child Labor Committee (fig. 39). The caption on this January 1912 photo of nine family members reads, "Manuel Sousa and family, 306 Second Street. On right end is brother-in-law; next him is father who works on the river; next is Manuel (appears to be 12 years old) wearing sweater and has arms folded. He has been a cleaner in the Holmes Cotton Mill for two years. John, Manuel's brother (next him in photo) works in City Cotton Mill. Next is sister. At left end is cousin. Small fry sprinkled around. All are very illiterate. John and Manuel are the only ones who can speak English and they only a little." The reference to the

Fig. 39. Portuguese immigrant family, 1912. Photograph by Lewis W. Hine. Courtesy of the Library of Congress (Reproduction no. LC-USZ62-64507).

Holmes Mill places the living quarters in the South End (Ward 6); many Portuguese lived near South Water Street at the turn of the century.[74] Since the Holmes Mill was built in 1909, young Manuel Sousa would have gotten his entry-level job just as the mill opened its doors. Called "forty-hour kids," because they could not work a full weekly schedule of fifty-four hours until they were sixteen, the limited income of boy sweepers nevertheless contributed to the household budget.[75] Child labor also kept the youths out of trouble while both parents worked in the mills, but generally it kept them out of school as well, in spite of night-school requirements. It also prepared (or sentenced) the next generation for employment in the mills.

Another of Hine's photos of workers' living spaces in New Bedford was taken in January 1912 (fig. 40). Here, the subject is of the French Canadian family of Alfred Benoit living at 191 North Front Street in Ward 1. Taken in the "kitchen/living room" a legend reads: "The U.S. Bureau of Labor Statistics published an index for the 'minimum budget necessary to maintain a workers' family of 5 in health and decency.' The average wage in New Bedford's textile industry covered about one-half of this budget." The necessity of other members of the family to work in order to augment the low wages paid in textiles is obvious. Here, as the caption notes, the boy is a sweeper in the Bennett Mils where his mother works. The father is a canvasser (Hine refers to him as "shiftless"). The baby being held is being cared for by another woman. This photo of a North End tenement also reflects that the principal living space was heated only by the cookstove. Here, a couch/daybed is also present to accommodate the sleeping needs of this seven-member family. As will be demonstrated shortly, many of the floor plans of New Bedford three-tenements only designated the kitchen space, allowing the remaining rooms to be arranged as needed. Most were used as sleeping space for family members and boarders with the water closet sometimes in the stair hall or

Fig. 40. Lewis W. Hine photograph of a kitchen/living room of the Alfred Benoit family at 191 North Front Street, New Bedford, in 1912. Courtesy of the Library of Congress (Reproduction no. LC-USZ62-73985).

basement. Given the 1900 U.S. Census figure quoted earlier of ten people per living unit in Wards 1 and 6 (where each of the photos discussed above were taken), a three-decker flat during this era would have held thirty individuals—ten on each floor level.

Worth noting, too, was the degree of geographic mobility of some of these working families. Alfred Benoit, for example, was listed in the 1910 *City Directory* as a bartender residing at 11 Logan Street (near Wamsutta Mills). There was no *City Directory* for 1911. By 1913, Alfred Benoit had moved to 229 State Street and was now listed as superintendent of the Public Baths. Meanwhile, all three families listed as residing at 191 Front Street in 1910 were replaced by *four* new families in 1914.[76]

Hence, while it is customary to think of corporate housing and rental flats as providing inexpensive shelter for the industrial work force of New Bedford, at the same time it is appropriate to think of these tenements as housing the working poor. The conditions of overcrowding due to maintaining "boarding-rooms" for relatives or co-workers was necessitated by the demand put upon these low wage earners to meet ever-increasing rental costs as the population swelled and housing was in greater demand.[77]

In spite of such staggering figures of housing density, city officials were reluctant to pass legislation addressing space requirements in building codes. Even housing reformers intent on expanding the awareness of the general public to issues of overcrowding were forced to express the requirement for space in unscientific terms using a ratio of people to the number of rooms in an apartment (such as those quoted above). By 1915 standards, overcrowding did not occur until there was more than an average of one and a half persons per room. Unfortunately, this figure was not based on any ideal of comfort, health, or safety, but more or less on the average found on current tenement surveys.[78] Existing conditions of over-crowding, then, became the appropriate standard for regulation, if such space requirements found their way into city building codes at all.[79]

Part of the reason for the absence of such legislation can be explained by the fact that there existed in every manufacturing city at the turn of the century a natural antagonism of competing interests. Progressive reformers, labor leaders, and some state legislators often sought better working and housing conditions, while manufacturers tended to respond with threats that excessive regulations jeopardized the very existence of the industry and related businesses within the city.

Interestingly, as such contrasts between living standards and conflicting ideologies grew most evident in the era of largest mill expansion, highest profit, and the greatest influx of immigrant population (from 1880 to 1921),[80] the public art of the city increasingly turned to depicting itself as a whaling community instead of as a textile urban center with 97 percent of its mill workers of foreign extraction. The bronze sculpture of *The Whaleman* presented in June 1913 to the city by William W. Crapo, at this juncture the president of Wamsutta Mills, was situated prominently outside the newly converted library, for example (fig. 41). It has become a symbol of the city ever since. Its inscription "a dead whale or a stove boat" is known to every school child, as is the image of the harpooner depicted with striking classical features in spite of the fact that traditionally harpooners were of Indian, African, or West Indian descent.

Similarly, on the inside of the library—significantly the former Greek Revival City Hall of the whaling era designed by Russell Warren—are large paintings of the city's whaling history at every turn. As a child, those images captivated me and reassured me of my regional identity, or so I thought. In choosing to commemorate the early whaling development of New Bedford to which the prominent families belonged, these same individuals conspired to construct an identity that denied the very reality of an evolving industrial landscape that they

Fig. 41. The bronze statue of *The Whaleman* was commissioned by William Crapo and made by sculptor Bela L. Pratt. It was presented by Crapo to the city on June 20, 1913. Used with the permission of the Board of Trustees of the New Bedford Free Public Library.

also helped to create. Thus, in the commemorative statue of *The Whaleman,* one may view public art as functioning simultaneously as a statement of regional power and prestige, and as an agent of illusion and myth. New Bedford's power elite, like vested individuals everywhere, succeeded in telling *their* view of history. In the process, they have selectively blended the historical and mythic pasts into a narrative with which they could identify most comfortably. This narrative has become, in large part, the "official" history. New Bedford does have a notable whaling heritage. What generally has been ignored in both historical and architectural accounts of the city, however, is life behind the "scrim": the veiled existence of immigrants screened either by factory smoke or the fine woven fabrics for which the city is also famous. These players in the city's cultural landscape are faceless and nameless in the official history. One sees only shadows of their deeds behind the scrim that divides the city. In contrast, the principal organs of

local and regional history display the "scrimshaw": the highly visible and deeply etched public statements incised in whalebone and public art of a more distant, sanitized, and "heroic" past.

One possible exception is the sculptural work dedicated in 1914 and placed in the vehicle rotary in Buttonwood Park—seen in its day as a setting for refreshing the "tired townspeople" of New Bedford (see chapter 4). Here a noble blacksmith, with chin and back erect, holds the gears of industry on a large anvil. Dressed in workman's attire, he rises above the shoulders of sea men and women positioned below. Bracketed by the two images of New Bedford's cultural and economic heritage, the inscription reads: "Dedicated as a tribute to the sturdy whaleman who early won fame for New Bedford and to their successors who, inheriting ideals and resourcefulness by creating a great manufacturing city" (fig. 42).

With such emblematic power, the city's forebears have been depicted as struggling in unison

Fig. 42. The inscription reads: "Dedicated as a tribute to the sturdy whaleman who early won fame for New Bedford and to their successors who, inheriting ideals and resourcefulness by creating a great manufacturing city." Sculpted by G. J. Zolnay, 1914, Buttonwood Park.

exists, instead, in the assortment of predominately Catholic churches, each bespeaking a different place of origin for its congregation and demonstrating the ethnic mix that eventually characterized the city; it is made known in the repeated visual couplings of mill and mill housing (though these, too, are quickly vanishing); it is echoed in the interwoven rhythms of backyard clotheslines connecting three-decker to three-decker in multiple layers of meaning (fig. 43). These images recall the social history of common landscapes and everyday life that the majority of New Bedford citizens lived particularly after the turn of the twentieth century.

Fig. 43. Louise Pitts behind the laundry deck at 90 Nelson Street in 1942.

against the "demons of the sea" and other opposing forces over which they eventually triumphed. In the process, the elite culture of the city has assembled a public identity that seemingly speaks of shared experiences and common goals that affirm a cohesive public culture, devoid of economic inequalities and political conflicts.

Essentially, the history of everyday life behind the scrim is everywhere in New Bedford *except* in the history books and public art.[81] This history

PART II

CORPORATE HOUSING AS AN INDEX TO SOCIAL CHANGE

HOUSING THE NEW INDUSTRIAL WORKFORCE

It has not been the policy of New Bedford businessmen to confine their city's enterprise to one class of industry, but the manufacture of cotton goods now holds the first place in extent and importance.

—William L. Sayer, *New Bedford, Massachusetts: Its History, Industry, Institutions and Attractions,* 1889

The whaling industry had required a sizable male labor force to maintain its offshore operations. But with the ten thousand crewmen on New Bedford whalers at sea for long periods few had families living in port.[1] Seamen's boardinghouses met the lodging needs of single men, while a limited amount of multifamily housing was available for whaling crewmen with families. In addition, dock workers, ship carpenters, and other tradesmen (such as riggers, coopers, caulkers, sailmakers, and ship chandlers) lived in cottages, above stores, in Federal Period mansions converted to boardinghouses, and in tenements located in older sections of the city among

Fig. 44. Gable-end, Greek Revival roominghouse (demolished) of the whaling era along South Water Street. Courtesy of Spinner Publications.

the maritime industries and along South Water Street to afford convenient access to the waterfront and downtown commercial district (fig. 44).[2] Such facilities were far too limited and too distant from the proposed mill sites to serve the needs of the textile industry, however. If skilled textile workers and mill operatives were going to be recruited to this infant industry in New Bedford, an adequate number of well-built, affordable, and conveniently located living accommodations needed to be provided by the textile corporations themselves.

Slowly replacing a working population in New Bedford of itinerant seamen dependent upon a share of the catch at the end of a two- to three-year voyage was a growing resident population after 1850 of mill workers receiving a weekly wage. Even during the earliest stages of corporate housing, textile workers—by their daily activities— began to define their lifeways within the spatially restricted context of mill districts, tenement housing blocks, and localized businesses. Collectively, these elements formed distinct working-class

neighborhoods dependent upon the life force of the mill economy. By degrees, the land set aside for textile production and housing for the ever-expanding mill population transformed New Bedford's outward expression from a seafaring village to an industrial city.

WAMSUTTA MILL HOUSING

In New Bedford, corporate housing was built as early as 1848 by the owners of the Wamsutta Mills to stabilize their workforce (fig. 45). Unlike earlier, more idealistic schemes elsewhere in New England—for instance, in Lowell, Massachusetts— that attempted to relate enlightened industrial village planning to social betterment, the first efforts toward providing housing for textile factory workers in New Bedford were the result of pure expedience.

As an 1892 source recalls, "After the [Wamsutta Mill] buildings were completed, all the overseers, machinists, carpenters and operatives were brought here from manufacturing localities in

Fig. 45. By 1848, these eight brick "four-tenements" were constructed for Wamsutta's skilled operatives. They were located between Hicks and Logan Streets along North Front Street (see map 3). Photograph from Jessamine Whitney, *Infant Mortality*, 1920.

Rhode Island, Connecticut, and central parts of this State. To provide homes for these people the company was obliged to build and maintain boarding houses and tenements, and this feature of the enterprise has been continued ever since."[3]

The design format for Wamsutta's 1848 brick double houses—like the initial workforce, materials, and design for the mill itself—was derived from other New England mill villages. The two-story, brick double houses built by Wamsutta (with paired central doors flanked by three windows on either side), for example, are nearly identical to the pitched-roof, brick double houses built along Worthen Street in Lowell, c. 1825. In turn, since labor politics shaped the perception of what type of housing was desirable (and appropriate) for skilled labor, the political culture of the times determined that the Lowell double houses resemble quality brick rows in leading English textile centers. Such improved housing, it was felt, kept the labor force from "floating." Also similar to the Wamsutta brick double houses are the wooden Great Falls Corporation boardinghouses, Broad Street, Somersworth, New

Hampshire, built c. 1826–30. Wamsutta's earliest corporate housing, therefore, would have been comparable to the facilities of some of the leading New England textile villages. Though smaller, the Wamsutta mill houses followed the same trend of some of the more recent model boardinghouses that were also being constructed of brick. See, for example, the contemporaneous double houses for factory overseers at Salmon Falls, and those built in Lawrence, Massachusetts, for the Atlantic Mills and Bay State Mills between 1846 and 1847.[4]

The 1871 *Walker Map of the City of New Bedford* situates the eight original brick double houses built by Wamsutta Mills (map 3). They were divided into two rows of four at the intersection of Logan and Front Streets opposite the freshwater pond. Of better construction and physically separated from the blocks of wooden multifamily tenements that were built concurrently between Purchase and County Streets, these brick units likely served as boardinghouses for the factory overseers that Wamsutta had recruited from nearby manufacturing localities. If they were like

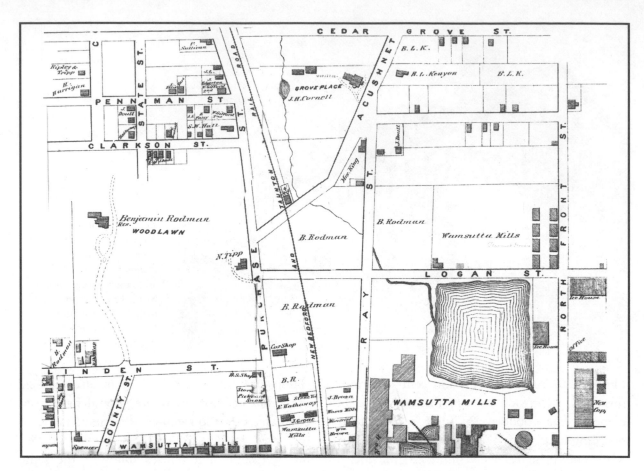

Map 3. 1871 Walker map, *The City of New Bedford,* Part of First Ward, showing the 1848 eight brick double houses (upper right).

surviving plans of the boardinghouses belonging to the Bay State Mills in Lawrence published in 1850, then the first floor would have provided space for a parlor, dining room, kitchen, and chamber (likely for the matron of the house), while the upper floor and a half provided sleeping chambers. Similarly, the rear yard likely would have had a well, cesspool, privy, and a space set aside for laundry and garbage.

The same area above the pond, where the eight brick double houses were built, continued to have wooden housing stock added as well. Several are visible on the 1876 C. H. Vogt, Lithographer from Wisconsin, *View of the City of New Bedford* (see fig. 49, insert upper right). Addi-

tional housing, built most probably in response to the demand brought on by Wamsutta's construction of Mills No. 5 and 6 in 1875 and 1882, continued to be built in the area of the brick boardinghouses into the 1890s. By the 1890s, however, it is likely that even the brick boardinghouses were now converted to family tenements. The 1911 *New Bedford Atlas* refers to the brick double houses, for example, as "four tenements," much like the rest of the corporate housing. These newer tenements are visible on the 1895 *Map of Bristol County, Massachusetts* (map 4).[5] One large housing unit was added to the northern end of each row of the brick double houses, beginning a new pattern of (5) tenement blocks to a row separated (at the rear) by a laundry court (fig. 50b). By 1895, twenty rental structures were grouped between North Front Street and Fulton Court (to the east and west) and bounded by

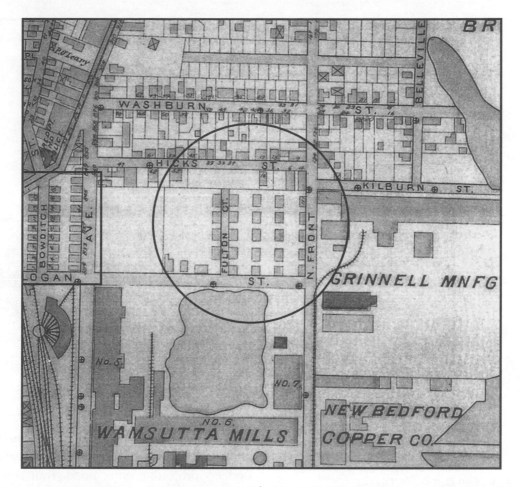

Logan Street to the south. Another five units of the same design were added to an undesignated street immediately to the west, joining two units of a different configuration. In all by 1895, twenty-seven tenement blocks were assigned to the area immediately north of Wamsutta's mills. A 1945 aerial photo indicates that all the brick units were gone by then, but twelve of the pre-1895 corporate housing units survived into recent years. The construction related to the 1967 John F. Kennedy Highway, however, destroyed the remaining evidence.

Beginning in 1848, Wamsutta also built large numbers of wooden multifamily tenements for the operatives and their families. Arranged five to a street front, they were located in the area bounded by Purchase and County Streets to the east and west respectively and continued in

Map 4. From the 1895 Beers *Atlas of Bristol County, Massachusetts,* showing three rows of Grinnell housing (left) and expanded rows of wooden four-tenements for Wamsutta (right). Used with the permission of the Board of Trustees of the New Bedford Free Public Library.

another grouping one-half block down from Linden Street to the north and to Hazard Street to the south (map 5). These units are currently four- and six-family tenements (fig. 46).

Throughout the 1870s, Wamsutta continued to expand its mill housing to the southwest of the mill site, and again invested heavily in the wooden multifamily house type. The 1876 *View of the City of New Bedford* indicates one-and-one-half-story and two-and-one-half-story double-tenements arranged in a horizontal format five to each side of the block (see fig. 49 top insert). These units were constructed as a cohesive architectural grouping

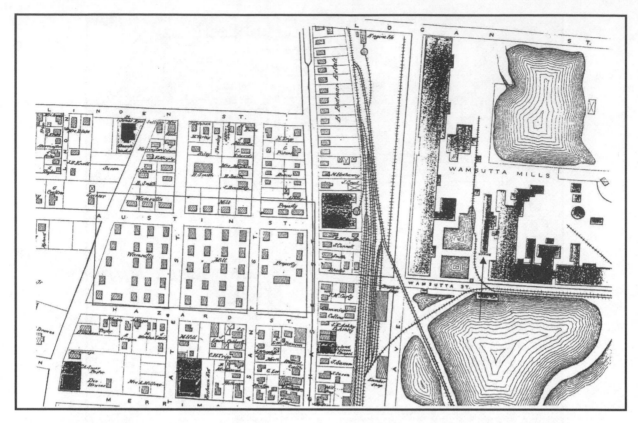

bounded by Hazard, Austin, County, and Pleasant Streets. In addition, eight housing units were sited one block east of this group to Purchase Street, providing at least thirty-eight multiplex units by 1876 in this area alone. Construction continued at a rapid pace and by 1887 the number increased to fifty-nine in this residential district with several other units in evidence running north and south between Purchase Street and the railroad tracks. When a 1913 field study was undertaken by the U.S. Department of Labor, the number of one-and-one-half-story and two-and-one-half-story double-tenements built to house Wamsutta's workers totaled eighty.

The general "pattern language" for these units consisted of two aligned front and rear doors located at the ends of the horizontal mass. Each entry was preceded by a stoop with four steps each under a projecting entry hood. Four sets of six-over-six sash windows were located on the first two floors between the entries, while half-window units (located directly above them) lighted the attic space. Two chimney flues (positioned toward the center of the gable ridgeline) served each of the double-housing units, while the clapboarded frame superstructure rested on a granite fieldstone foundation.

On the interior, one front and rear stair hall provided vertical circulation to the upper units on each side of the two-and-one-half-story double-house tenements, and served as ground-floor access to the front and rear principal living spaces. The stair hall, therefore, did not provide a through-passage for cross-axial movement from front to rear of the first-floor accommodations (fig. 46d). These units were rehabilitated in 1978 by the New Bedford Housing Authority for state-

Kitchen

Bath

Kitchen

Bath

Bedroom

Living Room

Living Room

Bedroom

Unit I

Unit 2

First Floor

subsidized housing, but the original plan is discernable.[6] Using the present room configuration to conjecture what the generic floor plan may have looked like, the front stair hall likely led directly into the parlor, followed by the kitchen. Two small spaces were located to the side of these "public" rooms, spliced between the front and rear entries, forming a four-room plan for the tenement units on the first two floors. (Thus forming "four tenements," as described in the 1911 *New Bedford Atlas*.) At least one of the smaller rooms was used as a sleeping chamber, while the smallest room may have served originally as a pantry or "sink room" for doing dishes in a dry sink and for storing food. Traditionally, the area marked "kitchen" on tenement floor plans was where the cast-iron cookstove was positioned. A dining table

Fig. 46. Front, rear, side elevation, and plan view of a Wamsutta two-and-one-half-story four tenement of the type built for Wamsutta Mills operatives between 1848 and c. 1889. Courtesy of Hresko Associates, Boston, October 18, 1985.

would have allowed this space to double as a food-preparation area and dining space, though it was not uncommon to find daybeds there as well, particularly when a member of the family was sick. In the center of the house plan (sharing a party wall) was a brick chimney flue, which served as stove hookups for both the kitchen and parlor stoves. This centralized heating core thus maximized the heat gain to all the other rooms. As for other environmental systems, it was not until 1888 that these apartments had inside plumbing installed. Even then, the toilets were placed in a dark cellar on each side of the double units for general usage via the rear stair halls. Prior to these improvements, members of the household went from the kitchen area, out the rear utility stair hall, to the rear yard, which provided all the facilities for drinking water, laundry, and human waste disposal. On the 1978 rehabbed plan, the rear sink room was converted to a bathroom, and a counter sink was added to the interior party wall of the original kitchen.

It is important to bear in mind, too, that even though these double-housing units are traditionally thought of in New Bedford as four- and six-family tenements (two families to each floor level of the adjoining units, with two additional attic apartments in the two-and-one-half-story type), at the peak of mill expansion these living spaces were often reconfigured into smaller sleeping spaces for maximum occupancy. As late as 1913, when the U.S. Department of Labor undertook an infant-mortality study in New Bedford, the following living arrangements were observed in the Wamsutta Mills area: "In a four-tenement, just north of the business center was found a family of seven, where lodgers were taken for 10 cents a night to help pay the $2.50 a week rental. The father, mother, and four children slept in one room, and one child in the kitchen; as many lodgers as possible were crowded into the other two rooms, which were filled solidly with cots, six in one room and four in the other. These were in use constantly for day and night shifts."[7]

The large number of four-tenements that continued to multiply in the North End was in direct response to the steady growth of the Wamsutta Mills. Between 1848 and 1893, seven mills were constructed with the total number of hands employed by 1889 reaching 2,600. As an 1889 source states, the corporation provided "for them well built, comfortable tenements of six and seven rooms each—over three hundred in number—and rented them from $6.50 to $9.00 a month. [The

operatives at this point in time were] principally English, Scotch, Irish, and French Canadians, with a slight sprinkling of Americans and a few other nationalities."[8] By 1892, the rents dropped to between $5.25 and $7.50 a month with the tenements now designed to accommodate five and seven rooms each. The average wage for operatives in the 1890s was $8.00 per week.[9]

The reference to tenements being configured "six and seven rooms each" is interesting, since the buildings themselves were referred to as "four-tenements." The 1913 study on infant mortality described the one-and-one-half-story and two-and-one-half-story tenements built by Wamsutta as follows:

These were [30] four tenement houses, three stories high, with two four room apartments on each side of the first and second floors, one on each side of the house. The occupants of each apartment had the use, also, of two rooms on the third floor, giving each apartment six rooms in all. A similar group of 50 houses lay to the west of those just mentioned. The houses of these groups were identical except that in the second group there were usually only two stories and two apartments of eight rooms each, four on each floor. . . . These houses were built in bleakly symmetrical rows with large undrained courts between, paved only with mud and decorated with clothes poles and fluttering rags. The toilets, damp and dark, were in the cellars, one for every two apartments.[10] (fig. 47)

The separate stair halls on the front and rear of the larger two-and-one-half-story units functioned, then, as zoned access; the front led to the attic rooms, while the rear led to the laundry yard and (by 1888) to the cellar toilets. These attic rooms (one on each side of the ridgeline), in turn, provided overflow living space for large families

Fig. 47. A group of fifty Wamsutta four-tenements in 1913. These smaller units had two floors and two apartments of four rooms each on each floor. Photograph from Jessamine, Whitney, *Infant Mortality*, 1920.

renting the bottom two apartments or, more often, served as an additional source of income when rented to boarders. Recalling the earlier 1913 description of Wamsutta's "four-tenement," this one apartment in the four-tenement rental unit not only accommodated a family of seven in the lower apartment, but also provided two attic units to serve an additional ten lodgers (charged at the rate of ten cents a person per night). Four cots were set up in one attic room, while six were placed in the other. The two stairwells also served as separated fire exits for these remote attic apartments. In some instances, it is likely that wash was taken in and meals were provided to offset the expenses of the principal renter. Even allowing for the fact that the attic overflow spaces were separated physically from the apartment units below—thus providing a degree of privacy—the living situation of seventeen lodgers in six rooms offers a far different perception of operative housing conditions than does the "official" corporate account in 1889 of "well built comfortable tenements of six and seven rooms each." Also, the density of the living accommodations very likely could not be surmised today by simply investigating the physical evidence of the four-room tenement plan as built. By combining physical and documentary evidence, a clearer picture of the daily life of some textile workers at Wamsutta Mills is revealed. Such data demonstrates, as well, how ordinary people retaliated against their restrictive social and economic circumstances and found ways of empowering themselves by reinterpreting their living environments to address their current living situation. As one older gentleman who was raised in Wamsutta housing said to me, "We were dirt poor, and never knew it. I was happy there."

While mill owners in Lowell were ridding themselves of the responsibility of investing in boardinghouses and tenements after 1848, why were New Bedford textile owners building such housing well beyond that era?[11] In a city so economically committed to and identified with whaling, there was a great deal of reluctance on the part of local investors and banks initially to shift economic support to a new industry. The first mills also lacked the workforce, materials, and real-estate infrastructure to support such an industry. It was incumbent upon the mill corporations, therefore, to provide the housing that was necessary to make the venture work. This requisite commitment to a broader capital investment (in the form of corporate housing) beyond the specific manufacturing needs of a textile mill may have been another contributing factor to why it took twenty-five years for another textile corporation to begin in New Bedford following Wamsutta's lead.

Thus, in the earliest days of textile development, standardized workers' housing formats, based on historic precedent from neighboring textile communities, were merely transferred to New Bedford to become part of its emerging industrial landscape. Over time, the large-scale and systematic construction of this building stock characterized New Bedford as a textile city. Such boardinghouses and tenements for the large workforce of mule spinners, weavers, loom fixers, and operatives were built in New Bedford at least up to the 1890s. The number of tenements Sayer counted in 1889, three hundred, perhaps needs clarification for a more reliable assessment of the nature and volume of workers' housing in the city. Each multifamily double house contained four apartments or tenements; hence, the eighty one-and-one-half-story and two-and-one-half-story "four-tenements" accounted for three hundred and twenty tenements. Though Wamsutta workers soon adopted a different type of operative housing, some of these lodging facilities remained in use as company housing at least through the 1950s.

POTOMSKA MILL HOUSING

The shoreline of the city extended along the west bank of the Acushnet River from the mill sites just to the north of the commercial center (where Wamsutta was located) and stretched to the south for a distance of 10.75 miles. The area known as Clark's Point was located at the farthest southern point in the city and was surrounded on both sides by water views of the Acushnet River to the east and Clark's Cove to the west. This favorable natural setting offered several recreational advantages by 1871. A "point drive" allowed pleasurable carriage drives along the shoreline past boathouses, past the Revolutionary War–era fort, and past bathing areas on the Acushnet River side. Because of its distance from the urban center of New Bedford, the area also included several charitable institutions, such as the orphans' home, the City Farm and Hospital (the former Perry Russell farm was sold in 1828 to be used as the City Work Farm), and the almshouse. Clark's Point will be analyzed later in connection with the Howland Mill. Worth noting at this juncture are the number of benevolent institutions that had been established in the city as an outgrowth of the Quaker economic and political leadership in the city (the Friends were greatly interested in education and human progress in secular as well as spiritual matters) and the rural nature of the terrain prior to the onset of South End mill incorporations.

Before 1871, this part of the city was relatively undeveloped. There were few roads or water hookups, and it would be over a decade before a railway system would serve this part of the city. Instead, these were large rural lots with a few homes owned by descendants of the city's founding families, summer residences, such as the 1840 Gothic cottage owned after the 1860s by Mrs. Rachel Howland (formerly the Congdon estate), municipal institutions, such as the work farm, and scattered businesses, such as a soap-manufacturing plant, a large nursery belonging to H. Eames and J. D. Thompson, and a slaughterhouse owned by S. T. Vial.

When the Potomska Mill was built on South Water Street in 1871 and began to manufacture "fine lawns, satteens, print cloths, cretonnes, and jeans,"[12] the mill owners had to construct rental property for its workers, since no lodging was available locally in the South End. It should be pointed out, too, that the Potomska Mill was not begun as competition for Wamsutta, but to augment its

Fig. 48. Potomska workers' housing located at the northeast corner of Rivet and Second Streets. This previously unacknowledged block of four-family tenements were among a group of six built in 1871. By the 1906 Sanborn Map, ten units in all enclosed an unpaved laundry court and housed a portion of the corporation's unskilled workforce.

products by producing coarser goods like shades, umbrellas, and jeans (in addition to print cloth) as opposed to the fine bleached sheetings and shirtings Wamsutta produced. Moreover, Andrew G. Pierce was the president of both concerns, while businessmen such as William J. Rotch, William W. Crapo, and Francis Hathaway served on both boards of directors. Business practices in New Bedford self-consciously avoided redundancy in products as well as competition among local businesses, particularly since these economic ventures often were supported broadly by capital from family and friends living in New Bedford.

In the first phase of tenement building, the management of Potomska Mill No. 1 built six three-story tenement blocks that were square in form and surmounted by a flat roof. These large wooden structures (six bays wide) were built at the intersections of Rivet Street and First and Second Streets—just three blocks from the factory (fig. 48). These three-story blocks probably followed Wamsutta's example of providing four-room tenements stacked two to a side with additional sleeping rooms on the third floor accessible through corner stair halls. This would make sense in light of the fact that the mill

management of both corporations was essentially the same and that Wamsutta was still building four-tenements throughout the 1890s. In spite of a stylistic change to the Italianate from Wamsutta's late–Federal Period handling, the massing formula and entry arrangements were basically the same in both examples (fig. 49a&c).

A second group of six frame tenements was located on an adjacent lot at the southwest corner of Second and Rivet Streets. These tenements, however, were three-deckers built during the 1870s. Corporation-owned three-deckers may have made their debut in New Bedford with the 1871 build of the Potomska Mill.[13] The Potomska three-deckers, which offered a separate living unit on each floor, were flat-roofed with Italianate brackets along the cornice. At least one three-decker had stacked front porches by 1876 (fig. 49b). These three-story "three tenements" measured 38 by 44 feet. As smaller, more private living accommodations, they likely were set aside exclusively for skilled workers who were married, while the large four-tenement blocks—as at Wamsutta—provided lodging for both families and bachelor boarders. Both types of Potomska housing are represented

Wamsutta Mill Housing, c. 1848

(Detail) *View of the City of New Bedford,* 1876. C. H. Vogt, lithographer, Wisconsin.

Potomska Mill Housing, c. 1871

Potomska Mill Housing, c. 1871

(Detail) *View of the City of New Bedford,* 1876. C. H. Vogt, lithographer, Wisconsin.

Fig. 49. Evolution of New Bedford Mill-Housing Typology.

in the 1876 *View of the City of New Bedford,* as well as in the 1888 Sanborn map. According to the *Record of Building Permits for the City of New Bedford*, on May 21, 1900, four of the original six three-deckers were still listed as belonging to Potomska Mills. But they were moved by the city at this time from Second and Rivet Streets by building mover John Borden to make way for the Ingraham Public School, which was being built to serve this South End mill district.

The original configuration of the six four-tenement blocks built to house Potomska operatives, on the other hand, formed an L shape with three built along Rivet Street, two down Second Street, and one down S. First Street. When Potomska built Mill No. 2 in 1877, it added one more square four-tenement block to the north along S. First Street. Two more were added north of the units along First and Second Streets by 1895. Between 1895 and 1906, a tenth four-tenement was added between the last two units to form a stylistically unified quadrangular arrangement that enclosed a central court (map 6). Facing outward around the four sides of an unpaved laundry yard, this previously unacknowledged group of tenement houses established the only visually cohesive housing units that Potomska built.[14] Subsequent construction reflected a wide variety of tenement housing alternatives (some built above saloons) that were scattered within a four-block area around the mill with very little attempt made to distinguish them as corporate housing.

During the 1870s and 1880s the South End was just beginning to undergo industrial expansion (unlike the North End, which began to industrialize thirty years earlier), and few urban amenities existed until South Water Street and, later, Rivet Street were established as business districts for the mill population. Scattered stores and saloons, therefore, sprang up around the Potomska Mills and tenement blocks to provide needed services close at hand, particularly following the addition of two more mill annexes for Potomska by 1880. Perhaps because of the short-age of such amenities, not all mill hands chose to live near their place of work. A review of the residential listings for the Potomska Mill workforce in the 1889 *New Bedford City Directory* reflects a rather broad distribution of the working population (table 1). By 1895, a rail line connected the South End mills to the central business district and North End residential communities, augmenting a trolley line which previously served the Potomska Mills. After this point, the better-paid working population gained access to even greater geographic mobility. By the 1890s, however, the workforce of Potomska had diversified beyond the English skilled workers who had been recruited predominantly from Lancashire, England. The French Canadian workers and, later, the Portuguese workers, as noted in the 1923 *Reconnaissance Survey of New Bedford*, preferred to walk to their place of work and to shop along South Water Street. These two ethnic groups established recognizable neighborhoods near the Potomska riverfront, while skilled English mule spinners, weavers, and loomfixers lived farther west.[15]

The 1892 *History of New Bedford* indicates that Potomska's mills employed twelve hundred male and female operatives and owned "twenty-six four tenement houses, which are rented at nominal rates to the help."[16] By dividing the number of operatives by the available housing—twenty-six four-tenements or one hundred and four living units—each four-tenement, hypothetically, accommodated approximately forty-six operatives or about eleven operatives per tenement. Given the rent structure described earlier at Wamsutta, it is assumed that this number represents both the family of the principal renter and the male boarders inhabiting the attic apartments. Even accounting for the operatives living outside of the mill district, the persons per living unit still would have been high—particularly since only the number of *operatives* was used to calculate the persons per living unit, not *occupants*. Children, therefore, would not have been included in these figures. As in the

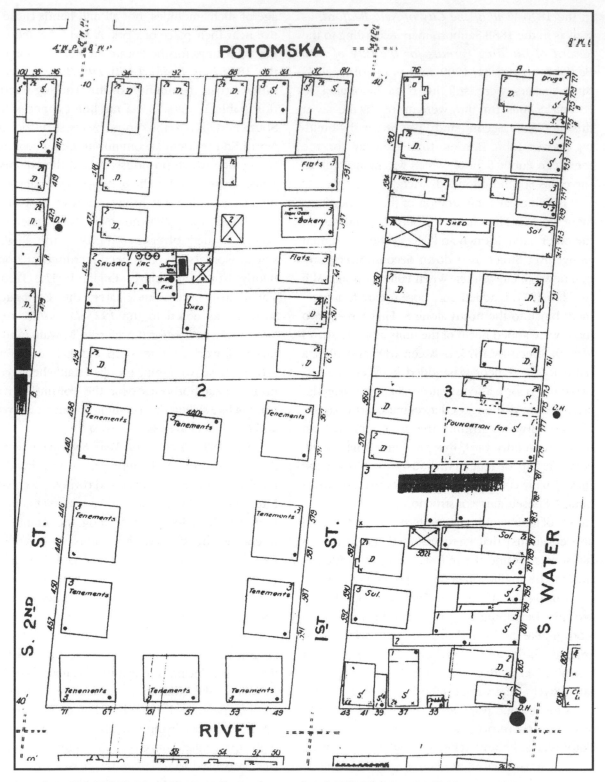

Map 6. A 1906 Sanborn Map indicating all ten of Potomska's four-family tenement blocks.
Used with the permission of the Board of Trustees of the New Bedford Free Public Library.

Table 1

HOUSING DISTRIBUTION OF POTOMSKA MILL WORKERS.

William Abbott	Loom Fixer	Warwick Street
Manlay Adams	Treasurer	42 South Sixth Street
John Allen	Clerk	94 State Street
Richard Birmingham	Loom Fixer	341 South Front Street
William Boardman	Machinist	101 Potomska Street
Horatio Bown	Machinist	273 Fourth Street
Eugene Bowman	Second Hand	262 South Front Street
James Brann	Overseer Dressing	Thompson Street
Joseph Brierley	Loom Fixer	88 Acushnet Avenue
John Broadbent	Second Hand	252 South Second Street
Samuel Broadbent	Third Hand	32 County Street
William Broadbent	Second Hand	Block 9 Rivet Street
Walter Card	Engineer	178 Fourth Street
Joseph Coldwell	Designer	2 Thompson Street
Cornelius Collins	Second Hand Spinning Room	Delano Street
George A. Collins	Overseer	178 Fourth Street
George A. Collins, Jr.	Slasher Tender	178 Fourth Street
Henry Cooper	Weaver	245 South Water Street
Patrick Cox	Loom Fixer	53 Blackmer Street
Ashton Demain	Loom Fixer	35 Acushnet Avenue
William Devoll	Paymaster	68 State Street
Richard Dunce	Section Hand	2 Thompson Street
William Fittz	Master Mechanic	115 Acushnet Avenue
Ralph Hill	Second Hand	Block 9 Rivet Street
Augustus Home	Overseer	Thompson Street
George Kilburn	Machinist	115 Acushnet Avenue
Charles Lanphear	Marker	92 Potomska Street
John McAuliff	Loom Fixer	99 Potomska Street

NOTE: Second Hands Broadbent and Hill reside in Potomska's large tenement Block 9 Rivet Street, while skilled machinist Horatio Bown lived further west on Fourth Street, and Clerk John Allen lived near the center of town. Compiled by the author from names listed in the 1889 *New Bedford City Directory* as being in the Potomska Mill employ.

Wamsutta tenement blocks, there is only an illusion of limited occupancy implied in the nomenclature of a "four-tenement house." Such terminology may have been used by the mill owners in their promotional literature for public appearances, obscuring the reality that, while these units may have been *designed* for smaller occupancy figures, once the operatives moved in and were faced with the economic constraints of mill life, these tenement blocks soon became collective, overcrowded living units. As early as 1887, both Potomska and Wamsutta were witnessing increased public criticism regarding operative housing conditions. The condition of overcrowding was particularly keen in the two decades following 1895, when the mill population swelled in response to new mill starts in the South End, and rents rose accordingly. Manipulating public opinion through promotional data released to local publications (such as the 1892 *History of New Bedford*) on the healthy status of the city's businesses and industries was, therefore, critical to the sustained economic success of the mills themselves.

Additionally, the use of domestic design features in the four-tenement "house," such as individual bracketed stoop entry hoods and modillions under the projecting cornice, served an emblematic purpose. In the particular context of the ten overcrowded tenement blocks built by Potomska beginning in 1871 and continuing through to 1906, the domestic features symbolized a healthy residential circumstance to the casual visitor and helped create the buildings' "public image." Interestingly, the aesthetic references to a contemporary popular style (the Italianate) and, particularly, the impressive scale of the workers' housing bore some resemblance to that of the mansions of the mill magnates, suggesting, however obliquely, social and economic parity among the full spectrum of the mill population that, of course, never existed.

By 1871, the transformation of New Bedford's southern reaches was underway as a new type of industry—textiles—entered the South End. Soon after, whale processing, more textiles, and the 1880 Pairpoint glass factory (started by Edward Mandell) established the core of a South End industrial environment in what prior to 1871 had been largely undeveloped, recreational, or city- and federal-owned land.

CHANGES IN HOUSING TYPE: THE GABLE-FRONT, SIDE-HALL WORKERS' COTTAGE

In contrast to the larger tenement blocks constructed by the Wamsutta and Potomska mill owners during the earliest stages of the industry, another tenement form became popular: the two-and-one-half-story, gable-front, side-hall workers' cottage. Sharing a visual affinity with its formal

antecedent (the single-family, temple-form house of the Greek Revival era), its gable end was oriented toward the street. Accordingly, access was gained to the two vertically stacked apartment units by way of the offset entry stair hall. Often, paired entries and a hall partition provided isolated access to the two individual apartments, while a rear service stair hall provided access directly into the kitchen areas of the two stacked apartments. The rear entry also led to the attic and cellar storage areas. As housing demands became more critical during the 1890s, attic spaces were often converted to smaller two-bedroom, third-floor living units—in many instances converting a two-family dwelling into a three-family tenement or flat.[17] (See chapter 5 for a discussion of the adaptation of this building type.)

This gable-front form began at least as early as the 1840s in New Bedford as a single-family residence. The popularity of this building type as a multifamily housing form, however, was most pronounced from the 1880s to the turn of the twentieth century in New Bedford (see table 2, which lists New Bedford's three-tenement construction patterns in chapter 5). This new type of rental housing was embraced only to a limited degree by the corporations themselves, and even then predominantly for its skilled workers. Instead, local developers took it upon themselves to meet the new market demand for large, inexpensive multifamily rental flats brought on by the consistent pattern of mill construction toward the end of the century. This shift in housing type was most likely in response to two external factors: first, the increased social criticism in newspapers (both locally and nationally) during the 1880s and 1890s regarding the squalor found in the large corporate tenements blocks; second, the changing nature of the workforce in response to improvements in mill technology by the 1890s. The first factor, public criticism, led to improved two-family housing for skilled workers initially, and to tenement block "upgrades" of the old corporate four-tenements for the less-skilled operatives. The second factor, improved mill technology, shifted the ethnic makeup of the tenement population and the types of jobs being performed in the mills.

CHANGES IN MILL TECHNOLOGY

When the cotton mills were first established in this city, the industry relied largely on a male skilled-labor force from England (most specifically from Lancashire and Yorkshire) and neighboring mill villages throughout New England. These workers were recruited by mill management and housed in double houses or four-tenements. Later, with the introduction of more efficient "fancy looms" the hiring emphasis shifted from skilled to unskilled labor. One would think that the more efficient looms would *reduce* labor demands. They did, of course, but the increased productivity and profit of the mills also spawned more mills, which, in turn, increased the demand for more common labor. Between 1882 and 1896, New Bedford was in the midst of its first of two mill booms. During the late stages of this boom, the rental population in the larger four-tenements became almost exclusively common labor, and also reached critical levels of overcrowding as reflected in the 1913 Infant Mortality study cited earlier.

As Gordon and Malone note in *The Texture of Industry*, such improvements as drop boxes for automatic shuttle selection (developed by George Compton and by Lucius Knowles by the late 1850s) led to the demise of American industrial hand weavers, which previously had dominated the production of fancy woven goods. Around 1870, an operating Furbush drop-box fancy loom was capable of being programmed to weave fancy patterns. The most revolutionary engineering achievement in textile machinery was the solution of changing bobbins in the shuttles of high-speed looms. With weavers having to stop looms up to a hundred times a day to replace empty weft bobbins by hand, an automatic bobbin changer that functioned while the loom was in operation was a long-desired goal. James H. Northrop, an Englishman working for the Draper Company in Hopedale, Massachusetts, eventually perfected the Northrop loom by 1894. Known as the Model A Draper, it greatly increased the speed of weaving cloth. Not only was the weaving process more efficient, but textile managers were also quick to increase the *number* of looms that a weaver operated, which made production soar. The strain on weavers and loom fixers having to manage more looms (coupled with factory speedups) became a consistent grievance leveled against mill managers during subsequent labor disputes. In the meantime, this new machinery translated to greater production, less-skilled labor, and lower operating costs.[18]

In most textile areas, the 1894 Model A Draper met the enormous consumer demands for print cloth during the last quarter of the nineteenth century. (Fall River, Massachusetts, as Mary Blewett notes in her recent text *Constant Turmoil*, was an exception, choosing instead to build its own signature looms to maintain market control.[19]) But while the Draper loom *did* make use of unskilled labor, it did so only during the intermediate phases of print cloth production (i.e., carding). By the 1890s, experiments that had been underway as early as the 1820s finally resulted in a perfected technique called ring spinning. These improvements produced the fine weft necessary for print cloth and began to replace the Draper/Northrup loom from the 1890s to the 1920s. Ring spinning offered two advantages to mill owners over the 1894 Draper/ Northrup looms. First, it provided a continuous cycle of production, whereas the Draper loom was discontinuous—requiring a stop in the line between spinning and winding. Second, ring spinning had the advantage of being operated by low-skilled labor as opposed to imported British skilled labor, which had a reputation for union militancy and required higher wages. Ring spinners were not only paid considerably less than mule spinners but were not represented by a powerful union.[20]

Whereas the earlier decision for skilled English workers to come to New Bedford was made in the context of the city's reputation as the leading center for fine woven goods, by the 1890s (as mule-spinning jobs began to disappear) English mule spinners were being discouraged from emigrating to New Bedford. As a result, English immigration into New Bedford virtually stopped by 1905, shifting the predominance of English representation among labor leadership.[21] Young boys were being trained now exclusively as ring spinners and were unable to enter the powerful National Cotton Mule Spinners' Association of America.[22] With the increased need for common labor in the cloth mills, there came a large influx of a foreign population into New Bedford. French Canadians came in greatest numbers between 1880 and 1910 followed by the Portuguese and Polish, most prominently between 1910 and 1920. Members of this new European workforce often had large families,[23] placing unprecedented spatial demands on the aging, corporate-owned four-tenements.

Interestingly, as the hiring demands shifted away from skilled labor and the new labor force represented diverse ethnic backgrounds, mill owners cut back greatly on the amount of corporate housing they built for their operatives. Unskilled labor was easier to replace than skilled workers for whom many of the smaller four-tenement blocks had been built, and mill owners in neighboring cities, such as Lawrence, had discovered by 1850 that grouping people of diverse backgrounds together in mill villages often led to disturbances.[24] Higher land costs, compared with the earliest stages of the industry, likely prompted a desire to limit the level of investment in corporate housing, particularly since such investment promised little cash return. As new mills continued to be built in the North and South Ends of the city and housing needs became evident, land speculators, developers, and builders took over the housing market for the textile workforce and thereby relieved the mill owners of this responsibility. The gable-front, side-hall workers' cottage initially became the preferred type from the 1880s to the turn of the century, only instead of a two-family unit (such as those built for company overseers), the scale increased to accommodate three or four families.

CHANGE IN SOCIAL PERCEPTION

Beyond the shift in technology and, hence, the labor force, other factors also had become evident. The emergence of detached, multifamily housing units that offered more privacy and better sanitation (such as the gable-front, side-hall workers' cottage represented) was part of a gradual evolution of thought among mill owners, housing officials, and social reformers who directed their attention to the changing textile workforce. This gradual shift is reflected in the fact that in 1874, the Massachusetts Bureau of Statistics of Labor conducted a study of mill housing in the state and praised the two New Bedford mills (Wamsutta and Potomska) for their corporate housing accommodations. By 1887, national and local newspapers and current periodicals of the time viewed the housing situation differently and charged that the early large tenement blocks were contributing to a poor quality of life for workers. In faint response to the complaints of the Massachusetts Board of Health in 1887, the Wamsutta Mills the following year attempted to improve both the aesthetic and sanitary conditions of their housing by painting the units six different colors to break up the monotony of the tenement blocks and by installing water closets in the cellars. The corporation also provided gardens for the workers near their tenements.[25]

In spite of such efforts, harsh public criticism aimed at the abhorrent living conditions in the Wamsutta Village continued through the next decade. The city's most prominent minister, the

Rev. William J. Potter, referred to the Wamsutta Village in 1892 as a "pestiferous excrescence," while similar criticism was leveled at the "squalor" that existed in the mill housing of the Potomska Corporation by the *New Bedford Daily Mercury* in 1894.[26] The *New York Evening Journal* for 1898, while covering the bitter New Bedford strike of that year, stated that the corporation housing included stairways and halls that were "more filthy than any New York tenement." The same year the *Boston Traveller* stated: "A walk in that section of the city shows that the houses owned by the mill men aren't fit to live in. The buildings are crumbling, the plaster on the ceilings and walls falling down, and every vintage of suspicion of paint was long obliterated." Interestingly, the area most depicted for ridicule by the newspapers in 1898 was Wamsutta's oldest—and formerly best—units, the brick boardinghouses now converted to four tenements (fig. 50). In response to such degraded living accommodations that were being provided to the mill operatives in New Bedford's largest (and wealthiest) mill complex, the more-skilled and better-paid operatives in New Bedford, according to *Outlook* magazine for 1899, chose to leave company housing and turned to privately owned and built three-deckers that were appearing, in increasing numbers, in the mill districts.[27] A view of

Fig. 50. "New England—Sketches among the Weavers." By the 1898 New Bedford textile strike, Wamsutta's oldest—and originally best—housing (refer to fig. 45) was now disparaged, prompting the increased popularity of the smaller, detached, gable-end, three-tenement shown over page. Widener Library, Harvard University, call no. XT51.

the Wamsutta Mills taken around 1892 looking south shows large numbers of the gable-end type and a few of the flat top three-deckers in place by this date (fig. 51).

Prior to the complete dependence on a speculative housing market, which was well underway during the 1880s, there were a handful of new corporations that experimented with "improved" housing. These housing experiments, it should be noted, took place *before* the technological improvements of the 1890s (discussed above) and before the commensurate reduction in skilled labor, but reflected an awareness by management that housing standards for skilled workers and overseers had to be improved if the city's reputation for fine woven goods was to be maintained. Owners of the newest mills, then, anticipated the

change. Corporate housing for Grinnell (1882), Acushnet (1882), and Howland Mills (1888) reflected the new preference for constructing one-and-one-half-story, two-story, and two-and-one-half-story detached cottages grouped in tidy mill villages to serve principally skilled workers. Perhaps with such improved housing, it was hoped, these new corporations of the 1880s would be exempt from the social criticism emerging in the press. In the process (particularly in the case of spinning mills, which still required a large proportion of skilled workers) the improved housing might lure skilled operatives away from established corporations around New England (fig. 52, see mill housing typology insert).

GRINNELL MILL HOUSING

On March 14, 1882, the Grinnell Manufacturing Corporation was organized, and soon produced over one hundred different styles of plain and fancy weaves. The mill complex was located immediately to the northeast of the Wamsutta Mills, adjacent to that company's block of eight brick double houses built in 1848 originally for

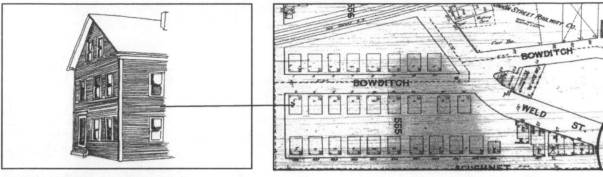

A. Grinnell Mill Housing, c. 1882

Grinnell Mill Housing from 1888 New Bedford Sandborn Map

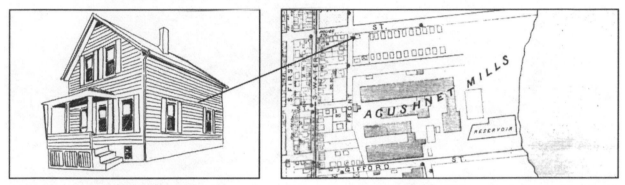

B. Acushnet Mill Housing, c. 1882

1895 Railroad and Reference Map for the state of Massachusetts

C. Howland Mill Cottage, c. 1888

1895 Railroad and Reference Map for the state of Massachusetts

company overseers. The Grinnell Mill employed eight hundred workers by 1889 and owned what was described as "twenty-seven two tenement houses."[28] These housing units were located just to the north of Logan Street, bounded to the west

Fig. 52. Evolution of New Bedford Mill Housing Typology.

Fig. 53. To the north of Grinnell's three rows of two-family corporate housing (now demolished) was the Weld Square Police and Fire Departments. Nearby were the city's trolley car barns (Union Street Railway Co.). Directly to the south was Wamsutta's Mill No. 5 and the Old Colony Railroad roundhouse. All contributed to the social stability as well as the urban clamor of New Bedford's North End mill districts. Photograph by Edmund D. Ashley, Jan. 1915. Courtesy of Spinner Publications.

by the tracks of the Old Colony railroad line, to the east by Acushnet Avenue, and to the north by the diagonal placement of Weld Street where it joined Acushnet Avenue.

Only the third textile mill incorporated (and the second in the North End), Grinnell offered a change in attitude toward mill village design that was rare in the city's architectural history. Three neatly aligned rows of detached, gable-end houses

facing each other established a cohesive block of corporate housing (fig. 52, see insert "A," and fig. 53). Unlike the unsightly dirt roads surrounding Wamsutta's tenement blocks, the major thoroughfares surrounding the Grinnell Mill Village were paved with New Bedford Belgian block (a granite, brick-shaped paving stone imbedded in sand).

This improvement was significant, for not until 1892 was the city beginning to consider it more economical to pave all streets with this material. As early as 1832, the first flagged sidewalks appeared in the city, and by 1838 a section of South Water Street was paved as an experiment. The following year the city paved a section of Purchase Street between Union and William—the heart of the commercial district—with cobblestone. By 1892, the city's density of population and industrial character required different measures. Cobble paving, it was argued at this time, while costing only fifty to seventy-five cents per square yard, was "the most crude and wasteful form of paving laid," since the wear and tear on horse-drawn vehicles was heavy. It was remarked that during the twelve years since 1880—the beginning of the first textile boom in New Bedford which, the newer mills like Grinnell had initiated—that the traffic on the main streets had increased many times. Whereas earlier the cost of renting a team to transport goods was charged by the day regardless of the load, all teaming was now done by weight or quantity. The sharp competition between teamsters had forced prices down so low that extremely heavy loads were being hauled in order to make a profit. As a result, loads went from four to six tons for four horses to six to twelve tons for the same number of horses. The concern was not for the horses, unfortunately, but for the hauling equipment. Since the widths of the wagons stayed the same, the concentrated loads shifted more often and hurt both paving (causing ruts) and the wheels. Block paving at two to three dollars per square yard on a sand foundation was more expensive but stood up better over time and, therefore, was perceived to be a better investment.[29] Grinnell's use of this paving material around its mill housing, then, was a significant step toward city and industrial improvement.

Beyond the street paving used at the mill village, granite curbstones defined a regularized transition from street to sidewalk to connected fence lines and to the houses themselves. The houses, in turn, provided a uniform horizontal cadence of house-sideyard-house until the block terminated at the diagonal introduced by Weld Street. Here, the tall masonry buildings belonging to the fire and police departments loomed at the end of the street vista as a symbol of protection and authority. The desire on the part of city and corporate officials to ensure police protection and fire safety among these mill districts is obvious, particularly in an era of escalating labor disputes.

The side walkways along each cottage allowed for a rear service entry into the kitchens of the two-family tenements, while the front entry served as the "public" entrance to the parlors off of the street access. These two-tenement houses were described in 1913 as having six rooms each with a toilet (no doubt later) adjoining the kitchen at the rear.[30] The conventional plan for this type included a parlor, dining room, and kitchen arranged in a row diagonally off of the front entry and three bedrooms located in a linear sequence directly behind the front stair hall.

In its overall effect, a disciplined and hygienic atmosphere of the mill village was achieved by the orderly appearance of these side-hall workers' cottages. Though restful in appearance as viewed in period photographs, this improved family housing did not exist within a tranquil setting. Daily household routines were interrupted regularly by the noises from the factory supply trains, whose tracks bounded the site to the west; by the factory whistles from Wamsutta Mills to the south announcing shift changes; and by the fire and police stations immediately to the north. In addition to the freight train and trolley traffic (the latter ran along Weld Street between the fire station and the Grinnell cottages), there was the constant noise of metal hitting the granite street surface from the wagon wheels and horse hooves of the delivery vehicles. All this visual and auditory commotion took place amidst a treeless, congested streetscape of stone, brick, and wood.

This was the new urban reality that replaced the pastoral setting Wall had depicted just thirty years earlier in his painting of *Wamsutta*. The attempt on the part of the Grinnell management to project rigid social and visual order through the uniform design of the mill housing was consistent with many of the "improved" mill villages of its day, where both the industrial product and factory premises exuded regimentation, standardization, and control. Nonetheless, the Grinnell housing, it should be said, set a high standard for later mills to follow in terms of limiting both the scale and density of its corporate residences. Of course, with eight hundred workers employed at Grinnell, these twenty-seven two-tenements provided lodging for only fifty-four families. This, no doubt, was not improved operative housing, but housing for factory overseers. The common worker turned, instead, to the growing number of larger, gable-end and flat-top rental units being built in the surrounding mill districts and designed to serve three and four families instead of just two. In recognition of such corporate housing improvements, however, the 1895 *New Bedford City Directory* listed the Grinnell Mill Housing among its "additional places of interest."

Unfortunately, as a result of the John Fitzgerald Kennedy Memorial Highway constructed during the 1960s, none of the Grinnell housing exists today. Because of such forces, the industrial history of the New England landscape increasingly is being preserved on paper rather than within its original physical and cultural context.

ACUSHNET MILL HOUSING

The Acushnet Mills Corporation followed Grinnell and also manufactured cotton cloth (silesias, satteens, and goods for the printer). It was organized in November 1882. The company employed about one thousand operatives by 1889, and "owned twenty-three tenements which they rented to the help" (see fig. 51b).[31] Similar to Grinnell, these two-and-one-half-story frame cottages with entry through the gable end were arranged in two aligned rows of housing—twenty-two facing Blackmer and two one-and-one-half-story cottages facing Front Street (one additional cottage was added along Front Street between 1889 and 1895). As late as 1913, neither Blackmer Street nor the wide laundry court between the rows of cottages were paved. Each of the two-and-one-half-story cottages contained "two apartments of

six rooms each," and by 1913 there was a toilet serving each apartment that was located in the hallway.[32] The smaller one-and-one-half-story cottages, on the other hand, bear a strong resemblance to the "reform housing" built by Lowell (such as those on Dane street dated by Coolidge to c. 1853, but probably actually built in the 1860s) and other textile communities such as Peanut Row, Harrisville, New Hampshire, 1864. Collectively, they indicate the gradual shift to smaller, more private corporate housing for skilled labor at this time throughout the industry.

In their scale and simplicity, the smaller Acushnet housing points to those built a year earlier for the Ludlow Manufacturing Association located near Springfield, Massachusetts (1879–81). Plans and elevations for these cottages were published in folio-sized plates as part of the "Report on the Factory Systems of the United States," bound with the 1880s U.S. Manufacturing Census. The model cottages were referred to as "housekeepers' houses," because they were planned from the point of view of ease of upkeep with "rooms wisely arranged, and plenty of stores and cupboards."[33] The lesson learned by the Ludlow management was similar to that of the New Bedford industries: "The experiment was made of building a few centrally situated modern blocks of flats, but in the words of the manager: this venture has not been successful at all so far, since no one apparently wants to live in a block no matter how modern or how well constructed. Cottages have had their educational value, and all prefer to live in separate houses."[34]

While it is perhaps easy today to discount such a shift in corporate attitude as a minimal gesture (namely, the decision to build cottages, rather than large tenement blocks), the subtle recognition of the worker's existence as a distinct individual—instead of as a hidden entity within an otherwise seamless stretch of workers' housing—was noteworthy. John Coolidge, in his groundbreaking study on Lowell, Massachusetts, between 1820 to 1865, notes a similar "spirit of experimentation" taking place in the shift to smaller wooden cottages as industrial housing after the great land sale in 1848 by Lowell's Locks and Canals Company. Here, he characterizes the greatest conceptual benefit of the rows of detached housing as residing in their "collective effect." As a group composition there was little difference, he felt, between the upper-class residential district of a Federalist seaport in New England and Belvidere—a row of more recent workers' cottages in Lowell. The layout of the residential districts of Federal Period seaports, he notes, were derived from English real-estate development practice. In contrast, the planned groups of uniform boardinghouses of Worthen Street in Lowell (representing the earliest form of barrack housing), with their repetitive, horizontal eaves line, unbroken plane of front walls, and practice of combining residential blocks in long strips, reinforced a "corridor aesthetic" down the streets typical of early corporate planning strategies. Whereas the sawtooth effect of the successive gables, strong plasticity of the façades, and emphasis on detached forms (as could be seen at Belvidere along Dane Street in Lowell) tempted Coolidge to investigate the buildings as "separate entities."[35]

The visual pairing of the large brick factory buildings for the Acushnet and Grinnell Mills, set against the orderly rows of wooden, detached family cottages located adjacent to them, began to establish a new urban pattern within the industrial precincts of the North and South Ends of the city. Recalling the Anglo-American wooden housing tradition of New Bedford's earlier village economy, these framed cottages stood in marked contrast to the former large tenement blocks and boardinghouses clustered around laundry yards that the city's earliest textile mill owners had constructed nearby.

Augmented by corner stores, area schools, and churches, and other forms of detached work-ers' housing, such as three-tenements, distinct mill neighborhoods slowly emerged around the newer corporations, permitting the mill districts to function as semiautonomous entities within the larger fabric of the city. Taken out of context (as the isolated photo of the Grinnell housing discussed earlier, fig. 53), these vestiges of small town community life—offered by images of tidy cottages surrounded by picket fences—present a delusion of residential scale that helped to retaliate against the exponential urban industrial development that lurked just beyond the model mill housing. The rows of Acushnet housing, for example, by 1895 were encircled by the police station (at the intersection of South Water Street and Blackmer), the corner park (shared by both the Acushnet and Potomska Mill corporations), and the public school (on Division Street), while mill hands had access to the bustling commercial district one block over on South Water Street. Farther west, at the intersection of Rivet and County Streets, were the Roman Catholic Church, St. Martin's Episcopal Church, and the Primitive Methodist Church, all on one corner and accessible by this date by the trolley, which passed by both the Acushnet and Potomska Mills, themselves part of a string of continuous mills along the southern reaches of the Acushnet River.

Today, only three of the Acushnet Mill housing units still survive (and they are of the one-and-one-half-story type), though by now even the Acushnet Mill is gone, leaving the requisite physical and socioeconomic linkage of mill to mill housing incomplete. The same is true of the Potomska Mill housing—among the earliest surviving corporate tenement blocks in New Bedford—now divested of its mill context and in a derelict state.

Perhaps the most socially progressive and speculative venture into mill housing in New Bedford, if not nationally at this time, appeared with the construction of the Howland Mill Village. It is, therefore, deserving of its own study.

Howland Mill Village
The Dashed Dream for an Industrial Utopia

Between the rigid social and visual order represented by the "improved" housing for the Grinnell and Acushnet Mills and the large-scale speculation that later created the triple-decker, a generation of capitalists and planners envisioned a less paternalistic scheme that melded the garden suburb and the mill. New Bedford's Howland Mill Village put in place a different relationship between capital and labor, and, had its parent corporation survived the financial crisis of the 1890s, it might well have set workers' housing on a radically different course.

Between 1888 and 1899, the short-lived Howland Mill Corporation offered its workers the option of either renting architect-designed model housing at reasonable rates (fig. 54) or purchasing building sites through a cooperative ownership housing arrangement. The single-family workers' housing was augmented by a curvilinear suburban

Fig. 54. The Howland Mill Village in 1996. The three variations of worker's cottage designs are all visible at left. The contour plan, the irregular placement of cottages, the wide streets with granite curbs, and the trees lining the sidewalk are all original design features.

plan, while additional "breathing places" were provided by generously proportioned, tree-lined streets. Space was also set aside for a proposed communal park that, had it been created, would have been part of a continuous chain of city parks and scenic parkways. These naturalistic planning elements were to provide the setting for an envisioned eight mill, state-of-the-art spinning mill complex connected to a transportation network of new macadam roads and an electric rail system.

In their desire to link technology and nature, as the earlier industrial planners of Lowell had sought to do, Howland Mill organizer William D. Howland and the newly established Boston architectural firm of Wheelwright and Haven provided their own progressive vision for an urban industrial utopia. Their creative synthesis of enlightened social policies, modern technological processes, and the pastoral ideal of the garden suburb tradition resulted in what was very probably the first picturesque workers' housing and naturalistic landscape scheme to be designed and built as part of a comprehensive industrial master plan in the United States. At the very least, the Howland Mill Village was among a select number of late-nineteenth-century experiments that influenced the renewal of progressive company housing and naturalistic industrial planning in the first quarter of the twentieth century—currently referred to as "new" company towns.[1] Further, the plan for the village differed critically from the paternalistic visions put forth earlier in New England, and in this regard the story of the village provides essential specifics for understanding the broader picture of workers' housing in the region. Its evolution traces not only the transition from company-built to speculator-built housing that ultimately brought the three-decker to New Bedford but also chronicles how ideas about laborers' housing had changed as the nineteenth century came to an end.

The Howlands in New Bedford

William Dillwyn Howland was born in New Bedford on March 27, 1853. The son of Matthew and Rachel Howland, he was part of a prominent Quaker family who, with a handful of other elites in the city, controlled the whaling industry, the emerging textile industry, banking, and, very often, local government. His grandfather, George Howland, was among New Bedford's earliest whaling merchants and the first president of the New Bedford Commercial Bank (later the National Bank of Commerce). His father, Matthew (1814–1884), and uncle George (mayor of New Bedford from 1857 to 1860) continued the family's involvement in the whaling industry until uninsured losses of its Arctic whaling fleet in 1871 and 1876 compelled family members to begin selling their remaining ships in 1881 (see chapter 1).[2]

The Howlands were close business associates of William Wallace Crapo, president of New Bedford's first textile concern, the Wamsutta Mills (1846), and a director of its second, the Potomska Mills (1871). William J. Rotch and his son Morgan, both one-time mayors of the city, were personal friends of the family. William J. Rotch also served on the board of directors of Wamsutta and Potomska Mills in 1889.

That a small group of people held unusual control over New Bedford's wealth and how it was allocated helps to explain how William D. Howland could achieve his detailed urban plan with such mechanical efficiency.[3] Within an otherwise conservative business atmosphere, Howland was able to carry out his progressive ideas in large part because he could rely on a close network of influential associates for support. The complex plan for his mills and workers' village—involving a wide range of planning issues from parks to trolley lines, from water and sanitation systems to progressive housing and modern thoroughfares—was able to proceed as a coordinated effort between business and government with relatively little bureaucratic intervention. Until municipal agencies appeared in New Bedford and other cities toward the end of the nineteenth century, urban-industrial planning, in the modern sense of the term, was often the end result of private business development.[4]

Little direct documentary evidence establishes Howland's specific role in the design of his mills and mill village,[5] but enough is known about his background to suggest why he in particular would implement a progressive workers' housing plan where and when he did. Howland's parents were lifelong leaders in the Society of Friends long after many prosperous New Bedford Quakers had become Unitarians or Congregationalists; his father served as an elder and a clerk of the New Bedford Monthly Meeting for approximately thirty years. The family was particularly active in philanthropic work. In 1870, Matthew Howland donated for public use an interdenominational chapel to serve the workers in the industrial North End where the Wamsutta Mills had been established in 1846. Such gestures of social concern cast an eye toward business and civic interests by attempting to create a layer of moral supervision in workers' areas, but they also suggest a peculiar brand of enlightened, ethical capitalism in association with Quaker goals for self-improvement.

Howland's grandmother and mother also played significant roles in the public sphere. His grandmother, Susan (Howland) Howland, had been a staunch antebellum supporter of abolition, prison reform, and education and aid to the Indians, as well as a proponent of the more equitable distribution of property. His mother, Rachel Collins Smith (1816–1902), was born into a leading Quaker family in Philadelphia and was a minister at Friends meetings for fifty-five years. Like many influential women in her day, she was active in such philanthropies as the City Mission, the Association for the Relief of Aged Women, and the Children's Aid Society.[6] But, unlike other prominent women in New Bedford, her social convictions extended to labor issues as well. In 1867, Rachel Howland served as a mediator when English skilled workers at Wamsutta Mills struck for a ten-hour workday, and she was instrumental in reaching a peaceful settlement.[7] According to a family relation, she viewed the well-known English social reformer Robert Owen as a hero for having bought up, with his partners, the spinning mills of New Lanark in Scotland and turning them into a model factory. This famous social experiment introduced modern machinery, reasonable working hours, good wages, healthy living accommodations, and a school near the factory.[8]

William D. Howland had not only the predisposition to investigate enlightened attitudes toward industrial labor but also the business training and opportunity to do so as well. Even though his father's whaling fleet was largely destroyed in the Arctic during the 1870s, when Howland had entered business after his graduation from Brown University in 1874, he was able to turn his professional ambitions to New Bedford's burgeoning textile industry, initially as a clerk, at Wamsutta Mills.[9]

By 1874 Wamsutta had realized a 300 percent profit on its original investment twenty-five years earlier, which proved the potential of cotton manufacturing in the city.[10] Howland, anxious to make his own mark as family resources were dwindling, began in 1880 speculating in printed fabrics made in the New Bedford mills and enjoyed impressive profits. With his five years at Wamsutta (from c. 1876 to 1881, attending to both the financial matters of the mill as well as repairing older machinery in the factories) and four months at Potomska Mills (spent drawing mill plans to accommodate new machinery), Howland established a firm business and technical knowledge of the textile industry. He supplemented this practical training during the winter of 1881–82 with several months of travel to research cotton yarn manufacture.[11]

NEW BEDFORD MANUFACTURING COMPANY

By the time Howland returned to New Bedford, it was evident from the rapidly growing number of weaving mills in the city—many of them specializing in fine woven goods—that a high market demand for quality yarn existed in the local cloth mills. However, he had not yet secured a solid managerial position in textiles which would allow him to meet this demand. In December of 1881, Howland attempted unsuccessfully to be appointed superintendent of a new mill being erected in New Bedford (likely the Grinnell Mill). Instead, he turned his attention to raising the stock revenue necessary to convert a flour mill in the city into a yarn mill. In addition to a core of local subscribers, outside investors from Providence and Boston provided the necessary capital stock of $125,000.[12] In March 1882, at the age of twenty-nine, Howland organized the New Bedford Manufacturing Company and became the company's treasurer.

Instead of refitting a flour mill in the city's North End, Howland built a new eleven-thousand-spindle mill just north of New Bedford's business center along the Acushnet River. The walls of the new mill were up by July 19, 1882. That day, Rachel Howland commented in a personal letter to an older son that "the building when done will be an ornament to this part of the city."[13] Her son's drive for perfection was beginning to manifest itself in built form as well as in business acumen.

By January 11, 1883, Kilburn, a stockholder, purchased cotton for his new Grinnell Mill from the New Bedford Manufacturing Company. Early signs were promising for Howland's first independent enterprise, as indicated by the Howland family correspondence. Rachel Howland held out great hope for her son's success: "Will is driving the Mill along finely and expects in a few weeks more, or by Christmas, to be making yarn, which there is every prospect he can sell at a good profit. He is sanguine that the stock will soon be above par." Matthew Howland was equally enthusiastic: "Tell Eugene that Willie's Mill stock, which he paid 95 for, has been bid at 98.87. Kilburn's crack mill, the Grinnell, has fallen from 105 to 101⅛, while Willie's has risen. Quite a feather in his cap. [Kilburn had been William D's boss at Potomska, and had received the appointment as Superintendent for the Grinnell Mill, which

William D. likely had sought]. Well, he drives early and late and means to make a success of it." In fact, Matthew Howland later commented on his expectations for dramatic profits at the New Bedford Manufacturing Company: "Willie is working away at the Mill, determined to make it pay. He wishes *it all* belonged to the family, since he is confident he can make it realize 15 to 25% profit per year."[14]

The correspondence indicates that these hopes for success were not unwarranted. Matthew Howland reported: "The Mill is doing all it can do, with orders as many as they can possibly fill. Yesterday was rather an exciting day for *me*. I had quite a long and interesting talk with William J. Rotch and Plummer about doubling the size of the [New Bedford Manufacturing Company] Mill, and I think something will be done about it soon. And then, in the course of the day, I exchanged 27 shares of Wamsutta stock for Mill stock, calling Wamsutta 107, the Mill 106. I expect to do more at the same rate or better." Matthew Howland, with his son's mill stock in hand, continued his optimism for the sustained growth of the area's yarn mill industries: "Business is very quiet here, indeed, and the cloth mills are not making any money, except Wamsutta. But although the stock of the Grinnell and Acushnet [both cloth mills] sells at 85 to 87, the Yarn Mill stock cannot be bought here at less than $110, and I am not sure any could be bought for that." Finally, he was able to reassure himself that William D.'s profits spoke for themselves: "Will is doing better and last month's sales were the largest yet—$13,000, as compared with $4 or $5,000 last year."[15]

At this stage, all business was being transacted on 81 Hawthorn Street, where William D. had converted the north room of his parent's Greek Revival mansion into an office. Perhaps this is fitting; with his father discussing a mill expansion with William J. Rotch and Plummer and his mother having helped to secure out-of-town investors for the final mill subscriptions this was becoming a family venture.

From the moment the first yarn was shipped in January 1883, it seems, investors realized that the demand for fine grades of yarn was greater than the single mill could supply. Confident of a sustained demand for quality yarns within the city's weaving mills, a second mill was built in the spring of 1886, a combing department was soon added to refine the spinning process, and in less than four years capital investment had increased to five hundred thousand dollars.[16] But, though the mill was proving successful to its original investors, William D. was not the principal stockholder of his first independent enterprise. He, therefore, received far less than his labor and leadership was worth. Nevertheless, this venture demonstrated Howland's business credibility and the strength of his influence and connections. It was evident that he understood yarn manufacturing and that he could see a large industrial project through to a profitable end. The same skills and business associations that he had brought to bear in incorporating the New Bedford Manufacturing Company were relied upon to make his vision of enlightened industrial capitalism real in the Howland Mills complex.

THE HOWLAND MILLS

In 1886, just as his New Bedford Manufacturing Company was expanding, William D. Howland, Morgan Rotch, and two other company officers organized the Howland Mills Corporation to supplement the city's existing spinning capacity.[17] Howland became the treasurer, and he and company president William J. Rotch and other investors purchased approximately 120 acres of land that had once been part of the estate of Cornelius Howland, Howland's maternal great-uncle. Two other contiguous parcels had most recently been farmland owned by Mr. W. Ashley (extending to the Dartmouth city line), and a large nursery operation, known as the Wasemequia Nursery, had been owned by Henry Howland

Crapo.[18] The large combined tract lay along the western head of Clark's Point, and jutted into the ocean just west of New Bedford's harbor at the southernmost extension of the city (map 7).

As has been noted in chapter 3, before 1871 Clark's Point was largely rural, the site of a wide pleasure drive, a handful of summer cottages on large lots, such municipal institutions as the work farm, hospital, almshouse, and orphans' home, a few scattered businesses, and, at its tip, the federal government's Fort Rodman. With the construction of the Potomska (1871 and 1877) and Acushnet Mills (1883 and 1887) in the South End along the western shore of the Acushnet River, this wooded area began to be transformed into an industrial landscape.

As evidenced by the 1875 *City of New Bedford* engineering survey maps (recently discovered by my research team), land speculation west of

Potomska's two South End mills had increased measurably since 1871, and as a result subdivision lots already had been plotted east of Crapo Street to County Street north of Cove Road (see map 7). This is the area formerly part of the Cornelius Howland estate which later was purchased by Howland Mills. This tract may have been under consideration as the building site for the Howland Mills, but would have encouraged a gridded arrangement of mill and mill housing similar to the Grinnell and Acushnet mills.

Map 7. Computer-enhanced detail of the 1875 city engineers' map showing the parcels purchased for the Howland Mills Corporation as well as Mill Roads No. 2, 3, and 4 laid out on the Crapo parcel. Engineering Survey Map of New Bedford, Wheelwright and Coggeshall, 1875. Courtesy of the Building Commissioner, New Bedford City Hall.

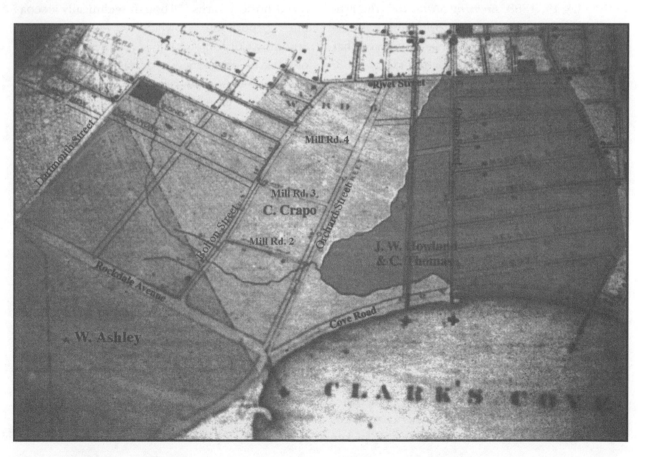

Instead, city engineers also had blocked out another parcel of land between Bolton Road and Orchard Street, for large mills separated by three numbered "Mill Roads" (see map 7).[19] In effect, the city government had zoned the South End for industrial development,[20] and the incorporators of the Howland Mills, when they purchased the two additional tracts, must have anticipated considerable growth as part of that transformation. "The idea of the purchase of so large a tract of land," the company stated in 1889, "was that the company might profit from the certain advance in the value of real estate in the vicinity of the mill."[21] Ultimately, the first two factories of the Howland Mills were constructed between Rockdale Avenue and what was designated Mill Road 2 on the 1875 engineering survey map.

The official announcement of the organization of the Howland Mills Corporation appeared in the May 19, 1888, *Evening Standard*. The article indicated that a four-story brick mill was currently under construction. It was anticipated that it would be in full operation by the fall of 1888, employing 150 hands. It was mentioned that the machinery, engine, and boilers were already contracted for, and when installed, the paper noted, "it will be the most extensive and thoroughly equipped mill of its kind in the country." The mill itself took only three months, from May 11 to August 14, 1888, to construct. The brick work of the main building of Mill No. 1 was completed by masons Brownell and Murklaud in just seven weeks—an indication of the high level of understanding that Howland and the superintendent of construction had attained for the highly specialized field of factory building (fig. 55).[22] The interior was fitted with maple floors, steam pipes, and—following the lead of Wamsutta's Mill No. 6 in 1882—"Edison wires."[23]

As with the New Bedford Manufacturing Company, mill expansion was almost immediate. By October 3, 1889, Mill No. 2 was completed. Adjoining Mill No. 1 was a new two-story picker house and a boiler house as an interconnected unit within the first designated mill parcel. By 1891, a second picker house was added to the mill complex, which created a symmetrical massing between the two mill complexes. A payroll/business office was constructed in 1898 to the south of the two mills along Orchard Street and immediately to the northeast of the large superintendent's house built for Bryan W. Card. This house (now gone) was built in 1889 at the corner of Orchard and Cove Streets looking out to the ocean (fig. 56). This ensemble completed the first stage of construction for the Howland Mills Corporation as a spinning mill complex (fig. 57).[24]

Beginning in 1892, Howland organized and had constructed to the north of Howland Mills two additional factories between Mill Roads 3 and 4 for the Rotch Spinning Corporation, which, with forty-two thousand spindles, also manufactured hosiery yarns.[25] Though technically a separate corporation, Howland viewed the Rotch Spinning Corporation as just another component of what he envisioned as an eight-mill industrial complex—two mills on each of the four mill parcels that, all told, would employ about twelve hundred operatives.

Aesthetically, this modern, thoroughly equipped factory complex was given the historical bearing of a medieval castle with its corbeled brick and crenelated towers; its medieval associations set against a picturesque, still largely rural, seaside landscape suggest a response to what English social critic John Ruskin termed "the dehumanizing, soul-destroying tasks of modern production."[26] Since the trappings of such dehumanizing industrial production were already in evidence in New Bedford, Howland self-consciously aimed at constructing an industrial setting for labor that would revitalize the worker, preserve his dignity, foster his productivity, and ensure his loyalty.

However, the Howland Mills was the first textile concern in New Bedford to choose an inland location away from the Acushnet River and

Fig. 55 (above). Howland Mill No. 1 under construction as seen from Cove Road, 1888. From William D. Sayer, ed., *New Bedford* (1889). Courtesy of the Building Commissioner, New Bedford City Hall.

Fig. 56 (left). Superintendent's house, 1889, with the **L**-shaped porch added later. The house (now demolished) faced the cove, not the workers' housing, keeping surveillance to a minimum. This view dates from c. 1912 when the Howland Mills was owned by the Gosnold Mills. Courtesy of Thomas Whittaker, Spinner Publications.

remote from existing housing and transportation. In order to induce a permanent, highly skilled workforce capable of operating the mill's sophisticated machinery and, in turn, produce top quality yarns, its planners sought to address both shortcomings with an integrated social and technological scheme. The newspapers of Howland's day gave him almost sole credit for the compre-hensive industrial plan which resulted, but in fact it melded Howland's ideas for technical efficiency and social improvement with the ideas and skills of architects similarly immersed in progressive planning at the time, including the Boston-area firms of Wheelwright and Haven, and Frederick Law Olmsted, who likely were in charge of the residential sphere of the master plan.

Fig. 57. View c. 1901 looking west from Cove Road. This photograph captures the Howland Mills at its furthest development. From left to right: 1898 payroll office, 1888 picker house, 1888 Mill No. 1, 1888 and 1891 engine houses on either side of the brick smokestack, 1891 picker house, 1891 Mill No. 2. From Dart and Bigelow, *New Bedford and Fairhaven* (1901).

HOWLAND MILL VILLAGE

Howland turned to the housing concerns as Mill No. 1 was being planned and constructed in 1888. While the mill-construction phase of the project made use of a preexisting site plan, the mill village design offered an original scheme. He commissioned the newly formed partnership of Wheelwright and Haven to design a village of operatives' housing amidst a series of wide, curvilinear streets on a gently sloping hillside immediately west of the factories.[27]

Edmund March Wheelwright (1854–1912) was only thirty-four years old when he and Parkman Balke Haven undertook the New Bedford project

as one of the firm's first, yet Wheelwright had already amassed impressive architectural experience. After graduating from Harvard in 1876, he began his training in architecture with a year's study at MIT (1876–77) and then worked as a draftsman with the prominent Boston firm of Peabody and Stearns. Firm principal Robert Swain Peabody (1845–1917) was a New Bedford native, closely identified with various projects of municipal improvement, and head of the Boston City Park Department. Both Peabody and Stearns, and McKim, Mead and Bigelow in New York, for whom Wheelwright also worked (c. 1878), distinguished themselves during the 1880s with a large number of fine suburban homes and country estates in the "modern-colonial" style. Wheelwright's training in these firms is apparent in the Shingle Style cottages and picturesque planning of the Howland Mill Village.[28]

The progress made on the mill village by August 14, 1888, was described in the *New Bedford Evening Standard* as follows: "West of the mill, cottage tenements are being built for the corpora-tion. There are to be about forty of them and they are designed for separate families and of better style than other corporation tenements in Bristol County. . . . The mill is east of the former line between New Bedford and Dartmouth, and the tenements are on the tract recently annexed from Dartmouth, [the W. Ashley parcel]."

An October 3, 1889, *Evening Standard* article added that the clear intent behind the model housing, neat furniture, bath tubs, flower gar-dens, and winding streets was to attract and secure the "best and most intelligent class of operatives," and to do so in part by avoiding the trappings of standardization associated with "the ordinary machine made village":

> The corporation houses built this year, 25 in number, have been going up at the rate of two per week since the contract was awarded to George W. Gay. The mason work is done by John B. Sullivan, and all the cellars are finished. Wheelwright and Haven of Boston are the architects, Edward A. Crane is their supervisor for this job. The hardware is furnished by N.P. Hayes.
>
> The houses are in three different styles, but all differing more or less in details of dormer windows, form of roof, and other semi-ornamental features. The roads in the mill village are slightly winding, and the houses are more or less irregularly placed, so that the general look is anything but that of the ordinary machine made village.
>
> Most of the houses contain a dining or sitting room, a kitchen, pantry, five bedrooms and a bath room. Every house contains a bath tub. . . . The company manufactures the finest quality yarns, and to do this is obliged to hire the best and most intelligent class of operatives. To get and secure them, [the corporation offers low rent as part of the] liberality of the

corporation in providing pleasant quar-ters, and second their efforts by providing neat furniture, and in some cases hand-some flower gardens.[29]

Initially, only three streets of the larger resi-dential site were developed (map 8), but by the end of 1889 the village featured fifty single-family houses, a large, gambrel-roof boardinghouse for bachelors (fig. 58), and a superintendent's house (see fig. 56).[30] Thirty-five of these cottages were of a gambrel-roof, central-hall form consisting of seven rooms excluding the pantry (fig. 59). The remaining fifteen were smaller hip-on-gable, and gable-front cottages with five rooms on two sto-ries (see fig. 52c). The houses' massing and orien-tation varied; occupants entered either through the side or through the gable end. The smaller cottages, which cost $1,000 each to build, rented for $8.50 per month—the same price as Wamsutta's four-tenement units. The larger dwellings cost $2,000 each to construct and rented for $10 per month generally to spinners, skilled workers whose wages averaged $16 a week in 1895.[31] Most tenants thus paid 15 percent of their earnings for rent, and because rents were deducted weekly from wages earned, the company lost nothing from rents being in arrears.[32]

Most of the cottages were offset on their lots, which accented their informality compared with the more spatially constricted corporation hous-ing earlier New Bedford textile mill owners had built for their employees. In addition, the houses occupied lots large enough for a rear laundry yard and a front garden, both thoughtfully oriented to allow access from the cellar laundry tub and food-storage areas from the back hall.

The cottages' interiors also were designed with care. In the Dutch Colonial houses, a columned porch opened into a stair hall, and a bedroom was designed into the first-floor plan to serve as an optional rental space for a boarder. A room that could function either as a dining or sitting room

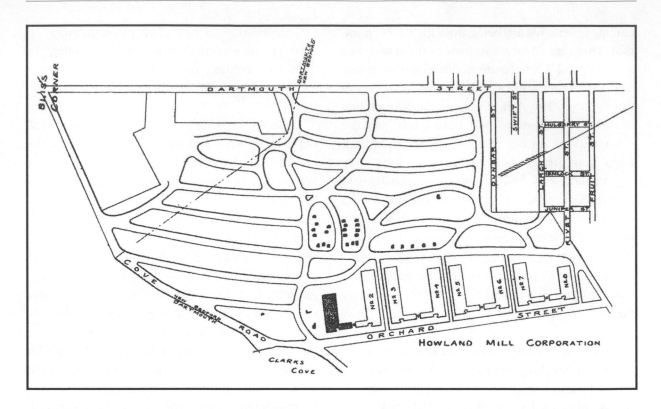

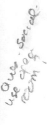

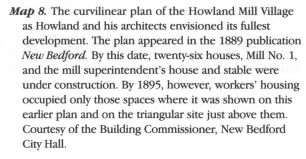

Map 8. The curvilinear plan of the Howland Mill Village as Howland and his architects envisioned its fullest development. The plan appeared in the 1889 publication *New Bedford.* By this date, twenty-six houses, Mill No. 1, and the mill superintendent's house and stable were under construction. By 1895, however, workers' housing occupied only those spaces where it was shown on this earlier plan and on the triangular site just above them. Courtesy of the Building Commissioner, New Bedford City Hall.

was located at the end of the front hall; this space was shared by both the primary renter and the boarder. To the left of the hall were grouped the kitchen and the pantry. The space designed for the cooking range was just below the second-floor bathroom, whose wall overlapped the kitchen's interior wall for the heat advantage. On the second floor were located four bedrooms and a bathroom. The cottages were each equipped with a flush toilet, a bathtub, hot and cold running water, and a marble washstand. The principal rooms were wallpapered. Such appointments were rare in workers'

housing—indeed, in most housing—in the 1880s and were in marked contrast to other New Bedford company housing built up to this point.

The design scheme for the mill workers' village, then, featured sophisticated concepts of reform housing architecture, sanitation, and suburban landscape design. It is also clear that Howland went to extraordinary lengths to ensure the quality of these improvements. For example, at considerable expense, the Howland and Rotch Mills had installed brick sewers through the unstable soil conditions around the salt marsh. According to the city's report from the Board of Public Works, the sewer needed a stone-and-cement foundation and required fourteen hundred tons of stone.[33] The Howland Mill Corporation also laid out and graded a road sixty feet wide and then offered to pay for building gutters on each side of it if the city's Board of Public Works, upon accepting the road, would macadamize it. The board applauded the corporation's "generous spirit" and noted its "pleasing contrast to the demands sometimes made on this

Fig. 58. Howland Mills boardinghouse, c. 1905 view. From Jessamine Whitney, *Infant Mortality* (1920). Courtesy of Spinner Publications.

department."[34] These street improvements in the immediate vicinity of the new mill complex prompted the city to provide additional access roads to the Howland Mill that, in effect, joined it to the city's street grid.[35]

Howland specifically requested macadam for his mill roads, for its even surface was found to be easier on horses' feet and carriage wheels alike; macadam (crushed stone in a tar and gravel bed) was just becoming a preferred paving surface in American suburbs and parks at this time, due particularly to the influence of the bicycle recreation movement. Perhaps more significant, macadam roads were among the improvements at Pullman's new model factory which caught the attention of *Harper's Monthly* in 1885.[36] Closer to home, the road surface was noticeably better than the Belgian block streets installed in front of Grinnell's (1882) "improved" workers' housing.

The wider streets in the Howland Mill Village also lessened the congestion of commercial traffic while creating, in concert with the tree-lined village thoroughfares and a proposed park adjacent to the factories, what Olmsted had termed "breathing places" (see fig. 52c). Together, these landscape features offered relief both to the mill worker and urban citizen from the otherwise predictable industrial realities of noise, congestion, and factory stench.[37]

At the same moment that the sewer and road systems were reaching completion, the city's Union Street Railway was expanding its service to the Howland Mill Village. The idea of extending rail service in conjunction with the ongoing mill construction was discussed as early as 1889, when Morgan Rotch served on the city's Board of Public Works. By 1894 the railway became a reality, and again the proposal was assisted by Rotch as a member of the Transportation Commission as well as a member of the Howland Mills board. Electric trolley service was extended literally to the front door of the mill complex.[38] Howland

Fig. 59. Howland Mills single-family housing for skilled workers designed by the Boston architectural firm Wheelwright and Haven. Courtesy of the Library of Congress.

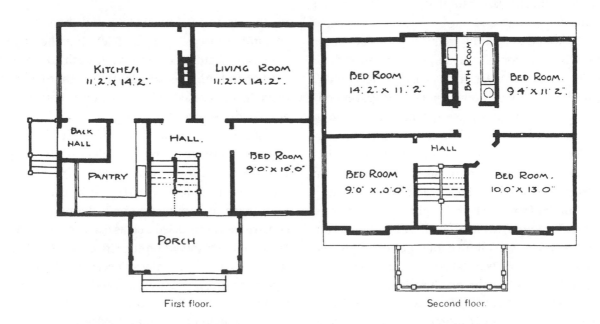

First floor.

Second floor.

HOUSE OF HOWLAND MILLS CORPORATION, NEW BEDFORD, MASSACHUSETTS.

PLAN NO. 54.

Fig. 60. The Bungalow, Wheelwright family cottage, Vinalhaven, in a 1986 view. Courtesy of the Maine Historic Preservation Commission.

Mill operatives who did not want to live in the village or wanted to shop in the city center could now easily do so; the railway stopped at the foot of Bolton Street and Rockdale Avenue, where the factories and cottages met. The original remoteness of the Howland Mill site was no longer an obstacle; in fact, the housing was now exceptionally convenient both to work and (with connections to the Globe Street Railway) to outlying commercial and recreational offerings. So strikingly different was the Howland Mill Village that the 1895 *New Bedford City Directory* listed it among "additional places of interest" and as a "very creditable village of mill tenements, conveniently arranged and of neat design."[39]

The Howland Mill Village was something of an anomaly in Wheelwright's career. His family paper manufacturing and printing business had exposed him to industrial facilities, and his business ledger indicates that he designed a boardinghouse during the 1880s for the Richmond Paper Company.[40] But until his term as Boston City Architect from 1891 to 1895, little architectural evidence exists of his commitment to social reform.[41] Despite Wheelwright's

training under architects who were well aware of progressive housing trends, it seems likely that the notion of model workers' housing was prompted more directly by Howland's labor-management philosophy as well as by the need amid growing competition to attract and retain the most highly skilled of the region's industrial labor force.

Wheelwright's more fundamental contributions to the village were probably its municipal improvements, for which his work was praised in its day, and its aesthetic qualities, about which too little was said. The markedly picturesque qualities of the cottages, their siting, and the neighborhood of winding roadways seem to recall Robert Swain Peabody's work in the Boston City Park Department and in private practice, but it should be noted that Wheelwright himself had been involved with resort architecture both on the coast of New Hampshire and in the Penobscot Bay region of Maine in the 1880s.[42] In 1883 he had led a group of Boston friends in the establishment of a vacation colony at North Haven, and his 1884–85 design for "Stormaway," a three-story summer home for Boston lawyer Moorfield

Storey, began his work in the Shingle Style in Maine. He also designed at North Haven the Islesboro Inn (1890, 1892); both the inn and the Wheelwright family cottage at Vinalhaven, Maine (fig. 60), employed the design strategy of intersecting cross-gambrel roofs. This distinctive design feature was apparently experimented with at the Howland boardinghouse, built the year before the Islesboro Inn (see fig. 58). The siting of the Howland Mill Village superintendent's house (looking out to the sea) and the massing formula of the men's boardinghouse, then, seem to have been strongly influenced by the elite architectural tradition exhibited in this contemporaneous seaside resort in Maine. Howland's sensibilities as an avid yachtsman would have been attuned to such visual associations. In fact, with his family's vacation cottages (in the Gothic Revival Style) located opposite Howland's new mill village in Clark's Cove, Wheelwright, in effect, was linking two landscapes—one of labor, the other of leisure—in the naturalist tradition.

The Mill Village in Cultural Context

That the Howland Mill Village was regarded not simply as workers' housing but as a prototype for a better way of life for industrial labor is clear in both local and national accounts of the time. One 1889 New Bedford history described the cottages as "models . . . designed for single families [and] attractive and varied architecture. . . . The territory has been laid out in accordance with modern ideas. It will be intersected by streets fifty and sixty feet wide, and breathing places, which may one day be fitted as parks, are provided for in the plans."[43] Six years later, an international study by the U.S. commissioner of labor cited the Howland Mill Village as one of six examples of "model small houses." It declared the houses' plumbing to be "of the most approved type" and noted that the designs created "thorough ventilation everywhere." "Waste water and refuse go into the sew-

ers," the report noted. "An unlimited quantity of water is allowed."[44]

The Howland Mill Village emerged in a particular climate of concern about the conditions in which the world's new industrial populations lived. By 1846, the perilous density of Boston's working-class neighborhoods had prompted Harvard Medical School's Henry Ingersoll Bowditch to investigate the public health aspects of existing workers' housing. Bowditch surmised that families of workingmen living outside Boston were healthier because they "have more room and better air, and the women and children might cultivate a small garden." His pioneering research on the causes of tuberculosis throughout the 1850s culminated in his 1862 *Consumption in New England* and helped cultivate an awareness that a significant relationship existed between local environment and all aspects of health. "It is impossible not to draw the inference," Bowditch argued, "that there is some intimate relation between the wise policy of separate homes . . . and the conditions of public health."[45]

The intensity of this critique grew stronger after the Civil War, when staggering losses from unsanitary wartime conditions and disease newly emphasized the problem. Mention has already been made (in chapter 3) of the criticism that was leveled particularly at the housing built by the city's two oldest textile corporations, Wamsutta and Potomska. At the center of concern were issues of poor sanitation and the monotony of standardized housing blocks.[46]

Out of this climate of concern grew reform that placed a high value on the introduction of design strategies aimed at preventing disease and promoting healthy living in the housing of industrial workers. Robert Owen's famous work at New Lanark, which he discussed at length in his 1813 *New View of Society*, had set the stage for industrial housing reform in Europe as well as in the United States. Surely, given his mother's interest in Owen, Howland was aware of the reformer's vision of a mixed-use community that provided a pastoral, aesthetic quality for the residential area opposite the mill and the potential economic benefit of reducing food expenses for the worker who chose to cultivate a vegetable garden. Howland's provision of garden space for each of the fifty Howland Mill cottages may have been influenced by Owen's ideas, as well as by the moral implications of the village improvement movement, which had recently extended its agenda to include industrial village life (to be discussed later in this chapter; see also notes 65 and 66).

Model workers' houses had been displayed at international trade fairs as early as 1851.[47] Throughout the century such expositions served as catalysts for the social improvement of corporate housing. Fourierism also stimulated the development of new forms of workers' housing on both sides of the Atlantic.[48] In 1853 British industrialist Sir Titus Salt, a disciple of Charles Fourier, created Saltaire, a town designed for the manufacture of alpaca woolens on the Aire River in northern England.

Model workers' housing began to appear more regularly in the United States after the Civil War. In 1871 Bowditch, who had helped establish the State Board of Health in Massachusetts several years earlier, worked with other prominent citizens to establish the Boston Cooperative Building Company to build and supervise houses for working men. Bowditch's studies and these houses influenced the establishment of statewide minimal room sizes and adjacent outdoor spaces in order to avoid overcrowding in housing for the American working population.

Two years earlier Olmsted had attempted to articulate, in his upscale Riverside Housing Community in the Chicago suburbs, the connection he perceived between landscape architecture and an improved quality of life.[49] At Riverside, Olmsted attempted to bring the advantages of the city into the countryside by creating convenient commuter rail access to Chicago and installing such amenities as gas, water, roadways, walkways, and drainage. Olmsted did not justify these amenities on humanistic principles alone; such "urban conveniences," he argued, would "give any farming land in a healthy and attractive situation the value of town lots."[50] To preserve the pastoral quality of the town, Olmsted recommended placing dwellings on lots fifty or a hundred feet or more apart and at some distance from the public road. Within the community, gently curving roadways were designed to suggest "leisure, contemplativeness, and happy tranquillity," and its open, landscaped "public grounds" provided space for recreation.[51]

After he created Riverside, Olmsted argued that just as urban amenities could enhance rural life, suburban features could improve city neighborhoods where workers lived. Urban neighborhoods might be improved by "the construction of good roads and walks, the laying of sewer, water, and gas pipes, and the supplying of sufficiently cheap, rapid, and comfortable conveyances to towns" and by the provision of "breathing places." "Man's enjoyment of rural beauty," he wrote, would be enhanced by foliage along the streets, which according to "modern science" purified the air and induced "health, virtue, and happiness." To allow foliage to reach maturity and the free flow of traffic, Olmsted suggested wider streets as well.[52]

By the early 1870s the principles that Saltaire and Riverside had put in place received official sanction by Edward Everett Hale, one of Boston's most famous ministers, in his *Old and New* (1870) and *Workingmen's Homes* (1874). The emphasis on landscaping in these neighborhoods of workers' cottages, Hale declared, "encouraged domesticity" and "promoted sociality, intercommunication, exercise, and the enjoyment of pure air."[53]

By the 1880s, public attitudes toward urban density and workers' living circumstances shifted, and the Massachusetts Board of Health and both local and national periodicals charged that large tenement blocks diminished the quality of workers' lives. In New Bedford, the growing social and legal pressure to improve the aesthetic and sanitary conditions of the existing mill housing (as noted in chapter 3) had impelled both the Grinnell and Acushnet Mills to build smaller, detached units in 1882.[54] While Howland Mills was not the first textile corporation in New Bedford to create detached housing for the city's workers, it was the first to break consciously from the gridlike unison of previous urban mill developments,[55] and it went a great deal further than other existing New Bedford corporate housing to address the well-being of workers. For example, the provision of indoor plumbing in single-family corporate housing—complete with flush toilets, hot and cold water, marble wash basins, bathtubs, and laundry sinks—was well beyond any explicit legal directives of the day.[56] The corporation's single-family housing was of recognizable quality; its indoor plumbing and heating were well designed; its extensive water, sewer, and roadway systems were markedly better than contemporary city standards; and the village avoided the criticisms of monotony and repetition. Indeed, the Howland Mill Village incorporated all the ingredients Olmsted had outlined as critical: it had wider streets bordered by foliage to purify the air, generous spacing between family dwellings, and a rail connection.

The significance of the Howland Mill Village becomes clearer when it is compared with the other groups of company-built "model small houses" cited as exemplary in the 1895 Federal Labor Commissioner's study. This report was undertaken by E. R. L. Gould, a political scientist specializing in municipal affairs. Entitled *The Housing of the Working People*, it was the first systematic survey of housing reforms in the United States and Europe. Among the list of noteworthy small model houses built in company towns were (in addition to the Howland Mill Village) those of the S. D. Warren and Company (Cumberland Mills, Maine); the Willimantic (Connecticut) Linen Company; Pullman's Palace Car Company

(Pullman, Illinois); Merrimack Manufacturing Company (Lowell, Massachusetts); and Robert Treat Paine (Boston).

Of these projects, Lowell, Willimantic, and Pullman housing predated Howland Mill Village, and both Willimantic and Pullman were influenced by the design principles put in place at Saltaire and perhaps Bournville and Port Sunlight as well.[57] Still, neither the Willimantic nor Pullman projects applied the principles of suburban-style landscape architecture and contour planning to workers' neighborhoods as consistently as did the Howland Mill Village which followed them.

George Pullman had hired a noted architect (Solon S. Beman) and landscape architect (Nathan F. Barrett) to design his model mill village in Illinois seven years before Howland hired Wheelwright and Haven.[58] At Pullman, the scale of the enterprise was much larger than at the Howland Mills: more than four thousand acres were acquired, and the size and variety of housing accommodations also ranged from detached housing to barrack tenements. But while there were wide, well-maintained, macadamized streets lined with young shade trees, most of the plan was laid out in a grid; picturesque landscape features were limited to the foreground space of the administration building (which, for example, fronted a human-made lake) and the Florence Hotel (map 9). This aspect of design was not overlooked by period observers. *Harper's* social critic, Richard Ely, applauded the variety of design which he found in the individual housing units where, for example, diverse roof forms avoided "unbroken uniformity." However, he disapproved of the fact that the lawns separating the houses from the street were always the same width, reinforcing the "regularity of form" in the street pattern. Also, he noted, "the streets cross each other at right angles" as a result of the grid. "Frightful monotony" was nevertheless avoided by breaking the regular pattern of the street grid with the insertion of a public square, an arcade, hotel, or market at right angles to the street. This changed the scale and rhythm of the street pattern and offered closed vistas affording points of visual interest (instead of long, unbroken corridors of industrial housing stock) when walking down the streets.

Considering that Pullman's industrial community plan was cited as a successful *social* experiment by *Harper's* reporter Richard Ely, the message sent to corporate planners, architects, and mill owners was that images of industrial regimentation (in both housing and landscaping) should be avoided. George M. Pullman's attitudes toward both the "civilizing effect" and "commercial value of beauty" also were evident as positive byproducts of carefully landscaped industrial settings.[59]

The Oaks, a neighborhood of forty workers' cottages planned by William Eliot Barrows for the Willimantic Linen Company in Connecticut in 1880,[60] on the other hand, hints at the contour planning principles of the romantic suburb tradition. In this regard it is the closest parallel to the Howland Mills complex. The Willimantic Linen Company began operations in 1857. Its Mill No. 4, built in 1880, was both the largest cotton mill in the world and the first textile mill to be designed and built to be illuminated by electricity.[61] Howland certainly would have known of this mill complex, as the lighting demonstrations in

Map 9. This plan of Pullman appeared as an inset to an engraving of the administration building and the Florence Hotel in an 1885 article in Harper's *New Monthly Magazine*. Curvilinear landscape design appeared only in front of the hotel, by the lake, and along two sides of the playground, not in areas where workers lived. From *Harper's New Monthly* 70 (Feb. 1885): 454

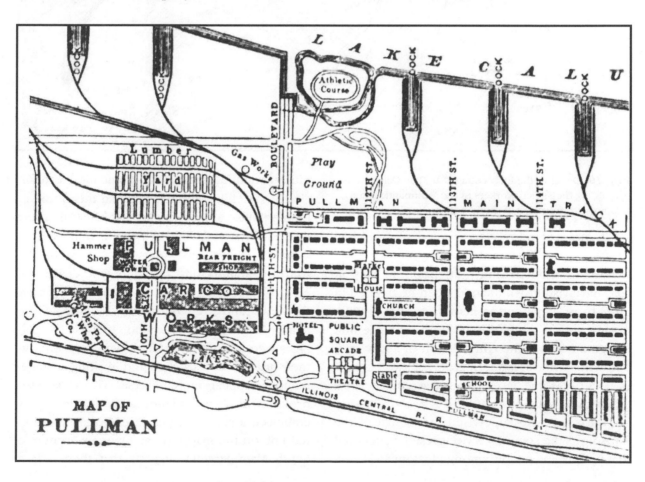

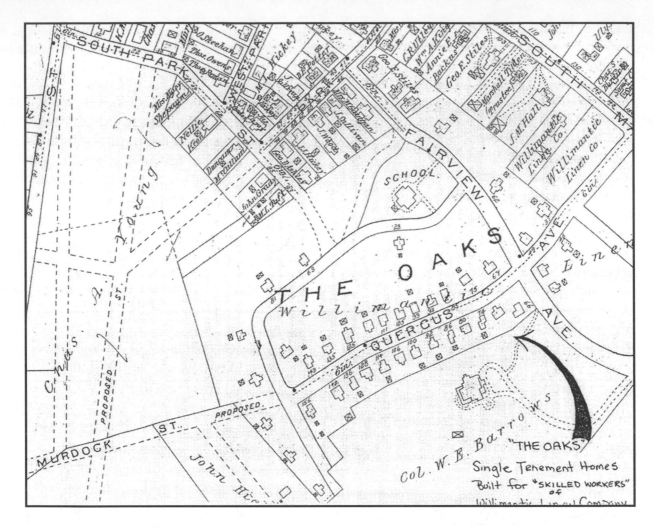

Map 10. Detail of the forty cottages at "The Oaks"
built for the skilled workers of the Willimantic Linen
Company. Courtesy of the Windham Textile and
History Museum.

themselves attracted much attention; he may, in
fact, have visited Willimantic when he traveled in
1882 to research cotton manufacturing. At Willimantic and at the Howland Mills alike, the mill
village paralleled the construction of a new mill,
and Willimantic's "modern group of forty houses"
of 1880 was the facet that attracted the labor
department's attention (map 10).

Barrows, who supervised the design of the
housing as the company's vice president, believed
that by "placing people among pleasant and beautiful surroundings they will become more careful,
cleanly, tasteful, and intelligent and therefore . . .
more valuable to their employers." The Oaks drew
on the physical layout of Saltaire, mid-century
designs for workers' housing at Lowell, the
romantic architectural and landscape designs of
Alexander Jackson Davis and Andrew Jackson
Downing, and even the rustic tradition of the
nearby Methodist campground (1860).[62] The cottages were of four different designs staggered in
their order of construction and in siting arrangement to appear more diverse. The Oaks also
broke with grid planning and tentatively
embraced a curvilinear design. Further, the dotted line on the map (linking Quercus Avenue to
South Main Streets) suggests that there was a

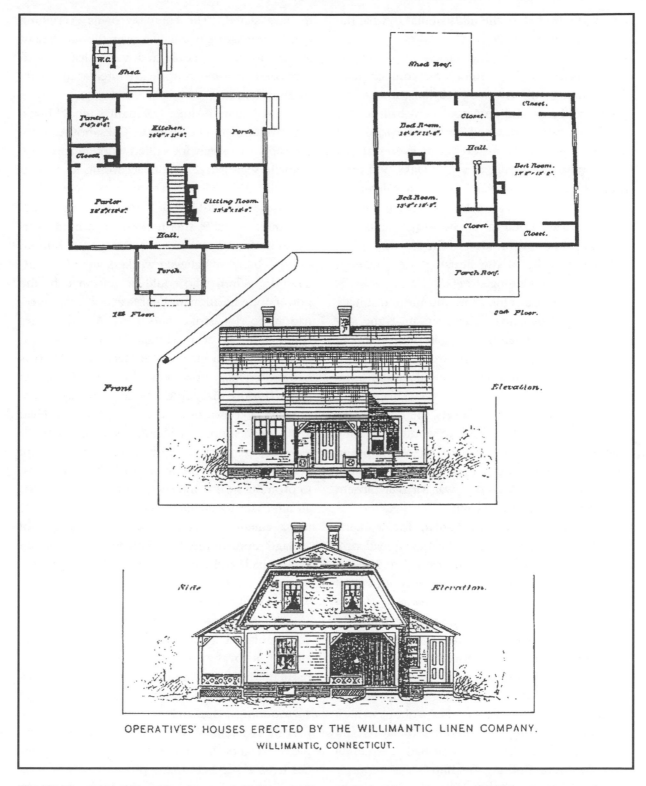

W.C.

Shed.

Pantry.

Closet.

Kitchen.

Porch.

Parlor

Sitting Room.

Hall.

Porch.

1st Floor.

Shed Roof.

Bed Room.

Closet.

Closet.

Hall.

Bed Room.

Bed Room.

Closet.

Closet.

Porch Roof.

2nd Floor.

Front

Elevation.

Side

Elevation.

OPERATIVES' HOUSES ERECTED BY THE WILLIMANTIC LINEN COMPANY.
WILLIMANTIC, CONNECTICUT.

Fig. 61. The Oaks, 1880, Willimantic Linen Company, Willimantic, Connecticut. From United States Census of Manufacturers, 1880. Courtesy of the Windham Textile and History Museum.

transportation link to the mills similar to what the Howland Mills later adopted.

Many features of the Oaks—from electric lighting in the mills to embryonic contour planning, single-family cottages, gardens, a streetcar system, a library, and an amusement hall—either existed or were proposed at the Howland Mill Village. Howland and his architects even planned forty cottages originally, as at the Oaks, and their design is strikingly similar to those at Willimantic (fig. 61). Still, the Oaks lacked the urban integration of parks, boulevards, housing, sanitation, industry, and transportation of the Howland plan, and the majority of the housing was clustered along only two winding streets.[63]

Perhaps more significant, and more distinctly revealing of Howland's progressivism, is the attitude toward industrial labor that its design embodied. Pullman and Lowell were both more thoroughly integrated with a sophisticated infrastructure than the Howland Mill Village, and Willimantic applied, if tentatively, the design principles of the romantic suburb to workers' housing slightly earlier. But the design of neighborhoods in these three projects made manifest a certain paternalism toward workers that was virtually absent from the Howland Mill Village.

Judging from the 1823 plan for workers' housing in Lowell, corporate authority had produced landscapes of unified control and visual order, while regulating nearly every aspect of operatives' lives as a means of ensuring a clean and morally upright industrial setting.[64] Similarly, prospective residents of Pullman had to apply at the agent's office and, if found to be of "good character," were permitted to sign a one-year lease, which among other things limited tenants' freedom to decorate their homes without written approval. The company attended to lawns and tenements; the Pullman resident had "everything done for him, nothing by him," one reporter observed after an October 1884 visit. One tenant at Pullman was later quoted in the *Cleveland Post*

to have stated, "The company owns everything and it exercises surveillance over the movement and habits of the people in a way to lead one to suppose that it has proprietary interest in [their] souls and bodies."[65]

At Willimantic Linen Company's model housing development known as the Oaks, houses were set aside exclusively for skilled workers and were spatially segregated on lots according to rank in the mill. Also, all forty cottages were situated under the watchful eye of Barrows, whose home, also built in 1880, was located on a bluff overlooking the village (refer to map 10, bottom right).[66] Barrows believed workers were like misguided children who could be reformed by the powers of education and culture away from inclinations to riot, strike, and drink. All employees residing in the forty cottages at the Oaks, for example, had to maintain gardens, and Barrows had garden inspectors under the guise of a garden club to ensure that gardens were properly tended. Barrows gave awards for the best gardens and had a gardener supply each home with cuttings. In essence, gardens in industrial settings were believed to rectify the image of industrial towns, to promote health and social interaction, and—as an alternate to owning a house and lot—to ally management and labor in the responsibility of "village improvement."[67] Barrows even placed exotic plants and stained glass in Mill No. 4 at Willimantic to soften the distinction between home and work as well as to boost morale.[68]

A pleasant built environment, it was thought, could enhance a company's public image, foster employee loyalty, and reduce labor turnover—particularly when well-designed company housing was augmented by attractive natural surroundings. But such amenities also could be part of a system of oppression when, for example, managers threatened to evict their employees from rented company property if they took part in union organizing.[69] In model company towns, aesthetic and cultural improvements often were linked, in some manner, to programs of social control and/or economic advancement on the part of management. The Willimantic Linen Company, for example, constructed a fashionable Stick Style building in 1877 with a company store on the first two floors and, as at Saltaire, a library and a reading room for employees and inhabitants of the town in the top story.[70] Forced upon the workers in response to a $345,000 increase in city taxes in 1877, the store took scrip only in exchange for goods, and while it turned a considerable profit for the corporation, the debt operatives incurred there tied them more closely to the control of the mill owners. Further, in 1882 Barrows announced that all linen company employees who could not read or write English by July 4, 1883, would be dismissed—unless they took free night classes in the Dunham Hall Library, in effect Barrow's own crucible for "social alchemy."[71]

As a reflection of the growing resistance to such corporate control at Willimantic, the 1895 labor commissioner's report noted, "In 1884 a well intentioned agent tried to get all employees under 16 to go from 9 to 10 in the morning to a room which was heated and well ventilated and provided seats, where bullion or milk and crackers were served free. The half hour following was given to play. It was found that the young people would not go voluntarily, and some so far objected to the practice that they left the works."[72] The study noted that women resisted being compelled to leave their working room and to eat their lunch in this space; some objected to mixing "with working partners of objectionable nationalities," while others were embarrassed by the comparison of their dinner pails.[73] Operatives also resisted the use of magnifying glasses given to inspectors of thread to protect their eyesight. "There is undoubtedly something in the American temperament, or perhaps one had better say in the temperament of laborers working in America, which is hostile to gratuitous help from employers," the study concluded. "The people dis-

like to feel that they are under control."[74] Such incidents were emblematic of a far-reaching attitude among labor to resist corporate measures aimed at the social welfare of the worker without the *consent* of the worker. In the end, as strikes in model company towns like Pullman, Illinois, and later Chicopee, Georgia, reflected, physical amenities in themselves were not sufficient to prevent unrest. As Malone notes, "Workers who enjoyed the appearance of their community were still capable of resistance to arbitrary work rules, inadequate wages, or excessive regulations of their private lives."[75]

The Howland Mill Village was flexible and democratic by comparison to both Pullman and Willimantic. The more emphatic use of contour planning within the cottage setting, coupled with the relative absence of company officials in the housing arrangement, softened surveillance and direct pressures of public performance. The village did include a mill superintendent's house, a relatively unassuming two-story, gable-front cottage, but it was not oriented toward the mill village and the adjacent factories as at Willimantic; instead, it afforded the mill superintendent an unobstructed view of the ocean and Clark's Point. While the more expensive gambrel roof cottages at the Howland Mill Village were rented by skilled workers, such as spinners, the fifteen smaller cottages were occupied by lower-paid operatives, such as doffers, comb-winders, and spoolers. Howland and his architects also never envisioned a company-controlled shopping district, relying instead on the trolley to provide access to shopping areas of choice.

Rents at the Howland Mill Village were reasonable and stable, not having been raised between the 1888–89 construction of the mill cottages and 1895. Tenants were permitted to sublet to other employees in the mills, and they were allowed to take in boarders to offset rent payments, which probably accounted for the fact that five of the seven rooms in the larger cottages were bedrooms. Not only could boarders be taken in, but renters did not have to be heads of families. Sons or daughters who worked for the Howland

Mills were entitled to have their parents live in corporate housing as long as a corporation employee paid rent through salary deduction. Coupled with a general shortage of worker housing in the South End, these provisions kept both the cottages and the men's boardinghouse full. The boardinghouse even realized an estimated profit of about 3 percent of the rental income.[76]

Tenants of the mill cottages could not become proprietors of the houses already built, but they could purchase vacant land from the corporation and build for themselves. Land was to be sold on what was then referred to as "long time" or a mortgage contract, and the company promised "every reasonable assistance . . . to help them to build."[77] Robert Treat Paine had made an early effort to establish building-and-loan associations to help Boston workers buy their own homes (they were located mostly in the Roxbury and Dorchester sections of Boston and dated from 1874 to 1891), but the practice of selling rather than renting workers' housing was still rare in the United States at the end of the nineteenth century; even at the later (1896) Bancroft Park housing development designed and built for the E. D. and G. Draper Company of Hopedale, Massachusetts, only the single-family houses rented by the managers could be purchased, and then only at the end of ten years.[78] Howland's workers, then, were allowed a far greater range of choices over the economic decisions confronting them, from taking in boarders to offset expenses to becoming independent homeowners within the industrial village. By such means, they were not just mill operatives working for the company, but (within a limited framework) also businessmen and businesswomen working on behalf of their own goals and visions for the future.

Howland's plan to create a park for workers at the Howland Mill Village also suggests his subscription to the progressive ideas most closely associated in his day with Olmsted and his one-time associate Charles Eliot, both of whom had major estate commissions in New Bedford in the 1880s and 1890s (see chapter 2).[79] Howland's family had long and actively pursued horticulture as an avocation, as had many of New Bedford's elite.[80] In 1892 he and his business associate Morgan Rotch, then a member of the New Bedford Park Commission, proposed to sell to the city land in the Howland Mill Village for a "Cove Park." It was situated along a parkway that the firm of Olmsted, Olmsted, and Eliot had proposed to create that year between three new parks in the city's extreme northern, southern, and western reaches (ultimately Brooklawn, Hazelwood, and Buttonwood Parks).[81] Thirty years later, one newspaper account held that because "the artistic side" of the model industrial complex "made strong appeal" to Howland, he had "secured famous landscape architects" to plan the park.[82] These architects have not been identified, but the close correlation of the Howland-Rotch proposal with the plans then being put forth by the Olmsted firm suggest the latter may have been involved.

By 1875, the city engineering study had already blocked out sections of the city for parks, including a "marine park" on Clark's Point, then the site of only two estates—the summer homes of William D. Howland and his mother, Rachel.[83] In the early 1890s the Olmsted firm submitted two proposals for creating an interconnected park-parkway system and for developing the "marine park" as an integral component of the system at the abandoned Fort Rodman, of which the city had been given custody in 1892 (map 11).[84] A stately promenade and an adjacent ten-mile, eighty-foot-wide scenic parkway—all told, 460 acres of scenic open space—would connect the industrial districts in the North and South Ends of the city. The plan envisioned that wagonettes, similar to those at Olmsted's Franklin Park in Boston, would carry workers for ten or twenty cents as far as the Fort Rodman property at Clark's Point.[85] Olmsted, Olmsted and Eliot emphasized the value of the plan to the city in terms of the rejuvenating effect

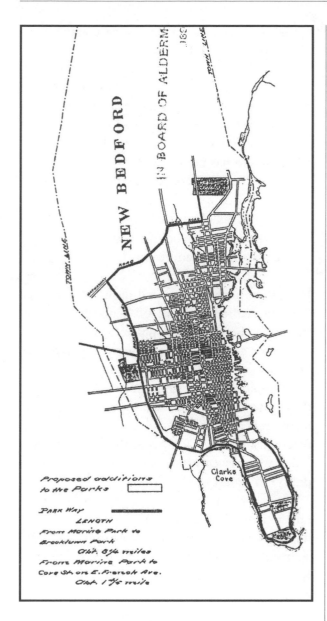

Map 11. Lost proposal of Olmsted, Olmsted and Eliots' plan for a "System of Parks" in New Bedford, dating from June 7, 1894. The system culminated in a Marine Park at the tip of Clarks Point. This scheme was designed to revitalize the city's "tired townspeople" after long hours in the mills. It linked the industrial neighborhoods of the North and South Ends together by way of a scenic parkway that offered bay views amidst a "pure rural landscape." Inexpensive wagonettes were envisioned by the firm to transport the city's workers to the string of public parks. Discovered by the author's research team. Courtesy of the Building Commissioner, New Bedford City Hall.

John C. Olmsted claimed New Bedford's marine park would be the "finest on the Atlantic Coast." The completed Olmsted, Olmsted and Eliot park/parkway proposal was estimated to cost two hundred thousand dollars.[87] In June 1892, the New Bedford Park Commission, created a year earlier, had sold bonds for the purpose of buying lands for the proposed "system of parks," and in 1895 it allocated five hundred dollars to the Olmsted firm to develop a preliminary plan and engineering study for Buttonwood Park.[88] However, facing new city leadership (Mayor Ashley served for thirty-three of the years between 1890 and 1937, shifting the city's political leadership from the Republican to the Democratic Party) and a national depression, the plans stalled. Brooklawn Park was created in the North End, independent of Olmsted's design influence, and by 1901 voters reluctantly agreed to fund Hazelwood Park on the former grounds of the Howland summer estates instead of a marine park at Clark's Point. In place of wagonettes on scenic parkways connecting these parks at both ends of the city, streetcars—then the icon of urbanism—carried workers through the city and to the parks. Only Buttonwood Park, west of the downtown commercial district, was built along the lines Olmsted, Olmsted and Eliot largely intended, and it too was connected to the city and outlying areas (like the neighboring textile city of Fall River) by the electric streetcar line.

that the scenic parkway would have on the city's workforce: "The Clark's Point property with its grand views of the bay is remarkably distinctive and fine. . . . Playgrounds, amusement houses, all constructions however useful, will be subordinated to the scenery, because of the well known fact that nothing is so refreshing to the tired townspeople as pure rural landscape, and because after acquiring such considerable areas it would be bad economy for the city to put them to any other than their highest use."[86]

Howland's vision of a model mill village had turned away from social control aimed at recasting the worker totally in the image of the corporation to an ideal of community where the identity (and, following the views of English social reformers John Ruskin and William Morris, perhaps even the joy) of the worker was encouraged in an atmosphere of greater personal freedom.[89] Perhaps the real significance of contour planning, whether in Olmsted's system of parks through New Bedford's working-class neighborhoods or in the Howland Mill Village itself, is the level of spatial and personal freedom it implied for the mill worker. Conversely, in Lowell and Pullman, the grid in which workers' housing was placed mirrored the rigidity of corporate control over the lives of its employees both inside and outside the mill setting.

There were pragmatic goals to these more liberal practices, however. As an 1891 article in the *Cleveland Plain Dealer* pointed out, the Howland Mill Village project was intended to attract and keep skilled workers and maintain agreeable labor relations without trade unions:

> How can we secure and retain the best class of operatives? Treasurer Howland laid before the directors his plan to secure these ends and the extent to which they have been carried out they have been remarkably successful. . . . In short, every effort has been made to attract to the mills . . . a most desirable class of help. In the whole scheme there has been nothing philanthropic or charitable but every move has been made on the broadest of economic ideas with a view to securing and holding the best efforts of the operatives and thus securing the greatest amount of work at the least possible cost and waste. . . . The corporation has paid excellent dividends [and] good wages have been paid. . . .
>
> Such an undertaking as this carried

out on such a broad plan shows that there need not be differences between capital and labor when both endeavor to live together in harmony. There is nothing cooperative in this scheme, as the term goes, yet the operators reap many good results from their steady careful work. Mr. Howland has done a great work in carrying out this undertaking and the benefits will be wide-reaching . . . a few more such ventures as this and we shall see the beginning of the end of the great struggle between capital and labor.[90]

Interesting here is the stated desire to exchange the paternalistic rhetoric of benevolence (e.g., "there has been nothing philanthropic or charitable") for economic rationality ("every move has been made on the broadest economic ideas . . . and thus securing the greatest amount of work at the least possible cost and waste"). Such statements reflect a shift in corporate thinking from paternalism (which following the 1894 Pullman Strike was viewed as an outmoded management policy) to progressivism.[91]

Yet, if we define "paternalism" as being the impetus for social, moral, physical, and economic improvement that originates from industrial management instead of from—or in concert with—the worker, then corporate paternalism certainly existed at the Howland Mills. As at Willimantic and Pullman, Howland had identified a future need for "annexes, such as libraries, reading rooms, or halls for social or literary reunions" and envisioned "a large brick building to contain a gymnasium, and evening school . . . and possibly a reading room or library; a club room or amusement room for men and helpfulness for women conducted on the general lines recognized in the working girls' clubs now organized so successfully."[92] These facilities were likely intended to be placed in the areas blocked out on the 1889 master plan at the intersection of Dartmouth Street and Cove Road (refer to upper left of map 8). Howland told the *Cleveland Plain Dealer* that he also hoped to create a cooperative insurance company "to provide against the sickness or disability of workmen and to aid their families in the event of their death."[93]

Thus, Howland arguably projected certain elite values about living and recreating onto his workforce (including the seaside resort image of the housing and the annual yachting excursion that Howland extended to his workers), and such benefits as long-term mortgages and health insurance kept workers tied to the workplace for long periods. The company also had discharged those "undesirable or troublesome operatives" who had attempted to organize a union at the mills in February 1891.[94]

Later events, however, demonstrated that Howland exerted a far less intrusive mode of social control than most industrialists of his time. And, more important, though it operated but a brief time, the Howland Mill Village provided the workers of New Bedford (and beyond) a very real glimpse of enlightened corporate leadership that demonstrated a genuine concern for the health and well-being of the workers. Had the Howland Mills survived, and Howland's Cove Park been built and linked to other urban recreational spaces within the city, such as the proposed marine park, a very different industrial landscape might have emerged than what materialized in the decades after 1900.

The End of the Howland Mill Village

The Howland Mills and its workers' village unraveled for the same reasons that enabled their construction to be initiated and executed so swiftly—Howland's connection with the city's business and political elite, coupled with his particular dedication to the welfare of his workers. By all accounts, Howland had a strong and supportive relationship with his operatives. Even as early as 1884, when he was operating the New Bedford Manufacturing Company, Howland's partnership with labor was recognized by William D.'s father: "[T]here are strikes and various kinds of troubles among the cotton mills. Willie's is running smoothly and making money still. The operatives are perfectly contented and happy."[95]

Later, when the state law mandating a ten-hour day was passed in 1892 (reducing the work week of certain mill employees from sixty to fifty-eight hours), most New Bedford mills cut wages to offset operating costs. Howland, however, honored the shorter workday and refused to cut wages. That same year, when many workers had to be laid off because of the sharp downturn in the textile market, Howland lowered the rent and in some instances did not collect it at all.[96]

Moreover, Howland did not follow the lead of the New Bedford Manufacturers' Association on August 14, 1894, when, in response to the severe downturn in the national economy the previous year, it shortened hours and announced two successive wage cutbacks totaling approximately 25 percent. The manufacturer's committee waited until Howland was out of town to elect to cut back pay rates, but Howland ultimately resolved to run his three yarn mills at the old pay rates so as not to sever "the smooth and friendly relations we have in our mills at the present."[97] As a result, Howland's workers did not strike with the rest of the city's ten thousand textile workers on August 20, 1894, and did not have to accept the 5 percent wage reduction other workers agreed to when the strike was settled by arbitration in October.[98] The *Fall River Globe* in August 21, 1894, quoted Howland as stating, "Our goods have a reputation and we have orders that must be filled . . . I cannot run a mill without the cooperation of the help. . . . [M]y silent spindles will not make money for the stockholders." Howland Mill operatives presented their mill manager with a certificate of merit for his attitudes toward his employees. The *American Wool and Cotton Reporter* observed of the Howland Mills in 1894: "A strike is as much an unknown incident in their whole career as an impairment of their credit."[99]

Within three years, however, Howland's credit was so substantially impaired that his mills and his housing experiment came to an abrupt and sensational end. The general downturn in the textile market related to the Panic of 1893 had brought several New Bedford corporations to the brink of economic disaster, including all three of Howland's enterprises (Howland Mills, New Bedford Manufacturing Company, and Rotch Mills). Like several other New Bedford Mills, they had expanded too quickly in anticipation of a continued high demand for goods and did not allow enough time to retrieve capital. Moreover, the mill village had come at a high price to the corporation. The land upon which the group of model dwellings had been built had cost only $3,500, but sewage, drainage, water connections, and other improvements totaled $38,000. By 1895, the corporation owned fifty houses at a total cost of $104,000 and a large boardinghouse that cost $36,000.[100] To these expenses were added the costs of the water system, additional road improvements, and perhaps even a share of the 1892 street railway extension. With only $5,000 received annually in rent from all the dwellings, increased revenues from the property were clearly needed to absorb the cost of the infrastructure. Finally, the most speculative part of the venture—the sale of lots to workers wishing to build their own houses—was structured in such a way as not to permit a quick capital return.[101] By 1897, the rapid expansion of the Howland Mills resulted in $2,069,732 in assets, but the corporation generated only $114,000 in profit and carried $965,000 as debt. With a $200,000 business note coming due, the company had only about $40,000 in cash with which to pay it. Howland was forced to request an additional $200,000 from area banks to cover the note.[102]

As treasurer of three separate corporations, Howland had allowed all of the mills to become overcapitalized and excessively indebted without revealing these facts to the board of directors. The "embarrassment" of Howland's financial mismanagement of three corporations (announced in the *Morning Standard,* April 24, 1897), following on the spectacular failure of the Bennett and Columbia Mills the previous week (announced in the *New Bedford Evening Standard,* April 15, 1897), shocked the textile interests of the city.[103] Given Howland's standing in the city, the so-called "deceptions of the treasurer" were handled in a kindly manner by the newspaper, but the corporations' excessive debt was anathema in the financial community.

Moreover, Howland's handling of the 1894 strike had created clear divisions within the New Bedford textile industry; the spinners union was said almost to have worshipped Howland, while such textile manufacturers as Andrew G. Pierce felt betrayed by Howland's actions during the strike relative to the agreement several corporations had worked out in his absence. This incident and his mills' indebtedness eroded Howland's earlier base of support among the business interests of the city.[104] The banks, whose board of directors were made up of the same mill owners who witnessed Howland's opposition to lowering wages when the ten-hour workday was instituted, were no doubt concerned about Howland's radical social agenda; by maintaining full production and paying full wages from 1893 to 1897, when other workers and mill owners were severely cutting back, Howland was, after all, going against the grain not only of the other mills in the city but also of the national economy in general.

On April 24, 1897, Walter Clifford, vice president of the National Bank of Commerce, which had done much of the Howland Mills business, told the local newspapers that the banks in the city intended to help Howland's corporations with the note coming due "provided the books showed a condition of things which would warrant it and an examination was begun." But the debt caused the banks to withdraw their offer, at which point the mills' financial difficulties were revealed to the public.

Then, on April 29, William D. Howland disappeared. Upon hearing the news and learning of the financial difficulties the mill faced, the operatives in the Howland and Rotch Mills took an "unprecedented turn" and "expressed their willingness, if it would relieve the stress on the corporation, to sustain a temporary cut-down, or even forego their pay days for a time, till such time as the corporations can better afford to make payment."[105] But on May 6, a week after he vanished, the *Evening Standard* reported that Howland's body had been found that morning under the North Street pier. He was still wearing his top hat and gloves and had important bank documents in his pocket. The newspaper added, "On Friday morning April 23, Mr. Howland had a conference with Otis N. Pierce of the National Bank of Commerce, when Mr. Pierce announced the decision of the bank to refuse further credit to the Howland Corporation unless the books could be opened to expert examination. . . . It is generally accepted that the despondent treasurer took his own life within half an hour after the time he left his office with Harry M. Pierce, his bookkeeper."[106]

In the end, more was lost than the three mill corporations under Howland's direction. Howland's death also signaled an end both to naturalistic planning and to other socially conscious schemes for housing mill operatives in the city. Regrettably, other corporations used Howland's earlier policies, such as his reluctance to lower wages in connection with the mandated ten-hour work day, as examples of how such practices inevitably led to corporate failure.[107]

The promise that the Howland Mill Village represented ended suddenly. Its influence, however, can be seen in workers' housing at Hopedale, Massachusetts, and Vandergrift, Pennsylvania, projects that followed immediately upon its heels and

that have previously been accepted as the benchmarks of picturesque industrial planning.[108] The E. D. and G. Draper Company of Hopedale had begun its company town in 1856. But until its 1896 Bancroft Park housing development the town had been laid out on relatively flat terrain in a grid pattern.[109] Warren Henry Manning (1860–1938), a member of the Olmsted firm from 1887 to 1896, had drawn up plans for grading and planting at Hopedale in 1888. By February 18, 1895, he is listed on Preliminary Plans (Olmsted Plan, job no. 1810–4) as superintendent of planting of Buttonwood Park in New Bedford. Even if he had not been involved directly in planning the Howland Mill Village, Manning was almost certainly aware of the contour plan put in place there, and this fact may have been a factor in persuading Hopedale Company officers to create a similar plan when he returned to that project site. The design of Hopedale's Bancroft Park (about 1898)—its shingled double-family housing sited on curved streets and walks, its twelve miles of macadam paving lined with stone curbing, and its nearly two miles of sidewalks—is indeed similar to that of the Howland Mill Village (fig. 62).[110] The expansive shoreline park Manning designed for Hopedale between 1898 and 1913 also had precedent in New Bedford's Cove Park and Marine Park schemes.

Similarly, the workers' village designed in 1895 by Olmsted, Olmsted and Eliot for the Apollo Iron and Steel Company at Vandergrift, Pennsylvania, relied heavily on contour planning and even sold industrial building lots to the workers, as did the Howland Mills. Vandergrift's hierarchical arrangement of mill agent and owner housing and its use of a rail system primarily to ship iron, steel, and lumber rather than to transport workers, however, made it more akin to the Oaks in these planning aspects than to Howland Mill Village. However, given the active roles that Olmsted's two sons played later in adapting naturalistic planning policies to large industrial sites—particularly following the firm's New Bedford's

Fig. 62. The duplex housing at Hopedale under construction about 1898. From Budgett Meakin, *Model Factories and Villages* (London, 1905).

parkway proposal of 1894—the Howland Mill Village now should be recognized as an important progenitor of the "new" company towns that developed in the first quarter of the twentieth century. Most closely associated are naturalistic planning schemes, such as Forest Hills Gardens, New York, designed in 1919 by Grosvenor Atterbury and Frederick Law Olmsted Jr., and Earle Draper's 1925 plan of Chicopee, Georgia.

The Howland Mill Village did not, however, survive the liquidation of the corporation in 1899. The mill assets were turned over to other parties, the receivers cut pay rates to match those that prevailed at other New Bedford mills, and the workers struck for the first time since the corporation was organized.[111] In 1899 the New England Cotton Yarn Company bought the corporation, including the mill housing, the open land along the Dartmouth city line, and a small piece of land on Clark's Cove.[112] The area beyond Dartmouth Street

planned for model mill housing ultimately became the site of the Sharp Manufacturing Company.

When New Bedford's economy recovered in 1901, it was clear to developers that textiles were in New Bedford to stay. Speculative builders took over the rental mill housing market almost exclusively from the corporations at this point. By 1902, the cottages designed and built for Howland Mill operatives became housing for middle management of the Gosnold Mill, which had purchased the mill holdings from the New England Cotton Yarn Company that year. Other speculation followed. The undeveloped area north of the Howland Mill Village, originally set aside for sale to Howland operatives, became packed with large, multifamily three-decker rental flats built predominately during the 1910s by local land developer Joseph T. Kenney to accommodate Sharp Manufacturing Company and Gosnold Mill employees.[113] The space laid aside for the proposed—but never completed— park in the Howland Mill Village was largely taken over by the Page Mill between 1906 and 1909. By 1920 the area the Olmsted firm proposed for a marine drive and park was described

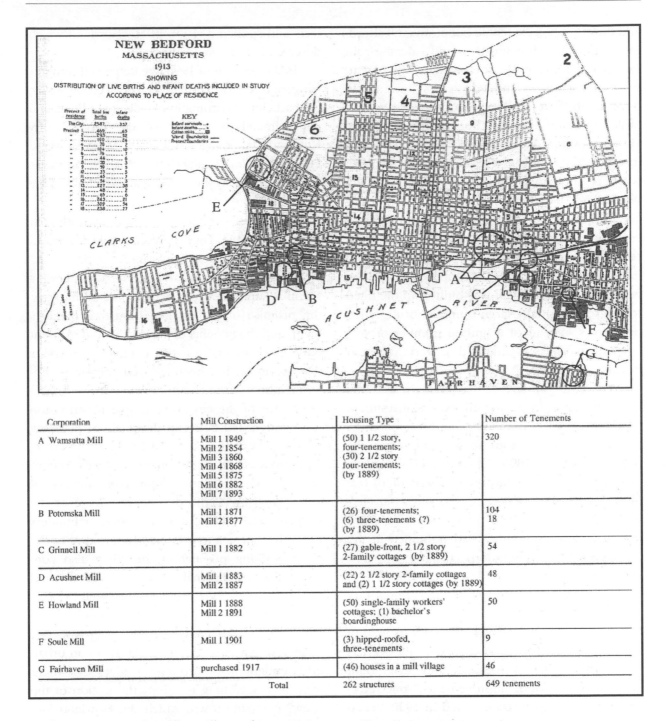

Corporation	Mill Construction	Housing Type	Number of Tenements
A Wamsutta Mill	Mill 1 1849 Mill 2 1854 Mill 3 1860 Mill 4 1868 Mill 5 1875 Mill 6 1882 Mill 7 1893	(50) 1 1/2 story, four-tenements; (30) 2 1/2 story four-tenements; (by 1889)	320
B Potomska Mill	Mill 1 1871 Mill 2 1877	(26) four-tenements; (6) three-tenements (?) (by 1889)	104 18
C Grinnell Mill	Mill 1 1882	(27) gable-front, 2 1/2 story 2-family cottages (by 1889)	54
D Acushnet Mill	Mill 1 1883 Mill 2 1887	(22) 2 1/2 story 2-family cottages and (2) 1 1/2 story cottages (by 1889)	48
E Howland Mill	Mill 1 1888 Mill 2 1891	(50) single-family workers' cottages; (1) bachelor's boardinghouse	50
F Soule Mill	Mill 1 1901	(3) hipped-roofed, three-tenements	9
G Fairhaven Mill	purchased 1917	(46) houses in a mill village	46
Total		262 structures	649 tenements

as being "covered with mills and tenement houses," and city residents spent leisure time at Acushnet Park, an "amusement house" of precisely the sort Olmsted had hoped to avoid.[114]

New Bedford's mill and housing practices were set, therefore, on a very different course,

Map 12. Map and listings of all the city's corporate-owned and -rented workers' housing available through documentary evidence. Base map from Whitney, *Infant Mortality* (1920); data overlay by the author.

and the city's biggest textile boom was still ahead. In the decade following Howland's death, from 1900 to 1910, New Bedford witnessed its greatest mill expansion and its greatest increase in population.[115] Yet, only two corporations would build company housing after the demise of the Howland Mill Village (map 12). In the particular instance of the Fairhaven Mills, a small village of workers' housing was constructed following World War I because of a general housing shortage in the city brought on by the returning servicemen. But, within a very brief time, they were sold off as private housing. The sheer volume of mills (seventy by 1923 as opposed to fifteen when the Howland Mill was built) and the need to house principally large numbers of unskilled operatives instead of a limited number of specialized workers demanded a very different housing response.

The entry of speculative builders into the housing market freed up mill owners' investment capital for new corporations and thus fanned the rate of mill expansion. In addition, after the precedent of the 1895 Whitman Mill, out-of-city investors began to incorporate New Bedford textile mills. The era of local governance over New Bedford's economic and physical destiny, which the city's leading families had fashioned in the eighteenth century, was thus challenged by new mill owners and housing developers alike. These developments, coupled with the temporary downturn in the national economy, doomed the Howland Mill Village. "Practical men took hold of the situation and then covered the mill districts with three and four deckers and sham built houses with modern improvements," one retrospective newspaper article noted in 1920. "Then the city came along and straightened the winding roads designed by Mr. Howland's landscape architects and spoiled a vision of Mr. Howland which deserved better consideration."[116]

In the summer of 1996, the Rotch Mill complex adjacent to the Howland Mills was razed. However, the bachelors' boardinghouse, albeit modified, and approximately forty-four of the original fifty Howland Mill cottages still stand, as do Howland Mills Nos. 1 and 2, adaptively reused for a time as retail space. Today the housing and the mills of the former Howland Mill Village are one of the city's few remaining complexes of mills and adjacent workers' housing. They represent, as well, a model mill village of national significance.[117]

Howland and his architects had offered a vision of unity between nature and technology, the promise of enlightened industrial management, and the benefits of a healthful and pleasant built environment for the company's workers that previously had been enjoyed only by wealthier members of the community living in the western sector of the city. This unique urban vision was sandwiched between paternalistic planning on the part of the powerful few, and the entrepreneurial efforts of the many that gave way in the end to an omnipresent commonality of design in New Bedford.[118] In the wake of the Howland Mill Village, the three-decker builders not only offered a new housing alternative to the city's working population, but they also constructed a new regional identity for New Bedford as a truly industrialized city. Ironically, at the very moment (1910) that New Bedford shifted most emphatically to a multifamily housing type that further accentuated the dense fabric of an urban grid, enlightened corporate leaders elsewhere were just beginning to adopt the notion of the "new" company town, which the Howland Mill Village had anticipated.[119]

PART III

FROM CORPORATE PATERNALISM TO A SPECULATIVE BUILDING MARKET

The Three-Decker in New Bedford

Front Elevation for Earl [...]
Proposed to be built at [...]
Drawn by Jacob Luippold, 8[...]

5

THE ANATOMY OF A NEW BEDFORD THREE-DECKER AND THE FORCES THAT SHAPED IT AT THE HEIGHT OF THE TEXTILE ERA

The vast majority of citizens . . . lived neither in a log cabin nor a mansion but a room or two in a city tenement.

—Renee Epps, vice president,
Lower East Side Tenement Museum,
Preservation (Jan./Feb. 1999)

As in physical weathering, the human transformation of the landscape (what I have termed *cultural weathering*) can be both an additive and subtractive process. Seen in these terms, the epoch of the three-decker builders in New Bedford clearly must be seen as a regionally defining moment in the transformation of this city's urban industrial character. In fact, it would be fair to say that the three–decker flat—the city's most characteristic building type—serves as a barometer to gauge the range of forces that New Bedford has undergone since the beginning of the textile era. Yet, historical references with regard to this late form of workers' housing in the city are scant, and the entire subject of the three-decker as a regional building form is under–researched.[1] Because the New Bedford mills and their related housing are so late compared with the earliest efforts in New England's textile history (representing as they do the post-1850, large steam-powered mills), they have been deemed by scholars of industrial history as less significant and, hence, less worthy of study. Further, the failure of the textile industry in the region following the economic downturn in 1923 and continuing through the Great Depression signals a steady economic decline for many of these manufacturing communities, and it is a story that most people are willing to forget. The rows upon rows of vacant (or adaptively used) mills and their housing counterpart, the three–decker, is for many an embarrassment. For such reasons, the three-decker (it is estimated that twelve hundred are extant in New Bedford) are conspicuously absent from all the tour guides and area studies of architecture. Additionally, very few historic districts comprising principally three–decker housing have been listed on the National Register in Massachusetts, in spite of efforts dating back to the 1970s.[2]

Beyond the limited sources available on the subject of mill housing in New Bedford and within the greater New England area, studies on flat buildings, tenements, or apartment housing are rare in architectural history as well. Carroll Westfall notes in his book review of Elizabeth Cromley's *Alone Together: A History of New York's Early Apartments*:

> Buildings that more than a single family call home have outnumbered houses in our major cities since the turn of the century. There have always been more of them than the commercial buildings that, along with single-family residences, dominate the received, canonic history of American architecture. . . . Perhaps the discipline is bound so tightly by the concept of style that the great mass of mediocre and uninteresting apartment buildings simply fails to stimulate any interest. . . . Or perhaps we neglect them because it is so difficult to accept their designers as successors of Palladio, Wren, and Schinkel, unless they are LeCorbusier or Mies and others who happened to illustrate their genius, their theorems, or their social programs in apartment buildings as well as other kinds of buildings.[3]

A similar prejudice exists abroad, as Frank Worsdall notes in his introduction to *The Glasgow Tenement*:

> The word *tenementum*—Latin: 'a holding'—takes us back both to the Romans and the feudal systems of the Middle Ages. The term originally referred to land and was synonymous with a steading, or plot of ground. . . . By the nineteenth century it was used with reference only to a specific type of building, namely a domestic building of more than one story, all the houses of which are reached by a common entrance and stair. . . . Tenement these days is a dirty word and is used almost exclusively to describe a slum property. It is this attitude of mind which has been responsible for the destruction of so much of our heritage— buildings which could, with a little foresight, have been reconstructed to provide continuing homes for their occupants.[4]

Within this existing critical framework, we now turn our attention to the subject of the three-decker flat and its appearance in New Bedford, Massachusetts.

Early Forms of Multifamily Housing

In 1880, census takers discovered that New York was the first American city to amass a population of over a million people; Chicago followed in 1890. The city was now clearly counted as the dominant force in American life. With the growth of American cities came the need to find alternative means of housing the full spectrum of city dwellers than was traditionally available. To serve the elite, architects turned to European models. Though there are accounts as early as 1853 of a small apartment house being built in New York City by Thomas Kilpatrick, the first multiple dwelling to launch the age of the apartment house was the *Stuyvesant*. Built in 1869 by Richard Morris Hunt at 142 East 18th Street in New York City, the building type was referred to as a "French or Parisian flat," having been an innovation of the French in the eighteenth century. (Examples can be found in the books of Jacques-Francois Blondel, 1705–1774.) The "moral" threat of sharing a building with so many other people, and the promiscuity encouraged by several families living on the same floor (the Stuyvesant was described in its day as containing "four complete houses" per floor to de-emphasize any associations of commingling) raised objections early on from many New Yorkers. In response, these first apartment buildings were self-consciously lavish in decor to attract highly respectable tenantry. To avoid associations of promiscuity, they also stressed spatially isolated living arrangements and circulation paths. On the upper end of the economic bracket was the Dakota, an eight-story luxury apartment house built for Edward Clark, president of the Singer Sewing Machine Company. Constructed by Henry J. Hardenbergh between 1880 and 1884, it boasted such innovations as a servant's entrance, special service stairways, and service and passenger elevators. In addition to providing two stairs for every two units (to further segregate the circulation spaces), there was a central courtyard and three air shafts to provide sufficient light and air to each room.[5]

Hydraulic elevators made apartments more convenient and more popular. In Boston alone, there were over two thousand elevators in a variety of buildings by 1884, aiding the "flat fever" construction boom. As Sarah Landau has noted, distinctions among various classifications of apartments soon became evident. French flats contained apartments for several families, but each had a private toilet and a hallway within each apartment (whereas tenements of the poor did not). If there were no private kitchens, and meals were served in a communal dining room, these structures might be classified as apartment hotels. The first "apartment hotel" is said to be the Hotel Pelham (1856–57) in Boston, designed by Alfred Stone of Arthur Gilman's firm, though others trace the hotel itself as an American building type back to the 1790s in Philadelphia.[6]

Tenement houses, on the other hand, served the new wave of immigrants. A prize-winning design in a plumbing magazine for 1879 served as a prototype for the "dumbbell" tenement. The long and thin shape, with the middle circulation core indented, led to the name "dumbbell." This tenement form took advantage of New York City's standard 25-by-100-foot lot to define its proportions. Usually four or five stories tall, with four families per floor and ten tenements on a block, some dumbbell tenement blocks contained as many as four thousand people. The building type (in spite of claims to the contrary) often skirted the 1867 Tenement Housing Law requiring that no more than 65 percent of the lot be occupied by the building, and that the space at the rear of the building be left open. Every bedroom was required to have a window opening out to natural air. Instead, the dumbbell tenements used largely 90 percent of its lot space, and bedroom windows often faced befouled airshafts instead of outdoor space. Such tenement blocks also were built increasingly closer together, further reducing the benefits of natural light and air. The dumbbell apartment, however, was an improvement on the former "railroad" flat which, by moving the stairs into the center of the plan (under a light shaft), created long, narrow apartments on each side. There were four apartments on each of the six floors with rooms arranged like cars on a train (hence the name); rooms opened directly into one another compromising privacy, and providing little in the way of light and ventilation.[7] Improved tenement design did not come about in New York until the Reform Law of 1901 (known as the Tenement House Act). The New England states often relied instead on the wood-frame "three-decker" to serve its urban working population.

THE THREE-DECKER: CHARACTERISTICS OF THE IMPORTED TYPE

The three-decker's earliest documented appearance is in 1855.[8] Most scholars agree that it is a descendant of the suburban side-hall house and the urban row house plan (figs. 63–64), though one 1916 source makes an interesting claim:

> The first-three decker, as we understand it, was built in Worcester. I am not here to defend the honor of the city, but the first three-decker was a mistake made by an architect and by builders that came from Fall River where they had built two story and a half houses with mansard roofs [fig. 65]. His estimate was less than what he could build them for, and he persuaded the party who was developing this little tract that instead of building a mansard roof, he should carry the walls up vertically and put a flat roof on it, thus giving more room in the upper story. That is the birth of the three-decker as we understand it, a building of three floors, all the

floors of the same area and each floor occupied by one family, with no spare room in the attic.

> Your three story decker in Fall River and Providence is a three story and attic or two story and attic, of which there are only a few in Worcester.[9]

Whether this contention is true or not, what becomes clear from its inception is that the limited goals of such builders and architects were to maximize the rental capabilities of small development tracts by building a frame, three-family dwelling vertically. In this regard, the type is different from other multifamily forms, like double or twin

Fig. 63. The 1840 Haile Luther house, located on the corner of Elm and Second Streets in New Bedford, is a middle-class, single-family dwelling of the gable-end, side-hall type.

Fig. 64 (left). According to Warner, these "cheap wooden imitations of the town row house may have inspired the three-decker" (photo augmented by the author). Courtesy of Sam Bass Warner, Harvard University Press.

Fig. 65 (below left). An early example of a two-and-a-half-story, mansard-roof three-tenement in Fall River, Massachusetts.

houses, which were built side by side sharing a common wall.

Though it is customary to think of three-deckers as housing for the urban working class, they were designed in many sizes to fit various price ranges, building contexts, and stylistic expressions. The earliest examples in Boston that Deedee Jacobsohn has traced through *Boston Building Inspection Reports*, dated 1880 to 1903, were small, boxy buildings (fig. 66a). They were smaller than eight hundred square feet, had only four or five small rooms, and generally did not have water closets. By the end of the 1880s, the more elongated plan emerged with a long interior hallway, five or six rooms, and a water closet[10] (fig. 66b).

In terms of organizational characteristics, the three-decker as it evolved after 1880 is designed as an elongated rectangular form generally assuming the proportion of 1:2. A common size is around twenty-five feet wide and fifty feet long. Unlike the single-family occupancy of the row house, the three-decker's interior volume of space provided three identical living units stacked one on top of

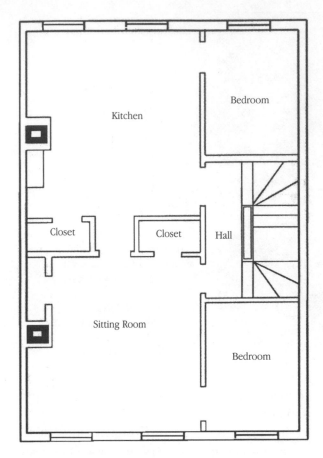

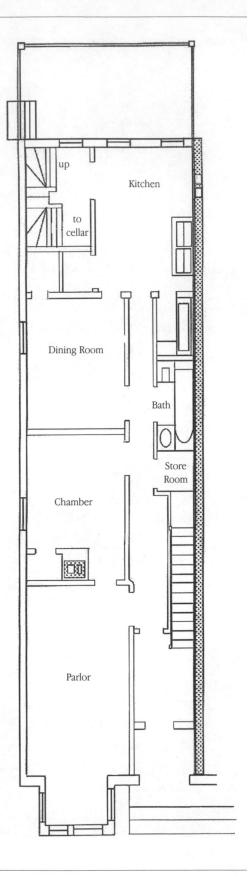

Fig. 66a (above). Second-floor plan of an early Boston three-decker (measuring 20 feet, 6 inches by 32 feet) at 36 Baxter Street. From Boston City Hall, *Boston Building Inspection Report* (1880), vol. 1: 99.

Fig. 66b (right). First-story plan of a three-family dwelling at 42 Laurel Street, Boston, Massachusetts. Note the early use of the corridor to separate principal social spaces and the awkward placement of the chamber off of the parlor (interior measurements are 21 by 45 feet, without rear piazza and front window bay). From Boston City Hall, *Boston Building Inspection Report* (1889), vol. 30, 108.

the other, providing lodging for one family per floor. The overall shape of the plan, narrow along the street frontage and deep into the lot, accommodated a linear progression of semipublic spaces leading from the front entry through a vestibule stair hall and continuing off axis into the parlor, sitting room, kitchen, and out through the rear stair hall. The bedrooms were arranged in a similar sequence opposite the path of travel, as were the pantry and water closet.

In middle- and upper-middle-class varieties, long, narrow halls leading from a reception vestibule separated the sleeping chambers from the public spaces. Such efforts not only ensured privacy, but also linked the units, by definition, to a better class of multifamily housing similar to the French flat or apartment house. These units were often referred to as two- or three-family apartments. As William T. Comstock notes in his *Two-Family and Twin Houses*, "[T]he two or three family house . . . belong to the same type. [But] under law a house is a tenement house when it affords accommodation for three or more families, while those of less accommodation rank as private houses . . . the great improvement in the planning of the tenement or the better class of tenement known as "the Apartment" dates back to late changes in the law as to light, air, and sanitation."[11] The nomenclature of a three-family "apartment," then, was not simply a gesture of pretension, but designated the dwellings as having individual toilets and hallways. Tenements, on the other hand, in addition to sharing a common entry among three or more families, often had toilets in the hall landing or not at all, while guests and renters entered from the stair hall directly into a parlor or dining room instead of down a corridor. Of even greater concern to social reformers when private hallways were eliminated from tenements by builders to save on interior space, was the fear that tenants passing through one room (namely a bedroom) to reach another would remove "the possibility of privacy and [open] up charges that tenements destroyed the morality of the home."[12] This was the principal concern regarding the plan of the railroad flats of the 1850s and 1860s.

Though generally placed on narrow urban sites to optimize land speculation, fire and health codes required that the wooden-framed and -sheathed multifamily house form be a free-standing struc-

ture.[13] As a result, the three-decker was surrounded on all sides by a perimeter of space which served as both a fire break and a defense against the spread of contagious diseases among the working population. Eventually, this self-contained, three-story housing form included three levels of porches on the front and an equal number of laundry "decks" on the rear: hence, the nickname three-decker.[14] This building type (referred to on architectural drawings in its day as a "three-family dwelling," and on New Bedford building permits simply as a "three-tenement") met the practical housing demands of the New England textile era and was readily adopted by many northeastern industrialized communities such as Worcester, Massachusetts (fig. 67), and Newark, New Jersey, where the building type appeared simultaneously during the 1850s. In South Boston, three-deckers appeared shortly after the tenement house law of 1868 as a way of avoiding the new building standards, which applied at that time only to tenements with *more than* three families.[15] Today, two- or three-decker flats are ubiquitous in "streetcar suburbs" and manufacturing centers throughout New England (map 13).

Often based on models published in trade journals as well as plans leased by local architects, these multifamily housing units were constructed largely during the last quarter of the nineteenth century and the first quarter of the twentieth century. The middle-class residents from inner suburban West Roxbury, Jamaica Plain, and Dorchester, Massachusetts, who adopted the housing type around 1880, for example, found the two- and three-deckers a useful housing alternative to the detached, single-occupancy house by optimizing construction costs on expensive suburban lots (in essence, three dwellings could be built on a lot for little more than the price of one house by stacking the living units upward).[16] Fashionable two- and three-family houses, then, were built in such burgeoning middle-class neighborhoods as Roxbury, Massachusetts, generally at a cost of about $3,600

Fig. 67. Cross-sectional stereoview of a gable-end, three-decker in Worcester, Massachusetts, taken following an 1868 gas explosion. Discovered by the author in the photographic archives of the Society for the Preservation of New England Antiquities, it is believed to be the earliest view of the type. Courtesy of the Society for the Preservation of New England Antiquities.

in 1894,[17] and often were owner-occupied (figs. 68–69). In urban industrial areas of Massachusetts, on the other hand, these multiple-family housing units were built on more restricted lots (and often with little variation) as rental lodging for the immigrant workforce that accompanied the New England manufacturing boom.

One example of the preference for this building type among the workers of an emerging manufacturing center is found in New Bedford, Massachusetts. Textile mills in New Bedford, as elsewhere in New England during this same time frame, had become synonymous with immigrant labor.[18] As a byproduct of a large transplanted unskilled labor force, the residential counterpart of the factory in this region became the multifamily dwelling.

~ New Bedford's textile development can be divided into two distinct phases. The first phase spanned from 1846 (with the founding of its first permanent textile mill, Wamsutta) to the cessation of mill incorporations by 1896 in response to the national depression (see chapters 3 and 4). The second phase began with the economic recovery in 1901 and continued up to the economic slowdown in textiles within the region that affected New Bedford by 1925. In terms of mill-construction "booms" per se, it was from 1882 to 1896 in New Bedford that the first great wave of mill incorporations occurred, accompanied by a large population surge. The corporate boarding-houses and four-tenement rental flats used by Wamsutta in the early years of the industry were rejected by the newer breed of mill owners

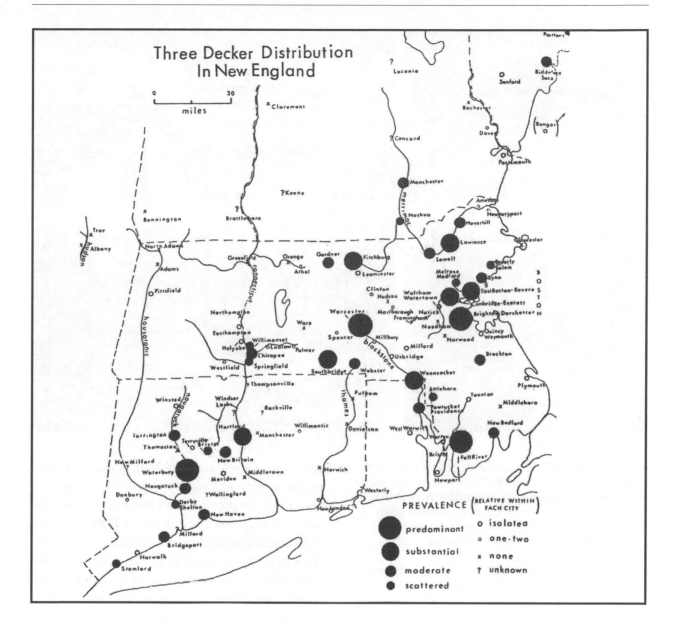

Map 13. Three-decker distribution map for New England based on Arthur Krim's 1967-70 field survey. Courtesy of Arthur Krim.

between 1882 and 1896. Instead, the shift to smaller, detached single- and double-family housing units was initially an effort among the spinning and weaving mills of the city to entice a relatively small but crucial resident population of skilled workers and overseers as competition grew within the region for an efficient and reliable workforce.[19] Since the textile mills essentially could not operate without the skilled union workers (particularly prior to the 1890s technological advances, which reduced the dependence

upon skilled workers), every effort was made by management to secure and retain top hands through the lure of good housing accommodations, benefits, and pay. The most fortunate skilled workers, such as spinners of the 1888 Howland Mills, as we have seen, were offered architect-designed, single-family residences with

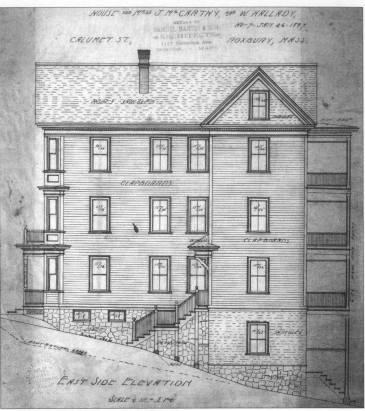

Fig. 68 (above left). Presentation drawing of a middle-class, three-family dwelling designed in 1894 by Jacob Luippold of Jamaica Plain, Massachusetts. Such drawings were offered to potential clients as representations of the architect's work. Courtesy of the Society for the Preservation of New England Antiquities.

Fig. 69 (above right). A gable-end, "Three-family dwelling" for J. McCarthy and W. Hallady designed by architect Samuel Rantin, 1897, of Roxbury, Massachusetts. Courtesy of the Society for the Preservation of New England Antiquities.

such interior appointments as marble hot water tubs and carefully landscaped surroundings.

At the same time, the weaving mills were replacing their old machinery with more efficient looms, like the 1894 Model A Draper automatic loom—one of the most important technological developments in the later phase of the cotton textile industry—and the ring spinner. These innovations reduced labor costs and utilized unskilled

operatives. They also boosted production and profits among area mills and led to a textile mill boom that, in turn, swelled the working population with unskilled labor. Between 1880 and 1910, New Bedford's population increased 300 percent. Many of the better-paid operatives in the new mills rented flats in three-deckers. This conspicuously omnipresent form of housing was produced in spurts of one, three, or seven at a time, and soon defined compressed pockets of mill workers' housing within walking distance to a factory. Though larger, more basic, and more densely populated than the detached cottages built for the industry's overseers and skilled workers (such as the two-and-one-half-story, gable-end, two-family dwellings built for the Grinnell and Acushnet Mills in 1882), the three-deckers offered markedly improved housing over Wamsutta and Potomska Mills' four-tenement blocks. In most three-tenement apartments by the late 1890s, for example, sanitary conveniences moved from the wash yards or cellars of the corporate tenement blocks to inside the living units, though this improvement until c. 1910 was limited to placement within first- and third-floor rear hallways. In addition to the sanitary improvements, the zoned living (created by the stacked flats) offered greater privacy, and the detached building forms also allowed for more abundant light and ventilation within each of the living units than did the four-tenements which shared a party wall. The new three-deckers also offered side yard and backyard semi-private living space, which summoned up references to private homeownership.

While the flat-roofed Italianate version of the three-decker made its debut in New Bedford as mill housing for the Potomska Mills during the 1870s, construction of this type of housing was done on a limited scale by the mill corporations themselves; other than the six three-tenements built by the Potomska Mills, c. 1871, and three built for the Soule Mill in 1901, there is no documentary evidence of three-deckers being built by New Bedford corporations for their workforce after 1893.[20] (The housing for Grinnell and Acushnet mill hands, though technically multifamily, were two-family dwellings.) Instead, responsibility for providing rental housing for the unskilled mill population and local service industries shifted gradually during the 1880s from mill owners to local entrepreneurs. Evidence of this shift was reflected in the popular press. The *American Architect and Building News* carried this announcement in its Building Intelligence Column under "General Notes": "New Bedford, Mass.—A Davis Ashley is to build a three-story building, 38 by 70 feet. It will be finished for two stores on the lower and four tenements on the upper floors. Caleb Hammond & Son [of New Bedford] are the architects."[21] The 1879–80 *New Bedford Directory* lists a grocery store at the 663 Purchase Street storefront, and a boot and shoe store owned by Ashley and Wilcox at the adjoining storefront on 661 Purchase Street. By the description given in the announcement, there would have been two two-story tenements above each of the stores designed as lodging rental units. Increasingly after 1880 the majority of unskilled labor turned to similar store tenements for their lodging needs (as was the European fashion), three-deckers, and other varieties of larger wood-framed four-, five-, and six-tenement housing units (fig. 70).[22]

It was during the second phase of the textile mill boom in New Bedford, however, that the three-tenement came into its widest use. The city witnessed the height of mill building between 1901 and 1910. Seventeen new corporations were founded during this time, with twelve mills incorporated in the years 1909–10 alone. It was clear to local builders that there was a pressing need to provide inexpensive housing for the flood of largely unskilled French Canadian workers, and later Portuguese and Polish operatives, who were being recruited as "common labor" to the mills. The answer was not only to revive the three-tenement, or "three-decker" as it later became known, from the previous mill boom but to optimize its rental capabilities, and to take over the building market for workers' housing from the corporations. Not surprisingly, three-decker construction roughly paralleled the growth of the mills. According to data compiled from the *New Bedford Record of Building Permits* (table 2), the most prevalent years of construction for the three-decker in New Bedford was between 1908 to 1913, of the 2,053 three-tenements constructed between 1893 to 1925, more than half (1,079) were built between 1908 and 1913. In 1910, the high point of mill construction, there were applications for 290 three-tenements: the city's all-time high.

In terms of formal characteristics, the gable-front, side-hall format popular among three-decker builders in Worcester and Roxbury, Massachusetts, had been the predominant type in New Bedford from c. 1880 to 1903 (fig. 71). Also in evidence was the flat-roof type preferred in South Boston and later in Lynn, Massachusetts (fig. 72). From the

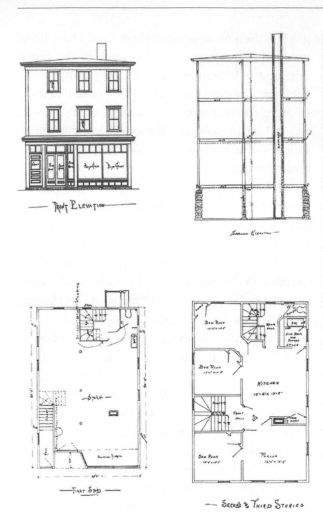

Fig. 70. Rare drawing by builder T. J. Moriarty for a store and tenements in New Bedford, 1904. Courtesy of the Building Commissioner, New Bedford City Hall.

Table 2				
NEW BEDFORD THREE-TENEMENTS, 1893–1930				
Date	Pitched	Flat	Hipped	Total
1893	6*	4	0	10
1894	14*	9	1	24
1895	24*	7	8	39
1896	43*	7	20	70
1897	28	2	32*	62
1898	3*	0	2	5
1899	6*	1	0	7
1900	5*	2	0	7
1901	14*	0	3	17
1902	40*	1	6	47
1903	85*	3	10	98
1904	21	1	40*	62
1905	19	1	62*	82
1906	19	3	42*	64
1907	14	0	76*	90
1908	5	1	136*	142
1909	4	1	259*	264
1910	0	1	289*	290
1911	3	1	148*	152
1912	8	0	114*	122
1913	8	0	101*	109
1914	2	1	95*	98
1915	6	0	71*	77
1916	3	1	88*	92
1917	0	0	1*	1
1918	0	0	0*	0
1919	0	0	1*	1
1920	0	0	0*	0
1921	0	0	2*	2
1922	1	0	4*	5
1923	3	0	15*	18
1924	0	0	10*	10
1925	1	1	14*	16
1926	0	0	0	0
1927	0	0	0	0
1928	0	0	0	0
1929	0	0	0	0
1930	0	0	0	0
Totals	**385**	**48**	**1,650**	**2,083**

NOTE: * Indicates the dominance of the three-decker roof form. (Compiled by Kingston Heath.)

recovery of the New Bedford textile economy in 1901 to its decline after 1925, the pyramidal, hipped-roof three-decker with front three-story bays increasingly became the predominant residential building type in the city (fig. 73). First appearing in the building permits in 1894, the hipped-roof form outnumbered the gable- and flat-roof varieties only once (1897) until 1904. From that year until the cessation of three-decker construction in the city by 1925 it was the preferred roof form. Most often, it measured approximately twenty-six feet wide by forty feet long—shorter

Fig. 71 (top). Side-hall, gable-end workers' houses across from the Dartmouth Mill (built 1895).

Fig. 72 (bottom). Flat-top three-deckers on upper Nelson Street (built 1892).

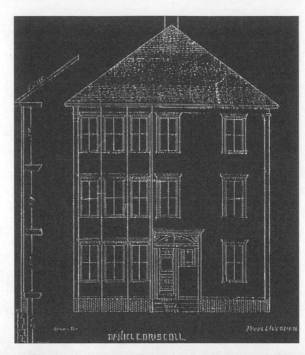

Fig. 73. This plan by the J. T. Richard Company of a hipped-roof, three-tenement for Daniel Driscoll is the earliest set of blueprints on file in the New Bedford City Hall for a three-decker. Without a front porch placed parallel to the projecting window bay, this scheme allows for four bedrooms instead of the customary three. Courtesy of the Building Commissioner, New Bedford City Hall.

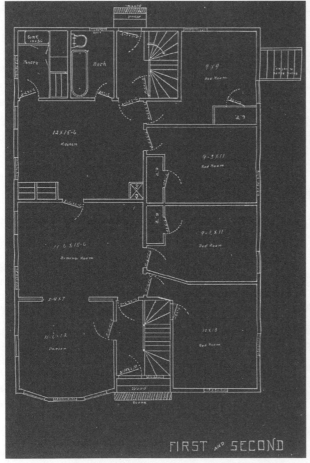

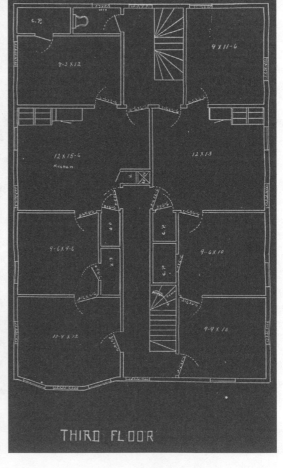

than the conventional type outside of the city. The purchase price ranged from roughly $3,000 in 1894, when the hipped-roof variation first appeared, to between $4,000 and $4,500 by 1910, when the building type had reached the height of popularity in the city. In 1890, male operatives earned $8 a week and women earned $4 a week. At these wages, the three-decker was too expensive for most unskilled mill operatives to own. Instead, this building type served as rental property for the city's working poor.

THE INFLUENCE OF MARKET FORCES ON THE BUILDING TYPE

Amidst the rapidly changing industrial context of New Bedford, where aging whaling vessels shared riverfront space with freshly minted factory buildings the speculatively built tenement house began to dominate the landscape at the far reaches of the city. Here, the three-decker was constructed largely as income property by local builders and architects for real-estate investors taking advantage of the new market trend related to the ever-expanding mill population. The practice was to build one or two three-tenements on adjacent lots for personal investment, or to build for clients who were buying housing lots in industrial areas. Some speculative builders, such as Michael E. Daley, hired "day work" and developed one complete side of Collette Street in the city's North End by building nine three-tenements during 1909 alone.[23] Others, like Nazaire Chaine, built between seven to ten units at a single time in response to new mill incorporations in the North End.[24]

Few architects' names appear in the *New Bedford Record of Building Permits* in connection with three-deckers. Architect John Williams designed three-tenements during the 1890s, then leased plans to builders in later years requesting that they be returned following the job. Similarly, architects S. C. Hunt and Caleb Hammond designed three-deckers occasionally, and the J. T. Richards

Co., an affordable-housing catalogue company out of Milwaukee, Wisconsin, provided plans locally as well. Most New Bedford architects, such as Oscar Crapo, did not design at this scale other than to produce plans and specifications for stores with tenements above, or to design double three-tenements, known locally as "six-blocks" (figs. 74–75). Instead, the three-decker was generally the realm of the speculative builder. John Sullivan, who began his career as a stone mason in the 1880s (working on such projects as the Howland Mill Village), often hired Fred Hazard to build three-tenements in both the North and South Ends of the city. Joseph Blier, Thomas Estiella, Joseph Motta, and Manuel Sylvia built in the predominately Portuguese and English South End. While Nazaire Chaine (also spelled "Nazare Chainay"), Alphonse Ricard, Joseph Langlois, and William Watling built in the Irish, English, Polish, and French Canadian neighborhoods of the North End. Here, even by the 1890s, the cultural associations tied to the three-decker flat were becoming fixed: housing for the poor, industrial, immigrant worker.

By the 1890s, the worsening working conditions in the mills, the shift to a largely unskilled labor force, and a drop in earning capacity (even among the skilled workforce) created a critical need for affordable housing among the city's textile population. The New Bedford mills, drawing upon financial arguments put forth by the powerful Arkwright Club of Boston (regarding the threat to New England by southern competition), took part in the regional wage cut on December 31, 1897. New Bedford operatives struck the following day. The *Boston Post* was one of the many papers that covered the strike. Its interview with weaver Mattin Offinger, who worked in the Acushnet Mills, points to some of the harsh economic realities facing the city's textile wage earners.[25]

Offinger emigrated as a boy with his parents from Germany to New Bedford in 1868. Meeting his future wife in the mills, they married in 1884. At that point, Mrs. Offinger earned thirty dollars a

Fig. 74. Six-block tenement built over a store: elevation and plans for client Desgardine. The plan for all three floors is a "rabbit run" apartment, sharing an interior party wall and allowing for two apartments per floor. Courtesy of the Building Commissioner, New Bedford City Hall.

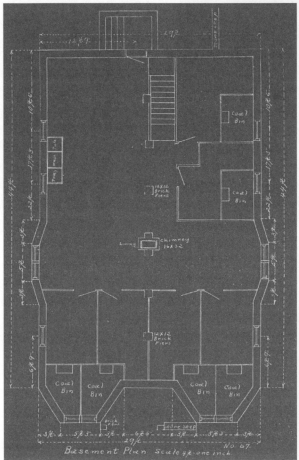

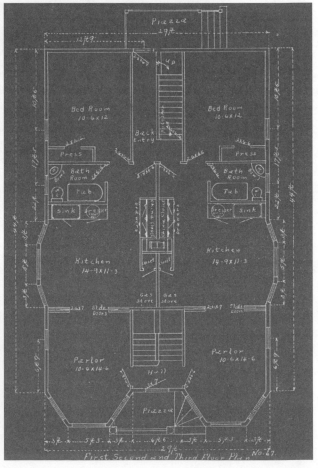

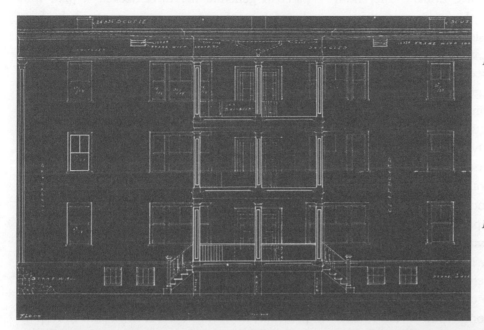

Fig. 75a (left). One of two Neo-Colonial six-blocks designed in 1924 by architect Oscar Crapo on the northwest corner of Crapo and Nelson Streets in New Bedford's South End. Courtesy of the Building Commissioner, New Bedford City Hall.

Fig. 75b (below). Elevation and plan view of the Neo-Colonial six-tenement in fig. 74a. Courtesy of the Building Commissioner, New Bedford City Hall.

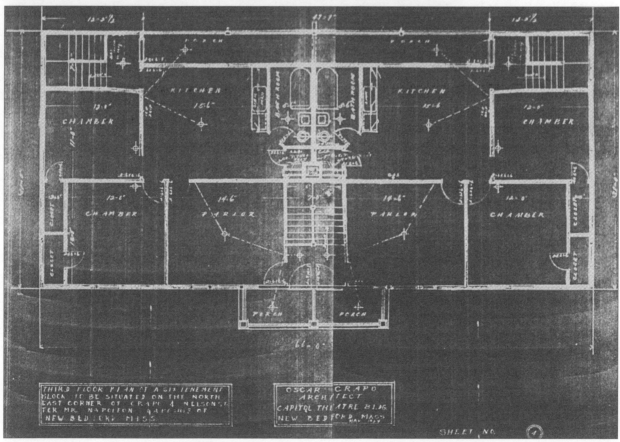

month as a weaver, as compared with her husband, who earned thirty-five dollars. They both tended four looms. With the succession of wage cuts during the depression years of the 1890s (there were 10 percent wage cuts in 1895 and 1897) and machinery speed ups to increase production, many were beginning to face lives of grinding poverty. Mr. Offinger tended eight looms at the Acushnet mills by 1897 and earned between twenty dollars and twenty-eight dollars a month. (After the birth of the first of two children, Mrs. Offinger left the mill). Not only was the workload doubled (tending eight looms instead of four) and the wages lowered (by approximately fifteen dollars a month compared with 1884 wages), a fining system introduced in the New Bedford mills after the Massachusetts Supreme Court declared the 1891 weaver's fining law unconstitutional, consistently lowered take-home pay even further through allegations of imperfect work. By the time all the wage adjustments were calculated, it was not uncommon for Offinger to make only $1.50 a week (or twelve dollars a month) for a family of four renting a three-room attic apartment for $1.50 a week. Living conditions, both inside and outside of the New Bedford mills, had clearly worsened since the paternalistic efforts undertaken just a decade earlier. Even the "improved housing" of the Grinnell and Acushnet mills was a source of derision in the papers during the strike, being depicted with sway-back roofs, only sixteen years after their construction. The new three-tenements, then, were designed to capitalize on the growing number of low-paid operatives desperate for affordable housing. For many renters, the realization that they would have to share their lodging with co-workers or in-laws to make rental payments was, by now, evident. Accordingly, three-decker builders consistently provided three- to four-bedroom apartments to meet this cooperative-rental demand (see chapter 1).

Unlike Dorchester and Fall River, where there was much experimentation in multifamily housing,

New Bedford by 1910 adopted a standard kit of parts to generate the three-decker: a plan with dimensions of approximately twenty-six by forty feet, a hipped roof, three-story bay windows, three-story front and rear porches, all for a cost of four thousand dollars. For most of the city's builders at this point, the three-decker meant architecture by the yard. As a result, by 1930 in New Bedford, two- and three-deckers made up 41.3 percent of the city's building stock, with 64.2 percent of the city's population living in dwellings designed for two or more families.[26]

Thus, during the textile heyday of 1901–25, the three-decker became the last vestige of mill housing in the city. As such, it continued to link the worker conceptually and physically to an adjacent industrial context as the earlier boardinghouses and four-tenements of Wamsutta had done. Its presence, however, represented a shift in responsibility away from the paternalistic visions of earlier mill owners for providing workers' housing to the entrepreneurial visions of the speculative builder in the late stages of the textile industry.

THE INFLUENCE OF THE BUILDER: LOCALIZATION OF THE REGIONAL TYPE IN NEW BEDFORD

The three-decker, as a Victorian-era solution for affordable workers' housing in New England, on occasion provided commodious, well-appointed living quarters for the better-paid working population of the city (fig. 76). More often, the building type was reduced to a simple commodity, and consequently the worker's needs were calculated by the builder within the framework of market demands. The three-decker (it is clear from reviewing the building plans) was a program-driven type in New Bedford. It offered in pitched, hipped- or flat-roof varieties a generic scheme of parlor, dining room, and kitchen in a linear arrangement with three to four bedrooms, a sink room, and a

water closet off to the side. Therefore, the city's more generalized nomenclature of "three-tenement" was appropriate for all three varieties, since by definition in New Bedford's city ordinance a "tenement" was any structure that provided lodging for three or more families, allowed for meals to be prepared on the premises, and had shared common entries. Also popular was a three- or four-room plan (called a "rabbit run" apartment) offering the requisite kitchen and parlor with one or two bedrooms; it was not uncommon, however, during the population booms for the parlor to be rented to boarders, leaving the kitchen as the sole "public" living space within the rental unit (fig. 74).

Many of the tenements prior to c. 1910 either had no water closets or they were located in the rear hallway or the cellar. The category for water closets did not even appear in the *New Bedford Record of Building Permits* until 1896, underlining how distinctly different the housing for Howland Mill's skilled operatives was: each single-family dwelling had hot water and a built-in bathtub. Access was gained through the front and rear stair halls of the three-deckers by piazzas

(partially enclosed porches), which began to appear regularly in New Bedford as renovations onto existing gable-ended, three-tenements during the 1890s. By the first decade of the twentieth century, the front piazza and rear laundry decks became standard features in New Bedford, in combination with the multi-story bay window, which allowed for a better climate response and additional recreational and work space for each apartment unit.

Before the general acceptance of the hipped-roof three-decker in New Bedford, there were subtle changes taking place in the design of the city's other forms of multifamily housing. The 1883 city building ordinance, restricting tenement construction in New Bedford to three stories, led to several resourceful measures for converting attic space into profitable rental property as the mill population swelled in response to its initial textile industry boom. There first appeared a cross-gabled roof massing on the gable-end, side-hall form. This design strategy gave way by 1894 to long shed-roof dormers (referred to as "Portuguese dormers" in the building permits because of their popularity

Fig. 77. A two-story three-tenement (with interior dimensions of 26 by 44 feet), with "Portuguese dormers" measuring 22 feet long and 8 feet high. This three-tenement is located in the South End mill district and was built in 1895 by Stephen Sylvia for Joseph Dias.

among this new group of immigrant builders) placed on both sides of the gable (fig. 77).[27] By changing the roof configuration in this manner, a builder could offer three rental units in a two-story tenement for about one thousand dollars less than the construction cost of a flat-roofed, three story three-tenement. The attic apartments, because of their diminished space due to the pitched roof, tended to be limited to two bedrooms instead of the customary three of the lower units, however. Finally, in 1894 the high, pyramidal hip roof was grafted onto the earlier and once more popular flat- and pitched-roof three-tenement floor plan to produce the characteristic New Bedford roof variation (fig. 78).[28]

According to city ordinance, wall elevations were not to exceed twenty-two feet in height from the sills to the plate in these combination-frame structures, but the maximum roof height could reach an additional fourteen feet. While low hipped-roof three-deckers were popular in Fall River by 1880, this high, pyramidal hipped-roof form effectively allowed for another floor of inhabitable space within local building codes and steadily gained in popularity. By 1897, this roof form was the most popular among three-tenement builders in the city. But, with the general slow-down in the textile economy of the city by 1898, the change in roof form did not prevail. As an indication of the critical point of renewed interest, in 1901 builder John Sullivan shifted from his earlier preference for pitched-roof multifamily housing and constructed three hipped-roof three-tenements in a single construction job for the Soule Mills. By 1904, the hipped-roof form was the preferred three-tenement type once again (refer to table 2). Builders maximized tenement space to such an extent that, by 1909, the fact that a new three-tenement contained "no attic rooms" was listed as an *exceptional* circumstance in the general notes of the city's building permits. (As Michael Daley's building ledger indicates, it cost only eighty-five dollars for attic rooms, and this was considered as part of his standard plan to the client.) These same building permits and blueprints on file indicate that builders rehabbed earlier Greek Revival mansions into tenement houses, added upper floors to one-story cottages, and even raised existing three-deckers in order to place commercial property below in response to the construction of new mills in the area (fig. 79).[29] Judging from the code restrictions precluding lodging space in cellars at this time, every usable space had rental potential in

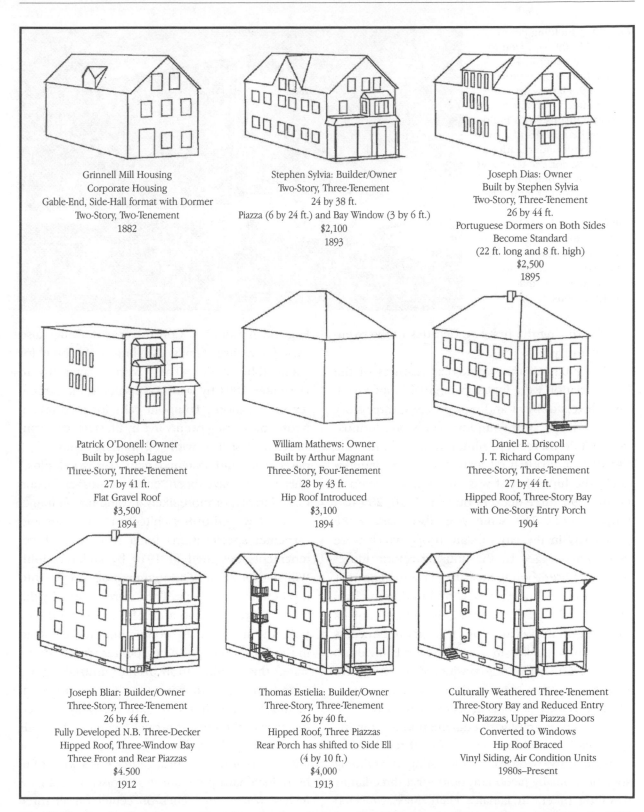

Fig. 78. The New Bedford three-tenement: formal and typological evolution. Drawing by Kingston Heath and Ed Portis, 1997.

Fig. 79. A building permit (No. 752-09) was filed for this tenement block by Alice Riding on September 8, 1909. Plans were submitted by architect John Williams for "a building to be raised and a store to be built underneath on the N. W. cor. Mc Gurk and Ruth." A second building was raised in order to place a store underneath for Mrs. Riding, which was located at 133 Ruth Street. By 1909, this new "commercial" site was surrounded by no fewer than five mill corporations.

the city during the first two decades of the twentieth century.

By 1904, all the typological features of the local variation were intact: pyramidal hipped roof, three levels of front and rear porches, three-story bay windows, and a random fieldstone foundation. While there were minor variations, like the use of a side porch ell instead of a rear laundry deck, the hipped roof was an imbedded feature. Of the 290 three-deckers built in 1910, 289 had hipped roofs. The same year also marked the popularity in the city of slate roofs, which were being encouraged by the housing reform movement as a fireproofing measure. This material was considered as an extra cost by builders such as Michael Daley, who charged one hundred dollars for the option. Because of the economic success of the three-decker in general, even individuals who previously had not considered themselves to be builders often converted to this trade because of the certainty of good investment returns.[30]

Written or graphic documentation for framing specifications seldom exists for three-deckers. Outside New Bedford, a full listing of building specifications by Jacob Luippold for a three-family dwelling (likely in Jamaica Plain, Massachusetts) survives at the Society for the Preservation of New England Antiquities. Construction drawings also exist for a three-family dwelling to be built for client John Zeller. They were drawn up in December 1891 by Jacob Luippold. In the carpenter specifications, Luippold calls for a "dwelling house" measuring twenty-five by fifty feet to be constructed of spruce with "all framing lumber . . . raised true and fastened with hardwood pins." This would have been either a post-and-beam braced frame, or more likely a combination frame.

In New Bedford, architectural drawings and carpenter specifications for a store with three-tenements designed in 1910 by architect John Williams for Zephir Quinten provide insights into local framing methods. They were located by the author in the storage attic of New Bedford City Hall. The structure was to be built on Nash Road in the North End. As the carpenter specifications state, this combination frame utilized "good sound spruce" and hard pine for its structural members—"all framed, pinned, and spiked together in the most thorough manner." Two sills (one to carry the walls and one to carry the floor joists) were 4 by 4 inches; center posts were of 6-by-10-inch hard pine; and floor joists were 2 by 8 inches, placed 16 inches on center on all three upper floors. The 4-by-6-inch corner posts ran

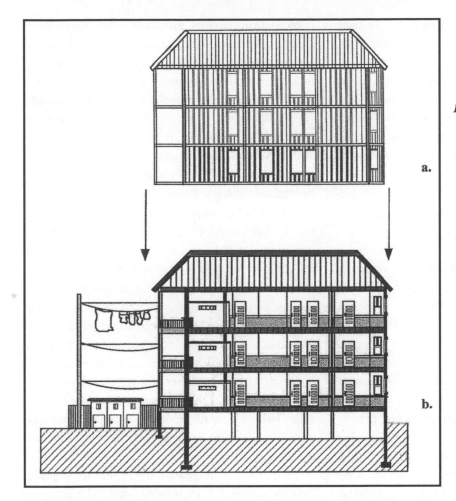

Fig. 80. Sectional Views: 1912 Three-Tenement. The conjectural structural section in a. is based on the carpenter specifications list submitted in 1910 by New Bedford architect John Williams to the City Building Permit Office. This combination frame utilized "good sound spruce" and hard pine for its structural members. The interior depicted in b. of a 1912 New Bedford three-tenement offered three identical living units stacked on top of the other, technically providing lodging for one family per floor. This sectional view shows the door entry leading into the parlor (to the far right), and the three bedroom spaces to the left, followed by the rear stair hall, and, finally, the rear laundry deck (to the far left). Drawing by Kingston Heath, Ed Portis, and Matt Jenkins.

uninterrupted through all three stories. End girts were 6-by-8-inch hard pine, while side girts measured 4 by 5 inches. The upper-story studs were 2 by 4 inches, placed 16 inches on center. Unlike the c. 1891 frame designed by Jacob Luippold above, there was no mention of corner bracing. The plates were 4 by 4 inch, made up of two 2-by-4 pieces spiked together and spiked to the top of the studding. Finally, the rafters were 2 by 6 inches, 20 inches on center, with the collar beams notched to each common rafter about 6 feet, 6 inches from the floor. Hollow brick infill was placed between the first-floor studding and around the front and rear stairways for fire protection. Worth noting is the persistence of the New England timber framing tradition, such as the "pinning" and "mortising" of the framing members. However, the plate was not made up of full 4-by-4 beams, but of two 2-by-4s spiked together, indicating a trend toward economizing on craft-intensive processes, such as hand-notching structural members, and the desire to use smaller gauge timbers to reduce costs (fig. 80).

In the twenty-five years following the 1901 economic recovery, most of the city's industrial landscape linked to textiles had been constructed. In the process, New Bedford emerged after World War I as the nation's leader in overall cotton textile production. Fed by the forces of large-scale European immigration (which provided a steady supply of affordable labor) and Corliss steam power (made more cost-effective by New Bedford's favorable location at the mouth of the Atlantic for inexpensive shipments of coal), the social and economic realities of industrial urbanism took hold. As New Bedford emerged as a smokestack city dedicated almost exclusively to textile production, the tenement builders followed—and sometimes anticipated—the construction of a new mill (refer to fig. 71).[31] Recognized as a vital component in this symbiotic economic relationship, the three-decker became the embodiment of New Bedford's industrial achievement—and subsequently its failure.

THE INFLUENCE OF POPULAR TASTE: THE BUILDER'S AESTHETIC INTENT

Though large in scale, the three-deckers retained the general character of a traditional, free-standing, single-family dwelling in the selection of design features, cladding material, and general massing. Inasmuch as the builders reflected the fashions set in upper-middle-class neighborhoods, they were similar to other middle-class alternatives to multifamily dwellings of the day. In addition, builders provided the requisite social and practical necessities of a late Victorian household. Three-deckers maintained the stylistic disposition of the current fashion in detailing and color; carried (by 1903 in New Bedford) a full complement of front and rear porches; the formal entry or "reception vestibule" led to a front parlor (separated from the dining room by sliding pocket doors, French doors, or curtain-like *portieres*); the dining/ kitchen area generally came equipped with built-in china cabinets with linen drawers below; building permits reveal that by 1913, gas cookstoves began to replace coal ranges in the new three-decker building plans, while basement boilers replaced coal-fired parlor stoves in some apartments; and, after 1910, most units were supplied with electric lights, cold running water, and indoor plumbing.

In New Bedford, this three- to four-bedroom, narrow, and deep housing format responded to the predictable urban density of a booming manufacturing center. It was the product of fast, cheap construction, narrow lots, and sewer connection charges based on street frontage. As one period observer put it, "[O]ne cellar, one water and gas main, [and] one plumbing shaft for three families."[32] At the same time, the housing type initially was designed to be an affordable, attractive alternative to the large-scale, repetitive boardinghouses and tenement blocks that the earliest corporations, Wamsutta and Potomska, had offered their operatives up until the 1890s. Hence, the primary rental market that the land developer and speculative builder needed to address was for married operatives with large families. Accordingly, these multifamily housing units were intended to read more like well-appointed, single- family houses conducive to social decorum, and more in keeping with the "ideal" of an independent single-family house not yet attainable by the renter. To make these large rental units seem more inviting as domestic space, builder Michael Daley provided such options as skylights in attic apartments, slate sinks (which cost fifty dollars), China closets and pantry (which cost forty dollars), and chair rails in the dining space.

William T. Comstock's 1908 builder's guide, *Two-Family and Twin Houses*, stated the compromise entailed for the speculative builder and the prospective client of such housing:

> The division by floors may not be the ideal dwelling, but it approaches it, and where the proposition is one of investment, gives much better opportunity for reasonable returns than the single house. While we recognize in the independent house, with its well cared-for grounds, whether it be a cottage or mansion, the more satisfactory American home, yet the conditions of life in our cities and towns are such that the cost of land is too great to afford such dwellings for all and the next step in that direction is the well-planned two-family house.[33]

The role these builder's guides often played was to establish the benefits of the new building type to the prospective buyer, and to offer recommendations for improvements on the type through leading examples by architects who addressed the major design constraints that the builder would face—from the need for efficient planning strategies to the desire for the individual zoning of energy systems. The examples shown, however, are often misleading as representations of the average type as built for the general population. What are displayed are high-end versions (often on suburban subdivision lots), exhibiting fashionable handbook ideals on the exterior in the form of mass-produced millwork, decorative shingle patterns, and stained glass. Similarly, the interior amenities include such accouterments as dumbwaiters, cellar to attic lifts for moving day, and talking tubes for receiving guests. In the hands of the builder-developer or small contractor of an industrial neighborhood, the "bottom line" became the norm. Stated concerns for amenities such as fancy piazzas, isolated entries, private stairwells, and individual systems for privacy, safety, and comfort were often solved in less effective ways when one addressed the economic realities of an exponentially expanding industrial environment that offered a rental market with limited resources.

THE INFLUENCE OF CULTURAL VALUES: THE SYMBOLIC IMPORT OF THE PIAZZA

As John E. Crowley notes, "[T]he porch/verandah—since the middle of the eighteenth century—[became] one of the strongest and most evocative images of comfort in North America."[34] He argues that the porch became an element of domestic architecture in a worldwide British culture during the eighteenth century and signified membership in a culture that gave priority to consumption in the domestic environment. Providing a fashionable means for comfortable heating and lighting or, conversely, cooling and shading was part of this new social membership.

But terminology became a problem. The Latin root of *porch* and *portico* emphasized "entering" the house, not remaining outside; further, porches historically implied spaces that were enclosed on all sides, and, while porticoes were open, the social use of such spaces were secondary to their monumental associations with classical architecture. "Piazza," in contrast, was a term earlier associated with a public space that was compositionally defined on all sides by arcaded buildings in Italian towns, but emerged in the eighteenth century as a partially enclosed domestic space. The word entered generic English usage in connection with the housefront arcades that Inigo Jones designed in the 1630s for two sides of Covent Garden.[35] Crowley credits John Plaw's *Sketches for Country Houses, Villas and Rural Dwellings* (1800) with introducing the term to an architectural audience.

I have attempted to assess the use of the term "piazza" as it was used on architectural drawings, builder's guides, and building ledgers during the late nineteenth and early twentieth centuries in connection with three-deckers. Jacob Luippold maintained an office at 89 Mozart Street in Jamaica Plain, Massachusetts, and prepared what amounted to an informal pattern book of sample designs, which he used to build three-deckers himself or leased to builders (stating on the drawings "plans to be returned to the architect at the completion of the job"). Many of the elevations, beginning in 1891, are color washes of neocolonial "dwelling houses of three-apartments," which attempted to capture Federal Period detailing in the Bulfinch manner (refer to fig. 68). Such work was clearly for middle-class clients, as evidenced by the more expansive floor plan, which often included a recessed entry, vestibule, hall (connected to a corridor), parlor, back parlor, dining room, kitchen, pantry, chamber, bathroom, back hall, and clothes dryer (fig. 81a). The

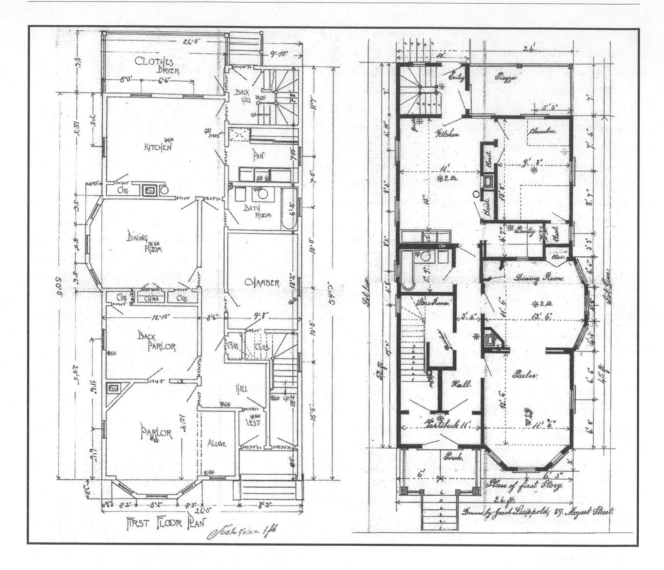

Fig. 81. Two first floor plans by Jacob Luippold for three-family dwellings; a. refers to the rear screened laundry porch area as a "clothes dryer," while b. refers to a front "porch" and rear "piazza." Courtesy of the Society for the Preservation of New England Antiquities.

notation on the plans for a "clothes dryer" is actually a twenty-six-foot-by-eight-foot-six-inch, semi-enclosed back porch or piazza off the back hall. On another plan (fig. 81b) the term "porch" implies a formal entry at the front of the three-family apartment, while the rear "piazza" was a functional entry where, as in the previous scheme, laundry could be hung.

During this era, more fashionable townhouses, such as the 1859 Catherine Hammond Gibson house (built in Boston's Back Bay at 137 Beacon Street), had wooden drying closets located in the cellar near the furnace to aid in doing the laundry service. Such functional facilities were, therefore, kept out of public view, allowing the rear alleyway to be used mostly for deliveries. This was in contrast to immigrant, working-class neighborhoods, where wash was hung unceremoniously over unpaved laundry yards from rear windows and porches connected to a laundry pole.

As multifamily units had increased laundry demands, this issue of the laundry room had to be

Fig. 82. Front elevations for two three-family dwellings located on Beech Street in Roslindale, Massachusetts. They were designed in November 1909 as speculative housing for Carl Scheorer by Jacob Luippold. Note the "clothes yard: placed on the roofs." Courtesy of the Society for the Preservation of New England Antiquities.

addressed in as inconspicuous a manner as possible within the social mores of Victorian society. A three-family dwelling built at North 58th and Alphonsus Street in Roxbury, Massachusetts, for client Henry Blitzer of Boston was begun on March 20, 1894. Fuchs and Wangler were the builders, and Jacob Luippold was the architect. While the front entry and vestibule doors maintained their formal character, the latter being "grained in oil to imitate oak and [had] a coat of coach varnish," the "clothes yard" was placed on the roof within an eighteen-by-thirty-foot area with a three-foot-high fence around it (fig. 82).

It would seem by these examples of middle-class three-decker plans that the porch implied an entry of higher social standing than the rear piazza; yet, in New Bedford three-deckers in working-class neighborhoods—where the laundry decks at the rear were clearly functional appendages—builder Michael Daley refers to both "front and back piazzas" in his account books. The strict distinction in terminology differentiating a porch as a formal entry as opposed to a rear piazza as a laundry deck, therefore, was not consistently applied during the building era of the three-decker. "Piazza" and "porch" can be thought of as interchangeable terms. The spaces themselves, however, did maintain different social connotations throughout, and both the front and rear porches eventually became necessities in New Bedford but for distinctly different reasons and with distinctly different aesthetic treatments.

It is fair to say that the front porch was viewed in elite circles consistently as a place for comfort, sociability, and public performance. Its associations, too, are clearly tied to the more elite tradition of the single-family residence. Yet, even the earliest documented three-deckers in New Bedford (the c. 1871–76 Potomska housing) had three levels of porches on the front of its workers' tenement.

Given the obvious economic constraints imposed on the building type, why would the client or speculative builder be willing to absorb the added expense of essentially three formal entries for a building to be placed amidst an industrial environment? In this regard, the porch or piazza was as much emblematic as it was functional for both the builder and the renter. Within the cultural context of the Victorian era, the stacked porches on the new three-decker flats signaled private ownership, civility, and good taste to the mill-operative family that could often only dream of owning a home.

From the speculative builder's point of view, the front porches, built selectively on the earliest three-deckers, were there in many instances merely as a social and stylistic contrivance of the day. Yet, as time went on and three-deckers became ubiquitous in New Bedford (as elsewhere in New England), the feature of the front porch began to function on many other levels. First, the porch laid claim visually to a residential space in a manner more personal than the stoop-and-entry hood of the larger working-class barracks, which in its physical context implied "mass" housing. Next, it allowed for the visual separation of each floor into private units, thus offering a touch of individuality amidst such overwhelming uniformity. Similarly, the design element signaled the builder's desire for complete physical "isolation" of families as a mitigating factor to sell the notion of compressed, vertically stacked living units to the renter—and eventually to social reformers, who saw the residents of these living units as being stacked "like drawers in a bureau,"[36] creating the potential for immorality. The editor's note to William T. Comstock's 1908 *Two-Family and Twin Houses*, which, despite the title, included a discussion of three-family units as well, is careful to point out Comstock's concern for "complete isolation" in multifamily dwellings: "As will be seen by a review of these designs, the planning has called forth much ingenuity to cover at the same time, the requirements of limited lot areas, ample accommodations and as complete isolation of families as possible." Further, the front porch served as a compositional device that stressed the horizontal lines of the unit to offset the inordinate vertical expression of the larger dwellings, allowing the three-deckers to blend into the area's lower-scale cottages and thereby preserving real estate values—one of the charges often leveled against the form (fig. 83).

With this allusion to private ownership firmly in place, the porch took on additional overtones of public performance for its users. The porch was very much an entrenched design feature for single-family residences in mid- to late Victorian culture, and it not only represented healthy communion with nature but also respectable domesticity in American society, as expressed in the prescriptive pattern books of the day, whether they were written by A. J. Downing or Catherine Beecher.

Downing, for example, extolled the virtues of both beauty and possession: "With the perception of proportion, symmetry, order and beauty, awakens the desire for possession, and with them comes that refinement of manners which distinguishes a civilized from a coarse and brutal people."[37] Beyond the visual association of the front porch with private ownership, the prominence of this feature in the later designs of the three-decker reflects as well a culture dominated by middle-class values, social convention, and

"appearances."[38] Consequently, the placement of the formal entry in connection with the "front" parlor was more an act of social propriety than of programmatic response tied to utility.

Interestingly, the front porches on the three-decker gained in popularity just as the three-decker became most suspect among social reformers. Perhaps it was a conscious effort on the part of speculative builders to attempt to ameliorate on the outside of the tenements the overcrowded living conditions within. For it is not until 1902 that the general interest in this design feature even warrants a category in the New Bedford building permits. The following year, the first hipped-roof three-tenement with three porches is recorded. (With the building up of the city's industries, New Bedford reached its maximum rate of population growth in 1905.) By 1907, there are consistent entries for new three-decker builds that incorporated three stories of

Fig. 83. Street view of 90 Nelson showing a 1912 three-family dwelling, flanked by a 1904 two-family dwelling, and a 1911 five-family dwelling. Often, the very use of the front porch as a design feature was designed to mitigate the inordinate scale of these tenement blocks, allowing them to blend into the area's lower-scale cottages. Unlike single-family residences, where the larger size of the house and lot implied greater prestige, larger multifamily dwellings reflected lower social standing.

piazzas. This new building trend brought a surge of piazza additions onto existing three-deckers at a cost of three hundred dollars for all three floors.

By 1907, there appeared to be a cultural consensus in New Bedford that required the inclusion of the piazza on this otherwise highly normative building form. Was the inclusion of this design feature merely a popular cultural urge that New Bedford builders were responding to as a means of attracting renters? Certainly, area

Fig. 84. By 1907, many piazzas in New Bedford were built as additions onto existing multifamily dwellings; here, they are used during the 1928 New Bedford labor strike. Courtesy of UPI/Bettmann and Spinner Publications.

builders were enjoying good returns on invest-ment real estate because of the textile boom and could well afford to accommodate such shifts in consumer tastes. But, if anything, there was a shortage of housing between 1907 and 1910 because of new mill starts, and such inducements were unnecessary on the part of the builder. There must be another explanation. Not surpris-ingly, it was at this very moment that the "menace" of the three-decker was being stressed by housing reformers, who would eventually push for their elimination. In 1907, the Massachusetts Civic League established a Committee on Housing that would eventually draft legislation to ban the con-struction of three-deckers. By 1912, Massachu-setts passed the Tenement Act for Towns, followed in 1913 by the Tenement House Act for Cities, which included restrictions on three-deckers designed to limit their construction. While orga-nizations such as the Massachusetts Civic League attempted to regulate three-tenement construc-tion, the Massachusetts Homestead Commission, formed in 1909, was pushing for low-interest loans and liberal state aid to fund single- and two-family houses for workmen in the suburbs as a means of providing an affordable alternative to the three-decker. The pressure was on three-tenement builders to change the image of these workers' dwellings.[39]

As John Kasson has noted, embedded in the urban consciousness of nineteenth-century life was a clear system of codes for appropriate behavior.[40] What today may appear to be a needless costume drama of Victorian conduct was at the time a dogmatic concern for social ceremonies and public rituals that were to take place in certain areas. These expectations inevitably extended into architectural decision making. Essentially, the structural and spatial accommodation of the formal entry and parlor were components of appropriate ritualistic response tied to "calling" during the Victorian era that produced such additional contrivances as hall stands and calling cards at the upper end of the economic bracket.[41] In Jacob Luippold's middle-class three-family apartments, such decorum was augmented in 1894 by electric door bells and talking tubes located outside the entry vestibule.

Seen in this context, the requisite paring of the front porch and the parlor bay window in moderately priced or low-cost housing was an attempt on the part of the builder-developer to transform social behavior through planning or to simply create the collective delusion to an ever-vigilant audience of reformers that such behavior already existed. The notion being offered was that "proper" design engendered proper human values. If the renters could be enticed to use the front porch, public surveillance—offered by the vantage point of adjacent piazzas—ensured appropriate behavior in these working-class enclaves by allowing neighbors to observe one another's conduct in a public arena (fig. 84).

But the three-decker endured harsh public criticism. Prescott Hall, in his 1916 address to the National Conference on Housing Problems in America, for example, stated his concerns that "vertical housing" allowed delinquent children to escape a mother's observation: "The late Judge Baker of the Boston Juvenile Court, was of the opinion that vertical housing is responsible for much of the apparent increase in juvenile delinquency; and for the very simple reason that the moment a child goes outside the door of a flat, it is on someone else's property. With a single cottage,

there is at least some yard where a child can play on his own land, and is more or less under the mother's observation. With the three-decker, occupying as it frequently does almost the entire area of the lot, the only playground is the street, and the opportunity to escape from control is increased."[42] The addition of the piazza on such "vertical housing" afforded parents the opportunity to monitor the actions of their children on the street.

Even though the renters seldom used these spaces as prescribed, the piazza or front porch was viewed by builders as a cultural necessity nonetheless. Conversely, the back porch was a practical necessity—begrudged by social reformers of the time, because of the corruptive human behavior that they assumed lurked in the darkness out of view of public surveillance. Because of such preconceptions of spatial usage (some associations, no doubt, were linked to conditions in English tenements during the early stages of the industrial revolution), there were continual efforts to change the behavior patterns of the industrial worker. Often in response to large families and spatial limitations of the tenements, these urban dwellers, for example, used the front entry for storage instead of for greeting guests. The cellar storage space, after all, was damp, and the attic was hot and somewhat inaccessible for large items. The back laundry decks, on the other hand, were in constant use for daily wash. Eventually, the rear decks were replaced by side-porch ells, which would be in clear view of the streetside onlooker, requiring laundry to be hung out rear kitchen windows on lines connected to laundry poles.

Thus, as an extension of the late Victorian value structure, the front porch became a calculated gesture of refinement—offered almost in the form of a "false front," like its commercial counterpart—implicitly prescribing social behavior for the New England immigrant industrial worker. Decorative features, such as neocolonial turned balusters, summoned references of pre-industrial

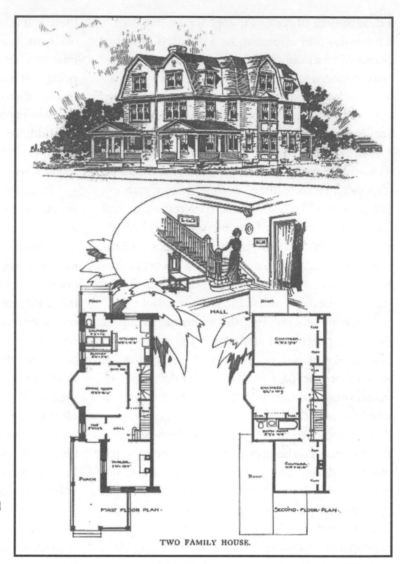

TWO FAMILY HOUSE.

Fig. 85. A two-family "twin" house by architect C. E. Schermerhorn illustrating the formal use of the entrance hall placed adjacent to the parlor. From William Comstock, *Two-Family and Twin Houses* (1908).

American domesticity and offered images of social stability, family harmony, and refinement.

Also projected onto the three-decker rental flats of the socially, economically, and politically marginalized renters of New Bedford during the first two decades of the twentieth century were notions of social success, privilege, gentility, private ownership, and Americanization, which the builder assumed his clientele demanded as a byproduct of national popular taste and dominant standards of public behavior.[43]

Many of the plans and elevations for the three-deckers were available from regional architects through the popular press and from local architects through leased plans that captured the normative cultural urges of the day. In addition, the pattern books—etiquette books in their own right—prescribed social values, either explicitly or implicitly, by playing upon the major image concerns of the day (fig. 85).[44]

While the front porch was a symbolic expression of ownership offered by the builder/designer, the ability to stress the *individuality* of the stacked living units was an act of independence claimed by the users. A common user accommodation took the form of landlords and long-term tenants painting their floor levels different colors. Such differentiation of living space was expressed originally by the change in color and texture offered by clapboards and shingles as was common in Queen Anne styling. Later, commercial siding predominated from composition shingles (particularly the 1920s), asbestos tile shingles (1930s–50s), and most recently aluminum and vinyl siding (see chapter 6). Even without such texture changes and color striations, these flats were clearly conceptualized by their users as single-story expressions of "home," in spite of the practical awareness that the renters occupied but one floor of the vertically stacked apartments.[45]

The Influence of Visual Order: Formal Characteristics of the Type within the Streetscape

Architecturally, the three-decker was often relegated to little more than an "architectural blank." Conceived in response to market demands as they related to the floor plan, rather than in response to any one stylistic idiom, aesthetic concerns in the New Bedford type are often considered parenthetically by its designer, except to the degree necessary to sell the product—though there are noticeable exceptions. The principal aesthetic expression of the builder's design was generally limited to the stylistic appliqué of the piazza in response to changing fashion. In fact, it would be fair to say that the essence of urbanity related to this building type was tied almost *exclusively* to the piazza (fig. 86).

On occasion, minor cornice, exterior window, and door moldings would extend the stylistic unity beyond the piazza, but generally such features were kept to a minimum. Additionally, the formal statement of the roof type, or the modulation of the façade treatment by projecting three-story window bays, vaguely reinforced the prevailing stylistic gestures of the day. To be sure,

such buildings in New Bedford were largely, but not exclusively, the dominion of the speculative builder. The emphasis on the porch as the principal decorative feature by the turn of the century was warranted not only by the desire to accommodate social and stylistic conventions, but also by the practical awareness that these narrow, vertical units were often so tightly compressed within their streetscapes that few would see a full view of anything *other* than the façade.

In this regard, it is worth noting that the three-decker was seldom intended to stand as an isolated figure within the mill neighborhood setting. Instead, the three-decker was often placed on restricted city lots, where it was difficult to secure ample outdoor living space beyond the four to eight feet required by local ordinances (fig. 87).[46] Even when the living units were built close together, the building type in its day (as a turn-of-the-century alternative to the urban mass-housing phenomenon) provided much more light, air, and room than, for example, the brick tenement houses found in the older sections of Boston and New Haven, which typically had only three or four interior rooms.[47] And, in contrast to the tenement housing conditions in England and Scotland during this time period, the three-deckers appear downright tame as an urban residential form for industrial workers.[48] Such tenements housed the poorer wage earners, who (unless they sublet bedroom spaces to family members or co-workers) could not have afforded the rent on an apartment floor in a three-decker. A 1911 source describing housing conditions in typical American cities, compared the different opportunities for New Haven, Connecticut, wage earners: "For skilled workers and others who can pay from fifteen to twenty-five dollars a month there seems to be a fair and increasing provision, but of a kind greatly to be deplored in a small city. The building of two- and three-family houses for this class has not ceased, but is far exceeded by the building of large tenements for six to eighteen families." This latter

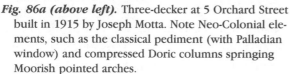

Fig. 86a (above left). Three-decker at 5 Orchard Street built in 1915 by Joseph Motta. Note Neo-Colonial elements, such as the classical pediment (with Palladian window) and compressed Doric columns springing Moorish pointed arches.

Fig. 86b (above right). Three-decker near the former Rotch Mill built during the teens with an elaborate piazza. As in the previous example, the gable treatment of the piazza disguises the hipped roof behind, serving literally as a "false front."

group paid between seven to fifteen dollars for rent, but had to contend with "privies in the dooryards" or "water closets in the cellars" and were "crowded as close as the present law permits against similar tenements or stores."[49]

In one respect, the three-decker shared a basic similarity with the tenements of industrial centers at home and abroad; the power of its presence was strengthened generally through *repetition* down long street vistas. The modular unit of the three-decker flat built up—by weave and cross-weave—the predetermined pattern of an interwoven fabric in much the same manner as did the even cadence of the power loom by which the mill operatives made their living (fig. 88). Such predictable patterns of living and visual order were very much in keeping with the institutional life of the mill itself, where individualism was suppressed in lieu of the "collective achievement" of the corporation. Orderliness, regimentation, and repetition thus were extended as governing principles from within the mill to the wider precincts of mill neighborhood (fig. 89).

Apart from the inevitable omnipresence of the housing type within its mill setting, variety (with regard to roof type, porch detail, scale, plan, style, and site orientation) was ensured initially by the fact that most of these housing units were developed

Fig. 87 (left). The New Bedford city ordinance required a minimum of eight feet between tenements. This side-yard condition of parallel sidewalks to rear entries did not allow for its later appropriation as a side-yard parking space. Note the unpaved foreground space to the right; paving the front walkways was the owner's responsibility.

Fig. 88 (below). The measured cadence of three-decker after three-decker formed wooden canyons of housing in the mill districts. This row of vertical housing is opposite the former Rotch Mill.

one or two lots at a time by local investors, who were taking advantage of the textile mill boom and the predictable need for rental housing.[50] Different design strategies were dictated often by sheer necessity, as builders were forced to respond to such design constraints as topographic changes and issues of orientation in an attempt to generate a profit out of even the least desirable building lots (fig. 90).[51] The regularized street grid superimposed on New Bedford's irregular topography

Fig. 89. Orderliness, regimentation, and repetition were extended as governing principles from within the mill to the wider precincts of the mill neighborhood. Photograph by Lewis W. Hine, Courtesy of the Library of Congress.

prevented the type of visual monotony which is more apt to take place on level sites, and is indicative of the lengths to which developers would go to optimize precious urban space (fig. 91).

Serving a broad cross-cultural user group, the "core structure" of the building type could be expanded to provide various "supratypes," such as double three-deckers called "six-blocks," and five-tenement "rabbit runs" capable of addressing moderately large multifamily housing needs with an efficient use of precious urban space. In turn, the type could be expanded further and adapted

in scale to contain stores, doctor's offices, and saloons on the first story to serve specialized commercial needs.

Between 1901 and 1925, streetscapes comprised almost exclusively of three-decker flats came to define the mill worker's sense of place. The incremental construction of these multifamily housing flats and store tenements by countless local builders and a handful of local architects eventually created long canyons of wooden tenements, terminated at the end of the block by the looming presence of a red-brick mill. Within these vertical neighborhoods, the tenement houses gained (through their accumulated numbers) the formal power necessary to offset the concentrated mass of the mill. On a conceptual level, this visual juxtaposition between the consolidated might of the mill—set against the incremental power of the

housing for its workforce—offers a metaphor for the internal politics of the corporation itself, which often pitted the power represented by management against the numbers represented by labor.

Fig. 90 (above left). An angled porch in response to the corner site condition in New Bedford's South End.

Fig. 91 (above right). Raised fieldstone retaining wall for a North End three-decker.

THE INFLUENCE OF THE SOCIAL SETTING: THE THREE-DECKER AS A COMPONENT OF COMMUNITY STRUCTURE

Once built, design issues such as "owned" or "isolated" spaces extended in more mundane ways beyond the front porch to the more practical laundry decks in the rear (which were a vital necessity in these cold-water flats). Other private spaces included the individual storage rooms and coal bins in the cellar, attic trunk rooms (built at a cost of twenty-five dollars as an "add on" in 1909), and separate garbage and ash can sheds in the backyard. The space utilization of rear and

side yard areas was determined by the occupants through prior use or through negotiations with the landlord and other renters. Additionally, the owners of the three-decker flats (who often occupied one floor of the building) were responsible for the decision to install and maintain sidewalk paving in front of the three-deckers. Thus, as a byproduct of its urban circumstance, once the three-decker flats were imbedded in the context of the mill neighborhood, the notion of private ownership extended out to the street itself in the form of the paving surfaces and, later, even to notions of tenant parking "rights."

The significant margin of success that the earliest textile corporations had achieved prompted a steady succession of mills to be built throughout the city, particularly following the recovery of the Panic of 1893 and the end of the crippling textile strike of 1898.[52] On the South End alone, the area directly south of the Potomska Mill and along the Acushnet River was completely taken up by mills by 1910. Recurring images began to define the character of the area as it developed into a mature mill district. Tall brick factory stacks laid claim visually to an area of industry. Such areas often contained back-to-back mills that were later annexes of a single corporation bearing carved granite identification plates that indicated the mill's number and sometimes the date. In the foreground space of the larger mills was a mill yard preceded often by a payroll office, gatehouse, and fence—spaces that were separated from the mill for security reasons, particularly during a strike "lock out." At a lower scale beneath a standard four-story brick mill and across a busy roadway, the wooden tenements were huddled together. Then, another horizontal mass of a brick mill asserted itself, followed by its incumbent neighborhood of workers' housing. This urban cadence of mill, mill housing, mill became an increasingly characteristic pattern of growth and development in the first two decades following the textile recovery. The very presence of a mill signaled the need for housing within walking distance, since few workers could afford to take the streetcar to work. Unlike streetcar suburbs such as Dorchester, where by the turn of the twentieth century the functional identities of the trolley and the three-decker were inextricably linked, the three-decker in New Bedford bespoke of factory life tied directly to an adjacent mill.

An image of the Whitman Mill taken shortly after its construction in 1895 on the South End clarifies the housing trend that would continue, then magnify, as New Bedford entered its second textile boom. Reaching out into the Acushnet River were the long, tendril-like loading docks for shipping out finished cotton cloth. Coal barges would often rest nearby. The sweeping horizontal line of the mill structure (which appeared to be more window than wall with its even placement of large industrial windows)[53] was pinned down compositionally by the vertical statement made by the chimney stack for the coal-fired Corliss engines situated within the boiler house below. Inside the Whitman Mill, Providence mill engineer C. R. Makepeace and architect Benjamin Smith pushed the spatial density for the number of power looms to their limits within the region. At five hundred, there were nearly double the number of looms in Lowell's early mills. Soon, separate weave sheds became common as a means of reducing the threat of structural failure due to the vibrations from the looms.[54] To the left of the mill was an uneven cluster of three-story mill tenements. Of the seven tenements present, only two were of the same design. In fact, the assortment represents nearly the full range of the building typology: the horizontal massing of the earlier Wamsutta four-family units, the flat-roof type of the 1870s found in Potomska and Wamsutta, the two-and-one-half-story gable-ended form similar to the Grinnell housing of the 1880s, and, finally, the hipped-roof, projecting bay massing that became the standard New Bedford type after 1904.

The cohesive building types that appeared with the corporate housing of the early textile era (no doubt prompted by favorable construction costs achieved by maintaining uniformity), yielded to greater diversity within the New Bedford building stock after the 1880s, but the city ultimately established its own design conformity as mill incorporations and housing demands reached a critical mass. With greater regularity, speculative builders developed full sections of a block with just the announcement of a new mill incorporation like speculative builders C. E. Cook and A. P. Smith, who in 1896 filed for sixteen contiguous building permits adjacent to the Dartmouth Mill

Fig. 92. The Washington Social and Music Club, 1905, designed by S. C. Hunt. This workingmens' club (now demolished) accommodated English born workers or those of English parentage who were Protestant. Courtesy of the *Standard-Times*/Spinner Publications.

that was incorporated the previous year. The growing immigrant population also prompted ethnically linked builders to develop certain areas of the city almost exclusively for certain ethnic groups, encouraging the segregation of the city.[55] Eventually, entire mill neighborhoods were spawned from a limited range of the three-decker design schemes. Long three-decker streetscapes were bounded at the ends of the block by mills, and anchored on each cross-street by stores, saloons, and shops—forming largely autonomous neighborhoods of industrial housing within the city.

Because the house form of the three-decker was directly related to the economic base of such textile communities, it remained a vital component in the operation of the mills. In turn, the social environments within the mill neighborhoods remained linked to the same industrial landscape. As long as the mill function and the workforce remained basically the same, cohesive neighborhoods grew up around the mills. These neighborhoods were interconnected further by stores that carried ethnic foods and by shopkeepers who spoke the prevalent language of the neighborhood and exchanged the currency from the homeland. Additionally, taverns and ethnically linked social clubs, such as the Washington Social and Music Club built in 1905 by architect S. C. Hunt on Rodney French Boulevard to serve the English workers in the South End, served as social centers after working hours (fig. 92), while churches established yet another layer of invisible boundaries in the form of belief, social standing, and ethnic origin (fig. 93). For example, a person could ask what Catholic parish an individual was

Fig. 93. Mt. Carmel Roman Catholic Church, 1903, Kelly and Houghton Architects, Brooklyn, New York. This church predominately served Portuguese residents in the South End.

from and immediately know, by association, the ethnic group, social standing, and level of economic empowerment that the person likely held within the community and, generally, within the mill hierarchy (fig. 94).[56]

The church parish, school district, mill location, and corner store established—on a practical and conceptual level—the parameters of a mill neighborhood comprising multifamily housing. Together, these institutions formed several distinct

and semi-autonomous communities within the larger political entity of the city (fig. 95). People identified themselves as belonging to the "South End" or "Mt. Carmel Parish," and often had very little reason to venture into other parts of the city. Such boundaries defined the neighborhood in ways that people not immersed in the dynamics of the local culture would ever know.

Yet, while members of the city's workforce tended to limit their activities to the neighborhood setting, they were tied together—and isolated from one another—by an invisible and interwoven socioeconomic fabric that linked the North and South Ends of the city. This was where all the mills were and where the immigrant factory workers lived, worked, and shopped in a similar fashion. In turn, these same mill neighborhoods were distinctly separate from—and yet tied to—the politically and economically empowered wealthy wedge of the center of the city, where the mill owners lived (fig. 96). Within an even broader context, the characteristic grouping of side-by-side houses set amidst industrial surroundings linked New Bedford to other manufacturing centers in New England that shared similar patterns of living and whose sheer survival was tied to corporate competition and national economic trends. In such a manner, ties to place, while being born of separate experiences and identities, ultimately become intertwined historically with bonds of power stemming from regional economies.

Consequently, not only was the building type of the three–decker formally and spatially dependent on other adjoining three–deckers for the definition of yard space, but it was also dependent upon the street lines and the broader relationship (axially, economically, socially, politically) of the mill economy itself. The meaning of a three–decker as an autonomous object apart from these other spheres of context would seem to be incomprehensible.

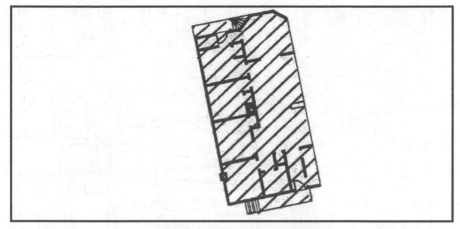

Home

Plan view of three-decker at lot 90 Nelson Street built 1912 by J. Blier for client F. Cardinand.

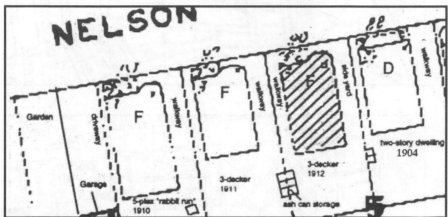

Yard

Plan view of the 90 block along Nelson Street showing the immediate side yards and adjacent multifamily housing that define circulation paths and social zones.

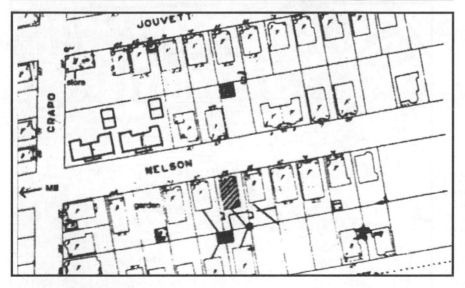

Street

Plan view of Nelson Street by 1924. Plan shows street configuration of various multifamily housing types and the variety of side/back yard conditions that create spatial corridors of community.

Fig. 94. Broadening Realms of Contextual Awareness—home to yard to street. Drawing by Kingston Heath and Todd Williams, 1993.

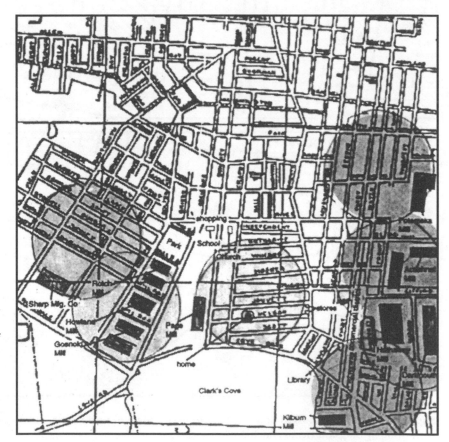

Neighborhood

The total environment of the workplace includes the mill complex itself, socioeconomic context of adjacent housing, commercial facilities such as corner stores, recreational and health facilities such as ball fields and clinics, sociopolitical institutions such as lodge and union halls, and surrounding engendering institutions such as schools, libraries, and churches.

District

Plan view of the South End mill district showing the broader industrial and cultural landscape. Mills are connected to prescribed areas of housing, education, shopping, worship, and leisure through land development, and spiritual and governmental mandates. Collectively, these areas form discrete, semi-autonomous working-class neighborhoods linked to the economic force of the mills.

Fig. 95. Broadening Realms of Contextual Awareness—neighborhood to district. Drawing by Kingston Heath and Todd Williams, 1993.

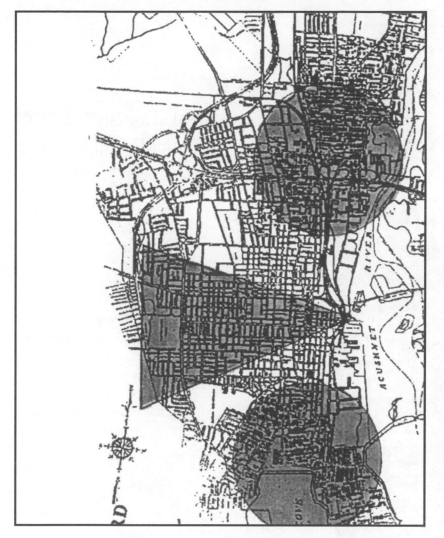

City

Plan view of New Bedford showing the social geography of the city. Here, the "wealthy-wedge" of elite residences lie west of the central business district and between South and North End industrialized neighborhoods.

The black dots represent a field survey of three-decker housing undertaken by Arthur Krim in 1989.

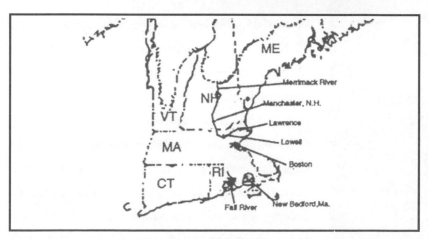

State and Region

Plan view of the state of Massachusetts with adjacent areas of competing New England textile communities as economic and technological reference points, stressing the interdependent bonds of a regional economy.

Fig. 96. Broadening Realms of Contextual Awareness—city to state and region. Drawing by Kingston Heath and Todd Williams, 1993.

Plate Glass

6

THE CULTURAL TRANSFORMATION OF THE THREE-DECKER AT THE CLOSE OF THE TEXTILE ERA IN NEW BEDFORD

Shall auld acquaintance be forgot,
King Cotton and his train?
'Tis up to you, each woman true
His prestige to regain.
Your kind co-operation give,
Make Cotton Week your pride,
Inaugurate a cotton shower,
Or be a cotton bride.[1]

—J. Edmund Estes,
"The Song of Cotton Cloth," 1924

In 1923, the year a reconnaissance survey of New Bedford was undertaken by a New York City engineering consulting firm to evaluate the financial health of the city, some seventy cotton mills operated by thirty-one corporations were functioning in the city and employing over 40,000 men and women.[2] The mills themselves were described as "models of their kind" almost without exception and run with a high degree of efficiency. In fact, the report was glowing, adding that the mill owners "have built splendid plants, have provided every facility for the safety and welfare of their employees, have paid good wages, have kept their equipment up to a high state of efficiency and productivity and have concentrated on the production of goods of the highest quality."[3] The mills were characterized as "solidly and well built" and "architecturally attractive," while their interiors were described as "orderly and well kept." Further, the survey team considered it an asset that the textile industries were almost entirely home owned—the invested capital coming primarily from the whaling profits of previous generations in New Bedford.

One of the concerns that was noted regarding the textile industry was the difficulty of securing common labor, which was ascribed, significantly, to the reduction of immigration.[4] In this regard, the report stated that "a large part of the city's common labor is performed by those of Portuguese stock. In the main, the highly skilled and more highly paid employees of the textile mills are of English birth or ancestry."[5] On the other hand, it was stressed as a business advantage that there was a very low rate of labor turnover, which added to the smooth running of the mills and, by extension, to the cohesiveness and social stability of the mill neighborhoods. The study, however, voiced a concern that New Bedford was "perilously near being a one industry city." (At this juncture, 82 percent of the city's workforce was employed solely in textiles.) Further, it was suggested that this industry had reached its high-water mark in terms of economic strength, and that growth of New Bedford's textile industry would not be in any way comparable to what it had been in the past. The recommendation was to diversify the economic base, since even the smaller local industries' markets did not extend outside the city, and generally fed the textile industry as well.

All in all, New Bedford in 1923 was described as a "great textile producing center and prosperous city." In the twenty years of the textile boom following the 1901 recovery, the population doubled (from 62,442 to 121,219), and the city's assessed valuation of property tripled. Its entire wealth was estimated in 1923 at nearly one-quarter of a billion dollars. However, what had contributed to the city's concentrated wealth contributed to its demise as well. Not only was the ownership of the textile industry in local hands, so too were its banks, street railway systems, and other related industries. In fact, the authors of the *Reconnaissance Survey of New Bedford* observed that nearly everything within its borders was owned by the people of New Bedford—"an exceptional state of affairs." There was an ominous ring to one statement in the report: "indeed, the city will be fortunate if it maintains its present prestige in the textile field, and if its present mills continue to prosper." New Bedford's best days were over.[6]

By 1924, concern about the regional decline in textiles began to be reflected in the local newspapers, as evidenced by the admonishment "each woman true/[King Cotton's] prestige to regain" stated in "The Song of Cotton Cloth" in the epigraph that opens this chapter. On the eve of New England week and the New Bedford Industrial Exposition, the mayor of New Bedford, Walter H. B. Remington, was concerned that the city's prominence as a national leader in the textile industry had not been made evident enough because the city's public image continued to be tied too closely to "her grand old whaling days." The headline for the September 14, 1924, *Evening Standard* read "SOFT PEDAL ON WHALING DAYS FOR TIME, SAYS MAYOR: Need of Boosting New Bedford as Live Manufacturing Center of Quality Cotton Goods Rather than as Home of Picturesque but Defunct Whaleships." Having full confidence in the *quality* of the textile goods produced in the city, the mayor saw the problem of sinking sales simply as being the lack of self-promotion. The recommendation was made to revive a 1909 proposal made by the mayor (as the former secretary for the old board of trade) for a common trademark. Reprinted by the *Evening Standard*, the label read: "Made in New Bedford, Mass. First in America For Fine Fabrics. Manufactures a Mile a Minute. New Bedford Products Lead The World." The hope was that if each of the city's cotton mills affixed this New Bedford label to its products, the added exposure would lead consumers to ask for New Bedford–made goods in preference to others when they went to buy—thus bolstering the local industry.

Others, too, looked to better merchandising as a means of offsetting the higher costs of New England–made cotton goods as opposed to those produced in the South. In the same issue of the *Evening Standard*, Prof. Arthur S. Dewing of the Harvard University Graduate School of Business Administration offered what he felt were three factors for the redemption of the New England manufacturing industry: "Better merchandising of New England–made cotton goods, more control of the finishing of its goods by the cotton mills, and more direct relations with the ultimate consumers." If proper attention was given to these three requirements, he concluded, "there is not only hope for the industry, but certainty of its rapid recovery and future prosperity in New England."

In the end, the problem of the sagging textile industry in New Bedford was not addressed by marketing strategies. The common trademark for New Bedford cotton goods, for example, was never adopted. Instead, conservative management practices in running the mills on the part of the local mill owners, interwoven financial networks of family-controlled mills and banking interests, and the allegations of increased competition of textile industries in the South led mill owners once again to slash wages, speed up machinery, and require operatives to manage more machines. Between 1918 to 1928, there was an accumulated 30 percent drop in salary.[7] In a city where low worker turnover had been one of its assets, eighteen thousand people left New Bedford between 1925 to 1930. In the years from 1926 to 1928, 50 percent of those were French

Canadians—the dominant labor force in the New Bedford mills since 1910. Whereas earlier New Bedford mill owners focused exclusively on fine woven goods (while the South produced coarse cotton goods), the New Bedford mills began to compete directly with southern mills both in the type of goods produced and in hiring practices, which now aimed at hiring the most recent immigrant wage earners as a means of addressing the lower wages paid to the southern factory worker.[8]

Additionally, maturation of the textile industry —by 1928 nearly eighty years old in New Bedford—demanded operational and physical changes to the mills. In turn, this state of affairs was mirrored in the condition of the area's building stock, which had been constructed to serve the textile industry. The 1923 *Reconnaissance Survey* made the following assessment:

> *While the housing conditions in the districts occupied principally by the foreign elements are better than most New England textile cities, there are far too many tenement houses and particularly houses of the 'three decker' type which are not up to the present standards of safety, sanitation and appearance* [author's emphasis]. In many cases the construction is bad and not only offers a serious fire risk, but a health menace. In many neighborhoods there exists a total inadequacy of light, air, and sunshine in and about the homes and an insufficiency of sanitary conveniences.[9]

Now heaped onto the three-deckers was the type of criticism leveled during the 1880s and 1890s at the large corporate tenement blocks that the three-deckers were designed to replace.[10] *All* workers' housing, particularly that serving the city's "foreign element," now seemed to be suspect. Similar to the action taken by Lowell mill owners after 1848 to retrieve capital, reduce expenses, and relieve ethnic tension, New

Bedford corporations began to divest themselves of rental tenements that had been constructed out of economic necessity at the dawn of the textile era. By 1928, only fifty tenements in New Bedford were owned by mill corporations.[11] One source states that Wamsutta Mills alone owned over three hundred tenements as of 1889.[12] Documentary evidence reveals that the entire number of corporate-owned structures in the city reached 262 by 1919, which translates to approximately 649 rental tenements (see map 13). Because of the demographic shift in the city's population and the abundance of rental property now available for sale or rent, many of the former mill tenements and speculatively built three-deckers constructed near the mills began to be populated by the newest and largest immigrant population to arrive in southeastern Massachusetts—the Portuguese.

THE INFLUENCE OF THE CITY'S CHANGING DEMOGRAPHICS: PORTUGUESE IMMIGRATION

While Azorean fishermen no doubt entered the port of New Bedford earlier, the first recorded Portuguese name to appear in the customs register of the city dates from 1817. By 1830, commercial ties between New Bedford and the Azores were being established. The first Azorean family to settle in New Bedford is said to have dated to about 1840. At the height of whaling in the city in 1857, men from Fayal were said to be "as plenty as whales' teeth" in New Bedford. Accordingly, there was a district at the south end of Water Street referred to as "Fayal Street" after the Azorean island where many of the first Portuguese seamen joined the American whaling fishery. By the end of the Civil War, the Portuguese population in New Bedford was more than eight hundred individuals.[13]

The small nine-island group of the Azores (scattered some 375 miles apart from Flores on the west to Santa Maria to the southeast) is approximately 2,300 miles east of Massachusetts, 700 miles off the coast of Portugal, and 750 miles from Africa. The archipelago of the Azores was discovered during the first half of the fifteenth century by Portuguese navigators. It is the only island chain in the mid-Atlantic; hence, they were ideally situated as a stopping point initially for Portuguese navigators and, by the nineteenth century, for the New England whalers bound for the southern fishery in need of supplies such as fresh fruits and vegetables. By the 1820s, these islands provided Azorean crewmen for the whalers. Much like the textile mill labor population that followed, less than half of the seamen employed in the American whale fishery were, in fact, "American." Melville notes in *Moby Dick:* "No small number of these whaling seamen belong to the Azores, where the outward bound Nantucket whalers frequently touch to augment their crews from the hardy peasants of the rocky shores. The whalers also cruised off the Portuguese-African colony of the Cape Verde Islands where they took on seamen."[14]

During the 1880s, the packet lines, such as the barkentine *Moses B. Tower,* made four regular trips yearly between New Bedford and the Azore Islands.[15] There was a distinguishable "Portuguese Quarter" by that time just half a mile north of the Potomska Mill. Many Portuguese kept stores in this section, or were involved in the fisheries (mainly the cod and mackerel fisheries) instead of working in the mills.

While whaling and the fisheries in general continued to be a source of income for the Portuguese into the next century, by the first two decades of the twentieth century, textiles provided additional job opportunities and served as a catalyst for further immigration. Largely in response to the New England textile boom, 89,732 Portuguese immigrated to the United States in the decade of 1910–20. Of that number nearly one quarter (19,338) settled in New Bedford—at this juncture the leading center of cotton textile production in the country.[16]

This factor relates directly to Portuguese immigration patterns. Jerry Williams notes that

the Portuguese immigrants living in the United States in 1870 were highly concentrated, not just in a few states, but in and around a relatively small number of communities within those few states. Former whaling centers, such as New Bedford and San Francisco had become the focal point. Massachusetts (with 2,555 Portuguese) accounted for thirty percent of the U.S. total, while California (with 3,435 Portuguese) accounted for forty percent. Gradually, however, Massachusetts became the ideal destination for many of the new immigrants. A sizeable Portuguese population already resided in the state; it was one of the easiest locations to get to from the Azores, which meant lower transportation costs; and employment opportunities were readily available. By 1900, Massachusetts had surpassed California and could lay claim to having the largest Portuguese population in the country.[17]

At first, the Portuguese worked in limited numbers in the mills, and were restricted from joining the labor unions because of language barriers and prejudice. But whereas half of the French Canadian population went back to their native country or sought textile jobs elsewhere in the region because of wage cutbacks in the city, the Portuguese stayed and replaced the French Canadian textile workers as the largest ethnic labor force in the New Bedford mills.[18] Faced with language barriers, limited funds, and limited education, the newest Portuguese arrivals were unable to afford the 2,300-mile journey back to the Azores.[19] Instead, this new group of Portuguese Americans invested what they could save in their adopted home.

Portuguese immigrants from the Azore, Medeira, and Cape Verde Islands settled predominantly in the South End of the city, where many of the textile mills were located and where three-decker neighborhoods had been emerging at "alarming" rates over the last two decades. Such sentiments were implied by local newspaper editorials, which chronicled the transformation of New Bedford's rural landscape from earlier more genteel visions to one of smokestacks, tenements and immigrants.[20] The three-decker now loomed as an image (or cause) of crowded industrial living conditions that needed to be remedied as indicated by this 1920 newspaper account: "[T]hey covered the mill districts with three and four deckers and sham built houses with 'modern improvements.' The city has passed an ordinance prohibiting this class of houses and there might be expected to be a lack of dwellings as there has been little of this class of property added to the city of late. The operatives have solved their problem by doubling up in tenements."[21]

By 1925, the era of three-decker building was over anyway. While the official 1916 ordinance restricting frame housing in New Bedford to two stories was based on fire safety, the building type had been the subject of housing-reform attacks since the early teens (see chapter 5). The very term "three-decker" was exclusively pejorative during the teens and twenties, carrying connotations of poverty, overcrowding, poor living conditions, shoddy construction, and immigration.[22] Builders and residents preferred terms such as "three-family dwelling," "dwelling house of three apartments," "three-tenements," or "rental flats" instead.

Outside New Bedford, for example, the attack on the three-decker often took the form of a social revolt against the "invasion of immigration." As Jacobsohn notes, the types of concerns voiced against the construction of the three-decker revealed the range of biases imbedded in our culture during the 1910s and 1920s that contributed to stigmatizing three-deckers as a degraded form of housing: "When they spoke of fire hazards, they acted within the usual scope of the housing reform movement. When they spoke of filth, crime and other social evils, spreading with three-deckers, they preyed on the long-held associations of bad housing with immoral behavior and ignorant immigrants. When they complained of depreciated property values and the ugliness of three-deckers, they betrayed their disdain for speculative builders, and a middle-class aversion to multifamily housing—a distaste that later fueled the zoning movement."[23]

Basically, the arguments put forth by opponents of the three-decker ranged from concerns over the depreciation of adjoining suburban property in areas such as Lynn and Worcester, Massachusetts, to charges of "undesirable citizens" being harbored within. Various strategies were used to curtail and even ban the three-decker. Lynn attempted a zoning regulation in 1913 to restrict the construction of three-tenement houses from an area from Broad and Lewis Streets to the waterfront—Lynn's finest residential district. Interestingly, the ordinance (referred to by opponents as "class legislation") never passed, and apartment buildings were built on this area by 1915. As early as 1911, one bank in Worcester even refused to extend loans for three-deckers and offered instead favorable rates for single-family dwellings. According to the bank president, his refusal to lend money on such houses equated to "nothing short of a revolution in the housing development of small and medium-sized cities."[24]

Perhaps in response to such prohibitive economic measures on the part of area banks, some local builders in New Bedford, like Michael Daley, took to financing three-decker housing starts and building alterations himself.[25] For newly arrived immigrants with little collateral and low wages, their only opportunities to buy land and to build might be in the form of personal contracts negotiated with local builders. Daley's clients paid once or twice a year (October and February) a sum of about $100 toward the principal, and (at about 5 percent interest) paid around $114 yearly in interest initially. By 1909, Daley held six house mortgages, one land mortgage and, on one occasion, extended a second mortgage for alterations. Daley's estimated cost per three-decker plan was $5,425 by 1913.

However, there were other forces at work beyond building codes and bank lending restrictions that eventually put an end to the three-decker as a solution to the city's pressing problems of overcrowding. Following World War I, housing costs for three-deckers soared in New Bedford, taking them out of the reach of even the speculative builder. The *New Bedford Record of Building Permits* indicates that, in 1920, the cost range was from $11,000 to $30,000 for three-deckers, depending upon embellishments. Even at the lowest range, this cost was approximately twice the cost before the wartime housing boom. From 1921 to 1925, this figure leveled off to around $10,000. As a dramatic indication of the shift in building preference, 1919 was the second-largest building activity in New Bedford history. Of the 269 dwellings built, only *one* was a three-decker.

The housing trend was now toward small cottages and two-family dwellings, which gained in popularity in late 1918. Such two-family housing was built in large numbers during the 1920s near the Dartmouth line on what was the former western edge of the Howland Mill Village parcel. Manuel Tavares, for example, filed for a water permit on August 4, 1922, for the two-family dwelling he had just begun building at 181 Norwell Street. With their larger lot sizes, lower scale, front and side entries, and fewer but larger rooms, they offered a recognizable "zone of emergence"—a transitional living environment between the poor living conditions represented by the rows of three-deckers among the mill districts to the single-family dwellings near Olmsted's Buttonwood Park.

But not all New Bedford citizens could afford such dwellings. Instead, some Portuguese residents in New Bedford invested in older three-decker tenements. which were now less in demand as the mill population began to dwindle in response to the region's economic slowdown. Often, these new tenement owners sent for family members back in the Old Country to reunite their households, establishing chain migration patterns. Formerly, the rent structure in the city was based on residents on each floor paying rent to an absentee landlord. Now, the multiple floors of a two- and three-decker flat were conceptualized as part of a large, single-family residence by the new urban dwellers, whose relatives often occupied various floors and contributed rent toward the cost of the mortgage.

With the mass migration of Portuguese to New Bedford between 1910 to 1920 came the commitment to a better way of life in their adopted home and a desire to maintain cultural and aesthetic ties with their native land as well. Because of the changed socioeconomic dynamics at play, the old familiar form of the three-decker began to reflect new aesthetic expressions and social meanings than when the building form was first conceived.

ACCEPTING CHANGE:
RE-ENVISIONING THE TYPE TODAY

In chapter 1, I analyzed the relationship of the interior and exterior spaces of a 1912 three-decker flat in New Bedford that had been adapted to the needs of members of a Portuguese American family between 1939 and 1979. The social patterns as well as the meanings inherent in the activities that took place within adjacent spaces were discussed in terms of both family dynamics and New Bedford's evolving regional economy after the Depression and World War II. However, it is also instructive to trace how such building types and their adjacencies evolve into the present day. It is clear that it is not only the contemporaneous setting within which a work is built that holds importance, but also the building's reflected response to the evolving nature of

place and its accommodation of social change that have relevance as well. Such human responses to external forces constitute the social history and social "context" to which the full understanding of architecture is tied. Hence, to freeze the building type of the two- and three-decker flat in New Bedford in its original historical period of c. 1870 to 1925 by interpreting its historical significance exclusively in terms of such issues as the Neo-Colonial or Queen Anne "style" established by its original builders denies our sense of history as an ongoing process.[26]

By doing so, we would ignore the fact that an "evolving vernacular" is in evidence today in New Bedford. The great infusion of Portuguese immigrants, who arrived in the decade from 1910 to 1920 were joined by a second wave following the 1965 U.S. Immigration Act. While during the mid-1950s and 1960s, many older Portuguese neighborhoods were reverting back to an Anglo-American identity by Portuguese who were becoming acculturated into the mainstream of American life, the cycle of assimilation was broken by the large new influx of Portuguese immigrants. Pastel colors on the three-deckers, coupled with sideyard subsistence gardens and vineyards, began to appear in abundance in lieu of large lawns and more muted house tones. Today, 60 percent of New Bedford's population is Portuguese. As would be expected, this new generation of city dwellers who migrated from Portuguese village life does not draw from the history and culture of old New Bedford, where the three-decker tenement was the residential correlative of the mill. This was not their experience. They have no vested interest in—and do not link their identity to—that era of the city's history. Therefore, they are less motivated by the desire to keep the three-deckers as they were. The flats must meet *current* needs and realities as well as address Old World sensibilities from their inhabitants' Portuguese cultural experience. As a result, the city's three-decker flats and domestic

Fig. 97. South Water Street shopping district after the demolition to make way for the John F. Kennedy Highway "connector."

adjacencies are being reshaped not only by the presence of a new ethnic group and a changed set of economic circumstances, but also by a new value structure of what defines prosperity than when the building type was first conceived.

Even the North End, which was predominantly French Canadian up through the late-1950s, is now referred to as "little Portugal" and has its own "Luso-American" banks, restaurants, and social clubs. Additionally, the work being done in the mills is different. Instead of fine finished cotton and silk goods of the textile boom era, garment-manufacturing shops or "sweatshops" (as they are more commonly referred to) produce such items as printed cloth. Today, approximately eight thousand people—many recently arrived Portuguese immigrants—work in the garment factories.[27] The old textile mills that have not been torn down, succumbed to factory outlet stores (there are around two dozen in the city), converted to senior-citizen housing, or abandoned altogether operate principally as garment shops. The long rows of factory windows originally designed for maximum natural lighting and ventilation are now closed up

to lower heating and cooling expenses, to reduce window breakage by vandals, and to cut down on visual distractions for higher productivity by the garment industry workforce.

Perhaps most important, the role these mills once played in community life has changed as well. No longer the center of economic and social life today, the physical presence of the mill in these neighborhoods seems inconsequential—almost intrusive. The people who live in the adjacent mill housing are no longer tied directly to the mills for economic support. Because the jobs are no longer in the mills exclusively, people commute to work and do shopping outside the neighborhood.

Though the corner stores still function in many communities, larger traditional shopping areas have given way to state and federal projects. The South End shopping district of South Water Street, for example, was demolished in 1975 and replaced with a highway "connector" for the John

F. Kennedy Memorial Highway, fragmenting community ties even further beyond the closing of the mills (fig. 97). The mills that function as discount stores draw people from *outside* the area. Therefore, the mills themselves—once the life force of the adjoining neighborhood—today address an entirely different user group than those who live in their shadow.

Some large factory complexes, like the Rotch, Pierce, and Morse Twist Mills, have recently been torn down, leaving huge cavities within the city's urban core. These demolitions open up street vistas to adjoining neighborhoods not witnessed by the local inhabitants during their entire lifetimes and merge social spheres of the city previously recognized as being socially distinct (fig. 98). The rows upon rows of three-decker housing stock, now unrelieved by the adjoining mass of area mills, stand naked in the landscape and serve the broader housing needs of the city as a collective grouping rather than as part of a mill district. The former symbiotic relationship of mill-to-mill housing is now severed, having been replaced by a new

socioeconomic and physical context that lends the three-decker different meaning and sociohistorical relevance.

As a native of this historic city, observing—rather than living through—this juncture of change that threatens to eradicate the very vestiges of my childhood identity, it is tempting to embrace a position that resists any further dramatic governmental or social transformation. There is indeed a melancholy grandeur that is evoked by the remaining pockets of mill districts and three-deckers that have resisted the human and physical effects of time. There is both sadness and sublimity in their presence as they lie witness to the changing forces in their midst, and vouchsafe the patterns of the past. However, the changes underway allow for another epoch in New Bedford's history to express itself (figs. 99–100).

The communities that lie at the geographic extremities of the city offer an entirely different vision of cultural heritage than does the Waterfront Historic District tied to the whaling era (that most visitors see). These old neighborhoods—the last vestiges of the former immigrant mill districts—are more the province of the transplanted Portuguese mind today than of the memory framework of New Bedford's industrial past. And they are

Fig. 98. Demolition photograph of the Rotch Mill site exposing former mill housing in the Page Mill District.

FROM PATERNALISM TO A BUILDING MARKET

Fig. 99 (above).
Portuguese Feast of the Blessed Sacrament in New Bedford's North End. Courtesy of the *New Bedford Standard Times*.

Fig. 100 (left).
Sunbeam Bread shop-front advertisement (whose logo is a blond-haired, blue-eyed girl) is recoded to reflect the large Azorean Portuguese population in the city.

being reshaped accordingly. While it is regrettable to see the "decks" of the three-deckers being removed (essentially reducing the type to its core structure), there are broader issues to consider. With unemployment in New Bedford (since 1991) often ranking fourth in the country—the nearby textile city of Fall River, Massachusetts, also now predominantly Portuguese, frequently ranks fifth— these housing purchases and subsequent alterations should be viewed as acts of personal triumph and pride for these newly arrived immigrants amidst some of the most severe economic conditions in the nation. For many of the three-deckers used primarily as rental units, the distinctive porches have been removed because of age, decay, cost of replacement, and changed patterns of behavior. The rear laundry decks and front porches have given way to such technological improvements within the household as washers and dryers and window-mounted air-conditioners, while the laundry poles, in turn, are used on occasion as mounting points for satellite dishes (fig. 101).[28] Seeking lower life-cycle energy costs and maintenance fees, more energy-efficient windows are added, porch doors (no longer deemed necessary once the decks are removed) are converted to windows (figs. 102–3), and a vinyl skin in an array of pastel colors, favored by many Portuguese Americans, have modified their original Victorian identity and meaning.

To many preservationists, these modifications represent "loss of integrity." Such overt changes to the physical fabric of the city's three-deckers prompted the mayor's Office of Housing and Neighborhood Development recently to publish a brochure (in English and Portuguese) on *Synthetic Siding in New Bedford*. In their own words, the purpose of the brochure was "to help the homeowners of New Bedford protect and preserve the investment they have made." Also implicit in the photo juxtapositions and captions was the desire to preserve the original architectural integrity of the buildings themselves.

Fig. 101. A laundry pole now also serves as a mounting point for a satellite dish at 90 Nelson Street.

TRANSFORMED INTERSTITIAL SPACES

As the city's workforce began to embrace the automobile, cement-block garages began to be constructed behind large six-block units, like those built by architect Oscar Crapo at 99 Nelson

Fig. 102. Removal of piazzas and conversion of former porch doorways to more energy efficient window openings are among a few local indicators of social, economic, and environmental response.

Fig. 103. In-process cladding of the three-decker in vinyl siding—often in pastel colors preferred by many recently arrived Azoreans.

Street in 1924 (fig. 104). Others were built in long rows (referred to as "gang garages") along the street fronts as parking spaces for automobiles became critical. The *New Bedford Record of Building Permits* indicates that such car shelters began to appear in large numbers in 1917 at a cost of between $500 and $700 and increased in demand through the 1920s, whereupon the price increased to $1,000. Today, they are inadequate to meet the needs of the local population. As a result, throughout the city's three-decker neighborhoods the side yard space, once set aside for Catholic yard shrines, tenement playground space, or lawns by earlier generations of New Bedford cit-

izens have been paved over, enclosed by a chain-link gate, and used for private resident parking. With several people in the household on each floor owning a car, parking has become a critical issue. John Ventura stated the situation: "the parents, when they arrive want to own a house; our children want a car." The side yards have been sacrificed (fig. 105).[29]

Given different site conditions, however, the space utilization is different. For the Portuguese, wherever there is land, there is normally a garden or small vineyard. Azoreans are island people raised in small villages and on farms, where they are skilled at squeezing a subsistence living from a

Fig. 104 (right).
Cement block "gang garages" built in 1924 by architect Oscar Crapo for his six-block tenements at 99 Nelson Street.

Fig. 105 (below).
Side-yard living space appropriated for off-street parking by tenants.

small piece of land. Often, the fields are located immediately behind the tightly grouped village dwellings.[30] Issues of housing proximity and density of space found in the New Bedford setting are not major constraining factors, since these village dwellers are preconditioned to similar physical/spatial relationships prior to arrival. As a result, village farming patterns are transferred to the New Bedford urban context today often within a few feet of a former textile mill.

Joseph Soares, who lives in a two-decker built in the early 1920s on land near the Dartmouth line in the former Howland Mill parcel, purchased his house in the 1960s *because* of its adjoining lot (fig. 106). Here, he plants potatoes, red beans (for soup), fava beans, funchi, garlic, tomatoes, kale, string beans, parsley, green and red peppers, and some corn. He has a small vineyard for wine, keeps a few chickens, and freezes fish caught by his son. In such a manner, many Portuguese live by keeping to themselves and establishing a microeconomic system that overrides the local economy—and, in some cases, the federal banking system itself. Mr. Soares, for example, with his paint contracting business, paid his house off in just ten years. By paying bank (or personal) mortgage contracts off early to lower interest costs or, in some cases, saving funds

by living with relatives and paying cash for the house all at once to avoid indebtedness, the Portuguese "develop" stable, ethnically linked neighborhoods—one house at a time.

Interestingly, Christopher Koziol delivered a paper at the 1988 National Association of Collegiate Schools of Architecture in Chicago in which he discussed the 1909 Massachusetts Homestead Commission.[31] He described what he termed the "New England agrarian myth" of a proposal to encourage market gardens for immigrants to offset mortgage payments in addition to industrial labor. Early plans to deplete costs of rent through vegetable sales dated back to the 1870s. In 1895, there was a "working man's co-op" established in Roxbury, Massachusetts. Additionally, a site plan in Lowell, Massachusetts, for a homestead commission for industrial workers was planned. Of the hundreds planned with the goal of making mortgage payments easier by selling produce (and establishing a "home-like look" in the owner-occupied duplexes), only twelve were undertaken, and they all failed. Yet, in New Bedford, such gardens have long been standard practice because

Fig. 106. Joseph Soares in front of his two-decker and urban garden at the corner of Norwell Street and Bolton. Arriving in New Bedford from the Azores, he purchased this home in the 1960s because of its adjoining lot, which allowed him to have a subsistence garden and "cellar kitchen" to put up preserves.

of the cultural predisposition toward farming urban land on the part of the Portuguese.[32]

These gardens and vineyards, while economically important, are just as often a cultural imperative on the part of the recent arrivals from the Old Country. Antonio Medeiros, who arrived in the United States in 1900 at age fourteen, always put up preserves from his garden and made dinner wine for his guests though he never drank himself. His daughter, Gloria, during the 1970s visited Povacao, San Miguel, where her father was raised and noted on the back of a photograph displaying acres of planted fields and vineyards in the Azores, "Now I know why Papa planted gardens" (fig. 107).[33]

Many of the owner-occupied two-decker houses today have full working kitchens in the basement for food preparation, preserving, storing

Fig. 107. Gloria Medeiros (left) and Azorean relatives in Povacao, Sao Miguel, Azores, where her father, Antonio Jose Medeiros, was born. On the back of this photograph, she wrote: "Now I know why Papa planted gardens."

fruits and vegetables, making wine, or making sausage. Rear access into the cellar often leads directly from an adjacent planting field, vineyard, or side lot. The so called "cellar kitchens" are another way (through family and community cooperation) of bypassing the broader regional economy. Further, as part of the value structure and social patterns of the community, the cellar kitchens allow the homeowner to keep the entire main living area of the privately owned apartment space presentable to public display in case of unannounced visitors, while the large-scale food preparation can take place out of sight in the cellar.

Because of such entrenched social practices, Portuguese homebuyers in New Bedford today will often overlook newer homes with modern living spaces if they cannot accommodate a cellar kitchen. These culturally specific living patterns need to be addressed as an integral "contextual" issue. Such acts of human intervention within the

existing building stock can be telling indicators of cultural adjustment and adaptation within a landscape, though they may seem inconsequential on first viewing.

As part of our training in architecture, architectural history, or preservation, we have been taught to look for cohesive patterns of *stylistic* or *formal* development within a region. We reflexively seek patterns that are *visually cohesive*. However, the dynamics by which people govern themselves without apparent logic establish a deep structure that does not reveal itself at first glance. Unconscious acts translate often into a complex social structure that subtly defines the particularized nature of place. Landscape architects and cultural geographers have made us aware that the form a landscape takes is the result of complex, overlapping, and interweaving forces that imprint themselves on the built environment and collectively constitute the context of place. In these patterns on the land lie insights into how human values and behavior manifest themselves in built form within a regional society.

By observing such patterns it became evident, for example, that many of the city's wooden three-decker flats increasingly were being encased in modern vinyl siding, decorative brick, or "artificial stone." They were also being equipped (particularly in owner-occupied units) with wrought-iron grillwork for decorative embellishment reminiscent of Portuguese verandas in lieu of wooden porch balustrades (fig. 108). Or, in a reductive mode, they were being given a vertical compositional massing emphasized by the homogenous vinyl skin and missing porches that now exuded of a distinctly different cultural expression (fig. 109). This new expression combined mainstream American and imported influences into a simultaneous subversion and celebration of both conventions that produced its own cultural specificity. This process, too, is cultural weathering. In chapter 2 we witnessed New Bedford's elite culture "modernizing" their homes and subdividing their lots in response to changing

Fig. 108. Rebuilt piazzas on Norwell Street mimicking Portuguese wrought-iron verandas on owner-occupied, two-family houses as part of the locale's new "cultural weathering" process. Note the brick casing on the foundation and its use on the porch and fence.

Fig. 109. The "new vernacular" response to the traditional three-decker form in New Bedford.

fashion and new economic forces. In that instance, we saw the appropriation of objects and spaces by a local culture in direct response to changing regional forces. As evidenced here, we stand witness to the appropriation and transformation of an existing workers' landscape by successive waves of people with a different world view and cultural background.

In the process of cultural weathering, information, aspects of social practice, or design elements are dissociated from their original source. They are then reconstituted through the collective processing of ideas that are operational within a region to meet the particular needs of a new culture. This syncretistic blend can result in a "new vernacular," which, in turn, can distinguish a region or subregion. Grape arbors, for example, are often found today in the driveways of Portuguese American neighborhoods in New Bedford where they do double duty as a carport and as a shaded eating area—merging Old and New World practices (fig. 110). Hence, traditional living patterns have been transferred with seeming ease from rural to urban contexts and (from continent to continent), illustrating the resilience of cultural tradition.

Fig. 110. An adapted grape arbor is used here to serve as a carport and picnic area. Such cultural adaptations of nineteenth-century multifamily urban living spaces by Portuguese Americans arriving in the city after the 1965 U.S. Immigration Act are emblematic of how ethnicity is imprinted on the landscape. Note the American flag in the background.

Such expressions of cultural weathering within a landscape can offer architects the "specifics" of regional adjustment that the users of the built environment have felt compelled to express. Looking at the evolving vernacular informs the historian and designer *how* and *why* changing patterns are manifesting themselves in built form today. An architect examining the vernacular has the opportunity to probe changing social and environmental conditions for sensitive and meaningful responses that can offer more than emblematic references to a distant, safer past.

HOW AN ENVIRONMENT AND ITS PEOPLE NURTURE A SENSE OF PLACE

How does one assess the range of determinants that shape a regional setting? As viewers of—and participants in—our built environments, we choose to respond to only a fraction of what is available to us. What is selected, focused on, or edited out reflects our cultural biases and professional training. We experience far more of the built and natural landscape—weather, smells, sounds, colors, sky conditions, contours, patterns (patterns of the land, of building arrangements, of human behavior, of social change)—than we customarily acknowledge. The patina of place comprises the accumulated layers of these myriad tangible and intangible qualities that manifest themselves in physical form. To be sure, "Place" is more than geographically definable space. On an emotional level, it is a mental construct—different for each of us and tied, from youth, to personal experience. Yet, there are some recurring points of nexus that tie people and a locale together. They are born of shared social and spiritual values, shared working and recreational patterns, ethnic and socioeconomic ties that, in turn, produce shared mental attitudes, sensibilities, and associations.

To the residents of New Bedford's South End along Clark's Cove, the familiar presence of the surrounding natural and physical context is evoked, for example, by the heavy blanket of morning fog that reveals the landscape through a muted filter (fig. 111). At daybreak, this unifying element of fog is dissipated in Spring and Summer by the warm glow of the sunlight that the local fishermen know all too well. Slowly, the differentiation of the human landscape comes into clearer focus as the fog burns off, and the built environment reveals itself in the industrial anchors of the Howland, Page, and Kilburn Mills. The mill smokestacks, in turn, visually contain the patchwork quilt of polychromatic hip roofs that identify the rental flats once built to serve the mills. Looming in the dis-

tance is the spiritual anchor of the Mount Carmel Portuguese Catholic Church. Accompanying the visual experience of these neighborhood "signifiers" are the smells of the tide changes, the cool breezes off the ocean, and the sounds of the sea gulls, which remind us of the body of water that was exploited to create this industrial landscape.[34]

Beyond the physical landmarks and natural phenomena that define the locale to the outsider and native alike, then, is the experiential awareness of place that New Bedford citizens carry with them that make the city distinctive. Unknowingly, they partake in what Ed Hall refers to as the "dance of life," whereby people move and interact in their cultural contexts in synchronic patterns of behavior that require little or no discussion.[35] In such a way, a sense of place gains meaning through a multitude of overlapping and interweaving interactions and impulses that serve to define common "sets" of shared experiences among its inhabitants.

These sets of shared experiences can be as abstract as a certain comfortableness derived from

Fig. 111. Clarks Cove at dawn showing the Kilburn Mill's chimney stack as an artifact of regional expression from an earlier age. The spiritual anchor of the community, the Mount Carmel Roman Catholic Church (1903) looms in the distance through a veil of morning fog. Pyramidal hipped-roof three-deckers reflect the domestic sphere of these former mill neighborhoods built in the shadow of a nearby factory.

the visual density of an industrial environment that has been nurtured since childhood by the measured cadence of three-decker after three-decker. The impulses may take the form of recollections—so vivid that they are capable of transforming vacant space into meaningful human drama. The conjured image of compressed humanity within streetscapes and mill yards at shift changes, for example, is made possible through prior personal experience with local living patterns. In essence, these abstract notions of place take the form of a "memory landscape," whereby clear images of place are framed not only by the awareness of the locale, but also by situations that resonate with personal identity. These memories that spring forth from knowledge of life in the mills are capable of recreating visual and also olfactory and auditory impressions that, collectively, lend architectural space its human dimension. Such recollections may summon up lost elements that once characterized place; as we stare at a row of abandoned textile mills, the deafening sounds of hundreds of metal power looms that traditionally asserted themselves as part of the neighborhood's daily mantra suddenly fill in a missing sensory component so vital to our understanding of local lifeways.

Though the tangible manifestation of such reference points may no longer exist within the landscape or even within the documentary record, they are retrievable by tapping the collective memory of the residents within a locale through oral history interviews. Oral history (while not totally reliable as a research tool) can be helpful to verify documentary evidence, which may lead to a greater understanding of the system of spatial use and cultural experience within a region and to a reconstruction of building processes and lifeways.[36] Perhaps more important, oral history interviews introduce into the historical record the values, attitudes, and habits of the people who helped *create* the history and character of place from among a broad differential of cultural, age, and gender viewpoints. Oral history inevitably runs the risk of violating privacy, since one is uncovering the "truths" of a locale. But oral history also offers local residents access to *their* history by allowing another voice and perception beyond an investigator's viewpoint. In order for scholars to avail themselves to the many levels of meaning that exist within a particular setting, we need to see the landscape as much as possible through the eyes of the people who use it and shape it.

Further, by seeking to limit awareness of buildings only as they were originally designed (in an attempt to preserve the original design "integrity" or the imagined past), we deny the natural processes of cultural and environmental *patination*

that links the buildings to their setting and to their past (fig. 112). In the patterns of change that are embodied in building transformations over time lie the collective record of significant regional and subregional forces that constitute the history and identity of a locale. In acknowledging these evolving patterns within a landscape, we place alongside notions of place as history to be "viewed"— the history that is being "lived."[37] Such patterns of local and regional phenomena are not only significant expressions of place, but also critical to our understanding of the larger mosaic of evolving American life. If we fail to allow for different historical visions in our characterizations of the past, it raises the inevitable question: *"What* and *Whose* history are we preserving?"[38]

With regard to the notion of "cultural weathering," this work has spoken to the process by which Portuguese Americans took their memories of life in the Old Country and attempted to make them fit into a wholly different context. Along the way, the remembered images of place were altered to adapt to a new environment, while simultaneously those same individuals transformed their homes and neighborhood settings in a manner different from earlier visions of old New Bedford—including those visions of the Portuguese who arrived at the beginning of this century.

The Portuguese American transformations of the three-decker building type demonstrate the power of a subculture over physical form. Consequently, there is a shift in analysis away from the envisioning of domestic space as represented by the hand of an *individual author* involved in the original design (chapter 5), toward the *collective visions* of the use of space (in this instance by immigrant families), who adjust to a new surrounding by remaking those environs and investing them with new meaning.[39] By degrees, the three-deckers begin to take on the character of the land within which they reside and the values of the people who use them. In the process, the maker's intent

Fig. 112. The traditional (right) and adaptively used (left) three-family tenement standing side by side in the former Rotch Mill neighborhood.

has yielded to the user's affective response. The physical and spatial transformations of the three-decker bring into focus the emergent quality and developmental clarity of vernacular design, whereby the basic matrix of form and space is modeled to the needs of the user and the dynamics of place.

Finally, the notion of cultural weathering has been proposed in this study principally to describe how ethnicity is imprinted on the landscape. However, in a broader sense, the concept calls for redirecting our perceptions of architecture away from a singular reliance on formal analysis or stylistic embellishment to exploring buildings and their settings from the perspective of the interrelated sets of cultural determinants that shape them. Design seen in this manner becomes a socially regenerative notion. Original design concepts, which often anticipated the *generalized* needs of a user, are restructured to meet *particularized* needs of changing populations. Collectively, they

reflect the lifeways of the local inhabitants from which regional planning and design can follow in a socially meaningful way. Further, by exploring the living patterns of particular user groups, such as the Portuguese, in connection with certain building types, this additional information contributes to our cultural perceptions of the landscape. Such studies not only illustrate the shape of life in subcultural pockets that hitherto have been ignored in the characterization of a region, but also reveal the multifaceted nature of a regionally manifest building type that speaks to the often dichotomous characteristics of a locale. In their totality, these disparate cultural influences (expressed in built form) define the distinctiveness of a region such as New England.

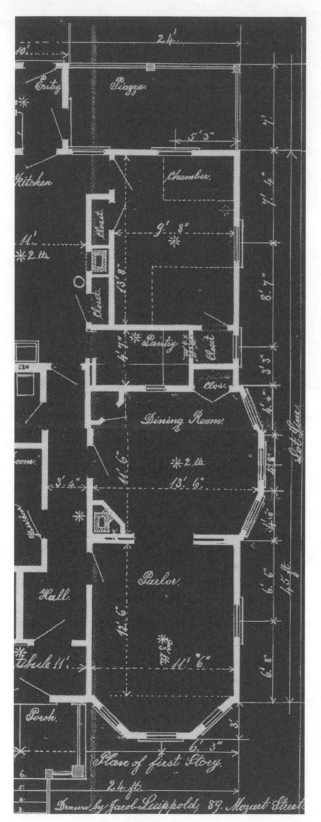

CULTURAL WEATHERING AS A VEHICLE FOR EXPLORING THE PROCESS OF PLACE MAKING

New Bedford, Massachusetts—like her sister textile communities of Lowell, Fall River, and Lawrence—is a city today of three-decker flats. Here, long street vistas of wooden, multifamily housing are linked visually and conceptually to the powerful presence of a red-brick mill that characteristically terminates the block. During the second and most productive phase of New Bedford's textile era, from 1901 to 1925, the three-decker became the most common form of urban housing for the largely unskilled labor force of the textile industry. By 1930, two- and three-deckers comprised over 40 percent of New Bedford's housing stock, while nearly two-thirds of the city's population lived in dwellings designed for two or more families.[1] Inside these rental flats, several generations of mill workers managed their lives in a collective-family living arrangement and carried out a full spectrum of social, economic, and religious rituals in the protective shadow of the mill. Life changed suddenly in 1923 with the collapse of New England's textile economy. The utility and regional significance of the three-decker flat did not end with the Great Depression, however—it merely changed. This work has chronicled that change.

It has also chronicled the construction and transformation of elite homes as the city's economic base shifted from whaling to textile production, as a new generation strived to establish *its* place in New Bedford's cultural hegemony. This work has discussed the cultural spectacle of freshly minted brick mills and their distinctive smokestacks replacing whaling vessels along the Acushnet River as artifacts of regional expression. The work chronicled those same mills as they became weatherbeaten by age and economic decline and were appropriated as sweatshops, as retirement homes, or as they were abandoned altogether and even destroyed. Finally, as part of the evolution of New Bedford's workers' landscape, this study traced the shift from corporate-owned housing for the textile workforce to a speculative housing market that produced the three-decker and discussed the form's utility up to the present. In the radical restructuring of the city of New Bedford from the status of near national icon during its whaling and textile eras to one of indeterminacy today, we have witnessed not the loss of architectural "integrity" in the cultural adaptations that took place, but a redefinition of this city's cultural heritage that speaks of a different record of habitation and a new collective identity of "place."

The focus of this study, therefore, has been largely on *change:* the need to recognize its importance as an ongoing determinant in built form, and the need to embrace it as a scholarly premise for understanding how buildings function in their settings after the architect or builder is absent from the sphere of control. Entire academic disciplines are structured around the principle of understanding the nature of buildings solely as the product of original design intention. More emphasis needs to be placed in design schools, architectural history programs, and preservation policy on the interrelated roles that cultural systems, historical circumstances, and the physical environment play as critical determinants in shaping our built environments and, more specifically, on the role ordinary people play as designers of the regional settings they inhabit.

We must recognize that architecture is seldom, if ever, the creative effort of one individual alone. Instead, architecture is the embodiment of a complex social process. In addition to the thousands of separate decisions involved in shaping buildings and their settings initially, there is a continuous array of adjustments that will accompany a building in its setting throughout its usable life; these adjustments grow out of the circumstances of the people who *use* these spaces.

Original design intention, then, represents only a brief snapshot of user accommodation. Further, the collective matrix of design forces that is involved in the generation and transformation of a building type is seldom limited to the confines of a building "site" or some other artificially imposed boundary. The building project inevitably becomes imbedded in—and is an extension of—a larger local and extralocal context of temporal and spatial influences.[2] As a result, every building and building group is a compilation of *many* histories, sets of intentions, and contextual relationships that serve to root a building in its specific setting.[3]

The value of a layered, contextual approach to the investigation of the built environment is that it not only acknowledges imported traditions and influences, such as design impulses from abroad, but also local design process and the systems which generate it.[4] By studying the built environment from the vantage point of what I have termed "cultural weathering," regional landscapes can become sources for exploring the manner in which human populations create, adapt, and transform their environments over time in response to personal sensibilities, human interactions, situational opportunities and constraints, and the forces of the natural environment.

THE NOTION OF CULTURAL WEATHERING

John Ruskin, the nineteenth-century architectural theorist and social reformer, acknowledged the innate capability of inanimate objects to serve as repositories for our memories and to provide inner richness to later generations through the evocative qualities of a building's "golden stain of time":

> [T]he greatest glory of a building is not in its stones, nor in its gold. Its glory is in its Age. . . . It is in [the walls'] lasting witness against men, in their quiet contrast with the transitional character of all things, in the strength which, through the lapse of seasons and times, and the decline and birth of dynasties, and the changing of the face of the earth, and of the limits of the sea, maintains its sculptured shapeliness for a time insuperable, connects forgotten and following ages with each other, and half constitutes the identity, as it concentrates the sympathy, of nations: it is in that golden stain of time, that we are to look for the real light, color, and preciousness of architecture.[5]

Implicit in the passage is the notion that somehow the original meaning of the work lies manifest, unchanged, through the ages. Hence, in spite of the recognition by the author of the natural weathering effects of age and vegetation (which imprint on a work their "glory" and sublimity over time) the original meaning, unlike the physical transformation of the object itself, is capable of being bequeathed, untarnished—"unstained," if you will—to later observers. In such a manner, it is assumed that the object is capable of serving, indefinitely, as a vessel of potential creative energy

and textual power from object to mind. This aversion in architectural education—to allow meaning and utility to change through time, as later authors and users add their collective inscriptions to a work—strikes at the heart of much of architectural analysis, historical interpretation, and preservation policy alike, even when addressing the common landscape.[6]

Obviously, the patination process of human beings, as with nature, can be viewed as either a positive or destructive force depending upon one's point of view. The critical issue of whether the collective re-inscriptions to an original work are an enriching component in the process of place making, therefore, lies in the primacy of a work as an *art object* or as a *cultural informant*. If we are to understand the nature of a locale, the record of ongoing change is as relevant as episodic moments of isolated achievement. Both are important to our understanding of a region, and neither should be seen in isolation. Change informs us about who we *are* as eloquently as our past deeds and accomplishments reflect who we *were*.

The point is not to celebrate the defacement of historic structures. There is a cultural necessity for "monuments." They anchor us into our landscapes, establish points of identification and define place, to a large degree, by signaling cultural moments as beacons of history. But, change too has its history and architects, in particular, may have a broader range of critical regional issues to address by not being tied exclusively to the visual references of historic precedent. Instead, there is much to be learned by focusing on how people use space in distinctive ways within a region in response to changing internal or external factors, and the meanings behind those interactions. After all, buildings, alone, do not define place; *people*, in their interactions with the natural and built environment, define place. As architectural scholars, our investigations need to reflect the awareness that architecture, like the landscape of which it is a part, is dynamic and ever changing. Not only does the physical nature of a building form change over time, but also the very meaning that it imparts changes as well.[7] Buildings, as physical evidence, have imprinted on them the forces of nature, the individual and collective acts of human behavior, and imbedded ideologies that situate them in their own distinctive ways at different points in time within their regional settings. To use an ecological analogy, a Coke bottle has a distinctive trademark shape that is tied to its corporate identity. Set adrift on the ocean, its labeling is worn off by the sea; its glass container becomes discolored by exposure to the sun; barnacles affix themselves to the container's surface until what finally washes ashore might be totally undiscernable to the culture that discovers it or produced it.[8]

Similarly, the architect or builder offers formal clarity and leaves a base pattern for later users to follow. Through extended use, the creative germ of design gains layers of social import which further illuminates the object, its setting, and its epoch. Given this construct, the relevance of architecture resides no longer solely in the understanding of the genesis of design but *also* in the recognition that architecture is inevitably a collective social act whereby the contexts, meanings, and uses of the object produced evolve through time.

Because architecture is the product of a continual act of creation, the changes evident in a building's form, plan, structure, or use significantly reflect the choices that people have made in adopting or adapting elements in their built environment in response to new regional realities and changing personal requirements. Such a process results in distinguishable regional forms that reflect this juncture of dynamic interface. Vernacular architecture represents a localized response to broad cultural systems, historical events, and environmentally determined regional forces. When manifested in built form, such buildings and their settings are capable of imparting a contextually rich bounty of learned cultural codes, patterns of behavior, local building processes, and social rituals.

This phenomenon of the gradual appropriation of objects by a local (or transplanted) culture and the process of altered meanings that ensue has been conceptualized in this study as "cultural weathering." Over time, the layering effect of these cumulative human adjustments that occur in response to an array of social, economic, and technological forces constitutes the patina of place that sets one locale apart from another. Artifacts, if we look at enough of them, can offer insights into these relational patterns of human behavior, belief, and natural phenomena, and lend greater clarity to our understanding of the cultural production of our built environments.

Recognizing these patterns of change in the physical fabric, as well as understanding less evident factors, such as the local dynamics that prompted the changes in the first place, requires insights into the internalized cultural language of the original and subsequent users. Such information grows out of the acquired knowledge of the culture: its social classes, politics, economics, rituals, aesthetic codes, and levels of situational power. Decoding such culturally transmitted information and determining how those factors express themselves in built form establish the basis of an increasing number of investigations by scholars of the vernacular.[9]

Such investigations, however, not only require immersion in the cultural milieu out of which the buildings came, but also demand a shift in the lens through which we view the evidence: we must move from seeing buildings as "objects on a site" to viewing building forms and spaces as integral conditions of the site and its people. The buildings and their settings, in turn, will prompt, modify, and extend the sets of questions posed, so that it must be understood that such an exploration process is itself dynamic because of the interaction between the questions being asked and the culture being investigated.

By shifting our focus from the object to the object in relation to its situational setting, we inevitably recognize that there is more than one vantage point to be addressed in the consideration of an architectural work. Traditionally, we explore architectural history from the point of view of the *architect* for an understanding of the set of creative ideas and aesthetic principles that a single individual has brought to the project that relates the work to others nationally or internationally. However, by understanding the same object or artifact from different points of view, one can gain deeper insights into a more comprehensive system of relationships that, in truth, govern our built environments.[10] For example, the *client's history* demonstrates how the architect's initial vision of the project is more often tempered by the client's particular needs, aspirations, and constraints.[11] The *builder's history* allows us to assess existing building technologies, programming decisions, or aesthetic choices within the framework of local or imported craft and aesthetic traditions, site conditions, economic conditions, legal constraints, and the particular skills of the builder (and other trades) that contributed to the ultimate success or failure of the project and its relationship to other works locally.[12] In addition, there is the *user's history,* which often redefines the use, meaning, and character of the building project over time as a result of various cultural systems that impact human behavior.[13]

A given architectural work is conceived, constructed, and used as a vital extension of its full environmental and conceptual context. Failing to acknowledge a wide spectrum of dynamics that shape such a work limits our understanding of its diverse and often complex nature and, therefore, does a disservice to the work itself. The goal is not to affirm that one state of a given work is better or worse than another, but to seek understanding of what such building influences reflect, collectively, about the fundamental nature of the object and of the setting within which the object resides.

From the analysis of such patterns of continuity and change within a landscape can come strategies for sensitive accommodation—an empathetic regionalism—that are tied to the current human situation as well as to the enduring character and meaning of place. As Dick Reynolds, geologist for the landscape architectural firm of Lawrence Halprin and Associates, notes: "If you can learn the history of a land over a hundred years, the knowledge can tell you what processes are at work in the region—both constructive and destructive. From these, you can learn how to use the land, how to plan a development; where to locate buildings, roads and plantings. You do not necessarily have to conform to the processes at work, but at least, if you choose to go against them, you are in a better position to estimate the consequences and the costs."[14]

INTRODUCTION

1. The number of wage earners associated with cotton goods in Massachusetts, for example, decreased by 42 percent between 1919 to 1929. There was a brief recovery from 1921 to 1923, then a steady decline. The dramatic collapse of Massachusetts's two major industries—textiles and shoes—is therefore reflected in the sharp downturn in the decade *prior* to the Great Depression. Between 1919 and 1929, Massachusetts lost 154,000 jobs in manufacturing and over 94,000 jobs in textiles and shoes alone. For some cities, like New Bedford, Massachusetts, where 82 percent of its workers were employed *solely* in textiles, the impact of the downturn in textile production was devastating. Richard Wilkie and Jack Tager, eds. *The Historical Atlas of Massachusetts* (Amherst: Univ. of Massachusetts Press, 1991), 39–42.

2. As is evident, most address mill villages built prior to 1860 that were built outside the major cities. The following provides an expansive list of both early and late studies on workers' housing in New England: Mary C. Beaudry and Stephen A. Mrozowski, "The Archeology of Work and Home Life in Lowell, Massachusetts: An Interdisciplinary Study of the Boott Cotton Mills Corporation," *IA (Journal of the Society for Industrial Archeology)* 14 (2) (1988): 1–22; Mary C. Beaudry and Stephen A. Mrozowski, *Interdisciplinary Investigations of the Boott Mills, Lowell, Massachusetts*, 3 vols. Cultural Resource Management Study nos. 18–20 (Boston: Dept. of the Interior, National Parks Service, North Atlantic Regional Offices, 1987 91); Thomas Beardsley, Thomas *Willimantic Industry and Community: The Rise and Decline of a Connecticut Textile City* (Willimantic: Windham Textile and History Museum, 1993); Richard M. Candee, "Architecture and Corporate Planning in the Early Waltham System," in *Essays from the Lowell Conference on Industrial History 1982 and 1983*, ed. Robert Weible (North Andover, Mass.: Museum of American Textile History, 1985), 17–43; Richard M. Candee, "New Towns of the Early New England Textile Industry," in *Perspectives in Vernacular Architecture*, vol. 1, ed. Camille Wells (Columbia: Univ. of Missouri Press, 1981), 31–51; Richard M. Candee, "The New England Textile Village in Art," *Antiques* (Dec. 1970): 910–15; Richard M. Candee, "Great Falls Industrial and Commercial Historic District," National Register of Historic Places Inventory—Nomination, typescript, New Hampshire Division of Historic Resources, Concord, N.H., 1982; Richard M. Candee, *Newmarket Revisited: Looking at the Era of Industrial Growth (1820–1920)* (Newmarket, N.H.: Newmarket Service Club, 1979); Richard M. Candee, "Newmarket Industrial and Commercial Historical District," National Register of Historic Places Inventory—typescript, New Hampshire: Division of Historic Resources,

Concord, N.H., 1980; Richard M. Candee, *Strafford Regional Planning Commission, Salmon Falls–The Mill Village Historic District Study for the Town of Rollinsford, New Hampshire* (Dover, N.H.: Strafford Regional Planning Commission, 1974); Richard M. Candee, "Salmon Falls Mill Historic District," National Register of Historic Places Inventory– Nomination, typescript, New Hampshire Division of Historic Resources, Concord, N.H., 1978; Richard M. Candee, "The 'Great Factory' at Dover, New Hampshire: The Dover Manufacturing Co. Print Works, 1825," *Old-Time New England* 66 (1–2) (Summer–Fall 1975): 39–51; Richard M. Candee, "Early New England Mill Towns of the Piscataqua River Valley," in *The Company Town, Architecture and Society in the Early Industrial Age*, ed. John S. Garner (New York: Oxford Univ. Press, 1992), 111–38; Richard M. Candee, *Atlantic Heights: A World War I Shipbuilder's Community* (Portsmouth, N.H.: Portsmouth Marine Society, 1985); Richard M. Candee and Greer Hardwicke, "Early Twentieth-Century Reform Housing by Kilham & Hopkins, Architects of Boston," *Winterthur Portfolio* 22 (1) (1987): 47–80; Gregory Clancey, "The Origin of the Boott Boardinghouse Plan and Its Fate after 1836," in *Interdisciplinary Investigation of the Boott Mills, Lowell, Massachusetts*, vol. 3: *The Boarding House System as a Way of Life*, ed. Mary C. Beaudry and Stephen A. Mrozowski, 7–21, Cultural Resources Management Study, no. 21 (Boston: U.S. Dept. of Interior, National Parks Service, North Atlantic Regional Offices, 1989); John Coolidge, *Mill and Mansion: A Study of Architecture and Society in Lowell, Massachusetts, 1820–1865* (New York: Columbia Univ. Press, 1942); Margaret Crawford, *Building the Workingman's Paradise: The Design of American Company Towns* (London: Verso, 1995); Robert F. Dalzell Jr., *Enterprising Elite: The Boston Associates and the World They Made* (Cambridge, Mass.: Harvard Univ. Press, 1987); Alan Dawley, *Class and Community: The Industrial Revolution in Lynn* (Cambridge, Mass.: Harvard Univ. Press, 1976); Thomas Dublin, *Women at Work: The Transformation of Work and Community in Lowell, Massachusetts, 1826–1860* (New York: Columbia Univ. Press, 1979); Thomas Dublin, ed. *Farm to Factory: Women's Letters, 1830–1860* (New York: Columbia Univ. Press, 1981); Steve Dunwell, *The Run of the Mill* (Boston: David R. Godine, 1978); John S. Garner, *The Model Company Town: Urban Design through Private Enterprise in Nineteenth-Century New England* (Amherst: Univ. of Massachusetts Press, 1984; John S. Garner, ed. *The Company Town: Architecture and Society in the Early Industrial Age* (New York: Oxford Univ. Press, 1992); James L. Garvin, "Academic Architecture and the Building Trades in the Piscataqua Region of New Hampshire and Southern Maine, 1715–1815" (Ph.D. diss., Boston Univ., 1983); Richard

Greenwood, "A Mechanic in the Garden: Landscape Design in Industrial Rhode Island," in *IA (Journal of the Society for Industrial Archeology)* 24 (1) (1998): 9–18; Laurence Gross, *The Course of Industrial Decline: The Boott Cotton Mill of Lowell, Massachusetts, 1835–1955* (Baltimore: Johns Hopkins Univ. Press, 1993); Duncan Erroll Hay, "The New City on the Merrimack: The Essex Company and Its Role in the Creation of Lawrence, Massachusetts" (Ph.D. diss., Univ. of Delaware, 1986); "Industrial Housing at Hopedale, Massachusetts, Robert Allen Cook, Architect," reprint from *Architectural Review* (Apr. 1917); Gary Kulik, Roger Parks, and Theodore Penn, eds., *The New England Mill Village, 1790–1860* (Cambridge and London: MIT Press and Merrimack Valley Textile Museum, 1982); Gary Kulik, Roger Parks, and Theodore Penn, "Pawtucket Village and the Strike of 1824: The Origins of Class Conflict in Rhode Island," *Radical History Review* 17 (1978): 5–37; Steven David Lubar, "Corporate and Urban Contexts of Textile Technology in Nineteenth-Century Lowell, Massachusetts: A Study of the Social Nature of Technological Knowledge" (Ph.D. diss., Univ. of Chicago, 1983); Thomas McMullen, "Industrialization and Social Change in a Nineteenth-Century Port City: New Bedford, Massachusetts, 1865–1900" (Ph.D. diss., Univ. of Wisconsin, 1976); Thomas McMullen, "The Coming of the Mills: Social Change in New Bedford in the Late Nineteenth-Century," Lecture in a series for the New Bedford Bicentennial, New Bedford Free Public Library, 1987; Thomas McMullen, "Lost Alternative: Urban Industrial Utopia of William D. Howland," *New England Quarterly* 55 (1982); Daniel Nelson, *Managers and Workers: Origins of the Twentieth-Century Factory System in the United States, 1880–1920* (Madison: Univ. of Wisconsin Press, 1995); William H. Pierson Jr., *American Buildings and Their Architects: Technology and the Picturesque, the Corporate and the Early Gothic Styles* (Garden City, N.Y.: Doubleday, 1978); Prude, Jonathan, *The Coming of Industrial Order: Town and Factory Life in Rural Massachusetts, 1810–1860* (Cambridge: Cambridge Univ. Press, 1983); Report: *Lowell National Historical Park and Preservation District Cultural Resources Inventory* (Boston: Shepley, Bulfinch, Richardson and Abbott, 1980); Special Textile Mill Issue *Old-Time New England* 66 (1975): 13–28; Robert Weible, ed. *The Continuing Revolution: A History of Lowell, Massachusetts* (Lowell: Lowell Historical Society, 1991); Francois Weil, "Capitalism and Industrialization in New England, 1815–1845," *Journal of American History* (Mar. 1998): 1334–54. For listings specifically on the three-decker building type, see the notes to chap. 5.

3. Donna Gabaccia, ed. *Seeking Common Ground* (Westport, Conn.: Praeger Press, 1992), x1.

1. Growing Up in a New Bedford Three-Decker

1. See introduction, n. 1.

2. See Joseph D. Thomas and Judith A. Boss, *New Bedford* (Virginia Beach, Va.: Donning Company, 1990), 186, 194. By 1939, 72 percent of the active spindles in the United States were located in the South compared with 24 percent in 1900. Regional wage differences were significant. From 1894 to 1927 the average southern textile wage was 40 percent below that of other parts of the country. See Margaret Crawford, "Earle S. Draper and the Company Town in the American South," in *The Company Town*, ed. Garner, 141–42.

3. For more on the notion of a consensus image of place see E. Relph, *Place and Placelessness* (London: Pion Limited, 1976). Whaling had ceased to be a primary economy in New Bedford following the discovery of petroleum in the 1860s and two successive disasters in the Arctic (1871, 1876) to ships and cargo whose owners did not have their fleet insured. Whaling, however, continued on a much diminished scale in New Bedford up to the 1920s. By this time other forms of Atlantic fishing like cod fishing and later scallop fishing prevailed.

4. Beyond folkloristic studies, social histories, and sociological analyses, which acknowledge the legitimate role of personal, family, and community history, the recent efforts in English literature in the form of experiential critical writing have drawn additional attention to this area of interest. Important contributors to this literary genre are Amy Tan, Susan Howe, Jane Tomkins, Mariana Torgovnick, and Charles Bernstein.

In addition, as James Clifford has pointed out, developments in modern anthropology in the early twentieth century addressed the notion of "ethnographic subjectivity." Basically, in attempting to provide cultural descriptions as a Science of Man, the scientific method applied to professional fieldwork created the ironic stance of "participant observation," or a state of being *in culture* while looking *at culture*. Clifford indicated how this approach permeates twentieth-century art and writing as well as an expanded view of cultural artifacts (which today is inclusive of language and a discrete system of signs). See James Clifford, *The Predicament of Culture, Twentieth-Century Ethnography, Literature and Art* (Cambridge: Harvard Univ. Press, 1988), esp. chap. 3, "The Ethnographic Self-Fashioning: Conrad and Malinowski." Further, Clifford Geertz states the problem as follows: "[I]f it isn't . . . through some sort of extraordinary sensibility . . . to think, feel, perceive like a native, . . . how is anthropological knowledge of the way natives think, feel, and perceive possible?" This query has led to discussions of the various formulations of "inside" versus "outside," "phenomenological" versus "objectivist," or what psychoanalyst Heinz Kohut (1971) refers to as "experience-near" and "experience-distant" concepts. See Clifford Geertz's "'From the Native's Point of View': On the Nature of Anthropological Understanding," in *Meaning in Anthropology*, ed. Keith Basso and Henry Selby, (Albuquerque: University of New Mexico Press, 1976) 221–37. Also in Clifford Geertz, *Local Knowledge* (New York: Basic Books, 1983), 55–73. The quotation above by Geertz is on p. 56. Further, Wolfgang Iser refers to the interchange between the reader and the text in literature as the "reader response theory." See his *The Act of Reading: A Theory of Aesthetic Response* (Baltimore: Johns Hopkins Univ. Press, 1978), and *The Implied Reader: Patterns of Communication in Prose Fiction from Bunyan to Beckett* (Baltimore: Johns Hopkins Univ. Press, 1974). For the notion of the hidden aspects of a cultural landscape see, Kent C. Ryden, *Mapping the Invisible Landscape* (Iowa City: Univ. of Iowa Press, 1993). Also worth noting is Gaston Bachelard, *The Poetics of Space* (Boston: Beacon Press, 1969), esp. chap. 1, "The House. From Cellar to Garret. The Significance of the Hut." This is a phenomenological analysis of the home to discover, in part, the "profound reality of all the subtle shadings of our attachment for a chosen spot." (4).

For cultural interpretations of "place," see Kenneth T. Jackson, *The Crabgrass Frontier: The Suburbanization of the United States* (New York: Oxford Univ. Press, 1985); Donald W. Meinig, ed., *The Interpretation of Ordinary Landscapes* (New York: Oxford Univ. Press, 1979); John R. Stilgoe, *Borderland: Origins of the American Suburb, 1820–1939* (New Haven, Conn.: Yale Univ. Press, 1988); and John Stilgoe, *Common Landscape of America: 1580 to 1895* (New Haven, Conn.: Yale Univ. Press, 1982). Barbara Allen and Thomas Schlereth, eds., *Sense of Place: American Regional Cultures* (Lexington: Univ. Press of Kentucky, 1990); J. B. Jackson, *Sense of Place: A Sense of Time* (New Haven, Conn.: Yale Univ. Press, 1994).

For more on the subject of retrieving place through memory, see the following: Peter Burke, "History as Social Memory," in *Memory: History, Culture and the Mind*, ed. Thomas Butler (Oxford: Basil Blackwell, 1989), 97–114; David Lowenthall, "Past Time, Present Place: Landscape and Memory," *Geographical Review* 65 (1) (Jan. 1975): 1–36. David Lowenthall, *The Past Is a Foreign Country* (New York: Cambridge

Univ. Press, 1985), 3–35; 185–263. See also Henry Glassie, *Passing the Time in Ballymenone: Culture and History of an Ulster Community* (Philadelphia: Univ. of Pennsylvania Press, 1982). For the notion of relational meaning, see Michel Foucault, "Of Other Spaces," in *Diacritics* (Spring 1986): 22–27. Structuralism, by Foucault's definition, is an effort to establish an ensemble of relations that makes them appear as juxtaposed as a sort of configuration whereby each act or space is implicated by the other.

5. For example, when the children were young my grandparents lived on the first floor for easy access to the tenement with young children and for carrying groceries from the corner store. As the children left home as adults, they moved to the second floor in 1966, because it was cheaper to heat, since essentially all the heat from the bottom apartment escaped upwards.

6. This tenement was built by a developer, Joseph Blier, on October 19, 1912, for his client Francis Cardinand (Permit no. 800). Blier was the builder of two three-deckers on adjoining front and rear lots that faced Nelson and Scott streets. The three-tenement on 90 Nelson was designed with six rooms and a bath, measured 26 feet by 44 feet, had a slate-hipped roof, and three stories of front piazzas (3 feet by 10 feet) off of a three-story bay and two rear piazzas (5 feet by 14 feet). Information from the *New Bedford Record of Building Permits.*

7. Conservative management practices in running the mills on the part of the mill owners, interconnected financial networks of family-controlled mills and banking interests, and increased competition of textile industries in the South forced mill owners to slash wages, speed up machinery, and require operatives to manage more machines. Between 1918 and 1928 in New Bedford, there was an accumulated 30 percent drop in salary. In a city where low worker turnover was one of its assets, 18,000 people left New Bedford between 1925 to 1930. Fifty percent of the French-Canadian population, which had been the dominant labor force in the New Bedford mills since 1910, left the city between 1926 and 1928. By the end of the 1920s, the Portuguese became the largest ethnic labor force in the New Bedford mills. See McMullen, "Industrialization and Social Change"; and his "The Coming of the Mills: Social Change in New Bedford in the Late Nineteenth Century," lecture series for the New Bedford Bicentennial Sponsored by the New Bedford Free Public Library, 1987 (the manuscript is among the holdings of the New Bedford Free Public Library, Special Collections). See also Jamie W. Katz, "Opportunity, Exclusion, and the Immigrants: Textile Workers in New Bedford, Massachusetts, 1890–1930" (B.A. thesis, Dept. of History, Harvard College, 1974), esp. 47–50.

8. Mary F. Sharpe, *Plain Facts for Future Citizens* (New York: American Book Company, 1914). This was, in fact, my maternal grandfather's citizenship training book. Antonio Jose Medeiros arrived in New Bedford from Povacao, San Miguel, Azores, in 1900 at age fourteen.

9. Because of the tendency of the users of space to subvert the spatial hierarchies intended by the designer, the purpose behind the streetscape and backyard neighborhood interpretive drawings is to animate the architectural space surrounding the three-decker by integrating separate but interrelated details otherwise difficult to record in other forms of documentation. Special thanks to Gregor Weiss for assisting me in the representation phase of this project.

10. In a similar way, Bernard Herman sees the Charleston single house less as a building type and more as an architectural strategy focused on the maintenance of complex social relationships. Moving through a household environment, he maintains, means encountering an array of experiences that affirm and challenge social relationships within a household. Similarly, to look at a building as "embedded" in a landscape provides for the study of spaces within and among buildings—especially spaces where actions and interactions occur and relationships are defined in ways that link domestic spaces with stratified and processional cultural landscapes. See Bernard L. Herman, "The Embedded Landscapes of the Charleston Single House, 1780–1820," in *Exploring Everyday Landscapes: Perspectives in Vernacular Architecture, VII*, ed. Annmarie Adams and Sally McMurry (Knoxville: Univ. of Tennessee Press, 1997), 41–57.

11. Bernard Herman refers to the close examination of such details as internal finish, room orientation, and condition in relation to other comparable spaces in nearby dwellings as "intrasite analysis." Herman, Ibid.

12. The 1890 U.S. Census for Wards 1 and 6 (the industrial sections of the North and South Ends of New Bedford) indicates ten people per living unit, or thirty people per three-tenement.

13. Interview with John Dias by the author, Mar. 13, 1992, New Bedford, Massachusetts. Mr. Dias lived on the upper floor of the 1912 three-decker on 90 Nelson Street during the 1940s. As a young man, he worked in the Acushnet Mills changing bobbins for the power looms during the late 1930s. These wages, he notes, were a big improvement over the wages he had earned

on his father's dairy farm in Dartmouth, Massachusetts. He married Elaine Pitts, who lived on the first floor of the same three-decker in 1947.

14. Beginning with the publication of *The Hidden Dimension* (Garden City, N.Y.: Doubleday, 1966), Edward Hall has addressed the subject of human perception and the use of space. He has demonstrated effectively how the built environment controls and reflects human relationships as an extension of the human psyche and culturally determined unconscious acts. Also, Edward Hall, *Dance of Life: The Other Dimension of Time* (Garden City, N.Y.: Anchor Press/Doubleday, 1983). For a systems approach that addresses the social dimensions of spaces as manifestations and reinforcements of social relations, see Peter Senge, *The Fifth Discipline* (New York: Doubleday, 1990). For a discussion of the relevance of spatial analysis to understanding cultural practice, and for a theory of spatial production, see Henri Lefebvre, *The Production of Space* (Oxford: Blackwell, 1991).

15. See, for example, Elizabeth Cromley's forthcoming book *Internal Affairs: A History of American Domestic Space*. Other works are forthcoming by David Scobey of the University of Michigan and Betsy Blackmar of Columbia University on issues of socially constructed space in New York and notions of official authority and surveillance related to those spaces. For a study of how objects in a home illustrate rules of a domestic environment, see Denis Wood and Robert J. Beck, *Home Rules* (Baltimore: Johns Hopkins Univ. Press, 1994). For an architectural design discussion of transitional space, see Herman Hertzberger, *Lessons for Students in Architecture* (Rotterdam: Uitgeveri, 1991), esp. the discussion of "In Between." For a discussion of different spatial cultures and experiences of space tied to different codes of comportment, see Richard L. Bushman, *The Refinement of America: Persons, Houses, Cities* (New York: Vintage Books, 1993). Diane Shaw's paper "Sorting the City: Socio-Spatial Dynamics in Mid-19th-Century Syracuse and Rochester, New York" (delivered at the Vernacular Architecture Forum's Annual Meeting, Columbus, Ga., May 8, 1999) illustrates how rules of etiquette were worn like a shield to protect genteel women from the cruder human element. Comportment, then, was used to preserve the "mantle of decency" and often led to spatial strategies such as a consciously constructed spatial order of movement, which conceptually structured social behavior within the cityscapes of Syracuse and Rochester during the early nineteenth century. These small cities, Shaw argues, led settlers "to construct functionally and architecturally segmented city-scapes," which she calls "compact–and-sorted cityscapes." Invisible social boundaries were relied upon to retaliate against the compact city, which otherwise was wide open and physically accessible to all. "Behavioral codes combined with architectural cues to forge a spatial culture that structured the social use of urban space." See also M. Gottdeiner, *The Social Production of Urban Space*, 2d ed. (Austin: Univ. of Texas Press, 1985). For issues of privatization and control within urban spaces, see Margaret Crawford, "Blurring the Boundaries: Public Space and Private Life," in *Everyday Urbanism*, ed. John Chase, Margaret Crawford, John Kaliski (New York: Moncelli Press, 1999).

16. For notions of the gendering of space, see Daphne Spain, *Gendered Spaces* (Chapel Hill: Univ. of North Carolina Press, 1992). Spain combines methods drawn predominantly from planning, feminist geography, and sociology to address notions of power and theories of stratification. Her study addresses implications of change in spatial arrangements with regard to the status of women over time and across cultures. For an example of gender mapping, see Thomas Hubka, *Big House, Little House, Back House, Barn* (Hanover, N.H.: Univ. Press of New England, 1984), 151, fig. 114. On gender-defined uses of space, see Mchaly Csikszentmihalyi and Eugene Rochbery-Halton, *The Meaning of Things: Domestic Symbols of Self* (Cambridge: Cambridge Univ. Press, 1981); Minh-Ha Trinh, *When the Moon Waxes Red: Representation, Gender, and Cultural Politics* (New York: Routledge, 1991).

17. For a discussion of thermal comfort from an experiential standpoint and the role of temperature contrast (versus steady-state systems) that add to the variety and content of place, see Lisa Haschong, *Thermal Delight in Architecture* (Cambridge, Mass.: MIT Press, 1979). Special thanks to Dale Brentrup in environmental design at U.N.C.C. for his assistance on doing a climate study analysis of the three-decker. For background sources, see G. Z. Brown, Bruce Haglund, Joel Loveland, John S. Reynolds, M. Susan Ubbelohde, *Inside-Out: Design Procedures for Passive Environmental Technologies* (New York: John Wiley and Sons, 1992), 5–12, 105–14, 167–70; see also G. Z. Brown, *Sun, Wind and Light Architectural Design Strategies* (New York: John Wiley and Sons, 1985), pt. 1: Analysis techniques "Climate as Context." An early groundbreaking study is Victor Olgyay, *Design with Climate: Bioclimatic Approach to Architectural Regionalism* (Princeton, N.J.: Princeton Univ. Press, 1963).

Works on the sense of place from the architecture, urban design, and planning professions include the following: Kevin Lynch, *The Image of the City* (Cambridge, Mass.: MIT Press, 1960), and *What Time Is This Place?* (Cambridge, Mass.: MIT Press, 1972); Nicholas Entrikin Jr., *The Betweenness of Place: Towards a Geography of Modernity* (Baltimore: Johns Hopkins Univ. Press, 1991); Jane Jacobs, *The Death and Life of the Great American Cities* (New York: Random House, 1961); Peter G. Rowe, *Making a Middle Landscape* (Cambridge, Mass.: MIT Press, 1991), esp. "Placelessness or Place," 56–60; Edward Ralph, *Place and Placelessness* (London: Pion, Ltd., 1976); Christian Norberg-Schulz, *Genius Loci* (New York: Rizzoli, 1980); Jory Johnson, "Regionalism and Invention: Codex World Headquarters," *Landscape Architecture* (Apr.– May 1988), 58–63; Kenneth Frampton, "Ten Points on an Architecture of Regionalism: A Provisional Polemic," *Center* (Mar. 1987), 20–7; Hertzberger, *Lessons for Students*; James Howard Kunstler, *The Geography of Nowhere: The Rise and Decline of America's Man-made Landscape* (New York: Simon and Schuster, 1993), esp. chap. 10, "The Loss of Community," 175–88; see also by Kunstler, *Home from Nowhere: Reading our Everyday World for the 21st Century* (New York: Simon and Schuster, 1996); John Agnew and James Duncan, eds., *The Power of Place: Bringing Together Geographical and Sociological Imaginations* (Boston: Unwin Hyman, 1989); Joseph Rykwert, *The Seduction of Place: The City in the Twenty-first Century* (New York: Pantheon Books, 2000); Francis Downing, *Remembrance and the Design of Place* (College Station: Texas A & M, 2001).

2. From Whaling Port to Leading Textile Center

1. William L. Sayer, ed., *New Bedford, Massachusetts: Its History, Institutions and Attractions* (New Bedford: 1889), 31; see also Henry Beetle Hough, *Wamsutta of New Bedford* (New Bedford: Wamsutta Mills, 1946), 18.

2. During the decade before the Civil War, New Bedford was the second-richest city in the state and one of the richest in the world in per capita income, since most of the poorly paid whaling crews lived at sea. McMullen, "Industrialization and Social Change," 6. Of the 735 vessels of all kinds in New Bedford, 250 were whaleships. In a single day, these whaleships were known to have brought in $300,000. In a year, the catch of oil and whalebone amounted to $10 million. The greatest receipts in any twelve months was in 1845—158,000 barrels of sperm oil, 272,000 barrels of whale oil, and 300,000 pounds of whalebone. See Hough, *Wamsutta of New Bedford,* 18.

3. Joseph Grinnell entered business in New York with his uncle John H. Howland in 1810 under the firm name of Howland and Grinnell. The firm failed, however, due to losses in shipping during the War of 1812. After 1815, Grinnell went into a partnership with his cousin Captain Preserved Fish. Following his cousin's retirement in 1825, Joseph took his brothers Henry and Moses into the New Bedford firm. At the time that Grinnell built his mansion on County Street in 1832, his estimated worth was $150,000. Grinnell's influence brought the New Bedford and Taunton Railroad to the city, a key factor in the later success of textile interests. Grinnell built two ships, had banking interest in the city, and was elected to the U.S. Congress. His influence shifted Wamsutta's charter from Abraham Howland to Thomas Bennett, who provided the leadership necessary to make textiles a success in New Bedford. See Hough, *Wamsutta of New Bedford,* 10–11.

4. Abraham Howland was elected mayor the year following the city's incorporation in 1846. He was elected four more times to that position. His estate on County Road was located almost across from the Grinnell mansion. Regarding the reluctant purchase of the estate, Hough quotes Howland as saying, "I tell you, Henry, I didn't intend to do it, but the agents were forever keeping after me, and to get rid of them I finally made an offer so ridiculously cheap I was certain they wouldn't take it. They took it" (Hough, *Wamsutta of New Bedford,* 18). With regard to Abraham Howland's experience as a ship's master, Hough states: "He had sailed several voyages on a whaleship, latterly, as master. . ." (Hough, ibid., 7).

5. Nicholas Whitman, *A Window Back* (New Bedford: Spinner Publications, 1994), 93.

6. Judith Boss and Joseph Thomas, *New Bedford* (Virginia Beach, Va.: Donning Co., 1990), 43.

7. These references came from the Arnold exhibit at the Rotch-Jones-Duff House and Garden Museum in New Bedford.

8. See Leonard Ellis, *History of New Bedford and Its Vicinity* (New York: D. Mason and Co., 1892). An image of the Arnold house (by 1889, it was known as the William J. Rotch house) in its natural setting can be found in Sayer, *New Bedford,* 67. References to Arnold's munificence were quoted from the Arnold exhibit cited in n. 7.

9. This original document is on display at the Rotch-Jones-Duff House and Garden Museum in New Bedford.

10. Abraham Howland, the original founder of Wamsutta Mills, was a political rival for a U.S. congressional post in 1848 with his relative and the first president of Wamsutta Mills, Joseph Grinnell. While Howland was a key political figure of the radical independent group known as the Barnburners, Grinnell belonged to the more moderate Whig Party, and Howland's brother-in-law, Captain Delano, was an ultra-conservative "Hunker"—the political opposite of the Barnburners. See Hough, *Wamsutta of New Bedford*, 9–11.

11. Pierson, *American Buildings and Their Architects*, 2: 297, 395.

12. A. J. Downing, *The Architecture of Country Houses Including Designs for Cottages, Farm Houses and Villas with Remarks on Interiors, Furniture, and the Best Modes of Warming and Ventilating* (New York, 1850), sect. II, entitled "What a Cottage Should Be." See Pierson, *American Buildings and Their Architects*, vol. 2, chap. 7, pt. 3 for further discussion. For more on the symbolic and social import of the Gothic Cottage, see E. Clifford Clark Jr., "Domestic Architecture as an Index to Social History: The Romantic Revival and the Cult of Domesticity in America, 1840–1870," *Journal of Interdisciplinary History* 7 (1) (Summer 1976): 33–56; Kathryn Kish Sklar, *Catherine Beecher: A Study in American Domesticity* (New Haven, Conn.: Yale Univ. Press, 1973). For a discussion of American Woman's Home, see David Handlin, *The American Home, Architecture and Society 1815–1915* (Boston: Little, Brown, 1979), 404–9. For a perspective which addresses Catherine Beecher as a leading advocate of "domestic feminism," see Dolores Hayden, *The Grand Domestic Revolution: A History of Feminist Designs for American Homes, Neighborhoods, and Cities* (Cambridge, Mass.: MIT Press, 1992), 54–63.

13. Alma McArdle, *Carpenter Gothic* (New York: Whitney Library of Design, 1978), 26.

14. Ibid. See also John M. Bullard, *The Rotches* (Milford, N.H.: Cabinet Press, 1947), 106.

15. William J. Rotch's first wife, Emily Morgan, died in 1861 following childbirth. William married her sister five years later. The mansion on County Street was left to William following the death of James Arnold in 1868.

16. Morgan Rotch's fondness for the Gothic cottage style is reflected as well in his decision to rent the cottage on Clark's Point belonging to family friends and business associates Matthew and Rachel Howland. The stone barn, later converted to a cottage, had been built in the Gothic style in 1840 by naturalist and banker Joseph Congdon. In 1865, the Howland family purchased the estate for summer use. By January 26, 1880, the cottage

is noted as being rented to Morgan Rotch (who three months earlier, December 5, 1879, had married a Grinnell). By 1883, Morgan Rotch (now mayor of New Bedford) moved into his father's 1846 Gothic cottage, having moved the dwelling back seventy-five feet to its present location. It had previously been owned by W. W. Crapo. Morgan, on May 9, 1883 hosted a wedding reception there for Belle Rotch. An 1857 addition by William Ralph Emerson maintained the Gothic style. See Matthew Howland to Matthew Morris Howland, Jan. 26, 1880; Mar. 3, 1880, Howland family correspondence, 1878–84, collection of Llewellyn Howland III, Jamaica Plain, Mass. For background on the Congdon Estate, see Ellis L. Howland, "Hazlewood, History of the City's New Park on Clark's Point" and "How Joseph Congdon's Industry Carved Out Its Beauty" *Standard Times*, July 27, 1901, and June 21, 1902.

17. Among just a few notables who either arrived in the city or were New Bedford natives were author Herman Melville, architects A. J. Davis, Russell Warren, Richard Upjohn, Robert Swain Peabody, and painters William Bradford, Charles Gifford, Albert van Beest, Albert Ryder, and Albert Bierstadt (during the 1860s Albert and his brothers Edward and Charles were largely involved with architectural photography of urban landscapes in New Bedford, Civil War battlefields, and Washington, D.C., rather than the large landscape paintings of the Rocky Mountain School for which Albert Bierstadt later was noted).

18. Herman Melville, *Moby Dick* (New York: Random House, 1950), 33.

19. See James E. Vance Jr., *The Continuing City* (Baltimore, Md.: Johns Hopkins Univ. Press, 1990), 355.

20. Ellis, *History of New Bedford*, 454.

21. Hough, *Wamsutta of New Bedford*, 14–15. Captain Thomas Bennett had been trained in the merchant service out of Fairhaven and New Bedford. Educated at Friends Academy and married to a Howland, he possessed the social connections necessary to function in New Bedford's financial circles. With his textile training in the South, it was said "he knew cotton in the bale, as it came from the gin, and . . . cotton manufacturing" (ibid., 9).

22. Ellis, *History of New Bedford*, 456.

23. Caroline F. Ware, *The Early New England Cotton Manufacture: A Study in Industrial Beginnings* (Boston: Houghton Mifflin, 1931), 107. Vance, *Continuing City*, 355.

24. Shortly afterwards, Rodman's company failed, and its assets were sold at auction in 1851. Daniel

Georgianna, *The Strike of '28* (New Bedford: Spinner Publications, 1993), 20–21; Hough, *Wamsutta of New Bedford*, 9.

25. This water source is referred to as the "ice pond" on the 1871 *Beers Map of the City of New Bedford*. Captain Delano had originally selected Fish Island at the mouth of the New Bedford Harbor as a mill site when Wamsutta was first organized under Abraham Howland. Hough, *Wamsutta of New Bedford*, 9. For the reference to Grinnell's support of the New Bedford and Taunton Railroad, see ibid., 11; 21.

26. Originally called "percall" and referred to as "Supercale" on Wamsutta labels, the closely woven cloth sheets were duplicated from samples brought into the New York store of Arnold Constable and Co. by a member of the Vanderbilt family in 1876. Hough, *Wamsutta of New Bedford*, 32–40. See also Georgianna, *Strike of '28*, 20–21.

27. Sayer, *New Bedford*, 149. Also, Hough, *Wamsutta of New Bedford*, 17.

28. Ellis, *History of New Bedford*, 456. Hough, *Wamsutta of New Bedford*, 22. Carpentry work was provided by Pierce and Wright, and Dudley Davenport for $19,560, and masonry work was done by Haile Luther for $16,395.

29. Ellis, *History of New Bedford*, 458. Even the company's first dividend, paid in January 1850, amounted to 5 percent of the stock value. Within twenty-five years the company's investment grew to $2,000,000 and paid a consistent 6 percent dividend. Interestingly, the original founder of the Wamsutta Mills, Abraham Howland, perhaps because of his political rivalry with Joseph Grinnell, never took a share of stock. Hough, *Wamsutta of New Bedford*, 11, 15; McMullen, "Industrialization and Social Change," 27–40; Georgianna, *Strike of '28*, 21.

30. Ellis, *History of New Bedford*, 460.

31. To be more precise, during the 1830s the mostly male workers in Fall River had joined with the working women in Lowell in sending petitions for the ten-hour workday to the Massachusetts State Legislature. See Georgianna, *Strike of '28*, 30; Hayden, *Grand Domestic Revolution*, 92 and 321n. 8. For more on the struggle on the part of labor to achieve a ten-hour workday, see Teresa Ann Murphy, *Ten Hours' Labor: Religion, Reform, and Gender in Early New England* (Ithaca, N.Y.: Cornell Univ. Press, 1992).

32. For more regarding labor protests, racial conflicts, and class struggles on board nineteenth-century American whalers, see Briton Cooper Busch, *"Whaling Will Never Do for Me": The American Whaleman in the Nineteenth Century* (Lexington: Univ. Press of Kentucky, 1994), which uses journals and ship logs. See also Elmo Hohman, *The American Whaleman: A Study of Life and Labor in the Whaling Industry* (New York: Longmans, Green and Co., 1928).

33. Sayer, *New Bedford*, 145.

34. For a summary of these early strikes, see Georgianna, *Strike of '28*, chap. 2.

35. Vital Records of New Bedford, MA., to the year 1850 (Boston, 1941), 3; *Census of Massachusetts* 1875 (Boston, 1877), 1: 274; *Census of Massachusetts* 1885 (Boston, 1887), 6: 220. These sources indicate that the foreign born population had increased by 4,309 people: a 73 percent increase over the 1875 figure, cited in Joanne Martha Dykas, "Whaling, Cotton, and the Howland Family: Reactions to Changes in the Economic Foundations of Nineteenth Century New Bedford, Massachusetts," (B.A. Thesis in History, Harvard Univ., 1980), 84–85.

36. As Boss and Thomas note: "The decline in the number of barrels of oil per voyage began in 1850 when the average take was 1693 barrels. By 1857, the year when the size of the New Bedford's fleet reached its peak, the average take was down to 796 barrels per voyage" (*New Bedford*, 70,76). See also McMullen, "Industrialization and Social Change," 6, 13; Georgianna, *Strike of '28*, 13; Everett Allen, *Children of the Light: The Rise and Fall of New Bedford Whaling and the Death of the Arctic Fleet* (Boston: Little, Brown 1973), 222; Barbara Clayton and Kathleen Whitley, *Guide to New Bedford*, (Montpelier, Vt.: Capital City Press, 1979), 117; Wilkie and Tager, *Historical Atlas of Massachusetts*, 116.

37. Allen, *Children of the Light*, 222; McMullen, "Industrialization and Social Change," 13; Hough, *Wamsutta of New Bedford*, 19.

38. Rachel S. Howland to her middle son, Matthew Morris Howland, 28 Sept. 1881 All citations listed for Howland family correspondence date from 1878–1884, and are in the collection of Llewellyn Howland III. The author is grateful for copies of these documents sent by Mr. Howland.

39. Richard S. Howland to William D. Howland, Dec. 23,1879.

40. Richard S. Howland to William D. Howland, Jan. 19, 1880.

41. Matthew Howland to Matthew Morris Howland, Jan. 31, 1880.

42. Ellis, *History of New Bedford*, 104.

43. Boss and Thomas, *New Bedford*, 104.

44. Ellis, *History of New Bedford*, 464–65.

45. Sayer, *New Bedford*, 154.

46. William Emery, *Ancestry of the Grinnell Family* (Privately printed, 1931), 20–23.

47. Sayer, *New Bedford*, 150.

48. McMullen, "The Coming of the Mills," 3.

49. For a discussion of the growth of the industrial city in America as it relates to New Bedford, see Vance, *Continuing City*, 353–61.

50. Allen R. Pred, *The Spatial Dynamics of U.S. Urban-Industrial Growth 1800–1914* (Cambridge, Mass.: MIT Press, 1966). Vance, *Continuing City*, 354.

51. Vance, *Continuing City*, 355.

52. To see how this factor relates directly to Portuguese immigration patterns, see Jerry R. Williams, *And Yet They Come: Portuguese Immigration from the Azores to the United States* (New York: Center for Migration Studies, 1982), 14–15.

53. Katz, "Opportunity, Exclusion, and the Immigrant," 25.

54. Technical Advisory Corporation, *A Reconnaissance Survey of New Bedford, Mass.* (New Bedford: A. E. Coffin Press, 1923), 291. This source notes that, following the Civil War and the sudden curtailment of the whaling industry, New Bedford had a population of 22,000. After that time, the rate of population increase according to Federal census in round figures were as follows: 1880–90, 45 percent; 1890–1900, 55 percent; 1900–1910, 56 percent; 1910–20, 25 percent.

55. Ellis, *History of New Bedford*, 453. Wilkie and Tager, *Historical Atlas of Massachusetts*, 35.

56. The French Canadians (numbering 8,559 in 1900) were joined by the English (5,389 in 1900, accounting for 21 percent), with the Portuguese (accounting for 19 percent) and the Irish (3,026 in 1900, making up 12 percent of the population, down from 24 percent in 1890). See Katz, "Opportunity, Exclusion, and the Immigrant," 32–33.

57. Ibid., 33.

58. *New Bedford City Directory*, 1911, 759.

59. Sayer, *New Bedford*, 153. By 1892, the figure would rise to 500 bales consumed weekly, 25,000 bales consumed annually, out of which was manufactured 24,000,000 yards of cloth. See Ellis, *History of New Bedford*, 461.

60. Katz, "Opportunity, Exclusion, and the Immigrant," 29.

61. Clayton and Whitley, *Guide to New Bedford*, 116–18; 159–61.

62. Rachel S. Howland to Matthew Morris Howland, Nov. 15, 1882.

63. Letter to F. L. Olmsted from Alice T. Mandell, Sept. 4, 1883. All correspondence quoted here can be located under Job File 672 in the Library of Congress, Manuscript Division.

64. Letter to F. L. Olmsted from Alice T. Mandell, Sept. 6, 1883.

65. Letter to F. L. Olmsted from Alice T. Mandell, Sept. 4, 1883. William Ralph Emerson designed the addition to the William J. Rotch Gothic cottage in New Bedford in 1857 shortly after starting his private practice. Between the years 1879 and 1887, the *New Bedford City Directory* has no listing under Emerson for anyone in the building trades. William Ralph Emerson, like Olmsted, was from the Boston area, and likely coordinated the construction progress by written correspondence. For more on William Ralph Emerson, see Henry F. Withey and Elsie R. Withey, *Biographical Dictionary of American Architects (Deceased)* (Los Angeles, Calif.: Hennessey and Ingalls, 1970), 198.

66. *New Bedford City Directory* entries for 1879 to 1889 under Edward Mandell. The 1889 entry, 292, was the first to establish the Hawthorn Street address. The Pairpoint Glass Company was begun in 1880 and built adjacent to the 1871 and 1877 Potomska Mills in the South End.

67. Matthew Howland to Matthew Morris Howland, Feb. 7, 1884.

68. Matthew Howland to Matthew Morris Howland, June 28, 1884.

69. See Job File 01381, Frederick Grinnell, Library of Congress, for the Olmsted legal contract for the job. The plans, however, can be located at the Frederick Law Olmsted Historic Site, Brookline, Mass., under the same job file.

70. Katz, "Opportunity, Exclusion, and the Immigrant," 29–30.

71. ISbid., 30–31.

72. Ibid., 31–32.

73. Ibid., 33.

74. The 1910 *New Bedford City Directory*, 405, lists a Manuel Souza, mariner, at 445 So. Water Street, while 404 lists a "fisherman" under the same listing residing at 20 County Street (where it meets Cove Road) in the same general area in the South End. The caption on the 1912 Lewis H. Hine photo of Manuel Sousa's family

lists the address as 306 Second Street, also in the South End.

75. Reminiscence by William Isherwood during an interview with M. Butler, North Dartmouth, Mass., Jan. 23, 1980.

76. Alfred Benoit is listed in the 1910 *New Bedford City Directory,* 977, and in the 1913 *Directory,* 384. The 191 No. Front Street address listing is in the reverse index for 1910 on p. 11.

77. This factor of overcrowding would continue, for as the 1923 Reconnaissance study on New Bedford revealed, rents remained high, despite the fact that adequate housing accommodations for the city's increasing population had kept better pace with the needs than was the case in many comparable cities. See Technical Advisory Corporation, *A Reconnaissance Survey,* 22.

78. David Handlin, *The American Home: Architecture and Society, 1815–1915* (Boston: Little, Brown, 1979), 364.

79. For a discussion of this issue in other locales, see Lawrence Veiller, "Tenement House Reform in New York City, 1834–1900," in *The Tenement House Problem*, ed. Robert W. De Forest and Lawrence Veiller (New York, 1903), 69–118.

80. See the "Industrial Beginnings" chart, which indicates the peak production years of New Bedford as extending from 1880s to 1921. Wilkie and Tager, *Historical Atlas of Massachusetts,* 30.

81. A noticeable exception is the recent sculptural piece of Lewis Temple, the African American blacksmith from New Bedford, who invented the revolutionary iron toggle harpoon tip in 1848. His image stands astride (though on a lower sculptural base) *The Whaleman* in front of the New Bedford Free Public Library.

As early as the eighteenth century, the whaling industry employed a high proportion of people of color, and New Bedford's African American population historically is second only to Boston's in Massachusetts. The more extensive foreground space of the library, which allowed the public art to be installed, was created by the Olmsted firm at the time of the original refurbishing of the former City Hall in 1912. Special thanks to Michael Steinitz of the Massachusetts Historic Commission for his background information on the African American involvement in whaling.

3. HOUSING THE NEW INDUSTRIAL WORKFORCE

1. McMullen, "Industrialization and Social Change," 3; Georgianna, *Strike of '28,* 12, 22.

2. Marsha McCabe and Joseph D. Thomas, *Not Just Anywhere* (New Bedford: Spinner Publications, 1995), 31. Some notable examples are the Mariner's Home, originally built as the private mansion of William Rotch Jr. in 1787; it was moved from the corner of William and Water Streets to Johnnycake Hill. In 1857, the mansion was donated to the New Bedford Port Society by James Arnold, son-in-law of Rotch, to provide shelter and a homelike atmosphere at a nominal fee for those who had been at sea for at least six months. Similarly, Friends Academy, built in 1810 on the corner of County and Elm by William Rotch, was sold in 1861 and moved to Elm Street for use as a tenement. And the Gideon Howland Jr. mansion, built in c. 1795 on the southwest corner of South Water and School Streets, was later used as a rooming house until its demolition in 1904. Boss and Thomas, *New Bedford,* 34, 47, 154.

3. Ellis, *History of New Bedford,* 456. James Vance has suggested that "Lawrence and New Bedford, both industrialized in the mid-1840s, demonstrate two distinct forms of industrial urbanism produced by contrasts in power sources and in labor recruitment." This much is true. However, he also adds: "An urban location [in New Bedford] with a generalized supply of housing was far more useful to their purposes than the boarding house system begun in Waltham" (*Continuing City,* 355). This latter point does not appear to be consistent with the evidence of large numbers of corporate boardinghouses and tenements being constructed in New Bedford beginning in 1848.

4. The side stairhalls make these units more akin to the one-and-one-half-story and two-and-one-half-story, four-tenement houses at Wamsutta, however. For more on corporate housing in New England, see Candee, "Architecture and Corporate Planning," 17–43. For specific discussions of the corporate boardinghouses mentioned, see Candee, "Early New England Mill Towns," 111–38. Images of the Dutton Street and Worthen Street housing in Lowell are represented in Coolidge, *Mill and Mansion,* figs. 4, 5, 9, 74. See also Steve Roper, "30 and 32 Atlantic Block, 401–403 Canal Street, Lawrence, Mass.: Architectural and Historical Research Report," typescript, Apr. 29, 1983; "Plans of the Boardinghouses Built for the Atlantic Cotton Mills," c. 1847, Essex Company Collection, Museum of American Textile History, Massachusetts Sanitary Survey Commission Report (Boston, 1850), appendix.

5. The reluctance to use brick for factory housing after the earliest corporate housing was constructed is understandable from an economic standpoint at this juncture, since the mills (until 1868) were constructed

of granite. Hence, any reduction in cost due to volume by building both the mill and the housing of brick would not have been a factor prior to 1868, when Wamsutta's first brick mill was constructed. The early investment in the brick boardinghouse format, therefore, must be construed as a competitive gesture on the part of Wamsutta's management to lure the best workers and overseers away from other area industries.

6. Plans and specifications for the units known as Wamsutta Village were prepared by the Boston architectural firm of Hresko Associates, Oct. 18, 1985, and were reproduced for the author through the assistance of Tony Souza of W.H.A.L.E. with permission of Hresko Association.

7. Jessamine Whitney, *Infant Mortality: Results of a Field Study in New Bedford, Massachusetts, Based on Births in One Year* (Washington, D.C.: U.S. Department of Labor, Children's Bureau, 1920), 55–6. Though the publication date is 1920, the actual field study was undertaken between 1913 and 1914. The housing report was written by Helen Wilson. As a regional comparison, John Luippold's findings for the 1900 Bibb Mill in Georgia (based on the 1920 U.S. Census) indicates twenty-four ten-room houses constructed for the mill's employees. Seventy-five percent of the houses had boarders, with an average of five boarders per house. Personal interview with John Luippold, Vernacular Architecture Forum Annual Meeting, Columbus, Ga., May 8, 1999.

8. Sayer, *New Bedford*, 153.

9. Ellis, *History of New Bedford*, 461.

10. Whitney, *Infant Mortality*, 56.

11. Beyond the issue of the speculative housing market in Lowell, which eventually took over the responsibility for housing the workers, is the problem of workers of different nationalities getting along in the boardinghouses. See "Memorandum of subjects to be brought to the notice of the Directors of the Salmon Falls Co. at their monthly meeting January 18, 1854," Treasurer's Report, Salmon Falls Manufacturing Company, 1854, A. A. Lawrence Papers, Massachusetts Historical Society. The topic of discussion was the "difficulty of keeping Irish and Americans together in an isolated village, . . ." quoted in Candee, "Early New England Mill Towns," 131. While this reference does not apply directly to Lowell, after 1848 the labor force at Lowell diversified greatly to include a wide assortment of nationalities. It is, therefore, reasonable to believe that similar problems of boardinghouse living in Lowell prompted the segregated housing districts

that later appeared in that city. In contrast, the Wamsutta skilled workers initially were mostly English; only after the Civil War, when the number of French Canadians workers increased, and into the 1880s did the workforce become more diversified in New Bedford. For a background of the boardinghouse system at Lowell, see Clancey, "Origin of the Boott Boardinghouse Plan," 7–21.

12. These products are mentioned by Ellis, *History of New Bedford*, 154. An earlier Potomska advertisement in the 1887 *New Bedford City Directory*, 6, included umbrellas and shades on the list.

13. Wamsutta employed this building type as well and, in fact, may have predated Potomska, but the Potomska three-deckers are the earliest *datable* examples of the type that could be uncovered because of the extensive fire damage and highway demolition that has taken place in the former Wamsutta tenement district. Photo documentation of the Wamsutta Mills indicates several rows of flat-roof three-deckers, but the photos date from the 1890s. Also, building permits in New Bedford do not begin until 1893, and those following this date do not specifically list Wamsutta as the client requesting the permit for a "three-tenement," while other corporations do. Wamsutta business records, half of which were destroyed by water damage, are not helpful in this regard either.

14. These previously unacknowledged Potomska Mill tenements are still extant, though in poor repair, and in danger of demolition due to recent fire damage. Some units maintain their original stylistic integrity. It is worth noting that due to the loss of the earliest Wamsutta housing in the Washburn area, the Potomska Mill housing dating from 1871 represents some of the earliest surviving examples of corporate housing in New Bedford, along with the Wamsutta Mill Historic District bounded by Hazard, Austin, County, and Pleasant Streets.

15. For a discussion of the ethnic makeup and housing types found in mill precincts 16 and 17 in 1913 where Potomska was located, see Whitney, *Infant Mortality*, 16–19, 55–56.

16. All twenty-six units can be located on the 1888 *Sanborn Map* by using the designation of "T" or tenement as the key. This denoted corporate-owned housing on *New Bedford Sanborn Maps*. An "F" denoted a flat on the "Description and Utilization Key to Symbols" on the *Sanborn Maps*, indicating single-family occupancy per floor. "R" was used for a roominghouse, which indicated a residential structure of more than ten rooms

used for lodging or boarding. Hence, on the early New Bedford Sanborns, a three-decker would be referred to as a tenement ("T") if it was an entity owned by a corporation, and a flat if it was a private rental unit. Similarly, a two-decker would be designated as a dwelling ("D") if it was a residential structure of not more than two families. As late as the 1906 *Sanborn Map*, Potomska was still building (within walking distance to the mills) such structures as saloons and stores with tenements above for the help. Ellis, *History of New Bedford*, 154. In "Coming of the Mills," McMullen states that "the Potomska Corporation also built two boardinghouses for single help "Coming of the Mills" (6), but there is no source for this information, and I found no other mention of the Potomska boardinghouses.

17. According to *New Bedford's Record of Building Permits*, the third floor was used frequently to provide additional lodging space by expanding the head room in the roof with cross gables and shed roof dormers during the 1890s through the 1910s. Today, the third-floor, two-bedroom plan is common in the gable-front, two-and-one-half-story type.

18. Robert B. Gordon and Patrick M. Malone, *The Texture of Industry: An Archaeological View of the Industrialization of North America* (New York: Oxford Univ. Press, 1994), 367–68. See also M. T. Copeland, *The Cotton Manufacturing Industry of the United States* (New York: Kelley, 1996), 86–88; William H. Chase, *Five Generations of Loom Builders* (Hopedale, Mass.: Draper, 1950), 13–19; William Mass, "Mechanical and Organizational Innovation: The Drapers and their Automatic Loom," *Business History Review* 63 (1989): 876–929.

19. Interview by telephone between the author and Mary Blewett, Sept. 22, 2000. See Mary Blewett, *Constant Turmoil* (Amherst: Univ. of Massachusetts Press, 2000) for a regional study of labor politics that includes New Bedford and Fall River.

20. In addition to the lower wages paid by the mills upon hiring, state regulations (known as the weavers' particular law) imposed on weaving in 1892 by the Massachusetts legislature affected the income of ring spinners. The law "forced textile mills to mark on tickets attached to warp beams all the specifications in the weaving process. . . . The act forbade arbitrary changes in piece rates in various styles and in lengths . . . along with weave specifications, the tickets stated wages to be expected." This was an effort to regulate the *amount* of work and, hence, wages paid by the mill to establish fair wage practices. In response, mill agents evaded the law by paying the weavers by the pound. The New

Bedford mills also had a punitive system of fines, whereby the entire process of textile production ended up on the bolt of cloth for final assessment. According to this system, any oil marks, defects, etc., that appeared earlier in the weaving process were the responsibility of the weaver as part of quality control. This could result in wage reductions from 30 to 50 percent for the weaver. Since only the weaver was fined, this caused division among the workforce. See ibid., chap. 10, esp. 320–22.

21. Ibid., chap. 10.

22. In 1890, the National Cotton Mule Spinners Association of America changed its name to be able to absorb ring spinners and to join with southern textile labor unions, thus hoping to establish national union representation. Fall River union leaders made a conscious effort, however, not to broaden the scope of the union because of regional and professional rivalries. See David Montgomery, *The Fall of the House of Labor: The Workplace the State, and American Labor Activism, 1865–1925* (New York: Cambridge Univ. Press, 1987). Special thanks to Mary Blewett for drawing may attention to this issue.

23. In 1900, the French Canadian population of New Bedford numbered 8,559. They were joined by the English, who numbered 5,389 (accounting for 21 percent of the population), the Portuguese (19 percent), and the Irish, 3,026 (12 percent, down from 24 percent in 1890). See Katz, "Opportunity, Exclusion, and the Immigrant," 32–33. For additional immigration patterns in New Bedford, see Ellis, *History of New Bedford*, 460. Compare the birth rates for each ethnic group in table III of Whitney, *Infant Mortality*, 18. More than one-third of all births in 1913 to foreign-born mothers (1,909) were to the Portuguese white population (685), followed by the French Canadian population (413), English (226), and Polish (223) as the largest figures. There were 753 births to all native-born mothers.

24. Refer to n. 11 above.

25. McMullen, "Coming of the Mills," 6.

26. McMullen, "The Coming of the Mills," 6–7. See also *New Bedford Daily Mercury*, Aug. 23, 1894.

27. These sources were cited in McMullen, "The Coming of the Mills," 6–7. On the 1898 strike, see the Scrapbook of Clippings Concerning the 1898 Textile Strike at New Bedford, 4 vols., Widener Library, Harvard Univ.

Such concerns about the living conditions within (and surrounding) tenement houses, of course, were shared broadly during the Progressive Era, and extended well beyond New Bedford. See, for example,

James Ford, "Housing and Disease," *Proceedings of the National Conference on Housing* 5 (1916): 190–97; James Ford, "Some Fundamentals of Housing Reform," *American City* 8 (1913): 473–81; Lawrence Veiller, "Tenement House Reform in New York City, 1834–1900," in *The Tenement House Problem,* ed. Robert W. DeForest and Lawrence Veiller (New York, 1903), 69–118; Marcus T. Reynolds, *The Housing in New York City* (New York: Columbia Univ. Press, 1890). This heightened concern exhibited by the popular press, housing officials, and scholars of the day helped establish a different "mental climate" toward mill housing that influenced the shift to building "model" housing in lieu of large tenements blocks.

28. Sayer, *New Bedford,* 157.

29. For a discussion of the earliest city paving strategies, see Boss and Thomas, *New Bedford,* 63. For the shift to Belgian block, see *City Document* no. 10, Jan. 1892, Board of Public Works under "Paving" (pp. 12–13).

30. Whitney, *Infant Mortality,* 56.

31. Sayer, *New Bedford,* 157.

32. Whitney, *Infant Mortality,* 56.

33. Budgett Meakin, *Model Factories and Villages* (London: T. Fisher Unwin, 1905), 26–27. Also similar in design to the Acushnet Mill cottages are the Andrew Dickhaut cottages on Bath Street, 1883, Providence, Rhode Island. These were single-family units built by a developer, however, and rented to employees at nearby industries. See David Chase, ed., *Providence: A Citywide Survey of Historic Resources* (Providence Preservation Commission, 1986), 31 and 139.

34. Meakin, *Model Factories and Villages,* 26.

35. Coolidge, *Mill and Mansion,* 91–93; 209n. 29.

4. HOWLAND MILL VILLAGE

1. See Crawford, *Building the Workingman's Paradise,* chap. 5.

2. Rachel S. Howland to Matthew Morris Howland, Sept. 28, 1881.

3. Morgan Rotch, a corporate officer of the Howland Mill Corporation, had been the mayor of New Bedford between 1885 and 1888, when the Howland Mill was being organized. Rotch continued to facilitate the company's expansion at critical points as a member of the board of public works, the transportation commission, and the park commission. He was also a close friend of Morris Howland, William D.'s older brother. William D.

Howland himself was a director of the National Bank of Commerce, which his grandfather had founded and of which his father was president. This bank handled many of the business transactions of all three of the corporations for which William D. Howland served as treasurer.

4. As in many urban areas up to the turn of the twentieth century, no administrative distinction was made between government and business; see, for example, the discussion of New York City's administrative structure in Christopher Tunnard and Henry Hope Reed, *American Skyline* (New York: Signet, 1956), 135. Such clarification of city government's power was just beginning to appear in New Bedford during the 1890s with such city agencies as the New Bedford Park Commission, established in 1891, and the Department of Building Permits, established in 1893.

5. Howland family correspondence from the 1870s exists in several collections, but none of William D. Howland's letters or business ledgers have survived. Additionally, the wealth of information in Matthew Howland's correspondence, cited elsewhere in this manuscript, ends with his death in 1884—four years before the incorporation of Howland Mills.

6. Rachel Howland's prominent social standing in Philadelphia allowed her direct access to people of political and intellectual import, from President Lincoln to Harriet Beecher Stowe, in her day. See William M. Emery, *The Howland Heirs* (New Bedford, Mass.: E. Anthony and Sons, Inc., 1919), 197.

7. Georgianna, *Strike of '28,* 31–32. See p. 53 for an informative chart listing "Prominent New Bedford Families on Bank, Mill and Other Board Directorates" by 1928. Though much later than Howland's era, the high degree of influence that this handful of prominent families wielded up to the collapse of the city's textile economy suggests a similar if not stronger business dynamic in Howland's time. See "William D. Howland, Noteworthy Career of the Unfortunate Mill Treasurer," *The (New Bedford) Evening Standard,* May 6, 1897, 1, 8; Emery, *Howland Heirs,* 197, 205–6; Allen, *Children of the Light,* 85, 148–49; Dykas, "Whaling, Cotton, and the Howland Family"; *New Bedford Evening Standard,* Mar. 5 and 6, 1867; *New Bedford Daily Mercury,* Mar. 5 and 6, 1867; McMullen, "Lost Alternative," 32. For more on labor relations in this era, see David Montgomery, *Beyond Equality: Labor and Radical Republicans, 1862–1872* (New York: Random House, 1967), 289–90, and his *The Fall of the House of Labor*; Nelson, *Managers and Workers.*

8. Llewellyn Howland III, telephone interview with the author, Oct. 3, 1995. Though often autocratic in his

management practices, Robert Owen (1771–1858) was also one of the pioneers of labor laws, the cooperative movement, and trade unions. In 1817, he put forth a report for the Committee for the Relief of the Manufacturing Poor and proposed an ideal settlement based on collective land use, self-sufficiency, and the mixed use of cultivated land and industry. Owen incorporated these principles of social reorganization in his planning of a model industrial city at New Harmony, Indiana, in 1825. As Norman Newton notes: "Of paramount interest here is Owen's conviction that environment affects character, that improved surroundings have a salutary effect upon workers, and that this in turn benefits industry itself. Although Owen is customarily regarded as the founder of modern socialism—a term he introduced in the 1830s—and was hailed by the workers as their champion, his early efforts were clearly paternalistic; that is, impetus for correction came directly from him, not from the workers." See Norman T. Newton, *Design on the Land: The Development of Landscape Architecture* (Cambridge, Mass.: Belknap Press of Harvard Univ. Press, 1971), 447; also see chap. 31 "English Town Planning and the 'Garden City'"; Leonardo Benevolo, *History of Modern Architecture* (Cambridge, Mass.: MIT Press, 1977), 1: 148–51; Hayden, *The Grand Domestic Revolution*, chap. 2; Edward K. Spann, *Brotherly Tomorrows: Movements for a Cooperative Society in America 1820–1920* (New York: Columbia Univ. Press, 1989), chap. 10.

9. Howland's 1874 graduation is verified by the Brown University Archives at the John Hay Library. The date given in Emery, *Howland Heirs*, 205–6, is 1879. Llewellyn Howland III suggests that Howland may have spent a year abroad and a brief time keeping the books for the Howland whaling fleet before beginning work at Wamsutta Mills. That Howland was probably promoted from clerk is stated in a letter from his oldest brother, Richard S. Howland, to him, dated Sept. 5, 1879: "Yesterday father said that you are feeling very well about your new position at Wamsutta and like the work—which is not so confining as formerly." That Howland was in charge of redesigning two of the Potomska Mills for new machinery is stated in a letter from his father, Matthew, to his brother Morris, Jan. 31, 1880; according to his father, William told mill owner Kilburn that "he would rejoice to do it, but that he had all he could do in the office. Then Kilburn said he should be released from that, so Will is rejoicing that perhaps he will have little if any more work as clerk in the office." Howland Family Correspondence.

10. Sayer, *New Bedford*, 146; Ellis, *History of New Bedford*, 458; Boss and Thomas, *New Bedford*, 150.

11. Richard S. Howland to William D. Howland, Dec. 29, 1878, Mar. 17 and Apr. 28, 1879; Matthew Howland to Matthew M. Howland, July 18 and Oct. 28, 1881, Howland Family Correspondence. Cited in McMullen, "Lost Alternative," 26. Regarding traveling "for several months, making a careful study of that specialty [the manufacture of cotton yarns]," see Sayer, *New Bedford*, 158.

12. Howland family correspondence indicates that "Horatio and Francis Hathaway have subscribed $5,000 each. L. A. Plummer and Capt. Delano each the same and perhaps Jonathon Bourne Kilburn, Andrew Pierce, and Joseph Grinnell have also promised to take some so that he seems quite encouraged. But I am afraid the last 30 or 40,000 dollars will come hard, after the recent subscription of $750,000 for Acushnet Mills" (Matthew Howland to Matthew M. Howland, Jan. 11, 1882). "Will is driving about trying to obtain the subscription to his yarn mill and we think that so far he has done remarkable well. The subscriptions amount to very nearly $100,000, so that Willie is pretty sure it will go. . . . Mother and Willie have gone out of town to see a rich man and ascertain if he will not take some of Willie's stock" (Matthew Howland to Matthew M. Howland, Jan. 27, 1882).

13. Letter dated July 19, 1882, Howland Family Correspondence.

14. Rachel Howland to Morris Howland, Nov. 15, 1882; Matthew Howland to Matthew M. Howland, Mar. 5, 1883; Matthew Howland to Matthew M. Howland, May 9, 1883; Howland Family Correspondence.

15. Matthew Howland to Matthew M. Howland, Mar. 11, 1884; Matthew Howland to Matthew M. Howland, Apr. 15, 1884; Matthew Howland to Matthew M. Howland, Sept. 8, 1884; Howland Family Correspondence.

16. The decision to construct a new mill instead of refitting the old flour mill came as a result of the offer made for the property being declined. Instead, a piece of land on the south side of Hillman Street, between North Second and Water Streets was purchased. The officers of the New Bedford Manufacturing Company were President Charles W. Clifford, replaced briefly by Edmund Grinnell and then Morgan Rotch; Treasurer William D. Howland; and Directors Oliver P. Brightman, Charles W. Clifford, Edmond Grinnell, Charles W. Plummer, Edward T. Pierce, William D. Howland, and David Wood. Later, Morgan Rotch replaced David Wood, and George E. Kingman replaced Grinnell on the board. Construction of the second mill brought the total num-

ber of spindles to thirty-seven thousand. By 1889, three hundred hands were employed. The dimensions of the second factory were 218 by 100 feet, three stories high. Bryan F. Card was the mill superintendent. The New Bedford Manufacturing Company not only met local demands for fine yarn. John M. Conway and Company, the oldest established yarn house in New York City, was the agent of the corporation and took the entire product. See Sayer, *New Bedford*, 158–62, and "Howland Mills Involved," *Morning Mercury*, Apr. 24, 1897.

17. The complete list of company offices and directors were as follows: William J. Rotch was chosen president, William D. Howland, treasurer, and Charles W. Plummer, clerk of the corporation. The directors were William J. Rotch, Horatio Hathaway, Thomas B. Tripp, Charles W. Clifford, Morgan Rotch, William D. Howland, and Charles W. Plummer.

18. "Howland Mills Corporation: An Organization of the Company Effected To-day," *Evening Standard*, May 19, 1888. The meeting of the incorporators of the new cotton manufacturing enterprise was held at the National Bank of Commerce, of which William D. Howland was a director. It was organized with capital stock of $350,000. The purchased tracts are indicated in the *Plan of City of New Bedford from Original Surveys by J.C. Sidney, C.E.* (Philadelphia: Collins and Clark, 1850). They appear as well in the 1871 Beers *Map of Bristol County*.

19. Comparing the 1871 *City Atlas* with the 1875 *City Engineering Survey Maps* makes clear that industrial subdivision lots had been platted between those years east of Crapo Street to County Street north of Cove Road. These subdivisions are shown on two maps published by Wheelwright and Coggeshall in 1875 as part of an extensive planning study. One was a civil engineering and sanitation map; the other was a plat map for present and future development. These maps were discovered in May 1996 by Ed Portis of my research team in the attic of the New Bedford City Hall. These 1875 maps also show the sites for Brooklawn, Buttonwood, Hazlewood, and the Marine Park; thus an urban plan for New Bedford was in place by this date. Olmsted may have worked from these maps to develop his system of parks in 1892.

20. Related to William D. Howland, Henry Howland Crapo II, son of William Wallace Crapo, was on the original board of directors for the Potomska Mill in 1871 and may have convinced his father between 1871 and 1875 to consider mill development, actual or speculative, in the South End. Hence, the incorporation and construction of the Howland Mills may have moved smoothly in

part because a spinning mill complex fit within the anticipated production needs of other mills in which the family and its relations had a vested interest.

21. Sayer, *New Bedford*, 165.

22. Howland had been in charge of repairing older machinery at Wamsutta Mills, and in 1880 he installed new machinery into Nos. 2 and 4 Potomska Mills, said to have saved "the labor of 50 operatives." These tasks, combined with his work in 1881 to draw up plans for a new mill at the Potomska complex, had surely given him ample background to understand a mill's technological needs.

23. For reference to the installation of artificial illumination into Wamsutta's new Mill No. 6 in 1882 in the form of three 250 light Edison dynamos and the social impact of artificial lighting in the mills, see Gordon and Malone, *The Texture of Industry*, 316–17. See also Harold C. Passer, *The Electrical Manufacturers, 1875–1900* (Cambridge, Mass.: Harvard Univ. Press, 1953), 78–104. For details on the mills' construction, see "Howland Mills Corporation," *New Bedford Evening Standard*, May 19, 1888; "The New Cotton Mills, Rapid Work in the Construction of the Howland Mill," *New Bedford Evening Standard*, Aug. 14, 1888; and "The Howland Mills," *New Bedford Evening Standard*, Mar. 15, 1889.

24. The plans for the 1898 payroll office, produced after the reorganization of the Howland Mill but before the corporation was liquidated in 1899, are on file in the attic storage of the New Bedford Building Department, New Bedford City Hall.

25. "Howland Mills Involved: Three More Cotton Corporations Found to be in Financial Straits," *Morning Mercury*, Apr. 24, 1897, 1, indicates that the Rotch Mills produced hosiery yarns. The 1889 advertisement in Sayer, *New Bedford*, xxix, reads: "Howland Mills Corporation, New Bedford, Mass. High Grade Cotton Yarns, Single and Twisted, Combed or Carded Hosiery Yarns, Chain Warps, Skeens, Spools, Cops, and Beams."

26. John Ruskin, "Nature of the Gothic," in *Stones of Venice* (1853). For an intriguing parallel to the Howland Mill Village with regard to the design of a workers' village according to the principles of Christian Capitalism, see Lisa Goff, "Graniteville, S.C.: William Gregg's Industrial Village," a paper presented at the Vernacular Architecture Forum Annual Meeting in Columbus, Ga., on May 8, 1999. Goff discusses how William Gregg, a wealthy Charleston merchant and Quaker, expressed his particular vision for a humane industrial village by constructing a tidy hamlet of

Gothic cottages in 1848. In an attempt to dispel the image of a mill village as a debased type, Gregg sought to improve the environment of the worker. Building upon the Gothic Revival era claims to the moral superiority of the style, which was believed to be capable of building character and devotion among its users, E. B. Bigelow and Richard Upjohn designed at least four different sets of plans in the Gothic Cottage style at Graniteville. Gregg contributed to the notion of a "community of workers" by also building a church and a school; attendance for children of mill workers was mandatory. No picturesque planning was used for the street layout, though cottage gardens were encouraged. The influence of the Gothic style on improving the workers' sensibilities and moral standards, Goff found, was negligible and in some cases was openly resisted by the workers. Gregg, however, employed innovative management practices for the time by instituting a joint stock ownership program.

27. *New Bedford Evening Standard*, Aug. 14 and Dec. 14, 1888; Jan. 1 and Oct. 3, 1889; Feb. 25, 1891; *Boston Globe*, Jan. 18, 1920, and Feb. 4, 1922, in *Boston Globe* Scrapbook, comp. Zephaniah Pease, New Bedford Free Public Library. See also McMullen, "Lost Alternative," 26. Edmund March Wheelwright's work is noted briefly in Douglass Shand Tucci, *Built in Boston: City and Suburb, 1800–1950* (Boston: New York Graphic Society, 1978), 195, and Carole A. Jensen, "Edmund M. Wheelwright," *A Biographical Dictionary of Architects in Maine* (1987), 4: 13.

28. Margaret Henderson Floyd indicated that Charles McKim formed the firm McKim, Mead and Bigelow (Bigelow was his brother-in-law) in 1874 and that Stanford White joined the firm in 1879. Also, Arnold Lewis indicates that "Bigelow was a partner with McKim and Mead in 1878 but left the firm to establish a private practice the following year. He retired in 1899." Hence, the date of Wheelwright's apprenticeship with McKim, Mead and Bigelow would have to have been prior to 1879. Since Wheelwright attended MIT between 1876 and 1877, the 1878 date seems likely. Edmund Wheelwright also traveled abroad in 1881. A letter from Alexander Wadsworth Longfellow Jr. (1854–1934), who joined Richardson's firm late in 1881 after three years at the École des Beaux-Arts, describes a trip to Normandy in 1881 with Wheelwright. Both sketched the Manoir d'Ango, whose picturesque tower-gable massing is said to have influenced the Glessner House. See Margaret Henderson Floyd, *Henry Hobson Richardson: A Genius for Architecture* (New York: Monacelli Press, 1997), 104, 121, 295n. 52. See

also Arnold Lewis, *American Country Houses of the Gilded Age* (New York: Dover, 1982), 18.

Wheelwright also worked for E. P. Treadwell in Albany, and following his study abroad between 1881 and 1882 he established his own architectural practice in Boston in 1883. Parkman Haven became his business partner in 1888, the year that the Howland Mill Village was commissioned. Also fortuitous was the hiring of Robert C. Spencer (of Prairie School fame). Alan Brooks notes that Spencer (1865–1953) "entered M.I.T. the year after [Dwight] Perkins; he was already in possession of a Bachelor of Mechanical Engineering degree from the University of Wisconsin (1886). He left the Institute without completing his studies, worked for Wheelwright and Haven and then Shepley, Rutan and Coolidge in Boston." Hence, the mechanical engineering skills and picturesque design sensibilities of Spencer were at the disposal of this young firm at the time that they undertook the Howland Mill Village. See H. Allen Brooks, *The Prairie School* (New York: Norton, 1976), 29. Little-known examples of Wheelwright's early efforts in "romantic primitivism" can be found in Lewis, *American Country Houses*, 60. For more on Wheelwright, Peabody, and the other principals in these firms, see Withey and Withey, *Biographical Dictionary of American Architects*, 273, 462–63, 568, 648–49. See also Jensen, "Edmund M. Wheelwright." According to Withey, Wheelwright began practice under his own name in 1885, not, as Jensen states, in 1883; Withey also states that Wheelwright was trained as well at l'École des Beaux-Arts, while Jensen contends Wheelwright never officially attended the school. Nonetheless, the Howland Mill Village would have been among the firm's first commissions. The date of the partnership of Wheelwright and Haven is variously given as 1888 and 1890. Since Jensen is working from the architect's original account books, we can trust her data over Withey. Information about Wheelwright's life and career can be found in the Wheelwright Family Papers at the Massachusetts Historical Society, Boston. For selected drawings, see the Haven and Hoyt collection at the Boston Public Library.

29. *New Bedford Evening Standard*, Oct. 3, 1889; see also Aug. 14, 1888. Sayer, *New Bedford*, 165–66, indicates that twenty-five of the cottages were built in 1888. Another twenty-five and the boardinghouses were completed in 1889.

30. "Mill Notes: The New Howland Mill to be Double the Size of No. 1," *Evening Standard*, Jan. 1, 1889. Several fine photographs of the superintendent's house and outbuildings as they appeared along Cove Road at

Orchard Street in 1912 are in the possession of Thomas Whittaker in New Bedford. Whittaker's grandfather had been the superintendent of the Gosnold Mill, which took over the Howland Mill shortly after it failed.

31. E. R. L. Gould, *Eighth Special Report of the Commissioner of Labor: Housing of the Working People* (Washington, D.C.: Government Printing Office, 1895), 325.

32. Ibid., 325.

33. "The brick sewer on Orchard Street, from the Howland Mill No. 2 to the Rotch Spinning Corporation, was rendered quite costly by the depth of the marsh mud which made it necessary to build a stone and cement foundation. This foundation was fifteen feet wide at the bottom and carried up half the height of the four-foot brick sewer" (*New Bedford City Documents* no.10, Dec. 1892, Board of Public Works, 26).

34. *New Bedford City Documents* no. 10, Jan. 1891, Board of Public Works, 12.

35. Ibid.

36. Robert A. Smith, *Merry Wheels and Spokes of Steel: A Social History of the Bicycle*, Stovkis Studies in Historical Chronology and Thought 16 (New York: Borgo Press, 1995). On macadam roads in New Bedford, see *New Bedford City Documents* no. 10, Dec. 1893, Board of Public Works, 13. For the notice in *Harper's*, see Richard T. Ely, "Pullman: A Social Study," *Harper's New Monthly Magazine* 70 (1885): 452–66.

37. The idea of designing "breathing places" into areas where workers lived gained currency in the work of Olmsted and other American landscape architects, such as Charles Eliot, during the 1880s and 1890s. Olmsted's article, "The Justifying Value of a Public Park," published in the *Journal of Social Science* in 1881, and his earlier presentation at Boston's Lowell Institute on February 1870, for example, called for extending the advantages of suburban neighborhoods into the city.

38. "Mill Notes," *New Bedford Evening Standard*, Jan. 1, 1889, reported, "The Dartmouth Street line of railway will soon be extended farther toward the Howland Mill village, and there is talk of extending the Old Colony railroad to the Potomska, Acushnet, Hathaway and Howland Mills." See *New Bedford City Documents* no. 10, Jan. 1892, Board of Public Works, under "Transportation Report." See also *New Bedford City Documents* no. 10, Dec. 1892, "Street Railways," 42. The line to Howland Mills was one of only two lines in the city operated by electric power. An electrified street-level line with an overhead conductor was successfully demonstrated in Richmond, Va., in 1887; by 1892 more than eight thousand electric cars ran on city streets in the United States. See Alan Marcus and Howland Segal, *Technology in America* (San Diego, Calif.: Harcourt Brace Jovanovich, 1989), 151–55, and Carroll Pursell, *The Machine in America: A Social History of Technology* (Baltimore, Md.: Johns Hopkins Univ. Press, 1995), 136.

39. *New Bedford City Directory* (1895), 60.

40. Special thanks to Carole A. Jensen for her letter to the author of Apr. 7, 1997, about entries in Wheelwright's ledger associated with social reform issues and workers' housing. Jensen bases her information on Wheelwright's business ledger, which is on loan to her. She informs me that there is a handwritten entry noting money paid to Wheelwright from the Howland Mills Corporation as well. Ms. Jensen has cataloged the only two known archival collections of Wheelwright's work and is currently working on a book on Edward March Wheelwright to be published by the Boston Public Library.

Ned Connors informs me that the Richmond Paper Company (for which Wheelwright designed a boardinghouse in the 1880s) was a short-lived but innovative paper manufacturer in East Providence:

> Richmond threw good money after bad at a chemical pulping process based on a Swedish patent. They built a large industrial site in 1882 on the Seekonk River and folded in 1887. In the meantime, however, they managed to work the bugs out of the sulphite pulping process that ended up dominating paper manufacture until the mid-20th century. The brains behind the operation was a Charles Wheelwright who had come down from Massachusetts to settle in Providence (marrying the daughter of Franklin Richmond, a paper and cotton dealer). Charles Wheelwright is also from the paper manufacturing family in Massachusetts and must be related to Edmund. (Personal correspondence, Ned Connors to the author, Mar. 12, 1998)

Connors raises the possibility that some of the factory housing of the Richmond Paper Mill site may be by Wheelwright. Given the limited dates of operation for the Richmond Paper Company, (1882–87), this project would have been undertaken just prior to the Howland Mill Village. The facility is still extant, in spite of the modifications by the wire manufacturing plant which purchased the site at auction in 1893.

41. See Jensen, "Edmund M. Wheelwright," in *A Biographical Dictionary of Architects in Maine*,

4: 13, published by the Maine Historic Preservation Commission.

42. Caroline T. Daniels, *Dark Harbor* (Cambridge, Mass.: n.p., 1935), and Jensen, "Edmund M. Wheelwright," 52. Also, as early as 1883, Wheelwright (in his first year of independent practice) designed a shingle and boulder seaside resort cottage called "Kelp Rock" in New Castle, New Hampshire. See Lewis, *American Country Houses*, 60.

43. Sayer, *New Bedford*, 165–66.

44. Gould, *Eighth Special Report*, 325.

45. Interestingly, Bowditch resisted the notion of workers living in the suburbs and argued that laborers wanted to live near their work, that railroads objected to lowering rates for laborers, and that passengers would find the large numbers of workers assembled at the depots annoying. Howland solved these problems by placing workers' homes near the mills, essentially bringing the suburbs to the workplace, and by providing a rail service predominately for the laborers, much like the "mill buses" of the modern era. For more on Bowditch, see Handlin, *The American Home*, 253–55, 256–58.

46. See McMullen, "Industrialization and Social Change," and McMullen, "The Coming of the Mills," 6, 7.

47. Model workers' housing was exhibited in London in 1851 and in Paris in 1867. The first international housing congress met in Paris in conjunction with the 1889 Paris Exposition, when Howland Mills was being planned. Two exhibition areas of model workers' housing were displayed at the World's Columbian Exposition in Chicago in 1893. Such international expositions continued, predominantly in Europe, through 1910. See Garner, *The Model Company Town*, 110–16.

48. Fourierism was based on the ideas of French socialist Charles Fourier (1772–1837), who believed in enhancing workers' lives by providing pleasant surroundings, offering good working conditions, and reorganizing the structure of society into cooperative communities. Believing that the private dwelling was one of the greatest obstacles to improving the position of women in civilization, Fourier argued that "the extension of the privileges of women is a fundamental cause of all social progress." In his view of the new industrial future, women would share equally in human activity and enjoy economic independence. Collective facilities, known as phalansteries, would offer the communal upbringing of children and would aim to overcome the conflicts between city and country, rich and poor, men and women by an enlightened arrangement of economic and social resources. For more on this subject, see Hayden, *The Grand*

Domestic Revolution, chap. 1. Brook Farm (1841–47) in West Roxbury, Massachusetts, was one of several antebellum utopian communities based on Fourierism.

49. The popular awareness of Olmsted's Riverside Park was almost immediate. Two years later, Lysander Flagg began a resort development in East Providence, Rhode Island, with a group of businessmen from Providence and Pawtucket. Flagg's enterprise, named the Riverside Land Company, was a miniaturized version of Olmsted's model American suburb. It grew into a flourishing resort over the next three decades and certainly would have been known to Howland because his oldest brother, Richard, was the publisher and editor of the *Providence Journal* during the 1880s. The irregular arrangement of the summer cottages and the use of patterned shingles may have had an influence on Howland's desire for simple worker's cottages similar to, but on a smaller scale than, those Wheelwright was building in Maine. See Richard Longstreth, "East Providence, Rhode Island" (Statewide Preservation Report, Rhode Island Historical Preservation Commission, September 1976), 36–39. Special thanks to Richard Longstreth for bringing this community plan to my attention.

50. Frederick Law Olmsted, "Public Parks and the Enlargement of Towns" (1870), reprinted in S. B. Sutton, *Civilizing American Cities: A Selection of Frederick Law Olmsted's Writings on City Landscapes* (Cambridge, Mass.: MIT Press, 1971), 52–59. See also Olmsted, "Public Parks and the Enlargement of Towns," *Journal of Social Science* 3 (1871): 1–36, and "The Justifying Value of a Public Park," *Journal of Social Science* 12 (1881): 147–64.

51. Olmsted, Vaux and Co., "Preliminary Report upon the Proposed Suburban Village at Riverside" (New York, 1868), 3, 7. For background on the precedents for the romantic suburb, see John Archer, "Country and City in the American Romantic Suburb," *Journal of the Society of Architectural Historians* 42 (2) (May 1983): 139–56.

52. Olmsted articulated these ideas in his February 1870 presentation at Boston's Lowell Institute and his 1881 article, "The Justifying Value of a Public Park."

53. Hale is quoted in Handlin, *American Home*, 246–58; see especially the sources listed on 247.

54. The Acushnet Mills owned twenty-three two-and-a-half-story frame cottages arranged in two rows that served as two-family residences for its operatives, while Grinnell provided a cohesive block of twenty-seven housing units neatly arranged in three rows of

gable-end, two-and-a-half story, two-tenement houses. See Sayer, *New Bedford*, 157.

55. In 1876, Olmsted had addressed the problem of erecting multiple dwellings in New York City, where the density of the population and the constricting pattern of the grid limited the placement of all buildings to one orientation. Additionally, the proximity of the houses limited access to the backyards. This was a problem particularly in the old urban contexts prior to the installation of gas, water, or sewage systems, and it created garbage, trash, and privacy issues for tenants when service people had to go through the connected side alleyways of the units. Olmsted preferred to alter this grid arrangement for urban multiple housing by providing greater space between buildings, introducing more variety in the design of the buildings, and adjusting their orientation to the street. See Handlin, *American Home*, 200.

56. While corporations were being pressured to address the sanitary conditions of their rental flats by the late 1880s, not until 1896 did the *Record of Building Permits in the City of New Bedford* even include "water closets" as a category in its building descriptions for the general population. A building permit issued on Jan. 3, 1896, to John Kothusau allowed George K. Teachmur to build two two-and-one-half-story, three-unit tenements in the North End mill district with *no* water closets. City codes clearly were slow to enforce regulations that affected local speculative builders. The federal census of 1890 indicates that there were approximately eight occupants per living unit in New Bedford's Ward 1, where Teachmur's tenements were. Thus, each three-unit tenement would have held approximately twenty-four inhabitants with no inside sanitary facilities.

57. Though he always denied any outside influence on Pullman, George Pullman likely visited Saltaire during his trip to Europe in 1873. Like Saltaire, Pullman provided impressive brick housing set amidst pleasant surroundings and offered such amenities as a library for the workers. More contemporary with both Pullman and the Howland Mill Village were the progressive picturesque village housing at Bournville (1879 to 1894), built near Birmingham, and Port Sunlight (1887), built on the outskirts of Liverpool, England. These workingmen's villages grew out of the English interest in the "smaller modern house," which has since become known as the romantic tradition in suburban planning

Initiating this tradition, Bedford Park (1877) became the first garden suburb. It was located on the western outskirts of London. Although its housing was intended as part of the lower-middle-class garden village architecture designed for the artistic property speculator Jonathan T. Carr (instead of as a community for industrial workers), many of its design features became major tenets for model mill village planning during the next decade. Hermann Muthesius noted, for example, in 1904 that there was an attempt to leave as many old trees standing as possible and to carry the pavement around them. Streets, therefore, were "pleasantly winding." Care was taken to provide every house with a small garden, while most of the houses were detached and designed with an eye toward "calculated variety."

Building upon Shaw's pioneering work at Bedord Park, the workmen's villages of Bournville and Port Sunlight drew upon English vernacular cottage designs for inspiration. At Bournville a workers' "estate" was built by George Cadbury, of the nearby cocoa and chocolate factory, as a housing and open-space plan. But the factory was actually *independent* of the Cadbury industry. The recreational facilities and residences (with gardens behind) were grouped around a central space. By 1900, the 330-acre site had 313 residences, administrated by the Bournville Village Trust. In cases where the occupants were only leaseholders, the rent exactly covered the cost of construction; in cases where they became owners (as Howland had planned) the purchase price equaled the value.

Instead of housing writers and artists, as Bedford Park had done, or building a planned housing development independent of the Cadbury industrial facilities, Port Sunlight provided housing specifically for workers at the Sunlight Soap Factory. W. H. Lever was a lover of architecture, and in 1887 he created a model workers' village and calculated the rent simply on the cost of maintenance. Muthesius notes that "the houses for Port Sunlight did for the workman's house what those at Bedford Park had done for the lower middle-class house; they provided an ideal combination of comfort, ease and artistic quality with the economic possibilities appropriate to their status. . . . As regards hygiene, . . . every house, down to the smallest, has a bath." In modern terms, the village utilized a "super-block arrangement," with open space for gardens and recreations. At the time Muthesius was writing, the community consisted of 230 acres.

In the case of both the Lever and Cadbury enterprises, neither of the company heads sought profit but merely expected interest at the lowest prevailing rate. Ralph Heaton designed all the houses at Bournville. Muthesius notes that they were built on the same principle as Port Sunlight but were not quite as varied. He added (in the spirit of Ruskin) that they were at the time "the only model villages of their kind in England, and succeeded in bringing art to the life of the working-classes." Perhaps most important, both Bournville and Port Sunlight represent early efforts on the part of industry to improve the quality of life for factory workers.

Ebenezer Howard continued the evolution of the garden city movement (begun at Bournville in 1879) with his 1895 publication, *Tomorrow: A Peaceful Path to Real Reform*. A second edition appeared in London in 1902 under the title *Garden Cities of To-morrow*. Hermann Muthesius's *Das Englische Haus* was originally published in three volumes by Wasmuth in Berlin in 1904, 1905. It has been reprinted in English as Hermann Muthesius, *The English House* (New York: Rizzoli International Publications, 1979), see 30–32; 58–60. Muthesius makes reference to a book by W. H. Lever published under the title *Buildings Erected at Port Sunlight and Thornton Hough* (London, 1902), and to a monograph containing plans and illustrations by W. H. Lever, *Cottages and Other Buildings Erected at Port Sunlight and Thornton Hough*. For general background readings on these industrial landscapes, see Philip Pregill and Nancey Volkman, *Landscapes in History: Design and Planning in the Eastern and Western Traditions* (New York: John Wiley and Sons, 1999), esp. 257–60. See also Newton, *Design on the Land*, esp. chap. 31, "English Town Planning and the 'Garden City.'"

58. For more on the planning of the town of Pullman, see Stanley Buder, *Pullman* (New York: Oxford Univ. Press, 1967), 25–27.

59. With regard to modern conveniences of operative housing, in Pullman the units had water closets, but they were located on the landing, not within the units proper. Other amenities included a gas cooking stove, gas fixtures for lighting, a sink, and a water tap. The apartments rented from eight to nine dollars a month, about twenty percent of the salary of a laborer and cabinetmaker. Garner, *Model Company Town*, 152; Richard T. Ely, "Pullman: A Social Study," *Harper's New Monthly Magazine*, Feb. 1885, 457.

60. The son of a distinguished theologian, Barrows had initially been hired in 1874 as an assistant treasurer to organize the Willimantic Linen Company's finances. Quickly gaining the support of founder Austin Dunham's liberal-minded son, he became vice president in 1877 and then president in 1882–83. See Thomas R. Beardsley, *Willimantic Industry and Community* (Willimantic, Conn.: Windham Textile and History Museum, 1993).

61. The Willimantic Mills acted as experimental workshops for the new electric light technology, and in 1882 they dispensed with the Brush arc light system and adopted Edison's "incandescent plant" throughout. Notably, this would make Wamsutta's No. 6 Mill (1882) the first to be designed and built with an Edison dynamo system from the start in the United States; the Howland Mills installed "Edison wires" six years later. See Beardsley, *Willimantic Industry and Community*, chap. 4. For more on other innovations in the artificial illumination of textile mills in America, see Gordon and Malone, *The Texture of Industry*, 316–17.

62. Barrows's Irish landscape gardener, Dwight Potter, is said in particular to have been influenced by the work of Downing and Davis. For more on Barrows's influence on Willimantic, see Beardsley, *Willimantic Industry and Community*, chap. 3.

63. For the 1880 period of housing development at Willimantic, see the *Special Federal Census Schedules for Connecticut* at the Connecticut State Library, Hartford, for 1880 under "Industry." The original volumes are in Vault 11 or microfilm 317.46 fc76c10ma. See also the U.S. Government's Tenth Manufacturing Census (1880), published in 1882. For a period perspective on Willimantic, see Meakin, *Model Factories and Villages*. Apart from naturalistic planning, the thirty single- and double-family cottages built by the Ludlow Associates in Springfield, Mass., 1879–81, rank among the best nineteenth-century workers' housing. Folio-sized plates appear in Carroll D. Wright, "Report on the Factory System of the United States," bound with the 1880 U.S. manufacturing census.

64. See Gross, *The Course of Industrial Decline*, and Vance, *Continuing City*, 83–85. Company-owned housing still accommodated one-quarter of the Boott Mill employees in 1888–91. Set policies governed the conduct of both residents and keepers, and the agent was free to exercise his power as he saw fit. Gross has noted, "Continued provision of housing allowed the agent, if he wished, to extend his power into the lives of the worker while in the community. . . . Eviction remained [Agent] Cumnock's ultimate rebuke. . . . Standards were based on Cumnock's beliefs, not work-related issues. . . . Despite the inherent difficulties of landlordism, Cumnock . . . [used] his position as an opportunity to purify the corporation." See also Richard Horwitz, "Architecture and Culture: The Meaning of the Lowell Boarding House," *American Quarterly* 25 (1) (Mar. 1973): 64–82. For a discussion of how Lowell's corporate executives and engineers carefully designed parks and promenades on a grand scale in an effort to recruit, retain, and control workers, see Patrick Malone and Charles Parrott, "Greenways in the Industrial City: Parks

and Promenades along the Lowell Canals" in *IA (Journal of the Society for Industrial Archeology)* 24 (1) (1998): 19–40. Malone and Parrott's research on naturalistic landscape gardening employed at Lowell during the 1840s and 1850s (particularly the tree-lined "greenways" along the Northern and Merrimack Canals, the rural cemetery, and parks) somewhat alters a view of a "rigid" physical and social setting, but these were not part of the original 1823 plan.

65. Ely, "Pullman: A Social Study," 452–66; resident quoted in Buder, *Pullman*, 99. Written criticism of the Pullman experiment had begun by 1885. See Buder, *Pullman*, 86–92.

66. In 1883 George Pullman lured Barrows away from Willimantic to aid in the further planning of his extensive industrial site for the Pullman Palace Car Company as its vice president. Pullman hoped that the ideal workers' community—with its lake vista and picturesque gardens in the public square—would help to ease worker unrest, but the disastrous strike at Pullman in 1894 proved otherwise. See Beardsley, *Willimantic Industry and Community,* 48. Barrows resigned from Pullman on December 5, 1884, and is suspected of having told Johns Hopkins University professor Richard T. Ely about the "benevolent feudalism" at Pullman. See Ely, "Pullman: A Social Study," 452–66. Buder, *Pullman*, 102, 104, makes reference to a *Walter* E. Barrows, not William E. See also Thomas J. Schlereth, "Solon Spencer Beman, Pullman, and the European Influence on and Interest in his Chicago Architecture," in *Chicago Architecture, 1872–1922*, ed. John Zukowski (Munich: Prestel-Vrelag, 1987), 173–88.

67. The association of gardening with social harmony and good moral standing within a community was a product of the mid-century village improvement movement, whose spokesman was the Rev. Birdsey Grant Northrop of Connecticut. In his *Rural Improvement*, Northrop recommended gardening as a way to create "better factory surroundings . . . cultivate public spirit and town pride [and] secure better hygiene conditions" and to make "factory buildings and tenement houses inviting, comfortable, and healthful" (Thomas Beardsley, interview with author, Oct. 9, 1995, Willimantic, Conn.). The author is indebted to Beardsley for the tour of the Willimantic "Oaks" and surrounding sites he gave to my students from the University of North Carolina at Charlotte and me. See also Beardsley, *Willimantic Industry and Community,* 33.

68. For the connection between these ideas and the "village improvement movement," see Handlin, *American Home*, 94, 115–16. For a large-scale example

of the achievements of village improvement as it came to represent industrial enlightenment and the maintenance of social and environmental harmony, see Garner, *Model Company Town*, 62–65, 68–77, on Fairbanks Village in Saint Johnsbury, Vt.

69. Patrick Malone, "Introduction to Green Engineering," *I.A. (Journal of the Society for Industrial Archeology)* 24 (1) (1998): 5.

70. Beardsley, *Willimantic Industry and Community*, 35–36. Other mill villages of the era offered philanthropic architecture as an opportunity for self- improvement for their employees. Hazard Memorial Hall in Peace Dale, R.I.; Cheney Hall in South Manchester, Conn.; the Fairbanks Museum in St. Johnsbury, Vt.; and the Town Hall and Bancroft Memorial Library in Hopedale, Mass., were designed as community facilities. Free libraries were built for factory employees at the Fairbanks Scale Works in Saint Johnsbury and the Ames Tool and Shovel Company of North Easton, Mass.

71. Beardsley, *Willimantic Industry and Community*, 39. The phrase "social alchemists" was used by Daniel Pidgeon, an English engineer and travel writer, in his book *Old World Questions and New World Answers* (London: Kegan, Paul, Trench and Company, 1884). Pidgeon had visited Willimantic in the spring of 1883 in time to view Barrows's social experiment.

72. Gould, *Eighth Special Report*, 328; Beardsley, *Willimantic Industry and Community*, 37–40.

73. Gould, *Eighth Special Report*, 328. According to Beardsley in a personal interview, the "objectionable nationalities," in the eyes of American workers of English descent, were probably Irish and French Canadian workers.

74. Gould, *Eighth Special Report*, 328. As late as 1909, Eugene J. Buffington, president of Indiana Steel division, wrote in *Harper's Weekly*: "fresh in minds of all of us is the failure of the Pullman Company to maintain its authority . . . the most successful attempts at Industrial betterment in our country are those furthest removed from the suspicion of domination or control by the employer" (Eugene Buffington, "Making Cities for Workmen," *Harper's Weekly* 53 [8 May 1909]: 15–17). For a discussion of parallel issues of social control over the lives of the mill operatives at Pullman from both a planning and management perspective related to social-welfare programs, see Crawford, *Building the Workingman's Paradise*, 37–45.

75. Malone, "Introduction to Green Engineering," 5.

76. Gould, *Eighth Special Report*, 326–27. Single male operatives were charged $4.00–$4.50 a week for

board, while day boarders paid $1.00 for five meals. The proprietor chose a person to operate the premises in exchange for rent and all profits accrued.

77. Gould, *Eighth Special Report*, 326. "Capital and Labor in Harmony: Howland Mills Held Up as a Model by the Cleveland Plain Dealer," reprinted in the *Evening Standard*, Feb. 25, 1891, stated, "These homes are sold to operatives who desire to purchase on reasonable terms," but Gould noted in 1895 that the cottages already built were needed for persons in the employ of the corporation and were rented instead.

78. French industrialist and philanthropist Jean Dollfus and Josiah Quincy of Massachusetts had also developed organizations to help workers buy homes on easy terms. Quincy's Homestead Clubs were Boston's earliest home-loan savings societies. Dollfus founded the Mulhouse Workingmen's Dwellings Company in France in 1853, which included a building-and-loan association and model houses designed by architect Emile Muller. Dollfus sold these houses rather than renting them. Another exception abroad is found in the model factory town at Bournville, although, in actuality, this housing facility was independent of the Cadbury factory and was administered instead by the Bournville Village Trust. Nevertheless, workers near George Cadbury's cocoa and chocolate factory (1879 to 1894) could become homeowners. Here the purchase price was equal to the cost of construction.

A proper system of easy home-financing extended to the industrial workforce remained an exception well into the twentieth century, however. In 1895, Apollo Steel hired the Olmsted firm—at this point in the midst of planning a park/parkway system in New Bedford—to plan its company town of Vandergrift, Pa. Like the Howland Mill Village, Vandergrift offered lots for sale and varied the design of the buildings that were set within a contour plan. In 1905, Gary, Ind., coupled a home-financing plan with an independent development company, the Gary Land Company, with mixed results. See Garner, *Model Company Town*, 112, 149; Crawford, *Building the Workingman's Paradise*, 43–44. See also Cynthia Zaitzevsky, "Housing Boston's Poor: The First Philanthropic Experiments" *Journal of the Society of Architectural Historians* 40 (2) (May 1983): 157–67.

79. In September 1883, Olmsted designed the grounds of the Hawthorn Street estate of Edward D. Mandell, a director for Wamsutta Mills. These plans are in the Frederick Law Olmsted Historic Site, Brookline, Mass., Job #672, and correspondence documenting the project is in the Library of Congress, Manuscript

Division. In all, Olmsted's firm proposed or undertook six projects in New Bedford. Only two are coeval with the Howland Mill—the Mandell estate and a May 1893 contract for specifications for a driveway and walks for the Frederick Grinnell estate on County Street between Bedford and Orchard Streets (Job #1381). Charles Eliot produced a landscape design for the extensive estate of New Bedford attorney James D. Stetson between 1883 and 1890. Stetson's home was adjacent to Matthew Howland's.

80. A. J. Downing, in *A Treatise on the Theory and Practice of Landscape Gardening* (New York: George P. Putnam, 1852), wrote of the environs of New Bedford generally (but of the residence of James Arnold, esq., in particular): "There is scarcely a small place in New England where the *pleasure-grounds* are so full of variety" (57). In 1846 George Howland Jr., John Howland, Abraham H. Howland, and William D. Howland's father, Matthew, signed the Articles of Intention for the New Bedford Horticultural Society, now in the collections of the New Bedford Free Public Library.

81. The proposal made to the New Bedford Park Commission "by one of our most prominent citizens" (likely William D. Howland) was to use thirty acres of marsh land as a dumping ground for twenty years as a business investment for the city and then convert it to a park. Its estimated worth was twenty thousand dollars, but it was never built. See undated minutes, New Bedford Park Commission, after June 1894, 3, located in the miscellaneous file, Building Permits Dept., New Bedford City Hall. See n. 83 below.

The concept of a system of pleasure grounds and parkways to refresh urban populations extended back to Olmsted and Calvert Vaux's works in New York City's Central Park and Brooklyn's Prospect Park, beginning in 1853. Olmsted's most inclusive plan for sylvan improvement of a metropolitan region were realized in the Buffalo and Boston park systems. In the Boston plan of about 1881, the parkway system was conceived of as a way of relieving a health menace tied to water drainage in the environs of Boston and of providing a convenient and pleasant passageway from the city to the suburbs. See Laura Wood Roper, *FLO: A Biography of Frederick Law Olmsted* (Baltimore, Md.: Johns Hopkins Univ. Press, 1993).

82. "Experiments with Mill Villages," Feb.4, 1922, *Boston Globe* Scrapbook.

83. On the 1875 *City Engineering Map*, the park is called "Clark's Point Park." On the transformation of Clark's Point, see Ellis L. Howland, "Hazelwood, History of the City's New Park on Clark's Point" and "How

Joseph Congdon's Industry Carved Out Its Beauty" *Standard Times*, July 27, 1901, and June 21, 1902. Special thanks to Joan Barney, Special Collections, New Bedford Free Public Library, for forwarding copies of these citations. In 1840 banker and naturalist Joseph Congdon built two stone buildings, one a Gothic cottage and the other a barn; both show the influence of Downing's design principles. Congdon transformed eighteen acres of forested land into a parklike setting with vantage points of the bay and created an orchard and a greenhouse. The Howland family purchased the north part of the estate in 1865. Rachel Howland summered in the converted stone barn, and William D. and his family lived in the other cottage after his father passed away in 1884.

84. At the suggestion of Olmsted, Olmsted and Eliot, the New Bedford Park Commission was to ask the city to purchase about 160 acres—the seventy acres of the Poor House Farm, about sixty acres of federal fort property at Clark's Point, and about twenty-eight acres of private land—for park purposes and to link a citywide park system. Charles Eliot advised the city to secure all beach rights around the marine park as well.

85. This June 7, 1894, proposal by Olmsted, Olmsted and Eliot was also lost. A typed facsimile with an illustration found its way into a miscellaneous file in the Building Permits Department at New Bedford City Hall. John Truitt, my teaching assistant, aided in locating it. There is no record of this plan at either the Olmsted National Historic Site or the Library of Congress.

86. Olmsted, Olmsted and Eliot to the New Bedford Park Commission, June 13, 1894. The communication was submitted and approved by the board of aldermen on December 13, 1894.

87. The parkway scheme was similar to the one the firm had designed for Boston but predated the plan Eliot and journalist Sylvester Baxter developed for Boston's metropolitan area. The New Bedford plan differed from the Olmsted firm's somewhat earlier plan for a marine park in South Boston (begun in 1869 and listed in February 1891 as "City of Boston, Plan of a Proposed Aquarial Garden") in that it intentionally linked the city's parks to its burgeoning industrial context. Planned in 1892, the South Boston park connected the marine park by a strandway to a residential area of Dorchester. See the eighty-three documents dating 1869–96 related to Job #926, Marine Park, Boston, and Job #931, Strandway, South Boston, Olmsted National Historic Site. On the Olmsted firm's proposal for this marine park, see undated minutes, New Bedford Park Commission, submitted sometime after June 1894, 1.

The author has since made copies of these minutes and the Olmsted correspondence regarding the New Bedford system of parks and placed them in the F. L. Olmsted Historic Site. They will be included with Job No. 01810 for the New Bedford Park Commission.

John Olmsted's plan for a marine park has not previously been acknowledged as well. The lost plan came to light on a research trip to the New Bedford Free Public Library with the help of Tina Furtado, assistant librarian in special collections, and Todd Williams, a research assistant for the author. See "The Late John C. Olmsted and the City's Park System," Feb. 29, 1920, *Boston Globe* Scrapbook, New Bedford Free Public Library. In the proposal, the city was to buy up the entire waterfront area outside the Rodney French Boulevard (at an estimated five to ten thousand dollars) to preserve the view of the Acushnet River and bay on both sides; the remainder was to be filled in with elite homes and picturesque, open spaces along the four-mile Point Road.

Though no plans have yet come to light for the marine park in New Bedford other than its inclusion in a planned system of parks, the idea continued to be discussed in the local newspapers well into the 1920s. By that time, however, a marine park was proposed for land to the northeast, abutting the Acushnet River near the bridge from New Bedford to Fairhaven, not for Clark's Point.

88. Documentation for this project exists at both the Library of Congress Manuscript Division (correspondence beginning July 9, 1894) and at the Olmsted National Historic Site (three plans from 1895, job #01810). The New Bedford Park Commission also paid an additional five hundred dollars for an engineering study of the water supply. It is not clear whether the third phase of the proposal—tree planting over three years—ever took place. This sketch is still extant at the park commission. In 1894 New Bedford underwent a major labor strike and felt the effects of the national depression triggered by the Panic of 1893, and it is possible that Olmsted's contributions ended with the sketch and engineering study, both completed in 1895.

Olmsted intended Buttonwood Park to include ballfields, tennis lawns, childrens' playgrounds, sandboxes, and even sheep barns.

89. Ruskin drew inspiration from the Bible (a form of Christian Socialism) and the social economic principles of Thomas Carlyle and Robert Owen. For selected discussions of Ruskin and Morris on the issues of political economy and the treatment of the "working producing class," see George P. Landow, *Ruskin* (Oxford: Oxford Univ. Press, 1985), chap. 3; William Morris,

News from Nowhere and Other Writings (London: Penguin Books, 1993); Charles Harvey and Jon Press, *William Morris: Design and Enterprise in Victorian Britain* (Manchester: Manchester Univ. Press, 1991), esp. introduction and chap. 6; and Eileen Boris, *Art and Labor: Ruskin, Morris, and the Craftsman Ideal in America* (Philadelphia, Pa.: Temple Univ. Press, 1986). For more on the specific nature of changing management practices in America, see Montgomery, *Beyond Equality*; and Daniel Nelson and Stuart Campbell, "Taylorism versus Welfare Work in American Industry: H. L. Gantt and the Bancrofts," *Business History Review* 46 (Spring 1972): 1–16. For more on the subject of paternalism, see Philip Scranton, "Varieties of Paternalism: Industrial Structures and the Social Relations of Production in American Textiles," *American Quarterly* 36 (1984): 235ff.

90. "Capital and Labor in Harmony." The New Bedford newspaper reprinted the *Plain Dealer* article in full.

91. Margaret Crawford suggests that this shift occurs with an organized "industrial welfare" program in 1898, when Josiah Strong established the League for Social Service and appointed William H. Tolman as director of industrial betterment. Crawford, *Building the Workingman's Paradise,* 48–52.

92. Gould, *Eighth Special Report*, 327; "Capital and Labor in Harmony." "Auditor's Report," *New Bedford City Documents* no. 8, 1891, indicates that sixty dollars of city funds were expended to support a baseball club for the Howland Mills.

93. Pullman, too, offered these cultural amenities, but he made it clear that the town operated as a business and charged fees for the use of the stables, library, and even the church. Eventually, however, the extreme example of paternalism Pullman offered was perceived by some as tantamount to modern-day feudalism and stigmatized company housing into the next century. See Ely, "Pullman: A Social Study"; Buder, *Pullman;* Crawford, *Building the Workingman's Paradise,* 37–45.

94. The large percentage of workers from Lancashire, England, had brought English versions of socialism and union activism into the city prior to 1867. Mill owners offered outstanding housing, wages, and benefits in order to temper the urge to organize.

95. Matthew Howland to Matthew Morris Howland, Feb. 7, 1884, Howland Family Correspondence.

96. McMullen, "Lost Alternative," 27. "Howland Mills Involved," *Morning Mercury,* Apr. 24, 1897, 1, noted, "Mr. Howland has always been exceedingly popular with the employees" and added that he had organized

and funded an "annual excursion" for them to Martha's Vineyard.

97. McMullen adds, however, that part of the incentive for such favorable employee relations was the difficulty of finding such skilled labor among the workforce. Also, with regard to Howland's actions in the 1894 strike was "the fact that the market for yarn was better that year than for cloth, the product of most of the other New Bedford mills. In addition, yarn manufacturers, whose products did not bear well-known brand names, were more hesitant than cloth makers to see production interrupted by a strike, since it would be more difficult for them to recapture their market" (*New Bedford Evening Standard*, Aug. 21, 1894, cited in McMullen, "Lost Alternative," 30–31). In addition the markets for each of the New Bedford products being different—viz., print cloth, fine goods, and yarn—divisions among the mill agents surfaced during this strike. As Mary Blewett notes, the New Bedford yarn mills (to which Howland's three mills belonged) "as a group employed three thousand, while the cloth mills had seven thousand operatives. One 'leading mill man' [likely William D. Howland] in New Bedford argued that no manufacturers' association should control their decisions. It is a serious matter for a yarn mill to lose a buyer as its product identity [unlike Wamsutta, which had a reputation for producing woven goods] is not known to the general public who purchases it under another brand name." Howland, then, was taking on Andrew G. Pierce, the power behind the manufacturers' committee and treasure of Wamsutta, in resisting this regional strike. Blewett, *Constant Turmoil*, 324–25. See also *Fall River Herald*, Aug. 21, 1894.

98. For a discussion of wage reductions during the textile era in New Bedford, see McMullen, "The Coming of the Mills," 5, 8, 9, 12, and McMullen, "Industrialization and Social Change."

99. *American Wool and Cotton Reporter*, Oct. 18, 1894, cited in McMullen, "Lost Alternative," 30.

100. Gould, *Eighth Special Report*, 327.

101. Ibid.

102. Cash and debts receivable for the New Bedford Manufacturing Company were listed as $36,399, the Howland Mills $40,991, and the Rotch Spinning Corporation $219,917. For a full disclosure of financial statements, see "Howland Mills Involved," *Morning Standard*, Apr. 24, 1897,1. Editorial notes at the end of the Howland family papers state that "Will, not wanting to repeat his mistake with the New Bedford Manufacturing Company, had arranged with William J.

Rotch, the titular President of both the yarn-mill and Howland Mill, to take his share of the $650,000 in new capital on margin; meaning that Rotch would put up the bulk of the cash for the new stock issue and Will would, out of the Corporation's earnings, gradually pay Rotch back and thereby realize the paid capital and benefit them both. . . . On mature, considered judgment Rotch decided to pull the plug" (176–77). Upon observing the expansion plans Howland had for the remaining elements of the village, Rotch perhaps felt he was spending too much on construction; given the slowdown in the economy, Rotch may have thought it prudent to call in his loan before more money was spent.

103. The Bennett Manufacturing Company built six mill buildings in 1889 alone. Henry Halcomb, who with Frank R. Hadley had founded Bennett Manufacturing, just three years later created the Columbia Spinning Mill; thus, the same industrialists were founding more than one company at about the same time and thus were tying up resources and collateral. In addition to the rapid expansion of these two yarn mills, local newspapers on April 15, 1897, revealed serious irregularities in the mills' finances, including the paying out of excessive dividends, charging expenditures to improper accounts, and falsifying indebtedness reports to state officials. In all, hundreds of thousands of dollars were embezzled, leading to the suicide of the company treasurer and the placing of the two mills in receivership. See New Bedford Evening Standard, Apr. 15 and 16, June 22 and 24, and July 9, 1897.

104. Given the threat that Howland's management policies (relative to the ten-hour day and to workers' living conditions) posed to the majority of other mills in the city, and Howland's direct opposition to Andrew G. Pierce's and Wamsutta's influence in the manufacturers' union, some foul play in connection with his disappearance, or at least with the failure of the bank (founded by his grandfather and earlier run by his father) to extend the loan, is not out of the question.

105. "Better than Feared . . . Mr. Howland Believed to Have Wandered Away While Dazed," Evening Standard, Apr. 26, 1897, 1.

106. Evening Standard, May 6, 1897.

107. New Bedford Evening Standard, Feb. 17, 1898; McMullen, "Lost Alternative," 36–37.

108. Because the New Bedford park plan was unknown to scholars, Garner noted that "no other company town or, for that matter, small industrial town had conceived such an extensive park system. . . . The Hopedale commission provided him [Warren Manning,

landscape architect] the opportunity on a small scale to do what Olmsted and Eliot did in Boston with the Muddy River development, which emerged as the nation's first regional park system in 1892" (Model Company Town, 192–94). In fact, the Hopedale commission more than likely provided Manning the opportunity to carry out what Olmsted, Olmsted and Eliot had envisioned for a New Bedford park system at least as early as 1894, when Manning was responsible for supervising that firm's designs for New Bedford's Buttonwood Park.

109. For a study of Hopedale, see ibid., esp. 152–56.

110. See ibid., 149, fig. 32. At Hopedale, the actual laying of the sewer line along Union Street was not begun until 1889, but by 1897 almost all of the houses were connected with "modern conveniences." Robert Allen Cook's 1896 designs for the Draper Company double-family houses at Hopedale received a silver medal at the Paris Exposition of 1900. Warren Manning and Arthur Shurtleff, who laid out the new Hopedale subdivisions of Bancroft Park and Lake Point, were both Olmsted alumni.

111. For reports of the reorganization committees see New Bedford Evening Standard, May 25, 1897.

112. The New England Cotton Yard Company also purchased the failed Bennett Manufacturing Corporation and the Columbia Spinning Mill—all spinning mills— which indicates the growing tendency toward corporate capitalism in New England textiles. Similarly, the British conglomerate Atlantic Thread Company (ATCO) absorbed the Willimantic Linen Company in 1898 along with other New England cotton mills, including some in New Bedford. With the consolidation move of ATCO came increased resistance to efforts of the American Federation of Labor to organize its employees. See Beardsley, Willimantic Industry and Community, 40–41, and Boss and Thomas, New Bedford, 132.

113. "50 Years Ago," Sunday Standard Times, July 6, 1958, stated that in July 1908 the New England Cotton Yarn Company sold to Joseph T. Kenney more than four thousand rods of land and that "a considerable section of the area was later to become the site of the Sharp Mill." The 1910 Walker City of New Bedford map shows that at this time the Sharp Mill was still called the New England Cotton Yarn Company. Kenney was indicated as owning more than five full city residential blocks bounded by Dartmouth, Sidney, Bolton, and Winsper Streets. The article stated that New England Cotton Yarn retained possession of the fifty Howland cottages when the other part of the property was sold. According to the New Bedford Record of Building

Permits, builder Joseph Motta built six three-unit tenements in the former Howland parcel in 1914–15 alone.

114. See "The Late John C. Olmsted and the City's Park System," *Boston Globe* Scrapbook.

115. The Soule Mill, designed in 1901 by Boston firm Lockwood, Greene, and Company and the first of the twentieth-century New Bedford textile mills to be incorporated, ended a five-year hiatus during which no new textile mills were incorporated in the city.

116. "Experiments with Mill Villages."

117. The Howland Mill Village became a Historic District on the National Register of Historic Places in 1997.

118. As reflected by the *Record of Building Permits*, the shift in New Bedford to the conventional hipped-roof three-decker was underway by 1894. Its full expression, with bay windows and three piazzas, was not standard until about 1907. Prior to this time, the flat-roof and gable-ended "three tenements" were prevalent. The high point of tenement housing in New Bedford, not surprisingly, was 1910, the same year that the greatest number of mills were incorporated in the city. In 1910, 639 houses were built containing 1,812 tenements. Of that number, 290 were three-deckers providing 870 tenements.

119. The new company town, according to Margaret Crawford, was generally a product of the first decade of the twentieth century. Following the disastrous 1894 strike at Pullman, which revealed to the public George Pullman's excessive and outdated paternalism, social reformers such as Jane Addams, Graham Taylor, and Richard Ely concluded that model industrial towns would succeed only if *independent* professionals—acting as buffers between capital and labor—took a larger role in their conception and planning. Two reform movements—the industrial betterment movement (c. 1898) and the campaign for housing reform—shaped the development of the new company town. Next, new methods of "social engineering" practiced by professional reform groups reorganized haphazard industrial paternal and philanthropic improvements of the previous century into systematic social programs. "Welfare capitalism" practiced by industry by 1898 now assumed a degree of responsibility for workers' safety and well-being in exchange, it was hoped, for loyalty. According to Margaret Crawford: "Planned industrial communities, financed by employers and designed by professionals, appeared to offer a comprehensive solution to urban and industrial problems. Employers, acknowledging their social responsibilities, would upgrade

working and housing conditions for their workers. Designers, using the garden city as a model, would create new types of communities away from urban areas. The resulting decentralization of industry and housing would reduce urban congestion, thus improving living conditions in cities" (*Building the Workingman's Paradise*, 76–77).

The Howland Mill Village may be seen as presaging (by at least ten years) the industrial betterment movement and embodying, as well, many of the comprehensive planning principles (particularly through the work of John C. Olmsted and Manning) of the new company town. In fact, the Howland Mill Village and the New Bedford system of parks represent a turning point in the Olmsted firm toward embracing large-scale industrial planning. However, by 1898 New Bedford had lost both elements of what could have been the beginning of a new model company town *movement* and an integrated park system based on Olmsted's naturalistic design principles. For more on the planning principles of the new company town, see Crawford, *Building the Workingman's Paradise*, esp. chaps. 3–5.

5. THE ANATOMY OF A NEW BEDFORD THREE-DECKER

1. As of this printing, two doctoral dissertations are underway on the subject of the three-decker outside of New Bedford. One is by Deedee (Rodolitz) Jacobsohn in the American Studies Department at Boston University on the subject of changing social patterns by residents of the three-deckers in South Boston; the other is by Kathy Long in the Art History Department at Brown University and is a typological study. Judy Smith's study, *Family Connections,* addresses the cultural transformation of the three-decker by Jewish and Italian immigrants and was an outgrowth of her doctoral dissertation at Brown University in American Studies. Earlier efforts include Janice Lee Morrill, "The French-Canadian Three Deckers of Southbridge, Massachusetts," undertaken as a master's thesis at the University of North Carolina at Chapel Hill in the Folklore Department in 1987, and Marilyn W. Spear, *Worcester's Three Deckers* (Worcester: Worcester Bicentennial Commission, 1977). Peter Barnett, "The Worcester Three-Decker: Form and Variation," *Monadnock* 48 (June 1974): 21–33. Dr. Peter M. Barnett has identified five basic types of three-deckers in his article "The Worcester Three-Decker: A Study in the Perception of Form," published in digest form in the quarterly magazine *Design and Environment* (Winter 1975). See also

Roger A. Roberge, "Three Decker: Structural Correlate of Worcester's Industrial Revolution" (Master's thesis, Clark University, 1965); Sam Bass Warner Jr. *Streetcar Suburbs, the Process of Growth in Boston, 1870–1900*, 2d ed. (Cambridge, Mass.: Harvard Univ. Press, 1978); and Douglass Tucci, *Built in Boston City and Suburb, 1800–1950*. (Boston: New York Graphic Society, 1978), esp. "French Flats and Three-Deckers," pp.101–30.

The French influence on the type is discussed in Michel Lessard and Huquette Marquis, *Encyclopédie de la Maison Québécoise, 3 Siécles d'habitations* (Ottawa: L'Homme Ltée, 1972). For a distribution analysis of the three-decker in New England see Arthur J. Krim, "The Three Decker as Urban Architecture," *Monadnock* 44 (1970). (See esp. fig. 1 from the 1967–70 field inventory.) Also, there have been several three-decker studies undertaken for the Massachusetts Historical Commission, including the 1981 *Worcester, Ma. Three-Decker Survey Report*, and a 1989 National Register Multiple Property Nomination that built upon the research and recommendations of the 1981 *Survey*, and listed 189 three-deckers, including several districts. For a Boston area study that reflects areas of three-decker housing see James Bradley, Arthur Krim, Peter Stott, and Sarah Zimmerman, *Historic and Archaeological Resources of the Boston Area* (Boston: Massachusetts Historical Commission, 1982). For a diffusion study of three-decker types in Dorchester, see Krim's *The Three-Deckers of Dorchester: An Architectural Historical Survey* (Boston: Landmarks Commission, 1977). For a flow diagram of the evolution of the type in North Cambridge, Mass., see Krim's "North Cambridge Vernacular House Types," *Northwest Cambridge Survey of Architectural History*, vol. 5 (Cambridge, Mass.: Cambridge Historical Commission and MIT Press, 1977). See also Ellen Rosebrock, *Historic Fall River* (Fall River, Ma.: Preservation Partnership, 1978), 42–47. Krim has also done a preliminary distribution study of New Bedford for W.H.A.L.E. in 1989 and is presently working on a three-decker inventory in Fall River, Mass. His work and that of Michael Steinitz (survey director of the Massachusetts Historical Commission) over the years have brought to the foreground an important urban vernacular form previously overlooked, in large part, by architectural historians, architects, and preservationists. The author is indebted to Arthur Krim and Michael Steinitz for their cooperation on this study.

2. For a discussion of this issue in preservation, see Dolores Hayden, "Placemaking, Preservation and Urban History," *Journal of Architectural Education* 41 (3) (Spring 1988): 45–51. On the problems of preserving three-deckers and similar urban industrial neighbor-hoods, Arthur J. Krim (then working for the Massachusetts Historical Commission) delivered a paper at the National Meeting of the Society of Architectural Historians in New Haven, Conn., in 1981. The session was on "Vernacular Architecture: Editing History Through Preservation," chaired by Dell Upton. Krim's paper was entitled "Recognition of the New England Three-Decker: The Preservation of Vernacular Urban Housing." In the paper he states, "Formal attempts to establish triple-decker preservation districts have been frustrated by locational problems within the older urban cores. . . . [There is] a reluctance to grant formal historical status because of its long-standing image as a vernacular housing type of the industrial period."

Of note are the preservation efforts of Michael Steinitz and Arthur Krim on projects in Worcester, Dorchester, and, most recently, in New Bedford and Fall River (see n. 1 above). The perception of three-deckers as a degraded type has begun to change, however. Michael Steinitz informs me that presently there are approximately five hundred three-deckers listed on the National Register as part of Historic District nominations and eighty-six listed individually; of that number, seventy-four are listed separately in Worcester, Mass., alone. Also notable is the forthcoming Rhode Island architectural guide written by William Jordy as part of the Buildings of the United States series sponsored by the Society of Architectural Historians in conjunction with Oxford University Press. Professor Jordy's survey of several three-decker neighborhoods is a refreshing change in the pattern of such tour guides. Museums, too, are beginning to recognize the architectural and social relevance of the three-decker as a regional signifier. There is a three-decker exhibit at the Woonsocket, R.I., Museum of Work and Culture, and a proposal to exhibit and interpret a full-scale three-decker within the walls of the Heritage Harbor Museum in Providence, R.I.

3. Carroll Westfall, Review of Elizabeth Collins Cromley, *Alone Together: A History of New York's Apartments* (Ithaca, N.Y.: Cornell Univ. Press, 1990) *Journal of the Society of Architectural Historians* (Mar. 1991) 50 (1): 94–95.

4. Frank Worsdall, *The Glasgow Tenement: A Way of Life* (Edinburgh: W&R Chambers Ltd., 1979), ix.

5. For more on the history of apartment and tenement housing, see Elizabeth Cromley, *Alone Together: A History of New York's Apartments* (Ithaca, N.Y.: Cornell Univ. Press, 1990); Mardges Bacon, *Ernest Flagg* (Cambridge, Mass.: MIT Press, 1986), esp. 234–67 ("Urban Housing Reform: An Incentive to Build"); Sarah Landau, "Apartment Houses" in *The Architecture of*

just after World War I, when housing shortages were a serious problem, the Fairhaven Mills built rental cottages (instead of three-deckers) as a means of securing employees. These were located in the north part of Fairhaven across the river from the mills. On a large tract of land, the mill built a village of forty-six houses. These were sold in 1922 to a Fall River speculator, who sold the houses individually at retail. See "Experiments With Mill Villages," *Boston Globe* , Feb. 4, 1922. The Sullivan data came from the *New Bedford Record of Building Permits* for 1901.

21. *American Architect and Building News* 5 (Apr. 12, 1879): ix. Special thanks to Deedee Jacobsohn for bringing this source to my attention. Caleb and Edgar B. Hammond were one of only four architectural firms listed in the *New Bedford Directory* (284) in 1879–80. Their office was listed at 129 North Water Street. The other three firms were those of John Allen, William Durfee, and Seth Ingalls. Ingalls built Wamsutta's first mill in 1847.

22. For the lowest-paid workers, these would include five-tenement rabbit runs and six-blocks mostly, with larger frame tenement and apartment houses also available.

23. Information gathered from the building ledger of Michael E. Daley in the possession of his grandson, Clement E. Daley of New Bedford.

24. On April 23, 1912, seven permits were issued to Nazaire Chaine, owner and builder, *for three-tenements* [sic] to be built on the north side of Bates Avenue, East of Acushnet Avenue. They were designed with five rooms and a bath, and measured twenty-six by forty feet. The tenement was three stories tall with a hipped shingle roof, bay window, front and rear piazzas. Three units cost $4,000, while the remaining four cost $4,500. Information gathered from the *New Bedford Record of Building Permits*. Courtesy of John Roza III, Deputy Building Commissioner of the New Bedford City Hall.

25. This newspaper account, as well as the circumstances of the January 1, 1898 strike, is covered in Blewett, chapter 10, esp. pp. 338–41. The interview itself and the illustration of Offinger's rental apartment can be found in the "Scrapbook of Clippings Concerning the 1898 Textile Strike at New Bedford," 4 vols. Widener Library, Harvard University, Call No. XT51. Special thanks to Mary Blewett for helping me locate this material.

26. Patricia Raub, "Another Pattern of Urban Living: Multifamily Housing in Providence, 1890–1930," *Rhode Island History* 48 (Feb. 1990): 6, table 5.

27. The earliest of these appeared on a three-tenement for Joseph Francis built by Frank Peters on July 16, 1894. One dormer was twenty feet long, the other fifteen feet long. The stated goal was "to finish the attic" likely for rental space.

28. The earliest hipped-roof three-decker listed in the city building permits was built by Arthur Magnant on Feb. 27, 1894, for William Mathews. This was the *only* hip roof constructed that year. Fall River, Mass., located just to the south of New Bedford, while more diverse in its three-decker forms, also had representative numbers of hipped-roof three-deckers by the 1880s, according to Arthur Krim. Their roof pitch is not as severe, however. Also a review of the factory constructions in New Bedford from the 1890s through the first decade of the twentieth century indicate consistent use of architects and mill engineers such as Charles Makepeace, Charles Praray (1847–1910), and F. P. Sheldon from Providence, R.I.— where the hipped-roof three-decker is also popular— who brought several mill innovations with them. The cross fertilization of three-decker building features makes sense in this context. New Bedford, then, seems to have experimented early on (c. 1870s to 1890s), until between 1904 and 1910, when the city stabilized its imported influences into a standard but distinctive building type.

29 Of note are two building permits filed for Alice Riding in 1909 (permit no. 752-09) with plans submitted by architect John Williams, Sept. 8, 1909, "of a building to be raised and a store to be built underneath on the N.W. cor. McGurk St. and Ruth for Mrs. Alice Riding." The second builiding was raised up in order to place a store underneath for Mrs. Riding. It was located at 133 Ruth Street. John Williams also submitted plans on Dec. 14, 1911, "to remodel and add an addition" (for apartments) to a former Greek Revival mansion at 115 Acushnet Avenue for Paul Pintor.

30. Michael E. Daley, for example, had previously worked for the Dawson Brewing Company before going into the business of building three-deckers around 1909, when he was in his forties (Correspondence with Clement Daley, Oct. 21, 1995). Of the 254 three-tenements built in 1909, nine were built for or by Michael Daley. Information gathered from the *New Bedford Record of Building Permits* for 1909, and the building ledger of Michael E. Daley, now in the possession of the Clement E. Daley estate.

31. See, for example, the rows of two-story, gable-end three-tenements built for John B. Sullivan by Frederick Hazard on the east and west sides of Cleaveland Street

south of Cove Road. They all measured 24 by 36 feet and were built for a cost of $2,000. Permits were issued on July 10 and Oct. 2, 1895. A permit to build the Dartmouth Mill was issued to J. W. Bishop and Co. the same day as developer Sullivan's second set of three-tenements, opposite the mill. Similarly, C. E. Cook and A. P. Smith, owners and builders, took out sixteen permits in the same block and the west side of Abbott on March 23, 1896, for two-and-one-half-story, gable-end three-tenements measuring 24 by 38 feet at a cost of $2,300 each.

32. Jane Holz Kay quoting a turn-of-the-century spokesperson in "Homey but not Homely: Portrait of a Three-decker," *(Cambridge, Mass.) Real Paper,* Sept, 3, 1975, 10, quoted in Jacobsohn, "Tenements in Context," 2.

33. Comstock, *Two-Family and Twin Houses,* 6–7.

34. John E. Crowley, "Inventing Comfort: The Piazza" in *American Material Culture,* ed. Ann Smart Martin and J. Richie Garrison (Winterthur, Del.: Henry Francis du Pont Winterthur Museum, 1997), 278.

35. Ibid., 279. The British also encountered the design feature in the indigenous domestic architecture of India during the seventeenth and early eighteenth centuries. Some scholars indicate that there are Portuguese, Spanish, Arabic and Persian origins as well.

36. See, for example, the period discussion by Richard Watson Gilder, "The Housing Problem—America's Need of Awakening," *The American City I* (1909): 34.

37. Quoted in Handlin, *American Home,* 236.

38. See John F. Kasson, *Rudeness and Civility: Manners in Nineteenth-Century Urban America* (New York: Hill and Wang, 1990). See also Bushman, *Refinement of America.*

39. "The New Massachusetts Homestead Commission," *The Survey: Social, Charitable, Civic* 26 (Sept. 19, 1911): 828. See also Jacobsohn, "Tenements in Context," 8–11.

40. John Kasson, "Semiotics of the City," a public lecture presented at the University of North Carolina, Charlotte, Mar. 25, 1994.

41. See Kenneth L. Ames, "Meaning in Artifacts: Hall Furnishings in Victorian America," in *Common Places: Readings in American Vernacular Architecture,* ed. Dell Upton and John Michael Vlach (Athens: Univ. of Georgia Press, 1986), 240–60. See also Lizabeth A. Cohen, "Embellishing a Life of Labor: An Interpretation of the Material Culture of American Working-Class Homes, 1885–1915," in ibid., 261–77. In this regard, Sam Bass Warner argues that the three-decker builders were driven by the ideology of the rural ideal, but "thought there were some similarities between the rich man's

estate and the cheap two families and three-deckers;" the lesser product resembled its model in details only. The lots were so small and the pattern of living so dense that the rural setting was lost altogether. . . . [T]he cramped suburban streets of three-deckers stand as an ugly joke against these modes: the picturesque houses set on garden lots" *Streetcar Suburbs,* 57–60. To mitigate the cramped urban spaces of workers' housing and still comply with the social rituals of the day, Clare de Graffenried in "Need of Better Homes for Wage-earners," *The Forum* 21 (May 1896): 301–12 begins her article by stating: "The two civilizing agencies of highest value for laboring people, next to industrial training and baths, are bay windows and front door bells." Special thanks to Alison K. Hoagland for this reference.

42. Prescott Hall, "The Menace of the Three-Decker," in *Housing Problems in America* (Providence, R.I., Fifth National Conference on Housing, 1916), 134–35.

43. Margaret Crawford states that "Cultural Americanization took the form of a self-conscious mythification of the Anglo-Saxon and colonial heritage. Simulating the architectural styles of the Colonial period allowed industrial managers to affirm the allegiance to pre-industrial cultural values and simultaneously repress the multicultural social reality on which the industrial economy depended" (*Building the Workingman's Paradise,* 112). See her chap. 6. See also Gerol Korman, *Industrialization, Immigrants and Americanizers* (Madison: State Historical Society of Wisconsin, 1967); John Higham, *Strangers in the Land: Patterns of American Nativism, 1860–1925* (New York: Atheneum, 1963).

44. A sample of authors who wrote pattern books that address the three-decker includes William T. Comstock, who published three-decker plans from five architects (one each from Boston and Worcester, and three from Waterbury, Connecticut) in the book *Two-Family and Twin Houses* (1908); Frederick H. Gowing, a Boston architect who advertised several three-decker plans for sale in his books *Building Plans for Modern Homes* (1911, 1914, 1920, 1921) and in *Building Plans for Colonial Dwellings* (1925); also, the magazine *Carpentry and Building* printed one set of plans for a three-decker, including framing plans and other details, each year between 1905 and 1908. I am indebted to Deedee Jacobson for bringing these references to my attention.

45. Richard Longstreth has related to me that upon asking a long-time three-decker builder in Providence, R.I., to define the building type, he replied, "It's just a bungalow, except there are three of them one on top of the other." This discussion took place in the mid-1970s,

when Longstreth worked for the Rhode Island Historic Preservation Office.

46. Chester E. Smolski, *Providence Journal,* Mar. 20, 1977, notes that in Providence, R.I., contractors sometimes built as many as nine three-deckers per acre. By analyzing classified advertisements in the *Providence Sunday Journal,* Patricia Raub cites prices ranging from about $6,500 to $10,500 in the late 1920s. See her "Another Pattern of Urban Living: Multi-family Housing in Providence, 1890–1930," *Rhode Island History* 48 (Feb. 1990): n. 45. For a discussion of the prejudice against this housing type in its era, see Gwendolyn Wright, *Building the American Dream: A Social History in America* (Cambridge, Mass.: MIT Press, 1981), 114–34.

In contrast, Victoria Newhouse notes in her biography of Wallace K. Harrison that Harrison, who grew up in a Worcester, Mass., three-decker, often looked back on the type "as an ideal solution when later he struggled with the problems of low-cost housing in New York City since it was inexpensive housing that provided ample light and air" *Wallace K. Harrison, Architect* (New York: Rizzoli, 1989), 32.

47. This factor, and the practical reality that rental fees of the other floors substantially covered the mortgage, made the three-decker a desirable purchase for first-time buyers. More recently, the same factors made it a suitable form for conversion to condominiums, at least until the glut in the condominium market in the Boston area in the late 1980s. By 1991, prices of three-deckers had dropped 15 percent. For current uses, rehabilitations, and new modular design based on three-deckers, see William A. Davis, "All Decked Out, the Humble Triple-Decker Finally Gets Some Respect," "At Home" section of the *Boston Globe,* Mar. 29, 1991, 37–38.

48. See Worsdall, *Glasgow Tenement.*

49. Emma W. Rogers, "The Foreign Invasion of a New England Town—New Haven," *The Survey: Social, Charitable, Civic* 26 (June 3, 1911): 373–74.

50. In Arthur Krim's study of three-deckers in Dorchester, Mass., he discovered that:

> usually there were three roles involved in the building of a three-decker: the landowner, the builder, and the architect. Often they would, in fact, be three separate men. Quite frequently, however, the builder would also own the land, design the three-decker, and construct it. Often the roles would be switched so that the same group or individual would perform different functions in different neighborhoods. Not surprisingly, building three-deckers was mostly the work of men, but often women, widows and spinsters, would buy the land and dictate the number and type of three-deckers constructed. And at least one three-decker was designed by a woman architect [Mary E. Farrell, who designed three-deckers in Adams Village].

With regard to the issues of design originality, he states: "Eventually, the stylistic individual ability of local groups disappeared as builders from different parts of Dorchester crossed each other's paths and exchanged ideas and designs. At the same time, these local groups themselves were absorbed into a larger, more homogenous building community. Thus, by the end of the First World War three-deckers throughout Dorchester showed a great similarity of design" (Krim, *Three-Deckers of Dorchester,* 64–66). In New Bedford, design similarity was reached by 1910.

51. Because of the predictable grid and the narrow, long lot sizes in many instances within the city, siting problems were among some of the most challenging design constraints faced by builders and architects. These issues persist today for both rehab and infill design for the building type. See some of the more innovative approaches taken recently by Cambridge, Mass., architect Americo Andrade to address issues of solar heating, natural lighting, and selective views. His work is cited in Davis, "All Decked Out," 37–38.

52. The Soule Mill designed by the Boston firm of Lockwood, Greene and Company led the recovery of the textile industry in New Bedford with the incorporation of its new cotton yarn mill in 1901. The construction not only ended a five-year hiatus in mill incorporations in the city, but the three hipped-roof three-deckers that builder John Sullivan provided for the Soule Mill operatives began a resurgence in that area of the housing market. Whereas in 1897 sixty-two three-tenements were built, between 1898 and 1900 no more than seven were built in a given year. By 1902, building starts for three-tenements again rose sharply.

53. From the 1880s on, the fire insurance manuals continually stressed the importance of natural or solar lighting for factories not only for illumination, but also for the "health and happiness" of the workers. Some texts used the term "etiolate" to refer to the withering effects brought on by the lack of natural light. See B. H. Thwaite, *Our Factories, Workshops, Warehouse, Their Sanitary and Fire-Resisting Arrangements* (London, N.Y.: E & F. N. Spon, 1882). Today, these large factory windows are often perceived by mill managers more as liabilities, and are boarded up to curtail heating and cooling costs, vandalism, or visual distractions to the workforce.

54. According to blueprints on file in the attic of the New Bedford City Hall, F. P. Sheldon and Company, an engineering firm with offices in Providence and Boston, seems to have led the movement toward separate weaving sheds in New Bedford. On Aug. 8, 1895, Sheldon submitted plans for Dartmouth Mill No. 5 with a two-story weaving mill. On Mar. 17, 1896, he designed weaving sheds for the Acushnet Mill with a sawtooth roof (apparently the first of this type in the city). The next technological improvement came with the integration of ventilation stacks with the sawtooth roofs on the weave shed addition of Wamsutta Mills on Sept. 8, 1906. Other information on the number of looms in the Whitman Mill came from interpretation information at Lowell National Historic Site.

55. Arthur Krim, for example, states: "[T]he existence of a community of builders—an informal alliance of tradesmen and speculators who worked for and with each other, borrow[ed] and invent[ed] designs . . . most of the three-deckers were constructed by newly emergent immigrant groups—Irish, Canadians, Jews and Italians, the very people the triple-deckers were meant to attract on the trolley" (*Three-Deckers of Dorchester*, 64–66). The appendix in that study lists major groups of Dorchester builders. Krim, who carried out a limited field inventory of New Bedford's three-deckers during the 1980s (which covered approximately two-thirds of the city's resources), has selective evidence for New Bedford of ethnically linked neighborhood development by builders, but research that I have undertaken in this area indicates that key builders, such as John Sullivan or Joseph Blier, worked in both the North and South End ethnic areas, and merely shifted their building crews accordingly. On the smaller scale, certainly ethnic builders built (on single or adjacent lots) three-deckers for members of the same ethnic group. See, for example, Stephen Sylvia, who is listed in the *New Bedford Record of Building Permits* as having built three three-deckers in 1893. He would continue to build exclusively for Portuguese clients, like Joseph Dias, for whom he built a three-decker on Independent and County Streets on May 8, 1895. Also, Wilfred Bernard came to New Bedford from a farm in Canada in 1914 and took part in the three-decker building boom. He constructed a rare brick three-decker for his family on 142 Deane Street in the city's North End (the blueprints are on file in the New Bedford City Hall) and built several others along Deane Street for French Canadian clients. The commonality in language for non-English-speaking clients would ensure such client-builder alliances.

As Olivier Zunz has observed in his study of Detroit immigration patterns and social organization within industrial communities, ethnicity and socioeconomic level determines residence patterns. Immigrant groups, therefore, are as likely to live (and build) near friends and relatives as they are to live in neighborhoods because of class and work bonds. See Olivier Zunz, *The Changing Face of Inequality: Urbanization, Industrial Development, and Immigrants in Detroit, 1880–1920* (Chicago: Univ. of Chicago Press, 1991).

56. See Katz, "Opportunity, Exclusion, and the Immigrant," 68 for a discussion of New Bedford's ethnic diversity.

6. THE CULTURAL TRANSFORMATION OF THE THREE-DECKER

1. This is the first stanza of "The Song of Cotton Cloth," which could be sung to the tune of "Auld Lang Syne." It was written by J. Edmund Estes and published in the New Bedford *Evening Standard* September 14, 1924, at the request of Fall River, Mass., Mayor Edmond P. Talbot during "Cotton Week." The rest of the song is as follows:

> *Boom cotton cloth both south and north*
> *With needle, coin and song;*
> *Change present style to one worth while,*
> *Impel the cause along.*
> *Long silent spindles then will hum,*
> *And shuttles fly again;*
> *Fulfill this plan of worried man*
> *For you should help the men.*
>
> *No cotton sale can ever fail*
> *Endorsed by lad and lass,*
> *Buy underwear and overwear,*
> *New cloth of every class.*
> *Help milkmen, merchants, employee*
> *The tariff, men will raise*
> *In ginghams, voiles, percales appear,*
> *Immortalize these days.*

2. Technical Advisory Corporation, *Reconnaissance Survey of New Bedford*, 13, 23.

3. Ibid., 3.

4. In response to the more than twenty-five million newcomers from foreign lands who had made their homes in the United States from the mid-nineteenth century up to the 1920s, a wave of protest to limit immigration occurred. Works by politicians and writers, like the 1926 *The Melting Pot Mistake* by Henry Pratt Fairchild, helped fuel the arguments behind the immigration restriction laws of the 1920s.

5. Technical Advisory Corporation, *Reconnaissance Survey of New Bedford*, 22.

6. Ibid., 23, 25.

7. By 1920, for example, the South had surpassed New England in the number of active spindle hours because of longer working days, lower wages, and lower transportation costs due to being closer to the source of raw material. See Crawford, "Earle S. Draper," 141–42.

8. By 1939, 72 percent of the active spindles in the United States were located in the South as compared with 24 percent in 1900. Regional wage differences were significant. From 1894 to 1927 the average southern textile wage was 40 percent below that of other parts of the country. See Crawford, "Earle S. Draper," 141–42. As Blewett notes, however, the "Southern Menace" of low wages was often exaggerated as a means of justifying wage cuts among the northern mills. In December 1897 following several wage cutbacks in Massachusetts, the editor of the *Fall River Globe* assigned reporter Walter N. Caswell to test the validity of such claims. After visiting several mill centers in the South, he found that wage differences were closer to 15 percent, but hours were longer. Blewett, *Constant Turmoil*, 346.

9. Technical Advisory Corporation, *Reconnaissance Survey of New Bedford*, 29.

10. Concerns related to lighting and ventilation, the minimum size of the rooms, and privacy (related to connected rooms and access to bathrooms) were voiced at the turn of the century regarding tenement design of any type. See, for example, the work of De Forest and Veiller, *The Tenement House Problem*.

11. Boss and Thomas, *New Bedford*, 115.

12. Sayer, *New Bedford*, 153.

13. See Jerry R. Williams, *And Yet They Come: Portuguese Immigration from the Azores to the United States* (New York: Center for Migration Studies, 1982), chap. 1. Leo Pap, *The Portuguese-Americans* (Boston: Portuguese Continental Union of the U.S.A., 1992), chap. 2, esp. 22–23, and nn. 1, 4, 5.

14. Melville, *Moby Dick*, 118. For other references in Melville to Azorean connections to whaling as early as 1807, see the two-volume edition published in 1922 by Constable & Co., vol. I: 149, 216, 219, 259, 293.

15. Williams, *And Yet They Come*, chap. 1; Pap, *The Portuguese-Americans*, chap. 2. See also Sayer, *New Bedford*, 65. McMullen, "The Coming of the Mills," 5, notes that the Portuguese arrived in New Bedford early in the nineteenth century. "There is a record of baptism of a Portuguese child in the city as early as 1824."

16. In 1900, the French Canadian population numbered 8,559 in New Bedford. They were joined by the English 5,389 (which accounted for 21 percent of the population), and the Irish 3,026 (which accounted for 12 percent of the population, down from 24 percent in 1890). See Katz, "Opportunity, Exclusion, and the Immigrant," 32–33. For more on the subject of Portuguese immigration, see Leo Pap, *The Portuguese-Americans*, chap. 2; Williams, *And Yet They Come*, chap. 1.

17. Williams, *And Yet They Come*, 14–15.

18. As Jamie Katz notes, nearly three-quarters of the Portuguese workers in 1911 had lived less than nine years in the United States. By 1920, however, the Portuguese were clearly the dominant ethnic group in New Bedford. See Katz, "Opportunity, Exclusion, and the Immigrant," 47–50.

19. For specific data on the financial conditions of Portuguese immigrants at the time of passage to New Bedford in the two decades from 1904 to 1924 and the illiteracy rate among this same group, see Stephen L. Cabral, *Tradition and Transformation, Portuguese Feasting in New Bedford* (New York: A.M.S. Press, 1989), 16, table 7, 18 table 8.

20. See, for example, Olmsted, Olmsted and Eliot's proposal to construct a scenic parkway along the ocean drive in the South End (in chap. 4). This proposal of 1894 was not carried out, and by 1920 the area was described as being "covered by mills and tenement houses." See "The Late John C. Olmsted and the City's Park System," Feb. 29, 1920, *Boston Globe* scrapbook, New Bedford Free Public Library, Special Collections.

21. "The Late John C. Olmsted." The ordinance limiting the height of frame dwellings was written in 1916.

22. According to Arthur Krim, the earliest use of the term "three-decker" to refer to a dwelling house with three separate family units appeared in the 1893 Worcester Centennial publication. The term was in widest use during the teens and twenties to connote a disparaged housing form.

As early as 1893 Portuguese builders joined the other principal ethnic groups in the city in exploiting the boom in tenement construction. Builders such as Thomas Estiella built several three-tenements during the teens in the former Howland Mill Village parcel. On Jan. 1, 1913, he took out permits nos. 1–3 to build three three-tenements with five rooms and a bath on each floor of a 26-by-40-foot floor unit. These tenements had slate-hipped roofs, an ell, a three-story 3-by-10-foot bay, and three-story 5-by-14-foot piazzas and were built at a cost of $4,000 each. It should be noted, however, that Portuguese builders, such as Stephen

Sylvia, are listed as early as September 27, 1893, in the New Bedford Record of Building Permits as having built three-tenements. Interestingly, on May 8, 1895, the three-tenement Sylvia built for Joseph Dias on Independent and County in the South End is described as having "Portuguese dormers" on two sides.

Of course, not all Portuguese lived in three-deckers nor in other forms of multifamily housing. The prosperous early New Bedford Portuguese Americans lived in single-family dwellings and, later, in two-family residences. John E. Luce Jr., for example, lived at 164 Grinnell Street with his wife, Mary Vera. The couple resided in what was described as a "charming white cottage well furnished and maintained." John E. Luce Jr. was described as being a "whaling captain and shareholder." The cottage plan included a parlor, sitting room, dining room, kitchen, and bedroom on the first floor. The second floor had additional bedrooms, which were connected to the first floor by a rear stairway. Special thanks to Lilian E. Avila for her correspondence of Apr. 26, 1996, describing the home of her aunt. Professor Avila stressed that *none* of her relatives ever lived in three-deckers, and she described other homes of relatives in New Bedford, including the one owned by Joseph Vera, who lived in "a handsome home (gabled), luxuriously furnished on the South Sixth street."

23. See Jacobsohn, "Tenements in Context," 11.

24. See, for example, "Exclude Three-Deckers from Residential Area," *Lynn Daily Evening Item,* July 11, 1913. For Lynn housing issues, see Naomi Rosenblum, "The Housing of Lynn's Shoe Workers in 1915," in *Life and Times in Shoe City* (Salem, Mass.: Essex Institute, 1979), 17–28. See also Hall, "Menace of the Three-Decker," 133–53. The Worcester bank president was Alfred L. Aiken of the Worcester County Institution of Savings. See "Housing Reform By Savings Bank," in *The Survey* 26 (May 27, 1911): 331.

25. See the building ledger of Michael E. Daley, currently owned by the estate of Clement E. Daley, New Bedford.

26. Today, there is an effort to preserve not only building and building contexts but *cultural* contexts. "Cultural conservation" recognizes the importance of safeguarding the more intangible aspects of place (e.g., lifeways, foodways, heritage, and tradition) that lend architecture its human component. Through such efforts, all historical periods and cultural expressions can be recognized as contributing to the fabric of American life. See Mary Hufford, ed., *Conserving Culture: A New Discourse on Heritage* (Urbana: Univ. of Illinois Press, 1994).

For a discussion of the various perceptions of place, see Relph, *Place and Placelessness,* and also, Jackson, *Sense of Place, Sense of Time.* For some new approaches toward preservation, see Elizabeth Cromley, "Public History and the *Historic* Preservation District," in *Past Meets Present,* ed. Jo Blatti (Washington, D.C.: Smithsonian, 1987), 30–36; Dell Upton, ed., *America's Architectural Roots: Ethnic Groups that Built America* (Washington, D.C.: National Trust, 1986); Michael A. Tomlan, ed., *Preservation of What, for Whom? A Critical Look at Historical Significance* (Ithaca, N.Y.: National Council for Preservation Education, 1998).

27. Boss and Thomas, *New Bedford,* 206–8.

28. Hot water tanks have been required by law since the 1970s for rental apartments and can be rented from the gas company. Washers and dryers, therefore, take the place of washtubs and clotheslines, making the once ubiquitous laundry decks less functionally significant. In addition, because of insert window air-conditioners and the threat of crime on the streets, few people use the porches recreationally. Those who do, rebuild them with a wrought-iron framework and corrugated metal under-decking which is more durable in the New England climate. The appearance of such elements as an air-conditioner, metal siding, flagstone porch cladding, and elaborate wrought-iron porches are merely reflections of a different set of criteria for "success" than those embraced by proceeding generations of three-decker dwellers.

Interestingly, the S-shaped iron balusters on the new porches simulate the old wooden forms from the 1910s, and approximate the iron verandas from the Azores that are more familiar to these Old World transplants as well. In Portugal, the verandas lent shade to apartments below, provided the primary outdoor space, and allowed inhabitants to communicate across apartment units or to the street vendors below. This cultural predisposition allowed for a ready transference of use to the piazzas when Portuguese immigrants inhabited these lofty, three-tiered living units, though the design was reconstituted to meet current sensibilities.

29. Interview by the author with John Ventura, Joseph Soares, Joseph and Ethel Couto, June 15, 1990, New Bedford.

30. For more on the architecture and living patterns in the Azores today, see the following: Francisco Ernesto de Oliveira Martins, *Arquitectura nos Açores: Subsídios Para o Seu Estudo* (Horta: Direcção Regional do Turismo, 1983); Maurico Abreu, *Açores: Paisagem sem Mácula* (Açores: Eurolito Lda., May 1987). The southern New England press, the *Spinner,* often carries articles on the Portuguese American influence in the region. A full-length text on this subject is forthcoming by *Spinner.*

31. Christopher Koziol, "Late 19th- and Early 20th-Century Philanthropic Housing," Association of Collegiate Schools of Architecture, Annual Meeting, Spring 1988, Chicago, Ill.

32. The 1923 *A Reconnaissance Survey of New Bedford, Mass.,* noted, for example, that one of the city's economic shortcomings was that there was little agricultural opportunity; however, the study notes that "on the outskirts of the city a few market gardens are operated, mostly by Portuguese" (21–22).

33. Most of the Portuguese in New Bedford came from such settings and practices rooted in traditional rural and village life in the Azore Islands—particularly San Miguel, Fayal, and Terceira. Often labeled "greenhorns" when they first arrive from the Old Country, their assimilation into the larger community of mainstream American life within the region is inhibited by the social infrastructure of Portuguese residents and family members, who assist them in adjusting to urban industrial life with as little trauma to old sensibilities as possible. With church services in Portuguese and Portuguese corner stores, banks, and doctors' offices there is very little need to even learn English. As a result, Portuguese life, culture, and values are imprinted on the city to at least the same degree as American life impacts imported customs.

34. The high annual humidity was ideal for countering static electricity in the cotton fibers, while the cove access enabled shipments of coal to be delivered for the furnaces and expedited the exportation of finished goods to New York (especially since the railroad served only the North End and Central Business District).

35. Beginning with the 1966 publication of *The Hidden Dimension*, Ed Hall has addressed the subject of human perception and the use of space, and has demonstrated effectively how the built environment controls and reflects human relationships as an extension of the human psyche and culturally determined, unconscious acts. See also Hall, *Dance of Life*. For a systems approach that addresses the social dimensions of spaces as manifestations and reinforcements of social relations, see: Senge, *The Fifth Discipline*.

36. For a good application of oral history used as evidence for understanding the social use of domestic space, see Michael Ann Williams, *Homeplace: The Social Use and Meaning of the Folk Dwelling in Southwestern North Carolina* (Athens: Univ. of Georgia Press, 1991). See also Edward D. Ives, *The Tape-Recorded Interview: A Manual for Field Workers in Folklore and Oral History* (Knoxville: Univ. of Tennessee Press, 1995).

37. Hegel in *Lectures on Fine Art,* trans. Bernard T. Knox (Oxford: Clarendon Press, 1975) and Schelling in *Philosophy of Art,* trans. Douglas W. Scott (Minneapolis: Univ. of Minnesota Press, 1988) were concerned with the evolution of historical cultures and the ways in which we grasp (without particular cognitive apparatus) what is real. Schelling puts forth the notion that what is real will change with the greater awareness of the viewer and the changing ideologies of the era in which the object is viewed. In art, Hegel argues that what is noted as being important is dependent on what matters to the interpreter, and hence, what is "seen." What appears to the viewer, then, calls attention to itself by the very process of what is selected and what is left unacknowledged. One may argue, using issues stemming from the psychology of perception, that aspects of a landscape do not even exist until the observer has developed the eyes to see them. In other words, the lenses through which we view the landscape define what we see and learn from it. Since the common experience of mill life in New Bedford was given a different reality as experienced through a different cultural filter of each of its participants, a variety of perceptions would be necessary to begin to define the spectrum of that collective experience.

38. Some additional references on this subject include A. Lee and R. E. Stipe, eds., *The American Mosaic: Preserving a Nation's Heritage* (Washington, D.C.: US/ICOMOS, 1987), esp. chap. 6, "Discovering Old Cultures in the New World: The Role of Ethnicity"; Susan Porter Benson, Stephen Brier, and Roy Rosenzweig, eds., *Past Meets Present: Essays About Historic Interpretation and Public Audiences* (Washington D.C.: Smithsonian, 1987); Perry Duis, "Whose City? Public and Private Places in Nineteenth-Century Chicago," *Chicago History* 12 (1) (Spring 1983): 2–27; 12 (2) (Summer 1983): 2–23; Tomlan, *Preservation of What, for Whom?*

39. Michel de Cerean, in *Practice of Everyday Life,* trans. Steven Rendall (Berkeley: Univ. of California Press, 1984), makes an interesting distinction in this regard between "strategies" (as imposed ideas for buildings and spaces by their original makers) and "tactics" (which are the subversive changes by the users). For an interesting study that attempts to understand the changing meanings of buildings by examining their uses and changes beyond their initial designs, see Barbara M. Kelly, *Expanding the American Dream: Building and Rebuilding Levittown* (Albany: SUNY Press, 1993).

CONCLUSION

1. Raub, "Another Pattern of Urban Living," 6, table 5.

2. While creative intent is a critical determinant of built form, architecture is most often a collective enter-

prise. Of the many individuals who will use or construct a particular work, a social mediation of ideas shape (and will continue to shape through the full term of a building's usable life) a given work.

3. For good demonstration models of architectural and social change in one city over several decades, see Gwendolyn Wright, *Moralism and the Model Home: Domestic Architecture and Cultural Conflict in Chicago, 1873–1913* (Chicago: Univ. of Chicago Press, 1980), and Warner, *Streetcar Suburbs*. In the latter work, Warner notes under the query "Who Built the Metropolis?" (3) that the growth of the metropolis is the "product of hundreds of thousands of separate decisions" by lower- and middle-class individuals, construction workers, builders, speculators, and architects with information and inspiration drawn not only from the architectural profession, but from the popular press, local and imported traditions and individual needs, sensations, and aspirations. To address this spectrum of thought, architecture is addressed by Warner within its social, economic, and political contexts.

4. For a demonstration model as it relates to building process in eighteenth-century eastern Virginia, see Dell Upton, "Vernacular Domestic Architecture in Eighteenth-Century Virginia," *Winterthur Portfolio* 17 (2/3) (Summer/Autumn 1982): 95–119.

5. John Ruskin, aphorism 30 of "The Lamp of Memory," in *The Seven Lamps of Architecture* (1849). For a further discussion of how the notion of the "stain of time" relates to Ruskin's discourse on the picturesque, see Michael Wheeler and Nigel Whitley, eds., *The Lamp of Memory: Ruskin, Tradition and Architecture* (Manchester, Eng.: Manchester Univ. Press, 1992), chap. 5.

6. See, for example, the difference between an iconological approach by H. Wölfflin, *Principles of Art History: The Problem and Development of Style in Later Art*, trans. M. D. Hotlinger (New York: Dover, 1932), which essentially argues for a singular meaning of an artistic element, and an iconographic approach by George Kubler, *The Shape of Time: Remarks on the History of Things* (New Haven, Conn.: Yale Univ. Press, 1962), which argues for the potentiality of an object to manifest and signal meaning in different ways through time. More recently, various works addressing the issue of cultural perceptions have redefined the notion of a fixed cultural meaning. See, for example, D. W. Meinig, "The Beholding Eye: Ten Versions of the Same Scene" in *The Interpretation of Ordinary Landscapes: Geographical Essays,* ed. Meinig, 33–48; John Berger, *Ways of Seeing* (New York: Viking, 1973), esp. chap. 1; Walter Benjamin, "The Work of Art in the Age of Mechanical Reproduction," in *Illuminations* (New York: Schocken Books, 1969), 217–51; Susan Buck-Morss, *The Dialectics of Seeing: Walter Benjamin and the Arcades Project* (Cambridge, Mass.: MIT Press, 1989); Philip D. Zimmerman, *Seeing Things Differently* (Winterthur Books, 1992). On more inclusive interpretations of the role of preservation policy today that accounts for change over time, see Cromley, "Public History and the Historic Preservation District," 30–36; Upton, *America's Architectural Roots*; see also the following by Dolores Hayden: "The Power of Place; "The Power of Place: Urban Landscape as People's History," *Historic Preservation Forum* 9 (2) (Winter 1995): 10–17; *The Power of Place: Urban Landscapes as Public History* (Cambridge, Mass.: MIT Press, 1995). On the notion of cultural conservation, see Hufford, *Conserving Culture*.

7. Michel Foucault argues, for example, that the present epoch is perhaps above all an epoch of space. "We are in the epoch of simultaneity; we are in the epoch of juxtaposition." Structuralism, by his definition, is an effort to establish an ensemble of relations that makes them appear as juxtaposed as a sort of configuration whereby each act or space is implicated by the other. "Today the site has been substituted for extension which itself had replaced emplacement. The site is defined by relations of proximity between points or elements; formally, we can describe these relations as series. . . . The problem of siting or placement arises for mankind in terms of demography. . . ." The problem of the "human site" is knowing what relations of propinquity, circulation, marking and classification of human elements should be adopted in a given situation in order to achieve a given end. "Our epoch is one in which space takes for us the form of relations among sites" (Foucault, "Of Other Spaces," *Diacritics* [Spring 1986]: 22–27).

8. "Ecology" as a term, according to Paul L. Tidwell, was coined in 1869 as a science-derivative discourse; today, through such methods as ecocriticism, which focuses on the human constructs of the land in terms of eco-systems and, in some cases, adaptive-survival strategies, the awareness that "everything is connected to everything else" is made paramount.

For a leading study that applies an ecological analysis to uncover long-term changes and modes of production that shaped colonial New England habitats, see William Cronon, *Changes in the Land: Indians, Colonists, and the Ecology of New England* (New York: Hill and Wang, 1983). See Bernard L. Herman, *Architecture and Rural Life in Central Delaware, 1700–1900* (Knoxville: Univ. of Tennessee Press, 1987), for a demonstration model of how buildings "speak" eloquently both of generations of gradual change and of radical transformations. For a significant study about how even a noted landmark, like Olmsted's Central Park, is used and changed and thus offers a shifting definition of its identity and social meaning that moves well beyond its primacy as an art object, see Roy Rosenzweig and Elizabeth Blackmar's *The Park and the People* (Ithaca, N.Y.: Cornell Univ. Press, 1992). For a discussion of the physical weathering of buildings as a result of natural forces, see Mohsen Mostafavi and David Leatherbarrow, *On Weathering: The Life of Buildings in Time* (Cambridge, Mass.: MIT Press, 1993). For a broad overview on how buildings change over time through human intervention, see Stewart Brand, *How Buildings Learn: What Happens after They're Built* (Middlesex: Penguin Books, 1994). In his discussion of the changing role and purpose of cities in Western society, and the processes used to create and transform the physical fabric of those cities, Vance uses the term "urban morphogenesis." See Vance, *Continuing City*.

9. Following a series of research seminars in Cambridge, England, in 1986, the theoretical perspectives of contemporary scholars such as Levi-Strauss, Clifford Geertz, Jacques Derrida, Paul Ricoeur, and Michel Foucault began to influence material culture analysis. Material objects, it was felt, functioned as texts, capable of yielding a contextual understanding of human behavior. Critical theory and deconstructionism stressed how situational power colored perceptions of the universe. Poststrucuralist scholars, in turn, sought to understand how meaning was "constructed" and contextually defined by social relationships and connected patterns of behavior. British archaeologist Ian Hodder argued for a "contextual archeology" that would establish the totality of the relevant environment for any given object and would establish the object's meaning. This contextual approach drew upon both documentary evidence and material culture, and covered broad-ranging time frames and disciplines. The goal was to link the act of creation to beliefs, situations, constraints, opportunities and available resources and to determine the cultural rules and local dynamics shaping the creative act. For readings related to critical theory, deconstructionism, landscape, and contextual approaches, see Christopher Tilley, ed., *Reading Material Culture: Structuralism, Hermeneutics, and Post-Structuralism* (London: Basil Blackwell, 1990); Clifford Geertz, *The Interpretation of Cultures* (New York: Basic Books, 1973), esp. "Thick Description: Toward an Interpretive Theory of Culture"; Christopher Tilley, "Interpreting Material Culture," in *The Meaning of Things: Material Culture and Symbolic Expression,* ed. Ian Hodder (London: Unwin Hyman, 1989); Ian

Hodder, *Reading the Past: Cultural Approaches to Interpretation in Archaeology* (Cambridge: Cambridge Univ. Press, 1986). Michael Kelly, ed., *Critique and Power: Recasting the Foucault/Habermas Debate* (Cambridge, Mass: MIT Press, 1994). For an effective overview of these methodological approaches, see Martin and Garrison, *American Material Culture*, 1–20.

10. Interesting in this regard is the anthology with commentary by Bruce Brooks Pfeiffer, *The Wright Letters* (Fresno: The Press at California State Univ., Fresno, 1984), which offers in three separate volumes "Letters to Clients," "Letters to Architects," and "Letters to Apprentices."

11. In this regard, architect and vernacular architecture scholar Thomas Hubka uses a method he describes as "deep contextualism" in his research on Polish wooden synagogues. Based on the anthropological writings of Clifford Geertz, Hubka stresses the inseparability of the architecture (artifact) and people (cultural studies) in seeking meaning in an architectural analysis. By setting a building and its people into a broad historical/cultural context, the insights drawn from the artifact and the cultural context inform each other in an ever-reciprocating manner. While such an approach is shared by many vernacular scholars, Hubka adds emphasis to these efforts by applying it to several investigative levels in his research on Polish synagogues as a means of speculating on issues such as the normalcy or uniqueness of timber-frame construction techniques found totally in relation to eastern European craft traditions. Further, Hubka's analysis of such issues as framing techniques for synagogue roofs extends to the ideals and range of options behind their application that were available to its makers. He states, "[T]hese synagogues existed in a complex cultural milieu that (in addition to Jewish mysticism) encompassed Baroque ideas and Baroque churches, a sustained Jewish material folk culture, Czarist threats, French chateaus, economic declines, and a Catholic peasantry. . . . Thus, a successful architectural analysis had to balance all the influences available to the builders of synagogues and then account for the reasons they selected, or were influenced by, particular sets of ideas; that is deep contextualism." See Thomas Hubka, "Deep Contextualism: An Attitude Toward Vernacular Architecture Research," Abstract: *Perspectives in Vernacular Architecture III* (Columbia: Univ. of Missouri Press, 1989), 242–43. See also Geertz, *The Interpretation of Cultures,* preface and chap. 1.

12. For a good account of the wide range of design applications that merge local and national phenomena in the hands of a regional builder, see Catherine

Bisher's account of North Carolina builder Jacob Holt in *Common Places*, ed. Upton and Vlach.

13. For an illustration of this issue, see Williams, *Homeplace*. In her study, for example, oral testimonials are used to assign regional meaning to room nomenclature, which sheds light on the system of spatial use and meaning within a region during a given period of time by different gender and age groups. Beyond identifying three common folk types in the region—the single pen, the double pen, and the center-passage plans—the functions of the spaces shifted over time as the users "rethought" their needs and aspirations. Hence, the meaning and utilization of space shifted with the user's changing mental structure. Similarly, Lisa Tolbert's dissertation, *Constructing Townscapes*, completed in 1994 under the direction of John Kasson in the History Department at the University of North Carolina, addresses the changing cultural condition of spaces as they respond to daily and seasonal rhythms. Dell Upton's "White and Black Landscapes in Eighteenth-Century Virginia," *Places 2* (1985): 59–72 addresses differing perceptions of a landscape based on spatial dynamics that are socially constructed and tied to vastly different spheres of situational power.

14. Dick Reynolds quoted in the article "Ecological Architecture: Planning the Organic Environment" (on the aims of the Sea Ranch developers), *Progressive Architecture* (May 1966): 122.

SELECTED BIBLIOGRAPHY

UNPUBLISHED SOURCES

Collections and Archives

Building Ledger of Michael Daley, Estate of Clement E. Daley, New Bedford, Mass.

Dept. of Building Permits, New Bedford City Hall, New Bedford, Mass.

John Hay Library, Brown Univ., Providence, R.I.

Howland Family Correspondence, 1878–84, collection of Llewellyn Howland III, Jamaica Plain, Mass.

Frances Loeb Library, Harvard Univ., Cambridge, Mass.

Library of Congress, Manuscript Division

Lowell National Historic Site, Research Dept., Lowell, Mass.

Lynn Historical Society, Lynn, Mass.

Mayor's Office Housing and Neighborhood Development, New Bedford, Mass.

National Archives and Record Administration, Washington, D.C.

New Bedford Free Public Library, Special Collections, New Bedford, Mass.

Frederick Law Olmsted National Historic Site, Brookline, Mass.

New Bedford Whaling Museum, New Bedford, Mass.

Parks and Recreation Office, New Bedford, Mass.

Society for the Preservation of New England Antiquities, Boston, Mass.

W.H.A.L.E., New Bedford, Mass.

Widener Library, Harvard University.

Windham Textile and History Museum, Willimantic, Conn.

Papers, Reports, and Theses

Auditor's Report. *New Bedford City Documents* no. 8, 1891.

Bahr, Betsy W. *New England Engineering.* Ph.D. diss., Univ. of Delaware, 1987.

Board of Public Works, 12. *New Bedford City Documents* no. 10, Jan. 1891.

——, 12. *New Bedford City Documents* no. 10, Jan. 1892.

——, 26. *New Bedford City Documents* no. 10, Dec. 1892.

——, 13. *New Bedford City Documents* no. 10, Dec. 1893.

Candee, Richard M. "Salmon Falls Mill Historic District." National Register of Historic Places Inventory–Nomination. Typescript, New Hampshire Division of Historic Resources, Concord, N.H., 1978.

———. "Newmarket Industrial and Commercial Historical District." National Register of Historic Places Inventory. Typescript, Division of Historic Resources, Concord, N.H., 1980.

———. "Great Falls Industrial and Commercial Historic District." National Register of Historic Places Inventory–Nomination. Typescript, New Hampshire Division of Historic Resources, Concord, N.H. 1982.

Crapo, Henry Howland. "The Story of Cotton and Its Manufacture into Cloth in New Bedford." New Bedford: Old Dartmouth Historical Sketches, No. 67.

Davidson, Lisa Pfueller. "Engineering the New South: A HAER Case Study." [Charles Praray after the dissolution of Co-Partnership with C.R. Makepeace & CO. of Providence in February 1898.] A paper presented at the Society for Industrial Archaeology, June 6, 1999, Savannah, Ga.

Dykas, Joanne Martha. "Whaling, Cotton, and the Howland Family: Reactions to Changes in the Economic Foundations of Nineteenth Century New Bedford, Massachusetts." B.A. thesis in History, Harvard Univ., 1980.

Goff, Lisa. "Graniteville, S.C.: William Gregg's Industrial Village." A paper presented at the Vernacular Architecture Forum Annual Meeting, Columbus, Ga., May 8, 1999.

Hay, Duncan Erroll. "The New City on the Merrimack: The Essex Company and Its Role in the Creation of Lawrence, Massachusetts." Ph.D. diss., Univ. of Delaware, 1986.

Jacobsohn, Deedee. "Tenements in Context: Housing Reformers and Boston's Three-Deckers." A paper presented at the Vernacular Architecture Forum, Lawrence, Kans., May 25, 1996.

Kasson, John F. "Semiotics of the City." A public lecture presented at the Univ. of North Carolina, Charlotte, Mar. 25, 1994.

Katz, Jamie W. "Opportunity, Exclusion, and the Immigrants: Textile Workers in New Bedford, Massachusetts, 1890–1930." B.A. thesis, Dept. of History, Harvard College, 1974.

Krim, Arthur J. "Recognition of the New England Three-Decker: The Preservation of Vernacular Urban Housing." Paper at the National Meeting of the Society of Architectural Historians. "Vernacular Architecture: Editing History Through Preservation." New Haven, Conn. 1981.

———. *The Three-deckers of Dorchester: An Architectural Historical Survey.* Boston: Boston Redevelopment Authority/Boston Landmark Commission, 1977.

Lubar, Steven David. "Corporate and Urban Contexts of Textile Technology in Nineteenth-Century Lowell, Massachusetts: A Study of the Social Nature of Technological Knowledge." Ph.D. diss., Univ. of Chicago, 1983.

McMullen, Thomas. "Industrialization and Social Change in a Nineteenth-Century Port City: New Bedford, Massachusetts, 1865–1900." Ph.D. diss., Univ. of Wisconsin, 1976.

———. "The Coming of the Mills: Social Change in New Bedford in the Late Nineteenth-Century." Lecture in a series for the New Bedford Bicentennial, New Bedford Free Public Library, 1987.

"Memorandum of subjects to be brought to the notice of the Directors of the Salmon Falls Co. at their monthly meeting January 18, 1854." Treasurer's Report, Salmon Falls Manufacturing Company, 1854, A. A. Lawrence Papers, Massachusetts Historical Society.

Morrill, Janice Lee. "The French-Canadian Three Deckers of Southbridge, Massachusetts." M.A. thesis, Folklore Dept., Univ. of North Carolina at Chapel Hill, 1987.

New Bedford Record of Building Permits. 1893–1930.

New Bedford City Directory. 1887, 1895; 1908–11.

"Paving." *New Bedford City Document.* no. 10, Jan. 1892.

"Transportation Report." *New Bedford City Documents* no. 10, Jan. 1892.

"Street Railways." *New Bedford City Documents* no. 10, Dec. 1892.

Office of Historic Preservation. "New Bedford Mills." New Bedford, 1977.

Olmsted, Olmsted and Eliot Proposal. *New Bedford System of Parks.* Miscellaneous file in the Building Permits Dept. at New Bedford City Hall. Minutes undated, c. June 1894.

Olmsted, Olmsted and Eliot Proposal. *New Bedford System of Parks*. Facsimile with illustrations has been placed in the Frederick Law Olmsted Historic Site, job no. 01810 for the New Bedford Park Commission.

Olmsted, Vaux and Co. "Preliminary Report upon the Proposed Suburban Village at Riverside." New York, 1868.

Report: *Lowell National Historical Park and Preservation District Cultural Resources Inventory*. Boston: Shepley, Bulfinch, Richardson and Abbott, 1980.

Roberge, Roger A. "Three Decker: Structural Correlate of Worcester's Industrial Revolution." Master's thesis, Clark Univ., 1965.

Roper, Steve. "30 and 32 Atlantic Block, 401–403 Canal Street, Lawrence, Mass.: Architectural and Historical Research Report." typescript, 29 Apr. 1983; "Plans of the boardinghouses built for the Atlantic Cotton Mills." c. 1847, Essex Company Collection, Museum of American Textile History, Massachusetts Sanitary Survey Commission *Report*. Boston, 1850.

Sandoval-Strausz, Andrew K. "For the Accommodation of Strangers. Nationhood, Aesthetics, Commerce, and Origins of the American Hotel." A paper presented at the Annual Meeting of Vernacular Architecture Forum, Columbus, Ga., May 8, 1999.

Shaw, Diane. "Sorting the City: Socio-Spatial Dynamics in Mid-19th-Century Syracuse and Rochester, New York." Paper delivered at the Vernacular Architecture Forum's Annual Meeting, Columbus, Ga., May 8, 1999.

Silvia, Philip T., Jr. "The Spindle City: Labor, Politics, and Religion in Fall River." Ph.D. diss., Fordham Univ., 1973.

Special Federal Census Schedules for Connecticut at the Connecticut State Library, Hartford, for 1880 under "Industry."

Tolbert, Lisa. "*Constructing Townscapes*." Ph.D. diss., History Dept., Univ. of North Carolina, 1994.

U.S. Government. Tenth Manufacturing Census (1880), published in 1882.

Veiller, Lawrence. "Industrial Housing." In the *Proceedings of the Fifth American Conference on Housing Problems in America*. Providence, 1916.

Wright, Carroll D. "Report on the Factory System of the United States." Bound with the 1880 U.S. manufacturing census.

PUBLISHED SOURCES

Builders' Trade Journals

Comstock, William T. ed. *Two-Family and Twin Houses*. New York: William T. Comstock, 1908.

Downing, A. J. *The Architecture of Country Houses Including Designs for Cottages, Farm Houses and Villas with Remarks on Interiors, Furniture, and the Best Modes of Warming and Ventilating*. New York, 1850.

Gowing, Frederick H. *Building Plans for Modern Homes*. 1911, 1914, 1920, 1921.

———. *Building Plans for Colonial Dwellings*. 1925.

Books

Adams, Annmarie, and Sally McMurry, eds. *Exploring Everyday Landscapes: Perspectives in Vernacular Architecture VII*. Knoxville: Univ. of Tennessee Press, 1997.

Allen, Everett S. *Children of the Light: The Rise and Fall of New Bedford Whaling and the Death of the Arctic Fleet*. Boston: Little, Brown and Co., 1973.

Atlas of New Bedford City, Massachusetts. Boston: George H. Walker and Co., 1881.

Bacon, Mardges. *Ernest Flagg*. Cambridge, Mass.: MIT Press, 1986.

Banham, Reyner. *A Concrete Atlantis, U.S. Industrial Building and European Modernism*. Cambridge, Mass.: MIT Press, 1986.

Basso, Keith, and Henry Selby, eds. *Meaning in Anthropology*. Albuquerque: Univ. of New Mexico Press, 1976.

Beaudry, Mary C., and Stephen A Mrozowski. *Interdisciplinary Investigations of the Boott Mills, Lowell, Massachusetts*. 3 vols. Cultural Resource Management Study nos. 18–20. Boston: Dept. of the Interior, National Parks Service, North Atlantic Regional Offices, 1987–91.

Beardsley, Thomas. *Willimantic Industry and Community: The Rise and Decline of a Connecticut Textile City*. Willimantic: Windham Textile and History Museum, 1993.

Beers Map of the City of New Bedford, 1871.

Benevolo, Leonardo. *History of Modern Architecture*. Cambridge, Mass.: MIT Press, 1977.

Benjamin, Walter. *Illuminations*. New York: Schocken Books, 1969.

Benson, Susan Porter, Stephen Brier, and Roy Rosenzweig, eds., *Past Meets Present: Essays About Historic Interpretation and Public Audiences*. Washington D.C.: Smithsonian, 1987.

Berger, John. *Ways of Seeing*. New York: Viking Press, 1973.

Biggs, Lindy. *The Rational Factory: Architecture Technology and Work in America's Age of Mass Production*. Baltimore, Md.: Johns Hopkins Univ. Press, 1996.

Blatti, Jo, ed. *Past Meets Present*. Washington, D.C.: Smithsonian, 1987.

Boris, Eileen. *Art and Labor: Ruskin, Morris, and the Craftsman Ideal in America*. Philadelphia: Temple Univ. Press, 1986.

Boss, Judith, and Joseph Thomas. *New Bedford*. Virginia Beach, Va.: Donning Co., 1990.

———. *New Bedford: A Pictorial History*. Virginia Beach, Va.: Donning Co., 1983.

Boston Manufactures' Mutual Fire Insurance Company. *Report Number 5: Slow Burning or Mill Construction*, 3d ed. Boston: Boston Manufacturers' Mutual Fire Insurance Co., 1908.

Bradley, Betsy. *The Works: The Industrial Architecture of the United States*. New York: Cambridge Univ. Press, 1999.

Bradley James, and Arthur J. Krim, Peter Stott, and Sarah Zimmerman. *Historic and Archaeological Resources of the Boston Area*. Boston: Massachusetts Historical Commission, 1982.

Brand, Stewart. *How Buildings Learn*. Middlesex: Penguin Books, 1994.

Brooks, H. Allen. *The Prairie School*. New York: Norton, 1976.

Brown, G. Z. *Sun, Wind and Light Architectural Design Strategies*. New York: John Wiley and Sons, 1985.

Brown, G. Z., Bruce Haglund, Joel Loveland, John S. Reynolds, and M. Susan Ubbelohde. *Inside-Out: Design Procedures for Passive Environmental Technologies*. New York: John Wiley and Sons, 1992.

Buck-Morss, Susan. *The Dialectics of Seeing: Walter Benjamin and the Arcades Project*. Cambridge, Mass.: MIT Press, 1989.

Buder, Stanley. *Pullman*. New York: Oxford Univ. Press, 1967.

Bullard, John M. *The Rotches*. Milford, N.H.: Cabinet Press, 1947.

Burgy, J. Herbert. *The New England Cotton Textile Industry: A Study in Industrial Geography*. Baltimore: Waverly Press, 1932.

Busch, Briton Cooper. *"Whaling Will Never Do for Me": The American Whaleman in the Nineteenth Century*. Lexington: Univ. Press of Kentucky, 1994.

Bushman, Richard L. *The Refinement of America: Persons, Houses, Cities*. New York: Vintage Books, 1993.

Butler, Thomas, ed. *Memory: History, Culture and the Mind*. Oxford: Basel Blackwell, 1989.

Cabral, Stephen L. *Tradition and Transformation, Portuguese Feasting in New Bedford*. New York: A.M.S. Press, 1989.

Candee, Richard M. *Newmarket Revisited: Looking at the Era of Industrial Growth, 1820–1920*. Newmarket, N.H.: Newmarket Service Club, 1979.

———. *Strafford Regional Planning Commission, Salmon Falls–The Mill Village Historic District Study for the Town of Rollinsford, New Hampshire* Dover, N.H.: Strafford Regional Planning Commission, 1974.

———. *Atlantic Heights: A World War I Shipbuilder's Community*. Portsmouth, N.H.: Portsmouth Marine Society, 1985.

Case, Willard. *The Factory Buildings*. New York: Industrial Extension Institute, 1922.

Chase, William H. *Five Generations of Loom Builders*. Hopedale, Mass.: Draper, 1950.

Chase, David, ed. *Providence, A Citywide Survey of Historic Resources*. Providence, R.I.: Preservation Commission, 1986.

City Engineering Survey Maps by Wheelwright and Coggeshall. New Bedford, 1875.

Clayton, Barbara, and Kathleen Whitley. *Guide to New Bedford*. Montpelier, Vt.: Capital City Press, 1979.

Clifford, James. *The Predicament of Culture, Twentieth-Century Ethnography, Literature and Art*. Cambridge, Mass.: Harvard Univ. Press, 1988.

Coolidge, John. *Mill and Mansion: A Study of Architecture and Society in Lowell, Massachusetts, 1820–1865*. New York: Columbia Univ. Press, 1942.

Copeland, M. T. *The Cotton Manufacturing Industry of the United States*. New York: Kelley, 1996.

Cowan, Ruth Schwartz. *A Social History of American Technology*. New York: 1997.

Crawford, Margaret. *Building the Workingman's Paradise: The Design of American Company Towns*. London: Verso, 1995.

Cronon, William. *Changes in the Land: Indians, Colonists, and the Ecology of New England*. New York: Hill and Wang, 1983.

Cromley, Elizabeth Collins. *Alone Together: A History of New York's Apartments*. Ithaca: Cornell Univ. Press, 1990.

Csikszentmihalyi, Mchaly, and Eugene Rochbery-Halton. *The Meaning of Things: Domestic Symbols of Self*. Cambridge: Cambridge Univ. Press, 1981.

Dalzell, Robert F., Jr. *Enterprising Elite: The Boston Associates and the World They Made*. Cambridge, Mass.: Harvard Univ. Press, 1987.

Daniels, Caroline T. *Dark Harbor*. Cambridge, Mass.: N.p, 1935.

Dawley, Alan. *Class and Community: The Industrial Revolution in Lynn*. Cambridge, Mass.: Harvard Univ. Press, 1976.

DeForest, Robert W., and Laurence Veiller, eds. *The Tenement House Problem*. Vol. I. New York: Arno Press, 1970.

Dublin, Thomas. *Transforming Women's Work: New England Lives in the Industrial Revolution*. Ithaca: Cornell Univ. Press, 1994.

———. *Women at Work: The Transformation of Work and Community in Lowell, Massachusetts, 1826–1860*. New York: Columbia Univ. Press, 1979.

———, ed. *Farm to Factory: Women's Letters, 1830–1860*. New York: Columbia Univ. Press, 1981.

Dunwell, Steve. *The Run of the Mill*. Boston: David R. Godine, 1978.

Ellis, Leonard. *History of New Bedford and Its Vicinity*. Syracuse, N.Y.: D. Mason and Co., 1892.

Emery, William. *Ancestry of the Grinnell Family*. Privately printed, 1931.

———. *The Howland Heirs*. New Bedford, Mass.: E. Anthony and Sons, Inc., 1919.

Fish, Gertrude Sepperly, ed. *The Story of Housing*. New York: Macmillan, 1979.

Floyd, Margaret Henderson. *Henry Hobson Richardson A Genuis for Architecture*. New York: Monacelli Press, 1997.

Gabaccia, Donna, ed. *Seeking Common Ground*. Westport, Conn.: Praeger Press, 1992.

Garner, John S. *The Model Company Town: Urban Design through Private Enterprise in Nineteenth-Century New England*. Amherst: Univ. of Massachusetts Press, 1984.

———, ed. *The Company Town: Architecture and Society in the Early Industrial Age*. New York: Oxford Univ. Press, 1992.

Geertz, Clifford. *The Interpretation of Cultures*. New York: Basic Books, 1973.

Georgianna, Daniel. *The Strike of '28*. New Bedford: Spinner Publications, 1993.

Gibson, James J. *The Ecological Approach to Visual Perception*. Hillsdale, N.J.: Lawrence Erlbaum, 1986.

Glassie, Henry. *Passing the Time in Ballymenone: Culture and History of an Ulster Community*. Philadelphia: Univ. of Pennsylvania Press, 1982.

Goode, James M. *Best Addresses: A Century of Washington's Distinguished Apartment Houses*. Washington, D.C.: Smithsonian Institution Press, 1988.

Gordon, Robert B., and Patrick M. Malone. *The Texture of Industry: An Archaeological View of the Industrialization of North America*. New York: Oxford Univ. Press, 1994.

Gould, E. R. L. *Eighth Special Report of the Commissioner of Labor: Housing of the Working People*. Washington, D.C.: Government Printing Office, 1895.

Gross, Laurence. *The Course of Industrial Decline: The Boott Cotton Mill of Lowell, Massachusetts, 1835–1955*. Baltimore, Md.: Johns Hopkins Univ. Press, 1993.

Groth, Paul. *Living Downtown: The History of Residential Hotels in the United States*. Berkeley: Univ. of California Press, 1994.

Haber, Samuel. *Efficiency and Uplift: Scientific Management in the Progressive Era, 1890–1920*. Chicago: Univ. of Chicago Press, 1964.

Hall, Edward. *Dance of Life, The Other Dimension of Time*. Garden City, N.Y.: Anchor Press/Doubleday, 1983.

Handlin, David. *The American Home, Architecture and Society 1815–1915*. Boston: Little, Brown and Company, 1979.

Harvey, Charles, and Jon Press. *William Morris: Design and Enterprise in Victorian Britain.* Manchester, Eng.: Manchester Univ. Press, 1991.

Haschong, Lisa. *Thermal Delight in Architecture.* Cambridge, Mass.: MIT Press, 1979.

Hayden, Dolores. *The Grand Domestic Revolution: A History of Feminist Designs for American Homes, Neighborhoods, and Cities.* Cambridge, Mass.: MIT Press, 1992.

———. *The Power of Place: Urban Landscapes as Public History.* Cambridge, Mass.: MIT Press, 1995.

Herman, Bernard L. *Architecture and Rural Life in Central Delaware, 1700–1900.* Knoxville: Univ. of Tennessee Press, 1987.

Hertzberger, Herman. *Lessons for Students in Architecture.* Rotterdam: Uitgeveri, 1991.

Higham, John. *Strangers in the Land: Patterns of American Nativism, 1860–1925.* New York: Atheneum, 1963.

Hindle, Brooke, and Steven Lubar. *Engines of Change: The American Industrial Revolution, 1790–1860.* Washington, D.C.: Smithsonian Institution Press, 1986.

Hodder, Ian. *Reading the Past: Cultural Approaches to Interpretation in Archaeology.* Cambridge: Cambridge Univ. Press, 1986.

———, ed. The Meaning of Things: Material Culture and Symbolic Expression. London: Unwin Hyman, 1989.

Hohman, Elmo. *The American Whaleman: A Study of Life and Labor in the Whaling Industry.* New York: Longmans, Green and Co., 1928.

Hough, Henry Beetle. *Wamsutta of New Bedford 1846–1946: A Story of New England Enterprise.* New Bedford: Wamsutta Mills, 1946.

Hounshell, David A. *From the American System to Mass Production, 1830–1932.* Baltimore, Md.: Johns Hopkins Univ. Press, 1984.

Howard, Ebenezer. *Garden Cities of To-morrow*, ed. F. J. Osborn. Cambridge, Mass.: MIT Press, 1965.

Hubka, Thomas. *Big House, Little House, Back House, Barn.* Hanover, N.H.: Univ. Press of New England, 1984.

Hufford, Mary, ed. *Conserving Culture: A New Discourse on Heritage.* Urbana: Univ. of Illinois Press, 1994.

Hughes, Thomas P. *American Genesis: A Century of Invention and Technological Enthusiasm, 1870–1970.* New York: Viking, 1989.

Hunter, Christine. *Ranches, Rowhouses & Railroad Flats.* New York: Norton, 1999.

Ives, Edward D. *The Tape-Recorded Interview: A Manual for Field Workers in Folklore and Oral History.* Knoxville: Univ. of Tennessee Press, 1995.

Jackson, John Brenckerhoff. *A Sense of Place, A Sense of Time.* New Haven, Conn.: Yale Univ. Press, 1994.

Kasson, John F. *Rudeness and Civility, Manners in Nineteenth-Century Urban America.* New York: Hill and Wang, 1990.

Kelly, Micheal, ed. *Critique and Power: Recasting the Foucault/Habermas Debate.* Cambridge, Mass: MIT Press, 1994.

Korman, Gerol. *Industrialization, Immigrants and Americanizers.* Madison: State Historical Society of Wisconsin, 1967.

Krim, Arthur J. *The Three-Deckers of Dorchester: An Architectural Historical Survey.* Boston: The Boston Landmarks Commission, 1977.

Kubler, George. *The Shape of Time: Remarks on the History of Things.* New Haven, Conn.: Yale Univ. Press, 1962.

Kulik, Gary, Roger Parks, and Theodore Penn. *The New England Mill Village, 1790–1860.* In *Documents in American Industrial History.* Ed. Micheal B. Folson, vol. 2. Cambridge, Mass.: MIT Press and Merrimack Valley Textile Museum, 1982.

Landow, George P. *Ruskin.* Oxford: Oxford Univ. Press, 1985.

LeBlanc, Robert G. *Location of Manufacture in New England in the 19th Century.* Geography Publications at Dartmouth, no. 7 (1969).

Lee, A., and R. E. Stipe, eds. *The American Mosaic: Preserving a Nation's Heritage.* Washington, D.C.: US/ICOMOS, 1987.

Lefebvre, Henri. *The Production of Space.* Oxford: Blackwell, 1991.

Lessard, Michel, and Huguette Marquis. *Encyclopédie de la Maison Québécoise, 3 Siécles d'habitations.* Ottawa: L'Homme Ltée, 1972.

Lewis, Arnold. *American Country Houses of the Gilded Age: Sheldon's "Artistic Country-Seats."* New York: Dover, 1982.

Licht, Walter. *Industrializing America: The Nineteenth Century.* Baltimore, Md.: Johns Hopkins Univ. Press, 1995.

Lowenthall, David. *The Past Is a Foreign Country.* New York: Cambridge Univ. Press, 1985.

Marcus, Alan, and Howland Segal. *Technology in America: A Brief History*. San Diego, Calif.: Harcourt Brace Jovanovich, 1989.

Martin, Ann Smart, and J. Ritchie Garrison. *American Material Culture: The Shape of the Field*. Winterthur, Del.: Henry Francis du Pont Winterthur Museum, 1997.

McArdle, Alma. *Carpenter Gothic*. New York: Whitney Library of Design, 1978.

McCabe, Marsha, and Joseph D. Thomas. *Not Just Anywhere*. New Bedford: Spinner Publications, 1995.

McGraw, Judith A., ed. *Early American Technology: Making and Doing Things from the Colonial Era to 1850*. Chapel Hill: Univ. of North Carolina Press, 1994.

Meakin, Budgett. *Model Factories and Villages: Ideal Conditions of Laborers and Housing*. London: T. Fisher Unwin, 1905.

Meinig, D. W. *The Interpretation of Ordinary Landscapes: Geographical Essays*. New York: Oxford Univ. Press, 1979.

Melville, Herman. *Moby Dick*. New York: Random House, 1950.

Montgomery, David. *Beyond Equality: Labor and Radical Republicans, 1862–1872*. New York: Random House, 1967.

———. *The Fall of the House of Labor: The Workplace, the State, and American Labor Activism, 1865–1925*. New York: Cambridge Univ. Press, 1987.

Morris, William. *News from Nowhere and Other Writings*. London: Penguin Books, 1993.

Mostafavi, Mohsen, and David Leatherbarrow. *On Weathering: The Life of Buildings in Time*. Cambridge, Mass.: MIT Press, 1993.

Murphy, Teresa Ann. *Ten Hours' Labor: Religion, Reform, and Gender in Early New England*. Ithaca, N.Y.: Cornell Univ. Press, 1992.

Muthesius, Hermann. *Das Englische Haus*. 3 vols. Berlin: Wasmuth, 1904, 1905. Reprinted in English, trans. Janet Seligman, as *The English House*. New York: Rizzoli International, 1979.

Nelson, Daniel. *Managers and Workers: Origins of the New Factory System in the United States, 1880–1920*. 2d ed. Madison: Univ. of Wisconsin Press, 1995.

New Bedford Illustrated, 1892.

New Bedford Semi-Centennial Souvenir Book, 1897.

Newhouse, Victoria. *Wallace K. Harrison, Architect*. New York: Rizzoli, 1989.

Newton, Norman T. *Design on the Land: The Development of Landscape Architecture*. Cambridge, Mass.: Belknap Press of Harvard Univ. Press, 1971.

Olgyay, Victor. *Design with Climate: Bioclimatic Approach to Architectural Regionalism*. Princeton, N.J.: Princeton Univ. Press, 1963.

Pap, Leo. *The Portuguese-Americans*. Boston: Portuguese Continental Union of the U.S.A., 1992.

Passer, Harold C. *The Electrical Manufacturers, 1875–1900*. Cambridge, Mass.: Harvard Univ. Press, 1953.

Pease, Zephaniah W. *History of New Bedford*. New York: Lewis Historical Publishing Co., 1918.

Pidgeon, Daniel. *Old World Questions and New World Answers*. London: Kegan, Paul, Trench and Company, 1884.

Pierson, William H., Jr. *American Buildings and Their Architects: Technology and the Picturesque, the Corporate and the Early Gothic Styles*. New York: Doubleday, 1978.

Plan of City of New Bedford from Original Surveys by J.C. Sidney, C.E. Philadelphia: Collins and Clark, 1850.

Pred, Allen R. *The Spatial Dynamics of U.S. Urban-Industrial Growth 1800–1914*. Cambridge, Mass.: MIT Press, 1966.

Pregill, Philip, and Nancey Volkman. *Landscapes in History: Design and Planning in the Eastern and Western Traditions*. New York: John Wiley and Sons, 1999.

Prude, Jonathan. *The Coming of Industrial Order: Town and Factory Life in Rural Massachusetts, 1810–1860*. Cambridge: Cambridge Univ. Press, 1983.

Pursell, Carroll. *The Machine in America: A Social History of Technology*. Baltimore, Md.: Johns Hopkins Univ. Press, 1995.

Relph, E. *Place and Placelessness*. London: Pion Limited, 1976.

Reynolds, Marcus T. *The Housing in New York City*. New York: Columbia Univ. Press, 1890.

Roper, Laura Wood. *FLO: A Biography of Frederick Law Olmsted*. Baltimore, Md.: Johns Hopkins Univ. Press, 1993.

Rosebrock, Ellen. *Historic Fall River.* Fall River, Mass.: Preservation Partnership, 1978.

Ruskin, John. *The Seven Lamps of Architecture.* New York: Hill and Wang, 1989.

———. *Stones of Venice.* 3 vols. New York: Wiley, 1881.

Ryden, Kent C. *Mapping the Invisible Landscape.* Iowa City: Univ. of Iowa Press, 1993.

Sayer, William L., ed. *New Bedford, Massachusetts: Its History, Institutions and Attractions.* New Bedford: Mercury Publishing Co., 1889.

Senge, Peter. *The Fifth Discipline.* New York: Doubleday, 1990.

Sharpe, Mary F. *Plain Facts for Future Citizens.* New York: American Book Company, 1914.

Sklar, Kathryn Kisk. *Catherine Beecher: A Study in American Domesticity.* New Haven, Conn.: Yale Univ. Press, 1973.

Smith, Robert A. *Merry Wheels and Spokes of Steel: A Social History of the Bicycle.* Stovkis Studies in Historical Chronology and Thought 16. New York: Borgo Press, 1995.

Spain, Daphne. *Gendered Spaces.* Chapel Hill: Univ. of North Carolina Press, 1992.

Spann, Edward K. *Brotherly Tomorrows: Movements for a Cooperative Society in America 1820–1920.* New York: Columbia Univ. Press, 1989.

Spear, Marilyn W. *Worcester's Three Deckers.* Worcester, Mass.: Worcester Bicentennial Commission, 1977.

Stein, Susan, ed. *The Architecture of Richard Morris Hunt.* Chicago: Univ. of Chicago Press, 1986.

Steinberg, Theodore. *Nature Incorporated: Industrialization and the Waters of New England.* Cambridge: Cambridge Univ. Press, 1991.

Stilgoe, John. *Metropolitan Corridor.* New Haven, Conn.: Yale Univ. Press, 1983.

Sutton, S. B. *Civilizing American Cities: A Selection of Frederick Law Olmsted's Writings on City Landscapes.* Cambridge, Mass.: MIT Press, 1971.

Technical Advisory Corporation. *A Reconnaissance Survey of New Bedford, Mass.* New York: A. E. Coffin Press, 1923.

Thomas, Joseph D. *Spinner: People and Culture in Southeastern Massachusetts.* Vol. I. New Bedford: Spinner Publication, 1980.

———. *Spinner: People and Culture in Southeastern Massachusetts.* Vol. 2. New Bedford: Spinner Publication, 1981.

———. *Spinner: People and Culture in Southeastern Massachusetts.* Vol. 3. New Bedford: Spinner Publication, 1984.

———. *Spinner: People and Culture in Southeastern Massachusetts.* Vol. 4. New Bedford: Spinner Publication, 1986.

Thwaite, B. H. *Our Factories, Workshops, Warehouse, Their Sanitary and Fire-Resisting Arrangements.* London, N.Y.: E. & F. N. Spon, 1882.

Tilley, Christopher, ed. *Reading Material Culture: Structuralism, Hermeneutics, and Post–Structuralism.* London: Basil Blackwell, 1990.

Trinder, Barrie, ed. *The Machine in America: A Social History of Technology.* Baltimore, Md.: Johns Hopkins Univ. Press, 1995.

Tucci, Douglass Shand. *Built in Boston City and Suburb, 1800–1950.* Boston: New York Graphic Society, 1978.

Tunnard, Christopher, and Henry Hope Reed. *American Skyline.* New York: Signet, 1956.

Upton, Dell, ed. *America's Architectural Roots: Ethnic Groups that Built America.* Washington, D.C.: National Trust, 1986.

Upton, Dell, and John Micheal Vlach. *Common Places: Readings in American Vernacular Architecture.* Athens: Univ. of Georgia Press, 1986.

Vance, Jr., James E. *The Continuing City: Urban Morphology in Western Civilization.* Baltimore, Md.: Johns Hopkins Univ. Press, 1990.

Ward, C., and D. Zunz, eds. *The Landscape of Modernity: Essays on New York City, 1900–1940.* New York: Russell Sage Foundation, 1992.

Ware, Caroline F. *The Early New England Cotton Manufacture: A Study in Industrial Beginnings.* Boston: Houghton Mifflin, 1931.

Warner, Jr., Sam Bass. *Streetcar Suburbs: The Process of Growth in Boston, 1870–1900,* 2d ed. Cambridge, Mass.: Harvard Univ. Press, 1978.

Weible, Robert, ed. *The Continuing Revolution: A History of Lowell, Massachusetts.* Lowell, Mass.: Lowell Historical Society, 1991.

Wheeler, Michael, and Nigel Whitley, eds. *The Lamp of Memory: Ruskin, Tradition and Architecture.* Manchester, Eng.: Manchester Univ. Press, 1992.

Whitman, Nicholas. *A Window Back.* New Bedford: Spinner Publications, 1994.

Withey, Henry F., and Elsie R. Withey. *Biographical Dictionary of American Architects (Deceased)*. Los Angeles: Hennessey and Ingalls, 1970.

Whitney, Jessamine. *Infant Mortality: Results of a Field Study in New Bedford, Massachusetts, Based on Births in One Year*. Washington, D.C.: U.S. Dept. of Labor, Children's Bureau, 1920.

Wilkie, Richard, and Jack Tager, eds. *The Historical Atlas of Massachusetts*. Amherst: Univ. of Massachusetts Press, 1991.

Williams, Jerry R. *And Yet They Come: Portuguese Immigration from the Azores to the United States*. New York: Center for Migration Studies, 1982.

Williams, Michael Ann. *Homeplace: The Social Use and Meaning of the Folk Dwelling in Southwestern North Carolina*. Athens: Univ. of Georgia Press, 1991.

Wölfflin, Seymore. *The Decline of a Cotton Textile City: A Study of New Bedford*. New York: Columbia Univ. Press, 1944.

Wood, Denis, and Robert J. Beck. *Home Rules*. Baltimore, Md.: Johns Hopkins Univ. Press, 1994.

Worsdall, Frank. *The Glasgow Tenement: A Way of Life*. Edinburgh: W&R, Chambers Ltd., 1979.

Wright, Gwendolyn. *Building the American Dream: A Social History in America*. Cambridge, Mass.: MIT Press, 1981.

———. *Moralism and the Model Home: Domestic Architecture and Cultural Conflict in Chicago, 1873–1913*. Chicago : Univ. of Chicago Press, 1980.

Zimmerman, Philip D. *Seeing Things Differently*. Winterthur Books, 1992.

Zukowsky, John, ed. *Chicago Architecture, 1872–1922: Birth of a Metropolis*. Munich: Prestel-Verlag, 1987.

Zunz, Olivier. *The Changing Face of Inequality: Urbanization, Industrial Development, and Immigrants in Detroit, 1880–1920*. Chicago: Univ. of Chicago Press, 1991.

Journal Articles

Archer, John. "Country and City in the American Romantic Suburb." *Journal of the Society of Architectural Historians* 42 (2) (May 1983).

Barnett, Peter M. "The Worcester Three-Decker: Form and Variation," *Monadnock* 48 (June 1974): 21–33.

———. "The Worcester Three-Decker: A Study in the Perception of Form." *Design and Environment* (Winter 1975).

Barrows, Robert G. "Beyond the Tenement: Patterns of American Urban Housing: 1870–1930." *Journal of Urban Housing* (Aug. 1982).

Beaudry, Mary C., and Stephen A Mrozowski. "The Archeology of Work and Home Life in Lowell, Massachusetts: An Interdisciplinary Study of the Boott Cotton Mills Corporation." *IA (Journal of the Society for Industrial Archeology)* 14 no. 2 (1988).

Candee, Richard M. "Millwright and Merchant." *Old-Time New England* 60 (1970).

———. "The New England Textile Village in Art." Antiques (Dec. 1970).

———. "The 'Great Factory' at Dover, New Hampshire: The Dover Manufacturing Co. Print Works, 1825," *Old-Time New England* 66, nos. 1–2 (Summer–Fall 1975).

———. "New Towns of the Early New England Textile Industry." In *Perspectives in Vernacular Architecture*, I, ed. Camille Wells, 31–51. Columbia: Univ. of Missouri, 1981.

———. "Architecture and Corporate Planning in the Early Waltham System." In *Essays from the Lowell Conference on Industrial History 1982 and 1983*, ed. Robert Weible, 17–43. North Andover, Mass.: Museum of American Textile History, 1985.

Candee, Richard M., and Greer Hardwicke, "Early Twentieth-Century Reform Housing by Kilham & Hopkins, Architects of Boston." *Winterthur Portfolio* 22 (1) (1987).

Clark, Jr., E. Clifford. "Domestic Architecture as an Index to Social History: The Romantic Revival and the Cult of Domesticity in America, 1840–1870." *Journal of Interdisciplinary History* 7 (1) (Summer 1976).

Ely, Richard T. "Pullman: A Social Study." *Harper's New Monthly Magazine* (Feb. 1885).

Ford, James. "Housing and Disease." *Proceedings of the National Conference on Housing* 5 (1916).

———. "Some Fundamentals of Housing Reform." *American City* 8 (1913).

Foucault, Michel. "Of Other Spaces." *Diacritics* (Spring 1986).

Gilder, Richard Watson. "The Housing Problem—America's Need of Awakening." *The American City I* (1909).

Graffenried, Clare de. "Need of Better Homes for Wage-earners." *The Forum* 21 (May 1896: 301–12).

Greenwood, Richard. "A Mechanic in the Garden: Landscape Design in Industrial Rhode Island." *IA (Journal of the Society for Industrial Archeology)* 24 (1) (1998).

Gross, Laurence. "The Importance of Research Outside the Library, Watkins Mill, A Case Study." *IA (Journal of the Society for Industrial Archeology)* 7 (1981).

Hall, Prescott. "The Menace of the Three-Decker." *Housing Problems in America.* Providence, R.I., Fifth National Conference on Housing, 1916.

Hayden, Dolores. "Placemaking, Preservation and Urban History." *Journal of Architectural Education* 41 (3) (Spring 1988).

———. "The Power of Place: A Proposal for Los Angeles." *Public Historian* (Summer 1988).

———. "The Power of Place: Urban Landscape as People's History." Historic Preservation *Forum* 9 (2) (Winter 1995).

Heath, Kingston Wm. "The Howland Mill Village: A Missing Chapter in Model Workers' Housing." *Old-Time New England* 75 (263) (1997), 64–111.

Horwitz, Richard. "Architecture and Culture: The Meaning of the Lowell Boarding House." *American Quarterly* 25 (1) (March 1973).

"Housing Reform By Savings Bank." *The Survey*. New York: The Charity Organization Society of the City of New York, 1909–37. Vol. 26, May 27, 1911.

Hubka, Thomas. "Deep Contextualism: An Attitude Toward Vernacular Architecture Research." Abstract in *Perspectives in Vernacular Architecture III,* ed. Thomas Carter and Bernard Herman. Columbia: Univ. of Missouri Press, 1989.

"Industrial Housing at Hopedale, Massachusetts, Robert Allen Cook, Architect." Reprint from *Architectural Review* (Apr. 1917).

Jensen, Carole A. "Edmund M. Wheelwright." *A Biographical Dictionary of Architects in Maine* 4 (13) (1987).

Kay, Jane Holz. "Homey but not Homely: Portrait of a Three-decker." *(Cambridge, Mass.) The Real Paper,* Sept. 3, 1975.

Krim, Arthur J. "The Three-Decker as Urban Architecture in New England." *Monadnock* 44 (June 1970): 45–55.

———. "North Cambridge Vernacular House Types." *Northwest Cambridge Survey of Architectural History.* Vol. 5. Cambridge, Mass.: Cambridge Historical Commission/MIT Press, 1977.

———. "Residential Building Types." *Northwest Cambridge Survey of Architectural History*. Vol. 5. Cambridge Historical Commission, MIT Press, 1977.

Kulik, Gary, Roger Parks, and Theodore Penn. "Pawtucket Village and the Strike of 1824: The Origins of Class Conflict in Rhode Island." *Radical History Review* 17 (1978).

Lowenthall, David. "Past Time, Present Place: Landscape and Memory," *Geographical Review* 65 (1) (Jan. 1975).

Malone, Patrick. "Introduction to Green Engineering." *IA (Journal of the Society for Industrial Archeology)* 24 (1) (1998).

Malone, Patrick, and Charles A. Parrott. "Greenways in the Industrial City: Parks and Promendaes along the Lowell Canals." *IA (Journal of the Society for Industrial Archeology)* 24 (1) (1998).

Mass, William. "Mechanical and Organizational Innovation: The Drapers and their Automatic Loom." *Business History Review* 63 (1989).

McMullen, Thomas. "Lost Alternative: Urban Industrial Utopia of William D. Howland." *New England Quarterly* 55 (1982).

Nelson, Daniel, and Stuart Campbell. "Taylorism versus Welfare Work in American Industry: H. L. Gantt and the Bancrofts." *Business History Review* 46 (Spring 1972).

Olmsted, Frederick Law. "The Justifying Value of a Public Park." *Journal of Social Science* 12 (1881).

———. "Public Parks and the Enlargement of Towns." *Journal of Social Science* 3 (1871).

Perry. Duis. "Whose City? Public and Private Places in Nineteenth-Century Chicago." *Chicago History* 12 (1) (Spring 1983).

Potter, E. T. "The Problems of Concentrated Residence." *American Architect and Building News* 25 (Oct. 5, 1889).

Raub, Patricia. "Another Pattern of Urban Living: Multifamily Housing in Providence, 1890–1930." *Rhode Island History* 48 (Feb. 1990).

Reynolds, Dick. "Ecological Architecture: Planning the Organic Environment." *Progressive Architecture* (May 1966).

Rogers, Emma W. "The Foreign Invasion of a New England Town—New Haven." *The Survey: Social, Charitable, Civic* New York. Vol. 26. June 3, 1911.

Rosenblum, Naomi. "The Housing of Lynn's Shoe Workers in 1915." In *Life and Times in Shoe City: The Shoe Workers of Lynn.* Salem, Mass.: Essex Institute, 1979, 17–28.

Scranton, Philip. "Varieties of Paternalism: Industrial Structures and the Social Relations of Production in American Textiles." *American Quarterly* 36 (1984).

Special Textile Mill Issue *Old-Time New England* 66 (1975): 13–28.

Upton, Dell. "Vernacular Domestic Architecture in Eighteenth-Century Virginia." *Winterthur Portfolio* 17 (2/3) (Summer/Autumn 1982).

———. "White and Black Landscapes in Eighteenth-Century Virginia." *Places* 2 (1985).

Weil, Francois. "Capitalism and Industrialization in New England, 1815–1845." *Journal of American History* (Mar. 1998): 1334–54.

Zaitzevsky, Cythia. "Housing Boston's Poor: The First Philanthropic Experiments." *Journal of the Society of Architectural Historians* 40 (2) (May 1983).

Newspaper Articles

"Better than Feared . . . Mr. Howland Believed to Have Wandered Away While Dazed." *Evening Standard*, Apr. 26, 1897.

Boston Globe, Jan. 18, 1920, and Feb. 4, 1922.

Boston Globe scrapbook, comp. Zephaniah Pease, New Bedford Free Public Library.

"Capital and Labor in Harmony. Howland Mills Held Up as Model by the Cleveland Plain Dealer." *Evening Standard*, Feb. 25, 1891.

Davis, William A. "All Decked Out, The Humble Triple-Decker Finally Gets Some Respect." *Boston Globe*, Mar. 29, 1991.

"Exclude Three-Deckers from Residential Area." *Lynn Daily Evening Item*, July 11, 1913.

"50 Years Ago." *Sunday Standard Times*, July 6, 1958.

Howland, Ellis L. "Hazlewood, History of the City's New Park on Clark's Point." *Standard Times*, July 27, 1901.

Howland, Ellis L. "How Joseph Congdon's Industry Carved Out Its Beauty" *Standard Times*, June 21, 1902.

"The Howland Mills." *New Bedford Evening Standard*, Mar. 15, 1889.

"Howland Mills Corporation." *New Bedford Evening Standard*, May 19, 1888.

"Howland Mills Corporation. An Organization of the Company Effected To-day." *Evening Standard*, May 19, 1888.

"Howland Mills Involved. Three More Cotton Corporations Found to be in Financial Straits." *Morning Mercury*, Apr. 24, 1897.

"The Late John C. Olmsted and the City's Park System," Feb. 29, 1920, *Boston Globe* scrapbook, New Bedford Free Public Library.

"Mill Notes: The New Howland Mill to be Double the Size of No. 1." *Evening Standard*, Jan. 1, 1889.

New Bedford Daily Mercury, Mar. 5 and 6, 1867, Aug. 23 1894.

New Bedford Evening Standard, Mar. 5 and 6, 1867, Aug. 14 and Dec. 14, 1888; Jan. 1 and Oct. 3, 1889, Feb. 25, 1891, May 25, 1897, Feb. 17, 1898.

"The New Cotton Mills, Rapid Work in the Construction of the Howland Mill." *New Bedford Evening Standard*, Aug. 14, 1888.

"William D. Howland, Noteworthy Career of the Unfortunate Mill Treasurer." *(New Bedford) Evening Standard,* May 6, 1897.

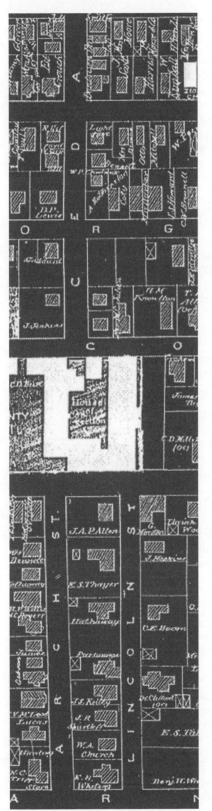

INDEX

Numbers in *italics* indicate figures.

Acushnet (early name for New
    Bedford, Mass.), 24
Acushnet (whaler), 33
Acushnet Mill, 38, 85, 91, 128;
    building smaller, detached units,
    102; housing, 80, *81,* 84–87
Acushnet Mills Corporation, 7, 84
Acushnet Park, 115
Acushnet River, 34, 35, 42, 70, 85,
    156, 183; developable space along,
    47; mills along waterfront, 44
adjacent lots, 14 , 174–75
Aire River, 101
Allen, Everett, 34
*Alone Together: A History of New
    York's Early Apartments*
    (Cromley), 120
*American Architect and Building
    News,* 129
American Woman's Home (Beecher
    and Stowe), 32
American Wool and Cotton Reporter,
    111
apartment hotel, 121
apartment house, 125
apartments, vs. tenements, 125
Apollo Iron and Steel Company at
    Vandergrift, Pa., 113
architectural education,
    acknowledging change, 184–85
architectural history, rarity of studies
    on flat buildings, tenements, or
    apartment housing, 120
architectural objects, formal and
    social readings, *12*
architectural space, human
    dimension, 179–80
architectural works, multiple
    perspectives on, 185–86

architecture: as cultural production,
    xvii–xxiii; culturally specific living
    patterns within, 176; embodiment
    of complex social process, 183,
    185; metaphor for labor-
    management struggle, 154–55;
    social context of, 168
Architecture of Country Homes, The
    (Downing), 31
Arkwright Club, 133
Arnold, James, 29, 30–31, 33
Arnold, Sarah (Rotch), 29
artifacts, offering insights into
    relational pattern of human
    behavior, 185
Ashley (Mayor), 109
Ashley, Davis, 129
Ashley, W., 90
Association for the Relief of Aged
    Women, 88
Atlantic Mills, 63, 64
*Atlas of Bristol County,
    Massachusetts, 64, 65*
Atlas of New Bedford, 29, 30
Atterbury, Grosvenor, 114
Azorean Stackhouse festival, 6
Azores, geography, 165

back porch, 144, 149
Bancroft Park, 108, 113
bank lending restrictions, 167
Baptists, 24
Barrett, Nathan F., 102
Barrows, William Eliot, 103, 104, 106,
    107
Bay State Mills, 63
bay window, 137
Beardsley, Thomas, xviii
Beecher, Catherine E., 32, 146
behavioral codes, 148–49
Belvidere, 85
Beman, Solon S., 102

benevolent institutions, 70
Bennett, Thomas, 33–34, 48
Bennett Mills, 54, 112
Benoit, Alfred, 55
Benoit, Alfred, family of, 54, *54*
Blewett, Mary, 77
Blier, Joseph, 7, 133, 190 n.6
Blitzer, Henry, 145
Blondel, Jacques-Francois, 121
Board of Public Works, 96, 97
boarders, 18, 52, 55, 69
boardinghouses, 95, *97*, 108, 126, 136; converted to
    family tenements, 64; uniform, 85
boarding income, 18
boarding room, 18
bobbin changers, automatic, 77
Borden, John, 73
Boston (Mass.), 121, 151
Boston Building Inspection Reports, 123
Boston City Park Department, 94, 99
Boston Cooperative Building Company, 101
Boston Post, 133
Boston Traveller, 79
Bourne, Jonathan, 39, 40, 51
Bournville, 102
Bowditch, Henry Ingersoll, 100, 101
breathing spaces, 97, 100, 101
Bristol Manufacturing Company, 48
Brooklawn Park, 109
Brownell and Murklaud, 92
builder, influence of, 136–41
builder's guides, 142–43
builder's history, 186
building codes, 167
building type, influence of market forces, 133–36
built environment, layered, contextual approach to, 183
Bulfinch, 143
Bungalow, *99*
Buttonwood Park, 56–57, *57*, 109, 113, 167

Candee, Richard M., xviii
Cape Verde Islands, 166
Card, Bryan W., 92
Cardinand, Francis, 7
Centennial Exposition (Philadelphia, 1876), 43
chain migration patterns, 168
Chainay, Nazare. *See* Chaine, Nazaire
Chaine, Nazaire, 133
Chicago, 121
Chicopee (Ga.), 107, 114
child labor, 53–54
child's perspective, 6
Children's Aid Society, 88
Christian Capitalism, 201 n.26

Christian home, embodiment of, 32
city, dominant force in American life, 121
City Cotton Mill, 53
City Directory, 55
city engineers' map (1875), 91, *91*
City Farm and Hospital, 70
City Mission, 88
City of New Bedford, The, 66
City Work Farm, 70
clapboard siding, *10*
Clark, Edward, 121
Clark's Cove, 32, 47, 70, 100, 114, 178, *179*
Clark's Point, 32, 70, 91, 107, 109
Cleveland Plain Dealer, 110, 111
Cleveland Post, 106
client's history, 186
Clifford, James, xix
Clifford, Walter, 112
climate context, 21, *22, 23*
collective achievement, 152
Columbia Mill, 112
Committee for the Relief of the Manufacturing Poor,
    200 n.8
common labor, housed in four-tenements, 77
company library and reading room, 107
company store, 107
Compton, George, 77
Comstock, William T., xxi, 125, 142, 146
Congdon estate, 31, 70
Congregationalists, 25
Constant Turmoil, 77
Consumption in New England (Bowditch), 100
contextual awareness, broadening realms, *159–61*
contour planning, 108–10, 113
Cook, C. E., 156
Coolidge, John, 84–85
cooperative-rental demand, 136
Corliss Steam Engine Company, 42
Corliss steam power, xvii, 33, 42, 43, *44*, 141
corporate authority, 106–8
corporate designer/planner, xxi
corporate housing, xx, 52; cutbacks on, 78; shift to
    smaller, more private, 84–85
corridor aesthetic, 85
cottages, 128
County Street, 25–28
*Course of Industrial Decline: The Boott Cotton Mills of
    Lowell, Massachusetts, 1835–1955, The* (Gross), xviii
Cove Park, 109, 113
Crane, Edward A., 95
Crapo, Henry Howland, 90–91
Crapo, Oscar, 133, 135, 172–73, *174*
Crapo, William M., 57, 58
Crapo, William Wallace, 31, 71, 88

Crawford, Margaret, xviii
Cromley, Elizabeth, 120
Crowley, John E., 143
cultural continuity, 15
cultural geography, 176
cultural-landscape analysis, xxii
cultural weathering, xviii–xix, xxiii, 119, 176–78, *177*,
    180–81, 183–86
curbstones, 83
Cushena, 24

Dakota (apartment building), 121
Daley, Clement, xxi
Daley, Michael E., xx, 133, 138, 140, 142, 145, 167
dance of life, 179
Dane Street (Lowell, Mass.), 84, 85
Dartmouth, 24–25
Davis, Alexander Jackson, 31, 32, 104
deep contextualism, 224 n.11
Delano, Joseph C., 31
Desgardine, 134
design concepts, restructured, 181
design-usage relationship, 16
Dewing, Arthur S., 164
Dias, Elaine (Pitts), 7, *15*
Dias, John, 7, *15*
domestic arrangements, variety of, 16–18
Dorchester (Mass.), 125
double houses, 62–64, 77
double parlor, 15, 16
Downing, Andrew Jackson, 30–31, 32, 104, 146
Draper, Earle, 114
Draper automatic loom, 128
Draper (E. D. and G.) Company, 77, 108, 113
Driscoll, Daniel, 132
drop boxes, for automatic shuttle selection, 77
dumbbell tenement, 121–22
Dunham Hall Library, 107

Eames, H., 70
economic rationality, shift from paternalism, 110
Edison wires, 92
Eliot, Charles, 51, 108, 109
elite homes, 183
Ely, Richard, 102–3
Emerson, William Ralph, 48–50
English immigration, stopped by 1905, 78
English labor force, 73, 77
enlightened industrial capitalism, 90
entrances, ceremonial and utilitarian, 11
estates: cultural weathering, 51; horticultural interests,
    48; ownership transfer from whaling magnates to mill
    owners, 48
Estiella, Thomas, 133

ethnic-particularism, xix
ethnicity, imprinted on landscape, 181
ethnographic subjectivity, 189 n.4
Evening Standard, 92, 163, 164
experience-near reading of place, 5

Fairhaven (Mass.), 33
Fairhaven Mills, 116
Fall River (Mass.), 44, 45, 77, 109, 136, 182; ten-hour
    workday won, 38; unemployment (1990s), 172
Fall River Globe, 111
false front, *152*
family size, average, 52
Federal Labor Commission, 102
Federal Period seaports, layout, 85
First National Bank (New Bedford, Mass.), 33
flat fever, 121
floor plan (rental hierarchy), *17*
Florence Hotel, 102
Forest Hills Gardens, 114
Fort Rodman, 91, 108
four-tenements, 5, *37, 63,* 126, 136; common labor
    housing, 77; English workers' housing, 77; plumbing,
    67–68; prevalence of, 68; use of domestic design
    features, 76
Fourier, Charles, 101
Fourierism, 101, 204 n.46
Franklin Park (Boston, Mass.), 108
French Canadian immigration, 78, 129
French Canadians, 38, 46, *46,* 73, 166
French (Parisian) flat, 121, 125
Friends, 70. *See also* Quakers, Society of Friends
Friends Academy, 32
front porch, extension of late Victorian value structure,
    149–50. *See also* porch
Fuchs and Wangler, 145
furniture rotation, 18

Gabaccia, Donna, xix
gable-end workers' housing, *80*
gable-front form, 76–77
gang garages, 173, *174*
garden city movement, 206 n.55
gardens, 173–75, *175*
Garner, John, xviii
Gay, George W., 95
gender, related to type of labor, 44
gender mapping, 21
gendering of space, 191 n.16
geographic mobility, 55
Gibson, Catherine Hammond, house of, 144
Gifford, Mrs. William, 31
Gilman, Arthur, 121
Glasgow Tenement, The (Worsdall), 120

Globe Street Railway, 99
Goodyear Tire Company, 9
Gosnold Mills, 93, 114
Gothic cottages, 31–32, *32*
Gothic Revival Unitarian Church, 31
Gould, E. R. L., 102
granite, dependence on, 41–42
grape arbors, 177, *178*
Great Falls Corporation, 63
Greek revival mansions, 26, 28, *28,* 29, 32
grid system, indicative of rigidity of employees' lives, 110
Grinnell, Art, 40
Grinnell, Frederick, 42–43; estate of, 51, *52*
Grinnell, Joseph, 26, 33–34, 51; home of, *28*
Grinnell Manufacturing Company, 80
Grinnell Mill, 38, 128; building smaller, detached units, 102; business with New Bedford Manufacturing Company, 89; expectations for dramatic profits, 90
Grinnell Mill Village: high standard for scale and density of corporate residences, 84; housing, *64,* 80–84, *81, 82,* 156; paved streets in, 82; urban reality of, 83
Grinnells, estate of, 40
Gross, Laurence, xviii

Hale, Edward Everett, 101
Hall, Ed, 179
Hall, Prescott, 149
Halprin (Lawrence) and Associates, 186
Hammond, Caleb, 133
Hammond (Caleb) & Son, 129
Hardenbergh, Henry J., 121
Harper's Monthly, 97, 102
Harrisville (N.H.), 84
Hathaway, Francis, 71
Hathaway, Thomas S., 48
Hathaway, William, Jr., 51
Haven, Parkman Balke, 94
Hayes, N. P., 95
Hazard, Fred, 133
Hazelwood Park, 109
Heath, Kingston Wm., *14;* environmental autobiography, 5, 6; family, 7, 14–18. *See also* Pitts, Amanda (Souza Paes); Pitts, Harold, Sr.
Hine, Lewis H., 53
Hine, Lewis W., 53–54
History of New Bedford, 41, 73, 76
Holmes Cotton Mill, 7, 53, 54
home design, decision-making process, 48–51
Homestead Clubs, 208 n.76
Hope Mill, 35
Hopedale (Mass.), xviii, 113, *114*
Hopedale Company, 113–14
horticultural interests, 48
Hotel Pelham, 121
housekeepers' houses, 84

housing: enticement for skilled workers and overseers, 127; shift to detached, multifamily housing units, 78
housing experiments (1880s), 80
Housing of Working People, The (Gould), 102
Howell Mill Village, costs and rental prices, 95
Howland, Abraham H., 26–28, 33, 48; desire to diversify economy, 39; difficulty financing cotton manufacturing, 34
Howland, Cornelius, 90
Howland, George, 88
Howland, Matthew, 31, 40, 51, 87, 88, 90
Howland, Matthew Morris, 40
Howland, Rachel Collins (Smith), 40, 48, 70, 87, 88–89; summer home, 108
Howland, Richard S., 40
Howland, Susan (Howland), 88
Howland, William Dillwyn, xx, 31, 51, 87–88, 89, 103; companies' credit impaired, 112–13; connection with city's elite, 111; dedication to workers' welfare, 111; disappearance and death, 113; eroding base of support, 112; financial mismanagement, 112–13; speculation in "prints," 40; success of business ventures, 89–90; summer home, 108
Howland Company, 40
Howland family: correspondence, 39–41, 48, 89–90; education, 40; religion and philanthropy, 88
Howland Mill Village, xx, 85, *87,* 94–100, 133; absence of paternalism toward workers, 106; cultural context, 100–11; encouraging personal freedom, 109–10; end of, 111–16; few tenant restrictions, 107–8; flexible and democratic compared to other mill villages, 108; goals of, 110; influence of, 113–16; interior design, 95–96; linking technology and nature, 87; new approach to workers' housing, 85–87, 94–100; offering model housing and purchase of building sites, 86; original design features, 87; park plans, 109; rents at, 107–8; significance of, 102; similarities to The Oaks, 103–6; street plan, *96;* surviving structures, 116; trolley access to, 107
Howland Mills Corporation, 32–33, 42, 86, 90–93, *91, 93, 94,* 112, 127–28, *178;* corporate housing for, 80; cottage, *81;* design of different industrial setting, 92–93; inland location, 92–93; layout of property and mills, 92; road surfaces compared to Grinnell, 97; sewers and street improvements, 96–97; superintendent's house, *93*
Hunt, Richard Morris, 121
Hunt, S. C., 133, 157
Hutchings and Co., 40
hydraulic elevators, 121

immigrant population, growth of, 156–57
immigration, xix, xvii, 141; importance to rise of manufacturing industry, 44; post-1960s, xxii; shifting patterns, 78

immorality, resulting from multifamily housing, 121, 146
incorporated companies, opposition to financing, 34
industrial housing, emerging diversity in, 156
industrial urbanism, 32; effects of, xvii; shift to, xvii;
    taking hold, 141–42
industrial worker, efforts to change behavior, 149
industrial workers' housing, xvii–xviii
Ingalls, Seth H., 35
Ingraham Public School, 73
intelligent specialization, 34
international expositions, 101
interpretive drawings, 90 Nelson Street, *9, 13*
intrasite analysis, 190 n.11
Iser, Wolfgang, 189 n.4
Isleboro Inn, 100

Jacobsohn, Deedee, 123, 166–67
Jamaica Plain (Mass.), 125
Jones, Inigo, 143

Kasson, John, 148
Kelly and Houghton, 158
Kennedy (John F.) Memorial Highway, 65, 84, 169–70
Kenney, Joseph T., 114
Kilburn Mill, 7, 18, 178, *179*
Kilpatrick, Thomas, 121
Kim, Arthur, 161
King Philip (Metacomet), 25
King Philip's War, 25
Knowles, Joseph, 48
Knowles, Lucius, 77
Kohut, Heinz, 5
Koziol, Christopher, 175
Krim, Arthur, xx

labor disputes, 77. *See also* strikes
labor movement, eviction threatened for proponents of, 106
Lagoda, 39
Lancashire (England), 44
land costs, 78
Landau, Sarah, 121
landscape architecture, 101, 102–3, 176
landscape gardening, 31
Langlois, Joseph, 133
Langshaw, Walter, 48
laundry, facilities for in early three-deckers, 144–45
Lawrence (Mass.), 63, 64, 182
Locks and Canals Company, 85
lot utilization, 11
Loudon, John, 25
Lowell (Mass.), 33, 45, 62, 63, 69, 84–85, 104, 106, 110,
    175, 182; boardinghouses, xviii; workers' protests, 38
Ludlow Manufacturing Association, 84
Luippold, Jacob, xxi, 128, 140, 143, 145, 149; plans of,
    144, 145

Luther (Haile) house, *122*
Lynn (Mass.), 129, 167

macadam roads, 96–97
Makepeace, C. R., 156
Mamomet Mill, *43*
Manchester (N.H.), 45
Mandell, Alice, 50
Mandell, Edward D., 48–51, 76; estate of, 48–51, *49, 50*
Mandell, Thomas, 48
Mandell (E. D.) and Company, 51
Manning, Warren Henry, 113
mansions, symbolism of, 4
manufacturing, steam power and immigration essential
    to growth, 44
manufacturing cities, competing interests in, 55
Map of Bristol County, Massachusetts, 64
Marine Park, 113
Marsh Island, 35
Massachusetts Bureau of Statistics of Labor, 78
Massachusetts Civic League Committee on Housing, 148
Massachusetts Homestead Commission, 148, 175
Massachusetts State Board of Health, 78, 101
Massachusetts State House of Representatives, 38
Massachusetts Supreme Court, 136
Massasoit, 24
material cultural analysis, xxi–xxii, 223 n.9
McKim, Mead and Bigelow, 94
Mechanics National Bank, 28, 43
Medeira Islands, 166
Medeiros, Antonio Jose, 6, 175, 176
Medeiros, Emilie, *10*
Medeiros, Gloria, 175, *176*
Melville, Herman, 33, 165
memory landscape, 179–80
Merchants National Bank, 28
Merrimack Manufacturing Company, 102
Metacomet. *See* King Philip
mill, orderliness in, *154*
mill districts, 156–58, *160*
mill technology, changes in, 77–78
mill villages: cultural context, 100–11; focus on, xviii
mill workers, wages, 133
mixed-use community, 100–101
Moby Dick (Melville), 33, 165
Model A Draper loom, 77, 128
model housing, 85, 101; examples of note, 102; intent of,
    95; Howland Mill Village an example of, 100
monitor roof, 51
Morgan, Charles W., 28, 31
Moriarty, T. J., drawing, *130*
Morning Standard, 112
Morris, William, 110
Morse Twist Mill, 170
Moses B. Tower, 165

Motta, Joseph, 133, 152
Mount Carmel Portuguese Catholic Church, 179, *179*
Mt. Carmel Roman Catholic Church, *158*
mule spinning, 44, *45*
Mulhouse Workingmen's Dwellings Company, 208 n.76
multifamily dwellings, controlling living environment through purchase of, 14–15
multifamily housing: design changes in, 137–38; early forms, 121–22; most common form of housing for textile industry, 182–83
multifamily rental flats, 52

Nantucket, 25
Nashawena Mill B, 7
National Association of Collegiate Schools of Architecture, 175
National Bank of Commerce, 88, 112, 113
National Child Labor Committee, 53
National Conference on Housing Problems in America (1916), 149
National Cotton Mule Spinners' Association of America, 78
National Register, 120
nationalities, relations among, 197 n.11
naturalistic planning, end of, in New Bedford, 113
Newark (N.J.), 125
New Bedford (Mass.), 3, *5*, 182; Central Wharf, *26*; change in economies, xx; changing demographics, 165–70; city divided, 47–57; city hall, 57; commercial district map (1815), *27*; conceptions of property ownership reflected in habitats of wealthy, 29; corporate housing, xx; delivery truck and work wagons, 8, *8*; despair following post-Depression years, 5; dichotomy of cultural landscape and official history, 56; early neighborhood planning the result of private business development, 88; early regional patterns, 24–33; elite society in 1800s, xx, 31; emergence of working-class neighborhoods, 62; era of greatest mill expansion and population increase (1900–10), 116; evolving regional character, xviii–xix; French-Canadian ethnic makeup, 8; growth rates (1890–1910), 45; height of mill building (1901–10), 129; history of everyday life "behind the scrim," 57; housing trend (1920s), 167; immigrant population growth in late 1800s, 39; immigration and changing settlement patterns, 45–47; importance in industrial history, 33; incorporation, 25, 33; largest center of cotton textile production in America, 46; library, 57; "little Portugal," 168; manufacturing suited to, 34; map and listings of corporate housing available (1913), *115*; material success of whaling families, 40–41; migration to the "hill," 26; mix of mills and mill neighborhoods, 6; nation's leader in cotton textile production, 141; new regional identity (1870s), 39–44; new three-tenements by year, *130*; North End, 37, 47, 68, 82, 88, 133, 158, *171*; Office of Housing and Neighborhood

Development, 172; one-industry city, 163; ordinance restricting frame housing to two stories, 166; park/parkway proposal, 109; planning and design, xx; population surge, 128; Portuguese culture in, 6; Portuguese immigration, 165–70; predominant industries, 3; preference for three-deckers, 126; prosperity in 1850s, 25; public art, 55–57; rail lines connecting South End mills to North End residential communities, 73; reluctance to abandon whaling, 37–38, 69–70; rise of textile era, 33–39; rural roots of ethnic population, 8; scarcity of automobiles, 8; segregation, 157; shift from whaling to textiles (1880–1910), 31, 41; skyline, 43; social geography, *161*; South End, 38, *47*, 47, 54, 70, 73, 75–76, 133, 158, 178; spatial segregation, 53; streets: —, Acushnet Avenue, 82; —, Arnold Street, 29, 51; —, Austin Street, 66; —, Blackmer Street, 84, 85; —, Bolton Road, 92; —, Bolton Street, 99; —, Collette Street, 133; —, County Street, 25–28, 29, 32, 48, 51, 63, 65, 66, 85, 91; —, Cove Park, 111; —, Cove Road, 91, 111; —, Cove Street, 92; —, Crapo Street, 91, *135*; —, Dartmouth Street, 111; —, Division Street, 85; —, Eighth Street, 29, 31; —, "Fayal" Street, 165; —, First Street, 71, 73; —, Fourth Street, 51; —, Front Street, 33, 34, 55, 63, 82; —, Fulton Court, 64; —, Hawthorn Street, 31, 48, 51, 90; —, Hazard Street, 65, 66; —, Hicks Street, 63; —, Linden Street, 65; —, Logan Street, 55, 63, 64, 81; —, Maple Street, 51; —, Mill Roads, 92; —, Nelson Street, 6–7, *8, 14*, 57, *131, 135. See also* 90 Nelson Street; —, Newton Street, 137; —, New Water Street, 41; —, North Front Street, 54, 63, 64; —, North Street, 7; —, Norwell Street, 167; —, Orchard Street, 29, 92; —, Page Street, 51; —, Pleasant Street, 66; —, Purchase Street, 63, 65, 66, 82, 129; —, Rivet Street, 71, *71*, 73, 85; —, Rockdale Avenue, 92, 99; —, Rodney French Boulevard, 157; —, Ruth Street, *140*; —, Second Street, 71, *71*, 73; —, South First Street, 73; —, South Water Street, 54, 62, 70, 82, 84, 85, 167, *169*; —, State Street, 55; —, Union Street, 29, 31, 137; —, Water Street, 26, 165; —, Weld Street, 82, 83; —, William Street, 26; system of parks, 108; textile development, phases of, 126–33; textile economy collapse, 3–5; textile-related industrial expansion, first phase, 37; transformation to fishing economy, 5; unemployment (1990s), 172; urban life and culture, evolution of, 37; use-segregated city, 47–48; view of the city, *72*; Ward 1, 52, 53, 54, *64*; Ward 3, 52; Ward 6, 52, 53; Waterfront Historical District, 170; West End, 137; whaling capital of the world, 25; working conditions, 38
New Bedford Atlas, 64, 67
New Bedford Board of Trade, 38
New Bedford City Directory, 51, 73, 84, 99
New Bedford Commercial Bank, 88
New Bedford Cordage Company, 32
New Bedford Daily Mercury, 79
New Bedford Directory, 129
New Bedford Evening Standard, 94–95, 112, 113

New Bedford Horticultural Society, 31
New Bedford Housing Authority, rehabilitation of
    Wamsutta Mills tenements (1978), 66–67
New Bedford Industrial Exposition, 163
New Bedford Institute of Savings, 32, 51
New Bedford Manufacturers' Association, 111
New Bedford Manufacturing Company, 89–90, 92, 111, 112
New Bedford Park Commission, 109
New Bedford Record of Building Permits, 7, 129, 133,
    137, 167, 173
New Bedford Steam Mill Company, 34
New Bedford and Taunton Railroad, 34
New Bedford Textile School, 7
"new" company towns, 87, 116
New England: agrarian myth, 175; change in regional
    economies, xx; cycle of industrialization in, xviii
New England Cotton Yarn Company, 114
"New England—Sketches among the Weavers," 79
New England week, 163
New Haven (Conn.), 151–52
New Lanark (Scotland), 89, 100
New View of Society (Owen), 100
New York, 121
New York Evening Journal, 79
Niger, 4
90 Nelson Street, 6–7, 8, 14–15, 16, *147, 159, 172*;
    changes in usage of, 19–23; floor rental hierarchy, *17*;
    rental during 1930s and 1940s, 18
North Haven (Maine), 99
Northrop, James H., 77
Northrop loom (1894 Model A Draper), 77, 128

objects, as vessels of creative positive energy, 184
Offinger, Martin (Mr. and Mrs.), 133–36
Old Colony Railroad, 82
Old and New (Hale), 101
Old Law tenement, 214 n.7
Olmsted, Frederick Law, 48–50, 93, 97, 101, 108–9, 115
Olmsted, Frederick Law, Jr., 114
Olmsted, John C., 109
Olmsted, Olmsted and Eliot, 51, 108–10, 113
oral history, 180
ordinary people, as designers of regional settings, 183
original design intention, 183
orphan's home, 70
Outlook magazine, 79
overcrowding, 51–55, 76–77
Owen, Robert, 88–89, 100–101
owned space, 10

Page (Paes), Charlie, 7, 16, 18
Page Mill, 7, 9, *10,* 114, 178
Paine, Robert Treat, 108
Pairpoint Manufacturing Company, 51, 76
Paisler, Charles S., 41–42

Palace Car Factory, 44
Panic of 1857, 39
Panic of 1893, 112, 156
Parker, John Avery, 25; estate of, *27, 29,* 48
participant observation, xix, 189 n.4
paternalism, views of, 110–11
patination, 180, 184
pattern books, 19, 146, 150
pattern language, Wamsutta Mills tenements, 66–67
paved streets, 82–83
Pawtucket (R.I.), 33, 42
Peabody, Robert Swain, 94, 99
Peabody and Stearns, 94
Peanut Row, 84
Perry, Dwight, 33
persons-per-dwelling, 52
persons-per-room, 52
Philadelphia, original site of hotel as American building
    type, 121
physical adjacencies, 11
physical space, vs. reality of socially constructed space,
    11
piazza, 11, *148;* additions onto existing three-deckers,
    147; cultural necessity of, 149; front, *10,* 11; front
    and back, 145; principal aesthetic expression of
    builder's design, 151; rebuilt, *177;* removal, *173;*
    social connotations, 145–46, *147;* symbolic import,
    143–51; vs. porch, 145
Pierce, Andrew G., 71, 112
Pierce, Harry M., 113
Pierce, Otis N., 113
Pierce Mill, 170
Pitts, Amanda (Souza Paes), 6–7, *8, 10, 14,* 16, *18*
Pitts, Harold, Sr., 6–7, *8, 10, 18*
Pitts, Louise, 7, *57*
Piva (Mr.), *15*
place: awareness of, 179–80; as mental construct, 178–79
Plain Facts for Future Citizens, 8
Plaw, John, 143
Plummer, 90
Plymouth General Court, 25
Polish immigration, 78, 129
popular taste, influence of, 142–43
porch: design features, 146; paired with parlor for social
    reasons, 149; social connotations, 146–47; vs. piazza,
    145
Port Sunlight, 102
Portuguese American culture, 6, 8–9, 16, 180
Portuguese dormers, 137–38, *138*
Portuguese Feast of the Blessed Sacrament, *171*
Portuguese immigration, 78, 129, 168
Portuguese workers, establishing residence near
    Potomska riverfront, 73
Potomska Corporation, public criticism of living
    conditions, 79

Potomska Mill, 38, 39, 40, *45,* 47, 88, 91, 142; beginnings, 70–71; Complex No. 1, 42; Complex No. 2, 42;
   density of housing arrangements, 73–76; distribution
   of workers, *75;* employment, 73; first phase of
   tenement building, 71; four-tenement blocks built in
   L shape, 73; housing, 70–77, *72,* 85, 146, 156; under
   Howland, 89; later housing construction undistin-
   guishable as corporate housing, 73; map of four-
   family tenement blocks, *74;* Mill No. 1., 71; praised
   for corporate housing accommodations, 78; products,
   70–71; public health concerns about housing, 100;
   relationship with Wamsutta, 70–71; style change from
   Wamsutta tenements, 71; three-deckers, 71, 129;
   workers' housing, *71*
Potter, William J., 78–79
Povacao, San Miguel (St. Michael), 6, 176
Pratt, Bela L., 58
Primitive Methodist Church, 85
privacy issues, 18–19
private space, 16
procession of spaces, reversal of, 15–16
promiscuity, associated with multifamily housing, 121
property rehabilitation, 139
Public Baths, 55
public and private ritualistic space, 16
public surveillance, 149
Pullman (Ill.), 107, 110
Pullman, George M., 102–3
Pullman's Palace Car Company, 102–3, *103,* 106

Quakers, 24, 25, 31. *See also* Friends, Society of Friends
Quinten, Zephir, 140

rabbit runs, 134, 154
rail lines, 85
railroad flat, 122, 125
Rantin, Samuel, 128
Rantin and Son, xxi
reader response theory, 189 n.4
rear deck, *15*
rear entry, 11, 15
rear passageways, 11
Reconnaissance Survey of New Bedford, 73, 162–63, 164
*Record of Building Permits for the City of New
   Bedford,* 73
reform housing, 84
Reform Law of 1901, 122
Remington, Walter H. B., 163
Rennselaer Polytechnic Institute, 42
"Report on the Factory Systems of the United States," 84
Republican Party, 32
Reynolds, Dick, 186
Ricard, Alphonse, 133
Richards (J. T.) Co., 132, 133
Richmond Paper Company, 99, 203 n.40

Riding, Alice, 140
ring spinner, 128
ring spinning, 77–78
Riverside Housing Community, 101
Robert Treat Paine, 102
Rodman, Benjamin, 34
Rodman, Samuel, 34
Rodman, William Rotch, estate of, 28, 48
Roman Catholic Church, 85
romantic naturalism, 31, 32
Rotch, Benjamin, 32
Rotch, Emily (Morgan), 31
Rotch, Joseph, 25
Rotch, Morgan, 33, 40, 88, 90, 97, 108
Rotch, William, Jr., 29, 30
Rotch, William J., 30, 31–33, 71, 88, 90
Rotch House, 31–32
Rotch Mill, 112; razing, 116; site demolition, 170, *170;*
   sewers, 96
Rotch Spinning Corporation, 92
Rotch Spinning Mill, 9
Roxbury (Mass.), 129, 145, 175
Ruskin, John, 92, 110, 184
Russell, Joseph, 25, 48
Russell, Joseph, III, 25
Russell, Perry, farm, 70

Salmon Falls, 63
Salt, Titus, 101
Saltaire, 101, 102, 104, 107
Sanborn, Dana A., xxi
Sayer, William L., 43
Schermerhorn, C. E., 150
screen inserts, *10*
seaman's boardinghouses, 61, *62*
Separatists, 24
shared experience, 178–79
Sharp Manufacturing Company, 114
shingle siding, *15*
shipbuilding, 25
shopfront advertisement, *171*
shrines, 11, 16
side yard, 11, 14
sidewalks, 10–11
single-family houses, 95, *98, 122*
six-blocks, 133, *134, 135,* 154
six-tenement, Neo-Colonial, *135*
Sketches for Country Houses, Villas and Rural Dwellings
   (Plaw), 143
skilled labor, 44; housing for, 76–77; leaving for privately
   owned and built three-deckers, 79
Slater's village (R.I.), xviii
Smith, Benjamin, 156
Smithy, A. P., 156
Soares, Joseph, 174, *175*

social conduct, reflected in housing design, 149
social context, 19–21
social control, 106–7
social engineering, 212 n.117
social perception, changes in, 78–80
socially constructed space, 191 n.15
Society for the Preservation of New England Antiquities, 140
Society of Friends, 31, 88. *See also* Friends, Quakers
Somersworth (N.H.), 63
"Song of Cotton Cloth," 162, 163
Soule Mill, 129
Sousa, John, 53
Sousa, Manuel, and family, 53–54, *53*
South Boston, 125, 129
South End Dartmouth Manufacturing Company, 48
space, epoch of, 223 n.7
space utilization, 173–78
spatial analysis, 191 n.14
spatial practices, subverting original design, 11
speculative builder, xxi, 116
speculative building, xviii, 7, 52
speculative housing market, emergence from corporate-owned housing, 183
Spencer, Robert C., 202 n.28
Springfield (Mass.), 84
St. Martin's Episcopal Church, 85
stacked living units, individuality of, 150–51
stair halls, purpose, 68–69
steam-powered mills, 42, 43, 44
Stetson, Thomas M., 31
Stone, Alfred, 121
Storey, Moorfield, 99–100
Stormaway, 99–100
Stowe, Harriet Beecher, 32
street vendors, frowned upon, 8
streetcars, 109
streets, as setting for reenactment of rural life, 8
strikes, 110–12, 114, 133, *148,* 156
structuralism, 190 n.4, 223 n.7
Stuyvesant (apartment building), 121
Sullivan, John B., 95, 138
superintendent's house, 95
Swift family, 40
Sylvia, Manuel, 133
Synthetic Siding in New Bedford, 172

Tavares, Manuel, 167
teaming, 83
Temple, Lewis, 196 n.81
tenement: etymology, 120; morality issues in design, 125; overcrowding, 53; reconfiguration into smaller sleeping spaces, 68; vs. apartment, 125
Tenement Act for Towns, 148
tenement blocks, growing criticism, 101–2

tenement forms, changes in, 76–77
Tenement House Act (1901), 122
Tenement House Act for Cities, 148
tenement houses, to serve immigrants, 121–22
Tenement Housing Law (1867), 121
textile industry: appealing dividends from, 39, 40–41; cessation of New Bedford mill incorporation, 126; concern about regional decline (1924), 163–64; criticism of workers' housing (1923), 164; difficulty of securing common labor (1920s), 163; divestiture of rental tenements, 164–65; early days of development, 70; emergence of working-class neighborhoods, 62; failure, 120; in Georgia, 33; immigrant labor synonymous with, 53; increased worker turnover in (1920s), 164; New England roots, 33; problems in maturation of, 164; regional wage cut, 133; shortage of labor, 38; wage differences among employee levels, 52–53; waterfront access important to growth, 43–44
textile mills: brick construction predominant, 41; conversion of, 169
Texture of Industry, The (Gordon and Malone), 77
The George and Susan, 40
The Oaks, 103–6, *104, 105*
The Whaleman, 57–58, *58*
Thompson, J. D., 70
"three-decker," increasingly pejorative term, 166
three-deckers, xviii, *152*; angled porch, *155*; arguments against, 167; attack on as form of revolt against immigration, 166; attacked by social reformers, xxi; availability of plans and elevations, 150; barometers of forces of change in New Bedford, 119–20; benefits compared to other types of industrial housing, 151; builder-financing, 167; builders' aesthetic intent, 142–43; builders and designers, 133; building of, 114–15; cadence of, *153,* 179; cement-block garages added, 172–73; changes in domestic landscape, 19–20, *20, 21;* climate context, *22, 23;* component of community structure, 155–58; constructed as income property, 133; core structure, 154; cost range for (1920), 167; cross-sectional stereoview, *126;* as culturally transformed living environment, xxi–xxii; cultural transformation at close of textile era, 162–81; demonstrating subculture's power over physical form, 180–81; distinguished from other multifamily forms, 122–23; early examples of, 123, *124;* economic and cultural context for, xix; 1871 debut, 71; etymology, 125; financing and costs, xx–xxi; first wave of building ended by 1893, 129; flat-roof type, 129, *131;* floor plan, *17;* floor rental hierarchy, *17;* formal characteristics, 129–33; gable-front, side-hall format, 129, *131;* ground floor used for commercial purposes, *140,* 154; hipped roof as standard feature, 140; housing reformers pushing for elimination, 148; improved living space, 129; improvement over four-tenement blocks, 128–29; increased occupancy by Portuguese immigrants, 165; influence of cultural values, 143–51; influence of social

three-deckers, *cont.*
setting, 155–58; influence of visual order, 151–55; kit for building, 136; last vestige of mill housing (1901–25), 136; little documentation for framing specifications, 140; living accommodations compared to four-tenements, 71; living spaces reinscribed by variety of human experience, 5–6; local framing methods for, 140–41; mill demolition exposing, 170; modern modifications, 172; modern transformation of outer appearance, 176; most prominent years of construction (1908–13), 129; New England distribution, *127*; New England's approach to housing urban working population, 122; new vernacular response, *177*; offering new regional identity, 116; organization, 11, 123–25; origins of, 122; pastel colors on, 168; period of building, xx; power of presence strengthened through repetition, 152; predominant time of construction, 125–26; primary rental market, 142; private spaces, 154; privately owned and built, 79; program-driven type of architecture, 136–37; purchase prices, 133; purpose of, 125–26; pyramidal, hipped-roof, 130, *132*; raised field-stone wall, *155*; re-envisioning the type, 168–72; removal of decks, 172; sanitary improvements, 129; side yards, new uses for, 173, *174*; sidewalks with, *153*; siting, 125; social life, location of, 14; social relevance definitions, 11; social significance, xx; socio-spatial dynamics of living environment, xix; space utilization of yards, 154; spatial dynamics, *19*; square footage, 11; streetscapes defining sense of place, 154; subsistence gardens and vineyards, 168; transformation, 183; transformations in type, xxii; transformative consumption of, xxii; transformed interstitial spaces, 172–78; typological features of local variation, 140; under-researched, 120; varieties in hipped-roof styles, 138; variety, 123, 125, 143, 152–53; vinyl siding added, *173*
three-family apartments, 125
three-family dwelling: front elevations for, *145*; gable-end drawing, *128*; presentation drawing, *128*. *See also* three-decker
three-tenements, *138*; early example, *123*; formal and typological evolution, *139*; general definition, 137; middle-class, *137*; old and new, side-by-side, *181*; sectional views, *141*; spaces undesignated, 54–55. *See also* three-decker
throstle-spinning, 44
Tirrell, Joseph G., 36
Titusville (Pa.), discovery of petroleum, 39
town row house, *123*
transition zone, 10–11
Treatise on the Theory and Practice of Landscape Gardening, A (Downing), 30–31
trolley service, 97–99
Tucker (John F.) Company, 51

two-deckers, modern cellar kitchens, 175–76
Two-Family and Twin Houses (Comstock), xxi, 125, 142–43, 146
two-family apartments, 125
two-family twin house, *150*
two-tenements, 83, 84

Union Street Railway Co., 82, 97
Unitarians, 25
urban estates, 25–33, *27, 28, 29*
U.S. Bureau of Labor Statistics, 54
U.S. Census (1900), 55
U.S. Department of Labor, 66
U.S. Department of Labor, infant mortality study (1913), 68, 77
U.S. Immigration Act (1965), xxii, 168
U.S. Manufacturing Census (1880s), 84
user's history, 186

Vance, James, Jr., 44
Vandergrift (Pa.), 113. *See also* Appollo Iron and Steel Company
Ventura, John, 173
vernacular, study of, 178
vernacular architecture, 185
vertical housing, perceived as contributor to juvenile delinquency, 149
Vial, S. T., 70
View of the City of New Bedford, 64, *65,* 71–73
village improvement, responsibility for, 106
village improvement movement, 101, 207 n.65, 66
Vinalhaven, *99*
vineyards, 173–75
Vogt, C. H., 64

Walker Atlas of New Bedford, 29, 31
Walker Map of the City of New Bedford, 63
Wall, William Allen, 35
Waltham system, 44
Wamsutta Mills, *4,* 24, 33, *35, 37,* 39, 40, 43, 44, 47, 48, 51, 57, 88, 126, 136, 142, 165; average wages (1890s), 68; construction, 34–35; density of housing arrangements, 75; density of living accommodations, 68–69; double-tenements, 65–66; four-tenements, *69,* 71; growth around, 36, 68; housing, *5,* 62–70, *72,* 156; Manufacturing Company, beginnings of, 33–34; Mill No. 1, *35, 36, 37;* Mill No. 2, *41;* Mill No. 4, *42;* Mill No. 5, 64, 82; Mill No. 6, 64, 92; pattern language of tenements, 66–67; praised for corporate housing accommodations, 78; products of, 34, 35; public health concerns about housing, 100; responses to Board of Health complaints, 78; site, 34; strikes at, 38; success in 1890s, 37; success under Howland, 89; tenement blocks assigned to, 65;

tenement environmental systems, 67–68; tenement rents (1880s–90s), 68; tenements, views of, *67*; Village, public criticism of living conditions, 78–79; wooden multifamily tenements, 65

"Wamsutta Mills" (Wall), 35–36, *36,* 83

Warren, Russell, 25, 26, 28, 57

Warren (S. D.) and Company, 102

Wasemequia Nursery, 90

Washington Social and Music Club, 157, *157*

Watling, William, 133

Watson (Lawrence) and Son, 50

Weld Square Police and Fire Departments, 82, 83

welfare capitalism, 212 n.117

Westfall, Carroll, 120

West Roxbury (Mass.), 125

whale oil, 25

whaling industry, 25, *26*; associated industries, 25; economic shifts in, 38–39; glut in market, 39; housing needs, 61–62; losses of fleet, 39; move to San Francisco, 39; prosperity's effect on landscape, 29–31; prosperity's effect on wharf area, 26; working conditions, 38

Wheelwright, Edmund March, 94, 99–100

Wheelwright and Haven, 87, 93, 94, 95, 102

Whitman, David, 34

Whitman Mill, *45,* 116, 156

Williams, Jerry, 166

Williams, John, 133, 140

Willimantic Linen Company, 102, 103–8, *104, 105*

wooden houses, added to Wamsutta Mills' housing stock, 64

Worcester (Mass.), 125, 129, 167

workers' cottages: gable-front, side-hall, 76–77, 78; side-hall, 83

workers' housing, public health aspects investigated, 100

workforce, changes in response to mill technology improvements, 76

working man's co-op, 175

Workingmen's Homes (Hale), 101

Worsdall, Frank, 120

Worthen Street (Lowell, Mass.), 85

yard spaces, 11

Zeller, John, 140

zoning movement, 167

THE PATINA OF PLACE was designed and typeset on a Macintosh computer system using QuarkXpress software. The text and titles are set in ITC Garamond and Gill Sans. This book was designed and composed by Cheryl Carrington and was printed and bound by Thomson-Shore, Inc. The paper used in this book is designed for an effective life of at least three hundred years.